D1708121

9/II

THE ESSENTIAL REFERENCE GUIDE

Stephen E. Atkins, Editor

ABC-CLIO®

An Imprint of ABC-CLIO, LLC

Santa Barbara, California • Denver, Colorado

Library of Congress Cataloging-in-Publication Data

Names: Atkins, Stephen E., editor.
Title: 9/11 : the essential reference guide / Stephen E. Atkins, editor.
    Other titles: Nine eleven
Description: Santa Barbara, California : ABC-CLIO, [2021] | Includes bibliographical
    references and index.
Identifiers: LCCN 2020037132 (print) | LCCN 2020037133 (ebook) |
    ISBN 9781440873027 (print) | ISBN 9781440873034 (ebook)
Subjects: LCSH: September 11 Terrorist Attacks, 2001. | Terrorism—United States.
Classification: LCC HV6432.7 .A106 2021 (print) | LCC HV6432.7 (ebook) |
    DDC 973.931—dc23
LC record available at https://lccn.loc.gov/2020037132
LC ebook record available at https://lccn.loc.gov/2020037133

ISBN: 978-1-4408-7302-7 (print)
        978-1-4408-7303-4 (ebook)

25   24   23   22   21   1   2   3   4   5

This book is also available as an eBook.

ABC-CLIO
An Imprint of ABC-CLIO, LLC

ABC-CLIO, LLC
147 Castilian Drive
Santa Barbara, California 93117
www.abc-clio.com

This book is printed on acid-free paper ∞

Manufactured in the United States of America

Contents

List of Entries

List of Primary Documents

Preface

Few events in American history have rivaled the September 11, 2001, attacks for impact on American society. Before that date most Americans had a hazy idea that the U.S. government was engaged in a war against terrorism, but there was little concern as long as terrorism was only a threat abroad. As the sole remaining superpower, the United States had few enemies that constituted a present danger to the American mainland. The collapse of the Soviet Union had ensured this. Although the United States and its government's policies were not universally admired in the international community, Americans felt safe behind their two oceans. This all changed on that fateful day of September 11. Much as December 7, 1941, was a day that transformed the history of the United States, September 11, 2001, has become a date that is a watershed in American history.

Little did most Americans realize that Islamist extremists had considered themselves at war against the United States for more than 30 years. Americans had been targets abroad of kidnappings and assassinations. The most obvious case was the killing of 241 marines in Beirut, Lebanon, by Hezbollah during the Ronald Reagan administration. Eighteen American service members were killed in a single incident in Somalia during the Bill Clinton administration. There were other attacks against Americans in Saudi Arabia, Yemen, and Africa. Representatives of the U.S. government had long been targets. American diplomats were not immune from assassination—the U.S. ambassador to Sudan, Cleo A. Noel Jr., and his chargé d'affaires, George C. Moore, had been assassinated in 1973.

One thing that characterized early terrorism was that much of it was state sponsored, so pressure could be applied by the United States against regimes aiding terrorists. This pressure worked particularly well against Libya and its mercurial leader, Muammar Qaddafi. With other states, pressure was less successful—Iran being the most noticeable failure. Even the Palestine Liberation Organization (PLO) responded to pressure. But in the last 20 years, a new brand of terrorism espoused by Islamic fundamentalists, or Islamists, has made its appearance. Adherents to this religious ideology have operated in independent nongovernmental organizations, making it more difficult for counterterrorism forces to isolate and overcome them. The most obvious example has been Osama bin Laden and Al Qaeda.

Bin Laden's hostility toward the United States began during the Afghan-Soviet War in the late 1980s. This hostility intensified as American troops were based on the soil of Saudi Arabia beginning with the 1991 Persian Gulf War. He issued two documents declaring war on the United States—one in 1996 and another in 1998. But none of Al Qaeda's early acts of terrorism took place on American soil. Most experts on terrorism, however, including Central Intelligence Agency (CIA) intelligence analysts, knew that it was only a matter of time before there was an Al Qaeda operation on American soil, but none of them could pinpoint an actual date or act. The fact that the terrorists devised a plan to use commercial aircraft as guided missiles surprised everybody in the intelligence and political community. Although there were hints of Al Qaeda's interest in using aircraft as a weapon in the mid-1990s, this information was never acted upon. In a comedy of errors and lost chances, the agencies of the U.S. government did little to prevent the September 11 plot from succeeding. This lack of attention to Islamist terrorism changed on September 11.

There has been a lack of objective resources available on the events surrounding September 11, 2001. Most objective have been inquiries by Congress, the 9/11 Commission, and a handful of journalists. They have pointed out major deficiencies in how government agencies handled intelligence about Al Qaeda operations prior to September 11. Besides establishing weakness, the inquiries have been most interested in reforming the American intelligence community so that there will be no future September 11ths. Despite these lengthy inquiries, questions still arise as to how the September 11 plot was carried out so successfully.

Several noteworthy books have appeared on bin Laden, Al Qaeda, and the hijackers, and they have been able to fill in some of the gaps of information about the September 11 attacks and the U.S. government's reaction. Less trustworthy books have also appeared, questioning the accepted facts. A growing industry of books has been published trying to debunk the official positions on the events of September 11. Conspiracy theories have proliferated at a lively rate. In the last few years these books have overshadowed the few accounts of events that reflect well on the victims of that day.

Opinions vary on who was responsible for not anticipating the September 11 attacks, and the debate continues to grow even twenty years after the event. There are five major theories, with the debate extending from the extreme Right to the extreme Left with variations in the middle.

- Official Position of the U.S. Government: No one was responsible because there was no credible evidence available that such an attack would take place. American intelligence knew something was up with Al Qaeda, but no one envisaged such an attack on American soil.
- 9/11 Commission Thesis: The members of the 9/11 Commission believed that the plot could have been discovered except for intelligence failures—in the Clinton and George W. Bush administrations, the CIA, the Federal Bureau of Investigation (FBI), the Federal Aviation Administration (FAA), and other government agencies—to cooperate and uncover terrorist operations both in the United States and abroad. September 11 was preventable, but systemic failures in the U.S. government allowed it to happen.
- Systemic Bungling Thesis: The actions of the U.S. government were negligent before September 11 because of turf wars between agencies, bureaucratic bungling, and overdependence on legal rulings

prevalent in the U.S. government. There was also a cozy relationship between aviation regulators and the airline industry, as well as interference from politicians over the years regarding ways to improve aviation safety. Those responsible for the bureaucratic bungling and sometimes deceitful conduct have never been held accountable, and in many cases received post–September 11 promotions.

- They Allowed It to Happen Thesis: There is the belief in certain circles that the Bush administration knew about the September 11 plot and allowed it to happen so that there would be a plausible excuse to expand American military might in the Middle East. The special target would be Iraq, but the Taliban in Afghanistan was also a prime candidate for removal. This thesis has been especially popular with the American and international extreme Left. They blame everything on the neoconservatives surrounding Bush. These left-wing adherents also believe that it was allowed in order to create an opportunity for the Bush administration to weaken American civil liberties.

- They Made It Happen Thesis: This thesis abandons the role of bin Laden and Al Qaeda in the September 11 attacks and places all the blame on the U.S. government. In the eyes of these conspiracy theorists, agents of the U.S. government carried out the attacks in a methodical manner in the pursuit of Bush's objectives for foreign and domestic policies. Believers of this thesis have concocted various schemes to explain how the U.S. government carried out the attacks that verge on the incredible.

The information collected in this work is intended to help the reader navigate and evaluate these theories. The reference entries and primary sources provided here will provide key evidence for analyzing and drawing your own conclusions about the failure to anticipate the September 11 attacks and, more generally, the causes and lasting effects those attacks have had in the United States and around the world.

The events of September 11 have produced a mass of data. This work is an attempt to bring some order to an otherwise undifferentiated mass of conflicting information. The book begins with six introductory essays covering: the impact of 9/11 on counterterrorism, on Muslim Americans, on civil aviation, on Islamic extremism around the world, on the civil liberties of Americans, and on the growth in America of the executive power of the presidency.

The A-to-Z portion of the book contains entries on people and events leading up to September 11, what actually took place on September 11, and the aftermath of September 11. This means that the participants in the September 11 plot are covered in some depth. The sequence of events on the day itself are covered in detail in various citations. Finally, the reasons why American intelligence and law enforcement agencies were unable to prevent September 11 are covered in considerable depth. Also of interest are the various conspiracy theories that have emerged in the aftermath of September 11, covered in an entry devoted to the topic. The goal overall is to present to the reader a comprehensive look at all aspects of September 11 so that it can be understood in its context. These A-to-Z entries are followed by a chronologically organized collection of key primary sources related to the events of September 11. Then comes a chronology, including a minute-by-minute recounting of events in the airplanes and in the towers. The project wraps up with an annotated bibliography.

A note needs to be made of spelling of Arabic names and groups. I have been uniform in the spelling of names, but other forms appear in the documents and in the quotes. In the course of the book, Osama bin Laden is also transliterated into Usama bin Ladin, or, in another variation, into Osama bin Ladin. This is also true of Al Qaeda, which is referred to as al Qaeda, al Qaida, or al-Qida in other sources.

Normally I dedicate a book to an individual or a group of individuals. This encyclopedia I dedicate to the victims and families of September 11, 2001. They became victims of a war that they had no part in. Let us hope that another September 11 will never happen.

A postscript: Stephen Atkins passed away in 2010 not long after finishing work on the first edition of his highly regarded *9/11 Encyclopedia*. Because of the first edition's success and valuable contribution to the study of the disaster, the encyclopedia was extensively updated and published in a second edition in 2011 on the 10th anniversary of 9/11. In the same spirit, this new project contains the core of the second edition's most important entries and documents in addition to the six brand-new essays assessing the impact of 9/11 on key themes. Once again, the entries have been updated (and new entries added) where events have warranted. The bibliography has also been updated.

Stephen E. Atkins (updated in 2020 by ABC-CLIO editors)

Introductory Essays

The Impact of 9/11 on U.S. Counterterrorism Efforts

In the weeks following the 9/11 attacks, President George W. Bush and the 107th Congress passed a number of domestic reforms. First, President Bush and Congress provided more than $40 billion in funding for reconstruction and recovery, strengthening domestic security, and compensating victims. Second, the administration strengthened immigration policies, designated 25 new groups as Foreign Terrorist Organizations (FTOs), and detained and tried noncitizens in a military tribunal (as opposed to civilian court). Perhaps, most importantly, President Bush signed an executive order targeting the finances of U.S. and foreign terrorist organizations. In this effort, more than 140 countries cooperated and worked with the United States to block terrorist financing. Third, Congress, citing the need to better protect Americans from the threat of terrorism, expanded the surveillance powers of the intelligence community, passing the USA PATRIOT Act.

In the years following 9/11, the domestic reforms continued. First, President Bush and Congress established the Department of Homeland Security in 2002, bringing together 22 separate agencies to enhance and better coordinate federal, state, and local capabilities in protecting the country from terrorist attacks. Second, President Bush and Congress established a commission in 2002, the National Commission on Terrorist Attacks Upon the United States, informally referred to as the 9/11 Commission, to investigate attacks and make recommendations. The 9/11 Commission made 41 recommendations in 2004, including the following: 1. reform of the intelligence community, which included the creation of the National Intelligence Director position and the creation of the National Counterterrorism Center, 2. the creation of joint homeland security congressional committees, 3. the enhancement of border security, which included biometric screening, new explosives screening capabilities, and "no fly" lists, and 4. the standardization of government identification, which included the REAL ID Act for setting driver's license standards.

After 9/11, President Bush emphasized that the U.S. counterterrorism strategy would target both terrorists and those countries that provide sanctuary for them. Moreover, the United States would act before terrorists could plan and carry out an attack against Americans. As such, the United States began to organize and prepare its military for large-scale overseas operations.

The United States, in terms of national consensus and strategy, moved from treating terrorism as a criminal matter to that of a national security threat. The United States subsequently adopted a policy of preemption, denial of sanctuary, and targeted killings.

The United States largely carried out the preemption and denial of sanctuary policy with overseas military operations. After signing the Authorization for Use of Military Force (AUMF) on September 18, 2001, President Bush began military counterterrorism operations on October 7, 2001, when U.S. and British forces began bombing military sites in Taliban-controlled Afghanistan. The focus of operations was on the fundamentalist Taliban government, which hosted Al Qaeda and Al Qaeda's founder and leader, Osama bin Laden. After toppling the Taliban government in December 2001, the United States tracked down bin Laden and Navy SEAL Team 6 killed him on May 2, 2011, at his compound in Abbottabad, Pakistan. In addition to Afghanistan, the United States conducted counterterrorism and counterinsurgency operations in the Philippines, the Horn of Africa, Pakistan, Yemen, and the Balkans. President Bush signed the Authorization for Use of Military Force against Iraq Resolution of 2002 on October 16, 2002, which cited Iraqi President Saddam Hussein's links with international terrorist organizations and weapons of mass destruction development efforts. President Bush subsequently built a coalition and invaded Iraq on March 20, 2003, deposing Hussein.

The United States largely carried out the targeted killing policy with the use of remotely piloted aircraft, specifically the Predator, which replaced the cruise missile as the weapon of choice for U.S. operators. The first use of a Predator was in October 2001, when the United States fired Hellfire missiles in a failed attempt to kill Taliban leader Mullah Muhammad Omar. The Central Intelligence Agency (CIA) was given broad authority for firing Hellfire missiles, and drone strikes increased during the latter part of the Bush administration. President Barack Obama ratcheted up the drone campaign, particularly in Pakistan, ordering 281 strikes in four years (2009 to 2012), averaging one drone strike every four days. The Bush administration, in contrast, averaged a drone strike every 40 days. Drone strikes were consistently carried out in Somalia, the Philippines, Yemen, and Pakistan, among others, which killed hundreds of extremists.

This policy of preemption, denial of sanctuary, and targeted killings continues today with each president citing AUMF to justify the use of military force. U.S. military forces now operate in dozens of locations in the Middle East, Asia, and Africa. But, Presidents Bush, Obama, and Donald Trump shifted from large-scale military operations to smaller-scale operations involving special operations forces, technology, and U.S.-provided capabilities in an effort to build partner capacity. This was a learned response—a crafted balance between the pre-9/11 mindset of treating terrorism as a criminal matter and the post-9/11 mindset of overreacting with a heavy-handed approach, which induced neutral parties to join violent extremist organizations.

The 2017 National Security Strategy (NSS) labels fighting terrorism as a long war, one in which the United States must defeat terrorists at their source, at their base of operations. The NSS cites the territorial defeat of the Islamic State and Al Qaeda as successes, while noting a terrorist threat will remain a long-term challenge. The 2018 National Strategy for Counterterrorism states the United States will protect its homeland against complex, diverse, always evolving terrorist threats using new technologies and tactics—all while optimizing resources and prioritizing its overseas operations.

Terrorist groups have adapted to U.S. counterterrorism efforts as well. The global jihadist movement now involves a proliferation of localized groups—AQAP, the Islamic State, Tekrik-e-Taliban (TTP), Al-Qaeda in the Islamic Maghreb (AQIM) and Al-Shabaab—in addition to the longstanding extremist organizations of Al Qaeda and Abu Sayyaf. These groups, operating under a franchise structure, form a loose alliance to topple governments and pursue an anti-Western agenda. Terrorist tactics and methods have also evolved, shifting away from centralized, complex operations to "lone wolf" attacks, such as active shooter attacks, homemade explosive devices, and vehicular manslaughter, carried out by individuals. From 2015 to 2018 in Europe and the United States, AQAP- and Islamic State–influenced individuals carried out attacks in Paris, San Bernardino, Brussels, Istanbul, Orlando, Nice, Berlin, London, Stockholm, Manchester, Barcelona, Strasbourg, and Liège.

Bradley F. Podliska

Suggested Reading

Alexander, Yonah. "United States." In *Counterterrorism Strategies: Successes and Failures of Six Nations,* edited by Yonah Alexander. Dulles, VA: Potomac Books, 2006.

Authorization for Use of Military Force. Pub. L. 107-40 115 Stat. 224. 18 September 2001.

Authorization for Use of Military Force against Iraq Resolution of 2002. Pub. L. 107-243 116 Stat. 1498. 16 October 2002.

Banks, William C. "Legal Sanctuaries and Predator Strikes in the War on Terror." In *Denial of Sanctuary: Understanding Terrorist Safe Havens*, edited by Michael A. Innes. Westport, CT: Praeger Security International, 2007.

Crenshaw, Martha, and Gary LaFree. *Countering Terrorism*. Washington, DC: Brookings Institution Press, 2017.

Hoffman, Bruce. *Inside Terrorism.* New York: Columbia University Press, 2006.

Innes, Michael A. "Cracks in the System: Sanctuary and Terrorism after 9/11." In *Denial of Sanctuary: Understanding Terrorist Safe Havens*, edited by Michael A. Innes. Westport, CT: Praeger Security International, 2007.

United States. Executive Office of the President. *National Security Strategy.* Washington, DC: Executive Office of the President, 2017.

United States. Executive Office of the President. *National Strategy for Counterterrorism.* Washington, DC: Executive Office of the President, 2018.

Williams, Brian Glyn. *Predators: The CIA's Drone War on al Qaeda.* Dulles, VA: Potomac Books, 2013.

The Impact of 9/11 on American Muslims

The senseless acts of violence waged on the United States on September 11, 2001, instilled fear, anger, and a sense of vulnerability in the minds of many Americans. Some people expressed their emotions by utilizing intimidation tactics, verbal assaults, and in many cases, physical violence against anyone who looked Middle Eastern or dressed in attire indicative of Muslim culture.

Immediately following the attacks, innocent American Muslims began suffering backlash for the atrocities committed by nineteen hate-filled radicals, members of the al Qaeda terrorist organization led by Osama bin Laden. Following the carnage of 9/11, anyone practicing the Islamic faith became a potential target.

Many Americans considered Islam evil and prone to violence long before 9/11. A significant factor that contributed to this xenophobic and narrow-minded view were the numerous attacks perpetrated by Muslims, specifically al Qaeda, against American civilians and interests overseas prior to 9/11. The 1998 Kenya and Nairobi embassy attacks are one example. For many Americans the 9/11 attacks merely confirmed preexisting fears and prejudices.

In the days following the attacks, Muslims became targets for systemic discrimination and profiling in many U.S. institutions including the legal system and news media. Therefore, many Muslims, fearing for their lives, barricaded themselves in their homes for weeks at a time.

Fear spawned by the media and online chatter within Muslim communities prevented many residents from going to work or attending school and some were afraid to shop for groceries or attend services at their mosques.

The media is a powerful tool capable of shaping public opinion and directing public discourse. In the era of 24/7 news coverage and online social networks, hate-filled speech and caricatures reach a global audience. As a result, people who heretofore internalized their fears and biases now feel emboldened to express their sentiments through verbal and physically destructive means.

In the days and weeks following the attacks, media coverage was intense and some news outlets focused their ire on the Islamic faith and its relation to global terrorism. Several news outlets as well as many American citizens viewed practitioners of Islam as potential terrorists. By way of contrast, the media often reports a mass casualty attack by an American-born lone wolf extremist as an isolated incident perpetrated by a mentally deranged and often racist individual.

Post-9/11 state and federal policies and legislation enacted to reduce incidents of violent extremism further stigmatized Muslim American communities and created an "us versus them" mentality that often led to acts of violence.

Two post-9/11 legislative efforts designed to mitigate the terrorist threat became law. The USA PATRIOT Act signed into law by President George W. Bush in October 2001 expanded the power of law enforcement to prevent terrorist acts and established penalties for perpetrators and supporters of terrorist crimes. The Countering Violent Extremism Program adopted by President Obama in 2014 attempted to deter U.S. citizens from joining extremist groups through collaborative community outreach programs designed to prevent violence primarily through education and intervention policies.

Whether by design or as a reaction to 9/11, the above legislation focused primarily on Muslims. Under the pretext of national security, Muslim Americans were arbitrarily arrested or detained, and their property was often seized. Deportations and unwarranted, intrusive surveillance of their communities and mosques were commonplace practices.

On January 27, 2017, President Trump signed a travel ban that prevented travelers from five predominantly Muslim countries (Iran, Libya, Somalia, Syria, and Yemen) from entering the United States. The ban, also referred to by some commentators in the media as the "Muslim ban," extended to two non-Muslim countries: North Korea and Venezuela. This, the third iteration of the ban, was upheld by the U.S. Supreme Court on June 26, 2018. The travel ban prevents Muslims residing overseas from reuniting with family members in the United States.

Hate-filled rhetoric from some evangelical Christian leaders as well as some politicians and others from the far-right fringe further alienated the minority Muslim population by spewing xenophobic comments that received national media attention. This undercurrent of hate imparted legitimacy to the verbal and physical violence perpetrated against Muslims in the post-9/11 world. Furthermore, racist comments by senior government officials fan the flames of hatred in this country by pitting one group of people against another.

Alienation of Muslims and other minority groups is rooted in ignorance. This mindset spawns prejudice and creates a fertile environment for discrimination and acts of violence. In this regard educating the public can help mitigate prejudicial attitudes by providing insight into Muslim culture and the Islamic faith. Research has shown that knowledge regarding ethnic group culture breeds tolerance and tolerance leads to acceptance.

A few facts regarding Muslim Americans need additional insight. First, not only did Muslim Americans die in the 9/11 attacks, many risked their lives during subsequent rescue efforts. Secondly, Muslim Americans have served and continue to serve in all branches of the U.S. military. Finally, Muslim Americans, many of whom have achieved acclaim in the fields of business, medicine and the sciences, contribute substantially to the U.S. economy.

In the divided America of 2021, it is critical that we lower the hate-filled discourse before tensions rise to the level of armed conflict between white Americans and Americans of color. The responsibility to eliminate the toxicity between diverse groups of Americans is the duty of every citizen. The history of the 20th century provides ample proof of the truth of the following statement: We overcome our petty prejudices and learn to live together in peace or die together in war.

Frank Shanty

References

Blumberg, Antonia. "How Being Muslim in America Has Changed since 9/11." *Huffington Post*. September 9, 2016. https://www .huffpost.com/entry/how-being-muslim -in-america-has-changed-since-911_n _57d1a61ee4b03d2d45992990.

Center for Constitutional Rights. "The Muslim Ban: Discriminatory Impacts and Lack of Accountability." January 14, 2019. https://ccrjustice.org/home/get-involved /tools-resources/publications/muslim-ban -discriminatory-impacts-and-lack.

Clay, Rebecca A. "Islamophobia." *Monitor in Psychology*, Vol. 48, No. 4. April 2017. https://www.apa.org/monitor/2017/04 /islamophobia.

Frumin, Aliyah, and Sakuma, Amanda. "Hope and Despair: Being Muslim in America after 9/11." *NBC News*. September 8, 2016. https:www.nbcnews.com/storyline/9-11anni versary/hope-despair-being-muslim-america -after-9-11-n645451.

Garofalo, Alex. "The United States after 9/11: 7 Ways America Has Changed since 2001 at 15-Year Anniversary."

International Business Times. September 8, 2016. https://www.ibtimes.com /united-states-after-911-7-ways-america -has-changed-2001-15-year-anniversary -2413197.

Kishi, Katayoun. "Assaults against Muslims in US Surpass 2001 Levels." Pew Research Center, Fact Tank. November 15, 2017. https://www.pewresearch.org/fact-tank /2017/11/15/assaults-against-muslims-in-u -s-surpass-2001-level/.

Levin, Brian. "Explaining the Rise in Hate Crimes against Muslims in the US." The Conversation. July 19, 2017. http:// theconversation.com/explaining-the-rise -in-hate-crimes-against-muslims-in-the-us -80304.

Levin, Brian. "FBI: Hate Crime Went Up 6.8 Percent in 2005; Anti-Muslim Incidents Surge to Second Highest Level Ever." *Huffington Post*. November 13, 2016. https://www.huffpost.com/entry/fbi-hate -crime-up-68-in-2_b_12951150.

Mallie, Jane Kim. "After 9/11, Immigration Became about Homeland Security." *U.S. News and World Report*. September 8, 2011. https://www.usnews.com/news /articles/2011/09/08/after-911-immigration -became-about-homeland-security-attacks -shifted-the-conversation-heavily-toward -terrorism-and-enforcement.

National Consortium for the Study of Terrorism and Responses to Terrorism. "Living in America as a Muslim after 9/11: Poll Trends 2001–2007. (Start 2009). https://www.dhs .gov/sites/default/files/publications/OPSR _TP_START_Research-Living-America -Muslim-After-9-11-Report_090818-508 .pdfneed date

NPR. "How Being Muslim in America Has Changed since 9/11." Talk of the Nation. September 8, 2011. https://www.npr.org /2011/09/08/140297257/how-being -muslim-in-america-has-changed-since-9 -11.

Powell, Kimberly A. "Framing Islam/Creating Fear: An Analysis of U.S. Media Coverage of Terrorism from 2011–2016." MDPI. August 28, 2018. https://www.mdpi .com/2077-1444/9/9/257.

Underwood, Alexia. "What Most Americans Get Wrong about Islamophobia." Vox. April 6, 2018. https://www.vox.com/2018 /4/6/17169448/trump-islamophobia -muslims-islam-black-lives-matter.

The Impact of 9/11 on Civil Aviation

On September 11, 2001, the U.S. National Airspace was closed to civil aviation and would not reopen for more than forty-eight hours (on September 13). Even a week later, 40% of commercial flights had not been restored, and those flights that were restored were experiencing delays due to enhanced security.

According to the U.S. Department of Transportation, commercial traffic after 9/11 took years to recover. While the number of passengers returned to its pre-9/11 peak in 2004, capacity (the number of seats sold by airlines) recovered more slowly. The International Aviation Transportation Association (IATA) reports that aviation did not return to profitability until 2006. Since 9/11, the market has shifted to a model more focused on low-cost carriers rather than traditional (known as "legacy") airlines.

Unsurprisingly, one response to the 9/11 attacks has been increased security measures for civil aviation. These measures include requirements for stronger locked doors to the cockpit to prevent hijacking; screening of all checked baggage; more careful screening of passengers and carry-on luggage; additional security officers (sometimes on board the aircraft); additional cargo security; and greater focus on limiting airport access and controlling airport perimeters. The collection and transmission of Advanced Passenger Information (API) for flights into the United States was also mandated by this legislation. Additionally, a $2.50 security fee was added to flights originating in the United States.

Prior to 9/11, there was no Transportation Security Administration (TSA). Passenger screening was carried out by the airlines, typically by contractors; security of airport premises was borne by the airports themselves. The TSA was created by the U.S. Congress in the Aviation and Transportation Security Act, which was signed into law by President George W. Bush on November 19, 2001. Within its first year, the TSA created a workforce of almost 60,000 employees. Initially, the TSA was part of the Transportation Department. The Department of Homeland Security was created in November 2002, and the TSA was subsequently transferred to that department in March 2003. While the TSA is most well-known for its security screeners at commercial airports, the TSA also has responsibility for highways, seaports, railroads, buses, and mass-transit systems.

Changes to civil aviation occurred at the international level in addition to domestic changes. The International Civil Aviation Organization (ICAO), which is a specialized agency of the United Nations, develops Standards and Recommended Practices (SARPs) to support "a safe, efficient, secure, economically sustainable and environmentally responsible civil aviation sector." ICAO was established in 1944 and now has 193 Member States. The SARPs developed by ICAO become Annexes, which are incorporated into the Convention on International Civil Aviation (known as the Chicago Convention), an international treaty that is legally binding on the 193 member countries. Annex 17 addressing aviation security was adopted in 1974 and was amended on December 7, 2001, as a direct result of the 9/11 attacks. "The amendment includes various definitions and new provisions in relation to the applicability of this Annex to domestic operations; international cooperation relating to threat information; national quality control; access control; measures related to passengers and their cabin and hold baggage; in-flight security personnel and protection of the cockpit; code-sharing/collaborative arrangements; human factors; and management of response to acts of unlawful interference" (ICAO). ICAO has also adopted a harmonized blueprint to integrate biometric identification information into travel documents that can be read by machines at the airport (for example, passports). ICAO also introduced an international standard in 2002 requiring hardened cockpit doors on any international flights with more than sixty passengers.

The Tokyo Convention of 1963 was an international effort to address hijacking and acts of unlawful interference in international civil aviation. Though it long predates the 9/11 attacks, it has been a valuable instrument in the post-9/11 world. The Montreal Protocol of 2014, developed partially as a result of post-9/11 changes to civil aviation and the difficulties that have continued to worsen regarding unruly passengers on commercial aircraft, further modernizes the international approach to the problem.

Though the 9/11 attacks were carried out using passengers on commercial flights rather than cargo, there were also changes to the air freight industry as a result of these attacks. There was a shift to the use of pre-shipment examination of exports, rather than just entry inspection of imports. A new set of protocols to the Kyoto Convention on the Simplification and Harmonization of Customs Procedures was introduced following 9/11, recommending that national customs administrations use electronic systems for review and clearance of cargo, use risk management techniques to determine which shipments to inspect, and ensure transparency of customs laws and regulations.

In order for commercial airlines to operate, they must carry insurance. One such form of insurance is a "War Risk" insurance, which covers damage due to acts of war (which generally includes hijacking). Though insurance may not be the first thought that comes to mind when reflecting on the 9/11 attacks, it was a major area of concern. All aviation insurers issued seven-day notices of cancellation to their insureds for this war risk insurance. This cancellation was a serious threat to the aviation industry. Some administrations took action at a governmental level to ensure the continuing operation of civil aviation, including the Federal Aviation Administration in the United States. The FAA continues to provide the war risk insurance that is needed by U.S. airlines. Though private insurers have returned to the market, albeit with more costly premiums for more limited coverage, the fact that governments are still in some cases providing this insurance has created distortions in the commercial aviation marketplace.

The attacks of 9/11 have caused changes to many aspects of our society. Perhaps least surprisingly, they have changed how individuals, governments, and the international community treat civil aviation (including both passenger travel and shipment of cargo). A concerted effort to increase security of civil aviation, at both domestic and international levels, has occurred in an attempt to remedy the gaps that allowed for the attacks to be carried out. Despite the significant damage to the industry following the attacks, civil aviation has managed to develop and expand, and has remained an incredibly safe means of travel.

Andrea Harrington

The Impact of 9/II on Attacks of Islamic Extremism

Contextualizing the Issue

Over the last several decades the Middle East has experienced an ongoing religious revival. In many ways this is part of a worldwide reaction to the secularizing trends of modern life. In the Middle East, many fundamentalist Muslims see secularization as the result of Western incursions and interference. Thus, here, religious revival and defiance of the West can be parts of the same process.

From the point of view of many Western governments, and particularly the United States, these incursions and interference, at least in their post–World War II manifestations, were necessary to protect vital economic resources such as oil or to confront the Soviet Union during the Cold War. Here are some specific examples of Western activity in this region: (1) Support by Western governments, particularly the United States, for secular, non-democratic regimes. For example, the governments in Egypt and Jordan. (2) Placement of military bases on Muslim land. For example, those in Saudi Arabia and Bahrain. (3) Support of Israeli policies toward the Palestinian people. Most Muslims consider these policies to be in violation of international law and Palestinian human rights. (4) Encouraging the spread of Western culture, which is seen as inherently secular and destructive of ancient traditions. Muslims are particularly sensitive to Western influence on gender roles. So, however the West might see it, these activities have frightened and angered Islamic fundamentalists.

During the First Gulf War (1990–1991) the government of Saudi Arabia invited American military forces into their country to help defend against a feared Iraqi invasion. Many Islamic fundamentalists interpreted this move as yet another opportunity for the West to undermine the independence and religious integrity of the Muslim Middle East. One of those who saw it this way was Osama bin Laden, the leader of the Islamic extremist movement, Al Qaeda.

An Extremist Response

By the year 1990 Osama bin Laden had already successfully fought one war against a Western power. That was the war in Afghanistan (1979–1989) that turned back an invasion by the Soviet Union. The forces that defeated the Soviet troops were "mujahideen" or Islamic fundamentalist fighters recruited from throughout the Muslim world. These fighters had no state affiliation, but rather saw themselves representative of the "umma" or Muslim society as a whole. After the Soviets withdrew from Afghanistan, Osama bin Laden turned his attention to the United States and its military and civilian presence throughout the Middle East. He labeled these Americans as invaders and called for them to leave. Then Al Qaeda began attacking American targets. For example, there were attacks on U.S. embassies, hotels, and warships visiting harbors in the Middle East. This process culminated in the attacks on the World Trade Center (WTC) and Pentagon on September 11, 2001.

Much like the expulsion of the Soviet Union from Afghanistan, the 9/11 attacks were seen as a great success and morale booster for bin Laden and the mujahideen. They considered the American victims of the 9/11 actions as casualties of war. They reasoned that many more innocent Arabs had been killed by America's aggressive policies than had died in the WTC. For instance, hundreds of thousands of Iraqis were reported to have died due to the sanctions imposed upon Iraq after the First Gulf War. Al Qaeda saw 9/11 as a counterattack. For them it was a tit for tat situation.

Opposing Perceptions

From the point of view of Osama bin Laden and those who supported him, the Western powers were enemies who had been aggressively exploiting the Middle East for centuries and, in the process, killing Muslims and undermining Islamic values. The mujahideen, in turn, were defending their homes and civilization.

However, most believing Muslims were very troubled by Osama bin Laden's tactics. And, though the Western media took little notice, leading Muslim scholars and religious figures insisted that Islam does not teach hatred or encourage violence any more than does Christianity or Judaism. They pointed out that the Quran specifically forbids attacks on non-combatants and their property, and therefore suicide bombers who believe they are doing God's work and will go to heaven are tragically mistaken. These Muslim leaders considered bin Laden and his followers as renegades.

Finally, from the point of view of the Western public, the September 11 attacks seemed almost inexplicable—as if it had to be the work of insane people following an insane religion. This was because the citizens in the West, and particularly the United States, had no accurate knowledge of the nature and history, and therefore the consequences, of their countries' Middle East foreign policies. National media and government sources of information had not accurately informed them of this history. Nor did most Westerners, including Americans, know anything about Islam, and so imagined the religion as one that preached violence and hatred.

Conclusion

The boost in morale given to the radical Islamic resistance survived the retaliation launched by the United States: the invasion of Afghanistan in October 2001 and the subsequent invasion of Iraq in March of 2003. While momentarily suppressing the violence of extremists, these invasions destroyed law and order along great swaths of Muslim territory. This, in turn, opened the way for new, and increasingly brutal movements. For example, brutal movements, such as the so-called Islamic State of Iraq and Syria. Al Qaeda and such offshoots like the Islamic State were eventually militarily defeated by efforts that involved intervention by the United States and other outside powers.

In the end the original goal of Osama bin Laden to push the Western powers out of Muslim lands was not achieved. However, the suppression of Islamic extremist movements is not likely to last. They are a product of certain historical conditions and as long as those conditions persist, these movements will have fertile soil in which to regenerate. They also have terrible precedents, such as the terrorist attacks on the WTC and Pentagon, to give them encouragement.

Lawrence Davidson

The Impact of 9/11 on Civil Liberties

The attacks of 9/11 shattered Americans' sense of security. For the first time in the living memory of many, Americans felt vulnerable to outside threats. America's relatively open borders and permissive laws, combined with the interconnected nature of life in the 21st century, caused many Americans to understand that the country could no longer hide behind two massive oceans to remain secure. As the dust settled on the World Trade Center, the Pentagon, and the field in southeastern Pennsylvania, Americans took a number of steps to prevent future attacks that impacted peoples' fundamental rights and freedoms under the Constitution, called civil liberties. In some instances, these steps came under attack as unjustified incursions upon the rights of individuals. However, the wake of 9/11 saw a response that was in some ways moderated compared to past conflicts, and the courts and other actors stepped in to prevent some of the worst incursions.

Governments—particularly democracies—often struggle with the question of how to balance security and liberty. Governments faced with new threats are often willing to curtail civil liberties in order to obtain new tools to combat those threats, and people who are afraid for their safety are often willing to allow this. This has been the pattern in conflict after conflict, including the Alien and Sedition Acts during heightened tensions with Britain in the late 1700s, President Lincoln's suspension of the right of habeas corpus during the Civil War, the internment of Japanese Americans in World War II, and the Red Scare during the Cold War. The tragedy of 9/11 raised this tension again.

Presidential powers, which had already been increasing for decades, grew significantly after 9/11. Congress provided the president with a broad authorization for the use of military force against those responsible for the attacks and any "associated forces." That authorization has served as the basis for wide-ranging military endeavors ever since 2001. The Bush administration—with Congress's assent—created the large new Department of Homeland Security, which imposed strict new airport screening rules and expanded domestic surveillance. Intelligence agencies grew markedly, with overall federal government spending on intelligence approximately doubling between 2001 and 2013. More aggressive interrogation and deportation of individuals residing within the United States led to complaints and lawsuits alleging the government was engaged in racial profiling.

The 2013 disclosures by former intelligence contractor Edward Snowden summarize some of the most significant government actions impacting civil liberties. While working at the National Security Agency (NSA), Snowden secretively gathered information on a number of secret NSA surveillance activities that he believed represented an abuse of government power. He leaked this information to the public, including information about a wide-ranging government effort to obtain metadata on Americans' cell phone activity and a data-mining program that granted the government access to large Internet companies' records. While the government sought to prosecute Snowden for his disclosures, an oversight panel created in light of Snowden's disclosures recommended a stop to mass collection of phone records and called for more oversight over other programs.

One of the most notable responses to 9/11 that impacted civil liberties was the "Uniting and Strengthening America by Providing Appropriate Tools Required to Intercept and Obstruct Terrorism Act of 2001," or, as it is more popularly known, the "USA PATRIOT Act" (later simply called the "Patriot Act.") In the weeks following 9/11, Congress passed the Patriot Act with broad support. The Act covered numerous areas, not all of which remained in effect for various reasons. The Act sought to enhance law enforcement investigatory tools to prevent terrorist acts, but it contained a number of controversial provisions that impacted civil liberties. For example, it expanded the list of offenses for which the government could eavesdrop on private communications under the Wiretap Act. The Act also expanded the government's ability to obtain a court order for surveillance, and permitted government lawyers to disclose grand jury matters to other parts of the government. The Act expanded the government's powers to obtain authorization from the Foreign Intelligence Surveillance Act Court for electronic surveillance, along with expanded powers for the FBI to issue subpoenas for information relating to foreign intelligence or international terrorism investigations. Despite the controversies many of these provisions raised, most court challenges to the Act proved unsuccessful. After a series of extensions, Congress in 2015 replaced the Patriot Act with the USA Freedom Act, pulling back several of the powers the Patriot Act granted to the federal government.

Soon after the 9/11 attacks, Attorney General John Ashcroft stated that the government would operate under a "new paradigm" that focused more on preventing future terrorist attacks than criminally punishing past ones. Under this paradigm, the United States employed harsh interrogation methods toward suspected terrorists, held suspects for years without criminally charging them, and released some to other countries to presumably be subject to torture. Just months after the attacks, the government authorized "enhanced interrogation" techniques after administration lawyers concluded the measures did not violate federal law prohibiting torture, and even if they did, the Constitution authorizes the president to approve such actions. These techniques included use of stress positions and prolonged standing, sleep deprivation, exposure to extreme temperatures, and most notably, waterboarding. Once discovered, these practices drew widespread condemnation, and a 2013 nonpartisan review firmly concluded that these practices constituted torture.

The Bush administration also made a decision soon after 9/11 to break from the traditional pattern of treating terrorism as a crime to be addressed through law enforcement and the judicial system. Instead, in November 2001, President Bush directed the establishment of military commissions to prosecute noncitizen suspected international terrorists or those who harbored them. Military commissions contained controversial procedures that led to legal challenges that slowed prosecutions. Following setbacks at the Supreme Court in 2006 and 2008, newly elected President Obama came to office in 2009 vowing to close Guantanamo Bay but was unsuccessful in fulfilling this pledge. To date, only eight of the hundreds of detainees at Guantanamo have been convicted by a military commission, and three of those convictions were later vacated. As of this writing, the commissions continue to be weighed down by procedural delays and legal challenges.

Eventually, the vast majority of prosecutions for terrorism-related offenses migrated to the Justice Department and federal civilian courts. One somewhat controversial issue impacting Americans involves use of the material support statutes to prosecute those who support terrorist organizations. Civil rights groups have criticized use of these provisions as violating the First Amendment because they are broad and potentially infringe on people's ability to distribute literature and engage in political speech. Nonetheless, the material support laws have become a key component of the Justice Department's prosecution efforts regarding terrorism. In 2010, the Supreme Court upheld the law against a First Amendment challenge, though it left open the possibility of future successful challenges.

Americans will long debate whether the tradeoff of civil liberties in return for security was worth it. On the one hand, proponents of the post-9/11 measures will note that America has not experienced another major terrorist attack since that day, something that seemed unlikely in the terrifying days following the attacks. (However, it is unclear to what extent the measures outlined above actually contributed to preventing terrorist attacks.) In addition, it is worth noting that despite voicing criticism as a candidate regarding the Bush administration's lack of respect for civil liberties, President Obama continued many (though not all) of the same policies as his predecessor. On the other hand, critics charge that by diminishing civil liberties, the government diminished America's standing in the world and played into the terrorists' hands by undermining the principles of American democracy. The attacks of 9/11 exposed deep divisions within America about the proper balance between security and liberty, divisions that remain to this day.

Jeremy S. Weber

Suggested Reading

Darmer, M. Katherine, Robert D. Baird, and Stuart E. Rosenbaum, eds. *Civil Liberties vs. National Security in a Post-9/11 World.* Amherst, NY: Prometheus Books, 2004.

Darmer, M. Katherine, and Richard D. Fybel eds. *National Security, Civil Liberties, and the War on Terror.* Amherst, NY: Prometheus Books, 2011.

Herman, Susan H. *Taking Liberties: The War on Terror and the Erosion of American Democracy.* New York: Oxford University Press, 2011.

Lane, Charles. "Debate Crystallizes on War, Rights." *The Washington Post*, September 2, 2002, A-1.

Liptak, Adam. "The 9/11 Decade: Civil Liberties Today." *The New York Times*, September 11, 2001, F-14.

Muller, Eric L. "12/7 and 9/11: War, Liberties, and the Lessons of History." *West Virginia Law Review* 104, no. 3 (April 2002): 571–592. doi:10.2139/ssrn.354761.

Samet, Elizabeth D. *No Man's Land: Preparing for War and Peace in Post-9/11 America.* New York: Farrar, Straus and Giroux, 2014.

Sinnar, Shirin. "Institutionalizing Rights in the National Security Executive." *Harvard Civil Rights-Civil Liberties Law Review* 50 (Summer 2015): 289–357. doi:10.2139/ssrn.2636326.

The Impact of 9/11 on Presidential Power

Throughout U.S. history, successive presidents have expanded the power and scope of their office during times of crisis or war. This pattern continued in the aftermath of the September 11, 2001, terrorist attacks. The U.S. Constitution and various legislation grant the president broad authority to defend the nation. Presidents serve as commander-in-chief of the military and have the authority to deploy troops, oversee strategy and covert operations, and manage domestic security efforts. In some instances, chief executives have drawn upon these powers in highly controversial ways. For instance, Abraham Lincoln suspended the constitutional right of habeas corpus in the midst of the Civil War in 1861, while Franklin D. Roosevelt ordered the internment of Japanese Americans through Executive Order 9066 in 1942 during World War II. Many of the actions undertaken by the post-9/11 presidents have been highly criticized for eroding the civil liberties of Americans, while simultaneously infringing on the traditional roles of the other branches of government, and, thereby, undermining the system of checks and balances that undergirds the U.S. political system.

Following the 9/11 attacks, members of the administration of President George W. Bush embraced an expansionist view of presidential powers. Led by Vice President Richard "Dick" Cheney, Bush's closest advisors argued that the executive branch needed broad powers to fight the War on Terror. In response, the president signed Emergency Proclamation 7463 on September 14, 2001, which expanded his military powers, including adding additional authority to deploy National Guard and reserve forces. This proclamation was renewed every year during the Bush presidency. President Bush also issued a series of executive orders and signing statements that set aside existing restrictions on the detention, interrogation and trial of prisoners, and authorized expanded domestic surveillance. The 2001 USA PATRIOT Act dramatically expanded the intelligence-gathering capabilities of the executive branch and gave law enforcement agencies new powers. Although some provisions of the Act were ended or reformed, other areas of the measure would be renewed in both the Obama and Trump presidencies. Bush further oversaw the largest reorganization of the federal bureaucracy since World War II through the creation of the Department of Homeland Security in 2003.

While the Supreme Court had generally deferred to the executive branch during periods of conflict, Congress had often taken a more active role in checking the expansion of presidential power. This pattern reversed itself in the post-9/11 era. Initially, during the Bush administration, both houses of Congress tended to grant the executive branch wide latitude on national security issues as many members sought to avoid allegations that they impeded the president's efforts to protect the homeland. Rising partisanship later made it difficult for Bush and his successors to achieve their domestic and international legislative priorities through Congress. Consequently, the chief executives instead turned to executive action to reach their national security goals. Meanwhile, the court ruled against a succession of Bush's initiatives, including the administration's system of military tribunals in the cases *Hamdan v. Rumsfeld* (2006) and *Boumediene v. Bush* (2007) (both cases reaffirmed the right of habeas corpus and the authority of federal courts to rule on the detention of suspected terrorists). The courts would continue to be the main check on presidential power during the presidencies of Barack Obama and Donald Trump.

Although he was highly critical of many of Bush's initiatives, Obama continued and expanded many of his predecessor's policies. Following his election in 2008, Obama did rescind permission to use some of the extraordinary interrogation techniques that had been permitted during the Bush administration. He also ordered the closure of the detention center at Guantanamo Bay, but that effort was blocked by Congress. However, the new president annually renewed Bush's state of emergency declaration. In addition, under Obama, the National Security Agency (NSA) implemented a far-reaching domestic surveillance program and dramatically expanded the use of aerial drones to target suspected terrorists overseas. In 2014, facing significant criticism, Obama issued a presidential policy directive that curtailed the NSA's mass surveillance program. In 2004, Bush had authorized the use of drones, but under Obama, drone attacks became one of the primary counterterrorism tactics. In more than 470 drone strikes in Libya, Pakistan, Somalia and Yemen, approximately 2,430 people were killed during Obama's tenure. Despite domestic and global criticism over the legality of such attacks under international law, the administration continued to utilize them. Especially troubling for civil libertarians were drone strikes that targeted U.S. citizens who were suspected of working with terrorist groups overseas. These attacks were undertaken without judicial oversight and were seen as a significant expansion of executive power. Obama also ordered conventional military strikes against Libya and the Islamic State without seeking congressional approval. The 2011 Libyan intervention helped topple dictator Muamar Qaddafi, but was criticized as a violation of the 1974 War Powers Act since the campaign was outside of existing authorizations in the War on Terror.

Trump also renewed Bush's 2001 state of emergency and continued a range of his predecessors' national security actions. He overturned Obama's order to close the detention facility at Guantanamo Bay. Trump's most dramatic steps to bolster his power occurred in trade policy and immigration. The president began enacting tariffs on a variety of goods leading to a series of reciprocal actions by other countries and a trade war with China. The administration used the tariffs to prompt a renegotiation of the 1994 North American Free Trade Agreement (NAFTA) between the United States, Canada, and Mexico, leading to the 2018 United States-Mexico-Canada Agreement (USMCA).

Concurrently, Trump increasingly linked immigration and asylum to national security and issued a series of executive orders to limit both. In 2019, the Supreme Court ruled that Trump could divert some $2.5 billion in military construction funds to the construction of a wall along the border with Mexico after he was unable to secure additional resources from Congress. Trump also increased restrictions on asylum seekers in 2019. Trump, like the other post-9/11 presidents, faced a Congress with at least one chamber controlled by the opposition party.

Nonetheless, like his predecessors, he was able to continue to expand the powers of his office by tying his efforts to concerns over national security.

Tom Lansford

For Further Reading:

Burke, John P. *Presidential Power: Theories and Dilemmas.* Boulder, CO: Westview Press, 2016.

Edelson, Chris. *Power without Constraint: The Post 9/11 Presidency and National Security.* Madison, WI: University of Wisconsin Press, 2016.

Fisher, Louis. *Presidential War Power.* Lawrence, KS: University of Kansas Press, 2004.

Pfiffner, James P. *The Bush Presidency and the Constitution.* Washington, DC: Brookings Institution Press, 2008.

Thurber, James A., and Jordan Tama, eds. *Rivals for Power: Presidential-Congressional Relations.* 6th ed. New York: Rowman & Littlefield, 2017.

A

Abdel Rahman, Sheikh Omar (1938–2017)

Sheikh Omar Abdel Rahman was the spiritual leader of radical Islamists' war against the United States. His reputation as a religious leader and his renowned militancy made him influential among many Muslims, to whom he issued two fatwas, or religious rulings, that justified war against the United States. His band of Islamist militants participated in the 1993 World Trade Center bombing. American authorities were eventually able to tie him to another plot to blow up facilities in New York City, sentencing him to life in solitary confinement without parole.

Abdel Rahman spent most of his life as an Islamist militant. He was born on May 3, 1938, in the small village of al-Gamalia in the Nile Delta region of Egypt. When he was 10 months old, he lost his eyesight, probably because of diabetes. After demonstrating early scholastic ability by memorizing the Quran at age 11, he was sent to an Islamic boarding school. He excelled there, and his academic achievements allowed him to enter Cairo University's School of Theology. There, and later, at the prestigious University of al-Azhar, Abdel Rahman earned degrees in Islamic jurisprudence. At al-Azhar, he was a good, though not brilliant, student, finding it an excellent place to establish contacts with others in agreement about the need for an Islamist state in Egypt. Abdel Rahman's compatriots shared the same agenda—an Islamic society created unilaterally and, if necessary, forcefully.

One of Abdel Rahman's compatriots at al-Azhar was Abdullah Azzam.

Soon after leaving university, Abdel Rahman, who had become a religious scholar with a militant Islamist agenda, started preaching against the secular regime of Egyptian president Gamal Abdel Nasser. In 1965 he preached at a small mosque on the outskirts of Fayoum about 60 miles south of Cairo, but his attacks against Nasser's regime led to his dismissal from his religious teaching post in 1969. This setback only intensified his hatred of Nasser and his regime. He then found work teaching at a girls' school south of Cairo, in Assiut. Perturbed by his mounting attacks, Egyptian authorities arrested him in 1970, and he spent eight months in Citadel Prison. After his release, Abdel Rahman was awarded a post as professor of theology at the University of Assiut, but, still under police surveillance, he decided to go into exile in Saudi Arabia.

Abdel Rahman helped launch the terrorist group Jemaah Islamiyah in 1976 with the goal of overthrowing the Sadat regime and establishing a theocratic Islamic state. This group began carrying out terrorist attacks in Egypt, and Abdel Rahman returned from exile in 1980. He was arrested a month before the assassination of President Anwar Sadat in October 1981. Because members of the Islamic Group had participated in the assassination, Abdel Rahman was tried for conspiracy to overthrow the Egyptian government; but, because the evidence was circumstantial, he was acquitted. He promptly sued the state for torturing him in prison, a suit eventually settled for $10,000. Despite his acquittal, the Egyptian government kept him under house arrest for the next six years, in 1985 allowing him to make a pilgrimage to Mecca. After his release from house arrest, Abdel Rahman's attacks on the Mubarak government continued, but gradually he turned his attention to preaching against the Soviets in Afghanistan. By this time Abdel Rahman had become, according to T. Bowyer Bell's *Murders on the Nile,* famous throughout the Middle East as the "spiritual mentor of the righteous gunmen of the new jihad."

After Abdel Rahman's release from house arrest, he made a visit to Afghanistan, where Abdullah Azzam introduced him to Osama bin Laden. Bin Laden held him in high respect because of his spirituality.

Although Abdel Rahman had achieved recognition as one of the leading Islamist scholars in the international Islamist movement, he faced difficulty in Egypt. A movement among other leaders of the Islamic Group tried to replace him because of his blindness. This attack did not prevent him from issuing a fatwa legitimizing the murder of Coptic Christians. Fearful of losing influence in the Islamic Group in Egypt, and finding the political atmosphere in Egypt too oppressive, Abdel Rahman moved to Sudan in April 1990. After bin Laden left Sudan, two of Abdel Rahman's sons went to Afghanistan to work with Al Qaeda.

Abdel Rahman decided to relocate to the United States, where recruits and money were available to advance the Islamist cause. Despite his reputation as a sponsor of terrorism, he obtained a visa in Khartoum without difficulty, arriving in the United States in July of 1990. In the United States, he found loyal supporters, but he also ran into dissidents, some of whom were unhappy with Mustafa Shalabi. At first Abdel Rahman supported Shalabi, but then the two disagreed over how to use the money they raised. Shalabi insisted that the funds go to Afghanistan to build an Islamist state there, but Abdel Rahman wished to finance efforts to overthrow the Mubarak regime. This disagreement ended with the murder of Shalabi. His murder case has never been solved. Shalabi's removal left Abdel Rahman in charge, and, in March 1991, Abdel Rahman received a permanent residence visa from the United States.

Abdel Rahman lived on the edge of several conspiracies. Several of his most militant supporters participated in the 1993 bombing plot that tried to bring down the Twin Towers of the World Trade Center complex in New York City. American authorities questioned him, but his involvement was mostly circumstantial. He claimed to have known Ramzi Yousef only briefly. His role in the plot to bomb other New York landmarks, however, was more pronounced, and he was arrested in August of 1993. American authorities charged him with a seditious conspiracy to wage a terrorist war against the United States. In January 1996 a New York City court sentenced him to life imprisonment in solitary confinement without chance of parole. After that, Abdel Rahman was held in a variety of maximum-security prisons in Missouri and Minnesota. He died due to complications from diabetes and coronary arterial disease at Butner Federal Medical Center in North Carolina on February 18, 2017.

Even in prison, he was charged with directing activities of his followers through his lawyer and translators. In 1998, he had a fatwa smuggled out of prison urging his followers to cut all ties with the United States and wage war against it. This fatwa gave religious justification for the September 11 attacks. His lawyer received a jail sentence for passing on information to Abdel Rahman's followers.

Abdel Rahman was regarded as one of the leading figures in the Islamist movement. Although he had no role whatsoever in the planning for September 11, or knowledge of it beforehand, his religious rulings offered justification for it. His association with Abdullah Azzam, Ayman al-Zawahiri, and, more indirectly, Osama bin Laden, helped produce the atmosphere that led to September 11.

Stephen E. Atkins

See also: Bin Laden, Osama; World Trade Center Bombing (1993); Yousef, Ramzi Ahmed; Zawahiri, Ayman al-

Suggested Reading

Bell, J. Bowyer. *Murders on the Nile: The World Trade Center and Global Terror.* San Francisco: Encounter Books, 2003.

Benjamin, Daniel, and Steven Simon. *The Age of Sacred Terror.* New York: Random House, 2002.

Lance, Peter. *1000 Years for Revenge: International Terrorism and the FBI; The Untold Story.* New York: ReganBooks, 2003.

Al Qaeda

Al Qaeda is the umbrella terrorist organization that planned and carried out the attacks of September 11, 2001. Osama bin Laden formed Al Qaeda in May 1988, near the end of the Afghan-Soviet War, from the Mujahideen Services Bureau. The idea for an organization to coordinate Islamist activities came from bin Laden's mentor, Abdullah Azzam. An organizational meeting

on August 11, 1988, and another on August 20, finalized plans. In November 1988, the existence of Al Qaeda was formally announced. From its beginning, Al Qaeda had an organizational structure consisting of four committees: military, religious, financial, and media. A consulting council headed by bin Laden oversaw the organization.

Leadership with Al Qaeda is highly selective. Only about 200 individuals have sworn loyalty (*bayat*) to bin Laden and provide the leadership cadre. Empty leadership positions caused by deaths and captures are filled by highly motivated subordinates. These leaders have extensive contacts in the Islamist world and communicate via the Internet.

Bin Laden recruited a large number of Afghan fighters into Al Qaeda at the end of the Afghan-Soviet War. Many of these recruits headed back to their native countries, where they formed indigenous terrorist groups. Among the more prominent groups affiliated with Al Qaeda are Abu Sayyaf (the Sword of God, Philippines), the Armed Islamic Group (the GIA, Algeria), Hezbollah (the Party of God, Lebanon), the Islamic Group (Egypt), Hamas (Palestine), the Islamic Jihad (Egypt), Jemaah Islamiyah (Indonesia), and the Moro Islamic Liberation Front (MILF, Philippines), along with at least 22 additional groups.

Al Qaeda believes in training its operatives in basic combat skills. As many as 110,000 trainees trained in Al Qaeda camps from 1989 to 2001. Probably about 30,000 have graduated during that period. About 3,000 trainees were assessed as capable of advanced training for terrorist operations. Graduates of these camps retain their affiliation with Al Qaeda when they go elsewhere.

Al Qaeda established various training camps in Afghanistan and Pakistan in the

1990s. Most of the instructors were Egyptians and had previous experience in the military or in security forces. After the U.S.-led Operation ENDURING FREEDOM and the loss of Afghanistan as a base, several of these camps were transferred to remote areas in Pakistan to join the Pakistani camps already there.

Instructors at the camps issue a training manual to the trainees that emphasizes teamwork, willing submission to leaders, and, above all, secrecy. Among its recommendations are that apartment living arrangements during a mission should be in groups of three. The manual also recommends that martyrdom missions have at least four targets for greatest effect.

Only a select few of the trainees were deemed worthy of a martyrdom mission. Psychological profiling was conducted by the instructors to select those most worthy. The best candidates were those who were highly religious and well educated. A graduate of the al-Masada Training Camp, Hasan Abd-Rabbuh al-Suraghi, put it another way, stating that instructors looked for candidates who were "young, zealous, obedient, and [who had] a weak character that obeys instructions without question." The instructors had no difficulty finding volunteers.

Western terrorist analysts have been confused over the extent of Al Qaeda's control over these groups. The only consensus is that Al Qaeda has been able to establish a degree of coordination among its member groups. Rohan Gunaratna, a Sri Lankan and a former research fellow at the Centre for the Study of Terrorism and Political Violence at the University of St. Andrews in Scotland, has described Al Qaeda as "a secret, almost virtual organization, one that denies its own existence in order to remain in the shadows."

Al Qaeda is a selective organization that rigidly oversees the selection of its members to carry out operations. It recruits only the most talented and motivated candidates, who then earn a modest salary of about $200 a month; those with great responsibilities may receive up to $300. Before the loss of Afghanistan in late 2001, Al Qaeda had trained more than 5,000 operatives in a dozen training camps to carry out terrorist operations. Recruits were processed through main training camps before being sent to various locations for specialized training. About 55 possible training locations existed.

Besides specialized training, political and religious instruction also took place. Bin Laden made regular visits to the camps, where he gave lectures and pep talks. He also held personal talks with those selected for special operations. Bin Laden met with Mohamed Atta, Marwan al-Shehhi, and Ziad Jarrah when they arrived for training in Afghanistan. Because of Al Qaeda's high prestige in the Muslim world, there are many Arabs—probably as many as 100,000—who are willing to join Al Qaeda if invited. This highly selective system is used to make operations resistant to foreign intelligence services penetration. Those agents who have attempted to penetrate Al Qaeda are killed when discovered or even suspected. In 2002 Al Qaeda had operatives active in 55 countries.

Financial support for Al Qaeda comes from a variety of sources. In the early years bin Laden used his personal fortune of $30 million–$35 million to support many of Al Qaeda's operations, but, after leaving Sudan, his personal fortune diminished, and other sources of income had to be developed. Other significant sources of funding have come from Islamic nongovernmental organizations (NGOs), such as

Islamic charities and foundations. After the attacks on September 11, 2001, Western authorities attacked these NGOs, and a considerable amount of funding for Al Qaeda suddenly dried up. For a time financial support came from state sponsors—Afghanistan, Iran, and Sudan—but these sources of funding have also mostly ceased.

Al Qaeda has conducted operations in a systematic way. It developed operations by using three types of operatives. Local militants were recruited for groundwork but had no knowledge of the details of a plan. Sleepers were sent to live and work in the area long before the operation. Finally, Al Qaeda specialists and martyrs were brought in at the final stages of the mission. Once the mission was accomplished, the survivors were to go underground again. This was the type of operation that Al Qaeda carried out in the African embassy bombings. Al Qaeda planners, however, are flexible and willing to improvise in case conditions change.

Al Qaeda's first terrorist operation took place in 1992. This was the bombing of a hotel in Aden, Yemen, on December 29, 1992, that barely missed its targeted U.S. troops. On June 26, 1995, an Al Qaeda–led group attempted to assassinate Egyptian president Hosni Mubarak as he visited Addis Ababa, Ethiopia. Al Qaeda cooperated with an Iranian group in a June 25, 1996, truck bombing outside the Khobar Towers in Dharhran, Saudi Arabia, that killed 19 U.S. servicemen and wounded 500 others. Its next operation was the bombing of the U.S. embassies in Nairobi, Kenya, and Dar es Salaam, Tanzania, on August 7, 1998, killing 234 people. A suicide bombing of the American warship USS *Cole* on October 5, 2000, killed 17 sailors and wounded 39 others. All of these attacks paled beside the havoc of the Al Qaeda–led suicide attacks on the World Trade Center's twin towers and on the Pentagon on September 11, 2001.

Since September 11, 2001, Al Qaeda has taken direct credit for or indirectly inspired a number of terrorist attacks. These included attacks in Bali (October 2002); Casablanca, Morocco (May 2003); Madrid (March 2004); London (July 2005); Amman, Jordan (November 2005); and Algiers (December 2007). Would-be suicide bombers linked directly or indirectly to Al Qaeda included the 2001 shoe bomber Richard Reid and the 2009 underwear bomber Umar Farouk Abdulmutallab. It can be difficult, however, to ascertain the level of Al Qaeda involvement in such attacks.

The collapse of the Taliban in Afghanistan in the autumn of 2001 was a serious blow to Al Qaeda's future operations. It lost its main base for the training of its operatives, as well as a secure staging area. Another important loss was Al Qaeda's military operations chief, Mohammad Atef. He was the victim of a Predator strike in the early days of the attack on the Taliban in Afghanistan. The survival of bin Laden and his second-in-command, al-Zawahiri, allowed Al Qaeda to reestablish operations outside of Afghanistan, although on a much more limited basis. Because of its decentralized command structure, Al Qaeda has been able to recover some of its strike capability by entrusting operations to subordinate groups. Despite this, Al Qaeda has been put on the defensive, forced to pursue operations prematurely or send operatives underground as sleepers for future operations.

Since 2003, Al Qaeda military forces have been fighting alongside Taliban forces in Afghanistan. Because bin Laden was aware in advance of the September 11 attacks, he began distributing Al Qaeda's fighting assets throughout Afghanistan so that Al Qaeda forces could survive the onslaught of American retaliation. It took the American military three weeks, until October 7, 2001, to begin offensive operations against the Taliban and Al Qaeda. During this interval, Al Qaeda dismantled its forces in Afghanistan and sent most of them into Pakistan and other central Asian countries. Most of the battles during the initial phase of Operation ENDURING FREEDOM—such as those at Tora Bora and Shahi Kowt—were delaying actions designed to allow Al Qaeda forces time to escape into Pakistan.

Besides fighting and planning future operations, Al Qaeda has become increasingly active on the Internet, where it contacts its operatives and recruits sympathizers. *Al-Neda* and *al-Ansar* have been the two most prominent websites for Al Qaeda. Information provided on these websites by Al Qaeda members gives justification for Al Qaeda operations. Al Qaeda operatives also use the Internet to post audio and video messages. Western intelligence services have tried, with only limited success, to close down these websites.

Al Qaeda and Taliban forces have made a military comeback since 2003. From secure bases in Afghanistan and Pakistan, military operations have been launched without fear of detection. The Afghan government has had to depend on North Atlantic Treaty Organization (NATO) forces for security, but parts of Afghanistan have fallen into the hands of the Al Qaeda–Taliban alliance. The continued presence of U.S. and coalition forces in Afghanistan, as well as ever-rising numbers of civilian casualties from NATO airstrikes, have increased popular support for Al Qaeda and the Taliban in recent years. But the continued instability in Afghanistan may prove to be the undoing of the Taliban–Al Qaeda alliance. In January 2010, Taliban leaders suggested that they were willing to break with Al Qaeda in order to bring about peace.

The loss of Afghanistan as a training and staging area has hindered Al Qaeda's terrorist operations. Immediately after the loss of its training camps, Al Qaeda's leadership began to look for alternative sites. An unlikely replacement has been Europe. An underground railroad of recruits for Al Qaeda has been set up from the Middle East to Germany and Great Britain. Both Germany and Great Britain have been more tolerant in their laws against suspected terrorists, although both have tightened their laws since September 11. After receiving training, many Al Qaeda recruits have returned to the Middle East and been smuggled into Iraq to join the Sunni resistance to the American occupation of Iraq, and to fight Iraq's Shiites.

The U.S. government estimates that it has captured or killed some two-thirds of Al Qaeda's top leadership. Suspected Al Qaeda members are kept at the Guantánamo Bay Detention Camp or at a network of secret Central Intelligence Agency (CIA) interrogation centers. Others have been put on trial in other countries, including Egypt and Syria, through the process of extraordinary rendition. The loose and secretive structure of Al Qaeda, combined with the revelation of certain operational errors within the U.S. military and CIA, has made it difficult to verify the two-thirds claim. For example, when Abu Zubaydah was captured in March 2002, he was believed to be third in Al Qaeda's hierarchy. After years of interrogation and torture, the U.S. government in September 2009 changed its position, asserting that it no longer believed Zubaydah had ever been a member of Al Qaeda.

On May 1, 2011 (May 2 Pakistani local time), U.S. Navy SEALs, acting on intelligence gathered over the course of several months, raided a compound in Abbottabad, Pakistan, where bin Laden was believed to be hiding. In the ensuing firefight, bin Laden and four others were killed. Western intelligence and security forces, however, continue to consider Al Qaeda a major threat, poised to strike at any time and anywhere with any type of weapon, from biological to nuclear. This threat was underscored by the fact that shortly after the announcement of bin Laden's death, members of Al Qaeda and other extremist groups promised retribution for bin Laden's killing.

Since 2011, Al Qaeda's leader has been Egyptian terrorist Ayman al-Zawahiri. The U.S. State Department offers a reward of $25 million for information that leads to al-Zawahiri's capture.

Stephen E. Atkins

See also: Bin Laden, Osama; Global War on Terror; London Underground Bombings; Madrid Bombings; Taliban; World Trade Center, September 11; Zawahiri, Ayman al-

Suggested Reading

Corbin, Jane. *Al Qaeda: In Search of the Terror Network.* New York: Thunder's Mouth, 2002.

Gunaratna, Rohan. *Inside Al Qaeda: Global Network of Terror.* New York: Columbia University Press, 2002.

Hassan, Hamdi A. *Al Qaeda: The Background of the Pursuit for Global Jihad.* Stockholm: Almqvist and Wiksell International, 2004.

Wright, Lawrence. *The Looming Tower: Al Qaeda and the Road to 9/11.* New York: Knopf, 2006.

American Airlines Flight II

American Airlines Flight 11 was a Boeing 767-223ER that was the first aircraft to crash into the North Tower of the World Trade Center complex in New York City on September 11, 2001. The pilot of the aircraft was John Ogonowski, a 52-year-old Vietnam veteran from Massachusetts, and its First Officer was Thomas McGuinness. Flight 11 departed from Boston's Logan International Airport nearly 14 minutes late, at 7:59 a.m., bound for Los Angeles International Airport. It carried slightly more than half its capacity of 181—81 passengers and a crew of 11—and had a full load of 23,980 gallons of aviation fuel at takeoff, which was routine.

The leader of the terrorist team, and its designated pilot on board Flight 11, was Mohamed Atta. Atta and other members of the hijack team—Satam al-Suqami, Waleed al-Shehri, Wail al-Shehri, and Abdul Aziz al-Omari—had bought first-class seats, which research conducted on other flights convinced them gave them the best opportunity to seize the cockpit and gain control of the aircraft. Two of the hijackers sat near the cockpit and two near the passenger section. Atta sat in 8D from whence he could command both teams.

The hijackers had little trouble passing through checkpoint security. American Airlines' security checkpoints at Logan International Airport were operated by a private company, Globe Security, which operated these checkpoints under a contract with American Airlines. Because American Airlines' desire was for passengers to be harassed at checkpoints as little as possible, the hijackers had no difficulty in passing through the checkpoints carrying box cutters and mace.

Instructions had been given by Al Qaeda trainers to the hijackers to seize the aircraft by force within 15 minutes of takeoff. Around 8:14, they did so, killing two attendants and a passenger, Daniel Lewin, immediately. Lewin, formerly an officer in the elite Sayeret Matkal unit of the Israeli military, was seen as a threat. The hijackers, who had apparently identified him as a potential air marshal, killed him as soon as possible. To allay suspicions, the hijackers lulled the passengers and crew into a false sense of hope by giving the impression that the plane would land safely and that the passengers would be used as hostages, a successful tactic of hijackers in the past.

Air traffic controllers received information from the cockpit via Ogonowski's radio, over which they heard a conversation between the pilot and a hijacker in the cockpit that made it evident that a hijacking was in progress. More ominously, they also learned from a hijacker's comment about plans to seize control of other aircraft. This information was the first indication of a plot to hijack numerous aircraft in flight.

The first concrete information about the hijacking came from Betty Ong, a flight attendant on Fight 11, who contacted the American Airlines Flight Center in Fort Worth, Texas, and related that two flight attendants had been stabbed and that another was on oxygen. A passenger, she said, had been killed, and the hijackers had gained access to the cockpit, using some type of mace-like spray to neutralize the crew.

Once the hijackers gained control of the aircraft, they took precautions to control the passengers, securing the first class section by intimidation, mace and pepper spray, and threats to detonate a bomb. The rest of the passengers, in coach, were led to believe a medical emergency had occurred in the first class section. The hijackers also told the passengers that the aircraft was returning to the airport. Another attendant, Madeleine Sweeney, contacted authorities and confirmed Ong's earlier message to the American Flight Services Office in Boston. She reestablished communication and was in fact on the line when the aircraft approached the North Tower of the World Trade Center. By the time the passengers realized what was happening, it was too late to do anything. Many hurriedly called their loved ones and said goodbye either by talking with them or by leaving messages.

The aircraft crashed at about 378 miles per hour between the 94th and 98th floors of the North Tower. The crew, passengers, and hijackers all died instantly from the force of the explosion and the fire that accompanied it. The force of the explosion alone shattered the aluminum wings and fuselage of the aircraft into pieces the size of a human fist.

The impact of the crash and the prolonged burning of aviation fuel weakened the structure of the North Tower, trapping those people above the 98th floor, who had no chance of escape. Those threatened by fire and smoke began to jump from the building. The North Tower collapsed on itself shortly after the South Tower fell.

Stephen E. Atkins

See also: Atta, Mohamed el-Amir Awad el-Sayed; World Trade Center, September 11

Suggested Reading

Aust, Stefan, et al. *Inside 9/11: What Really Happened.* New York: St. Martin's, 2001.

Bernstein, Richard. *Out of the Blue: The Story of September 11, 2001, from Jihad to Ground Zero.* New York: Times Books, 2002.

Craig, Olga. "At 8:46 AM, the World Changed in a Moment." *Sunday Telegraph* [London], September 16, 2001, 14.

9/11 Commission. *The 9/11 Commission Report: Final Report of the National Commission on Terrorist Attacks upon the United States.* New York: Norton, 2004.

Trento, Susan B., and Joseph J. Trento. *Unsafe at Any Altitude: Failed Terrorism Investigations, Scapegoating 9/11, and the Shocking Truth about Aviation Security Today.* Hanover, NH: Steerforth, 2006.

American Airlines Flight 77

American Airlines Flight 77, a Boeing 757–223, was the third aircraft seized by hijackers on September 11, 2001. It left Dulles International Airport, near Washington, DC, at 8:20 a.m., bound for Los Angeles International Airport with 58 passengers and a crew of 6. The pilot was Charles Burlingame and the First Officer was David Charlebois. Because of problems at the security gate, the flight was 10 minutes late taking off. The security checkpoint at Dulles International Airport was operated by Argenbright Security under a contract with United Airlines. Passenger screeners at Dulles International Airport were 87 percent foreign-born and mostly Muslim. Three of the hijackers failed the metal detector test, but, after passing hand-wand screening, were permitted to enter the aircraft. There was no indication that any of them were carrying prohibited weapons.

The five-person terrorist team was led by Hani Hanjour, who was also the team's designated pilot. Other members of his team were Nawaf al-Hazmi, Salem al-Hazmi, Khalid al-Mihdhar, and Majed Moqued, who had all bought first-class tickets to gain better access to the aircraft's cockpit. The hijackers used knives and box cutters to gain control of the cockpit sometime between 8:51 and 8:54 a.m., after which

On September 11, 2001, American Airlines Flight 77 slammed into the Pentagon in Arlington, Virginia, killing everyone on the plane and 125 in the building, including 74 Army personnel. (United States Army)

Hanjour turned the aircraft around and headed for Washington, DC. Like the hijackers of American Airlines Flight 11, the hijackers of Flight 77 calmed passengers by convincing them that the plane would land, after which they would be used as hostages.

Although by this time it was known that other aircraft had been seized and turned into flying bombs, authorities in Washington, DC, were slow to respond. Two passengers, Renee May and Barbara K. Olson, the wife of U.S. solicitor general Theodore Olson, made phone calls reporting the hijacking. She made two calls to her husband, giving him details of the hijacking. He told her the news of the two aircraft crashing into the World Trade Center.

By this time the Dulles air controllers were aware of an approaching unauthorized aircraft coming at high speed toward Washington, DC. They had been able to obtain a visual confirmation from a military transport, a C-141, as the hijacked aircraft headed toward the Pentagon. Between 9:37 and 9:40 a.m., Flight 77 crashed at 530 miles per hour into the ground at the base of the west side of the Pentagon, killing all passengers. Although much of the crash site contained recently renovated, unoccupied offices, the explosion and the resulting collapse of parts of the five-story building killed 125 people. The explosion did its greatest damage to the three outer rings of the Pentagon, but the two inner rings sustained damage as well.

Stephen E. Atkins

See also: Hanjour, Hani Saleh Husan; Pentagon Attack

Suggested Reading

Aust, Stefan, et al. *Inside 9/11: What Really Happened.* New York: St. Martin's, 2001.

Bernstein, Richard. *Out of the Blue: The Story of September 11, 2001, from Jihad to Ground Zero.* New York: Times Books, 2002.

9/11 Commission. *The 9/11 Commission Report: Final Report of the National Commission on Terrorist Attacks upon the United States.* New York: Norton, 2004.

Trento, Susan B., and Joseph J. Trento. *Unsafe at Any Altitude: Failed Terrorism Investigations, Scapegoating 9/11, and the Shocking Truth about Aviation Security Today.* Hanover, NH: Steerforth, 2006.

American Society of Civil Engineers Report

A committee of the American Society of Civil Engineers (ASCE) issued a report in the late spring of 2002 concerning the reasons for the collapse of the buildings of the World Trade Center complex on September 11. ASCE was founded in 1852 and is the oldest organization of its type in existence—and one of the most prestigious. After receiving a $1 million grant from the Federal Emergency Management Agency (FEMA), a 22-member committee was formed that contained specialists on metallurgy, fire, structural dynamics, and other relevant fields. Some of the biggest names in civil engineering participated in this study.

The chair of the ASCE committee was W. Gene Corley, senior vice president of an engineering research facility north of Chicago, whose PhD is in civil engineering. Corley had been the leader of the official engineering review of the 1995 Oklahoma City bombing of the Alfred P. Murrah Federal Building. He had a reputation as a fair and independent investigator of building failures.

Fires still burned amidst the rubble and debris of the World Trade Centers at Ground Zero two days after the 9/II terrorists attacks. (U.S. Department of Defense)

The final report of the ASCE committee was never intended to definitively analyze the entire situation but rather to understand how and why the buildings at the World Trade Center collapsed. Other pertinent issues, such as crowded stairwells and lack of egress for those above the damaged areas, were not included in the scope of the investigation. The investigators visited the World Trade Center complex site, but they found it too chaotic for normal surveying of materials. Even an examination of the steel proved disappointing. Instead, the investigators used known facts and computer simulations.

The investigators soon learned that the Twin Towers had been designed for lightness and efficiency—not for strength. The towers were essentially 1,362-foot-tall tubes. The architects had designed the

buildings to withstand winds of 150 miles per hour, and the decision to anchor them in bedrock gave them even more strength. There was some give in the building, and in strong winds people noticed some sway. Most of the support columns and elevators were in the middle of the building. The floors were built on thin steel trusses covered in concrete. The total weight of each tower, discounting people, furniture, and equipment, was around 600,000 tons.

The investigators came to understand the dynamics of the collapse of the South Tower best. It was relatively easy to calculate the force of impact of a Boeing 767 fully loaded with aviation fuel. The hijacker pilot, Marwan al-Shehhi, crashed the Boeing 767 at a speed of nearly 590 miles per hour into the south side of the South Tower, three-fourths of the way up the building. Because of its speed, the aircraft penetrated deeply into the building, severing as many as half the columns in the central core. The building might have survived except for the fire fueled by the aviation fuel. ASCE's final report claims that the South Tower would have remained intact even with the aviation fuel fire if the fire had not reached flammable material, such as furniture and paper, that intensified it, spreading it to six different floors. Molten aluminum began to flow down the building.

The investigators noted that the fire began to degrade the strength of the steel. Although the report ignored the issue, detractors had long charged that the fireproofing of the Twin Towers' steel was inferior. The fire burned at about 1,500 degrees. Structural steel begins to weaken at 300 degrees and at 1,100 degrees loses half its strength.

The fire could not be stopped. The building's sprinkler system was destroyed in the crash and would not have been powerful enough to put out such a fire anyway. Firefighters were eager but lacked equipment and a water supply sufficient to put out such a disastrous high-rise fire.

Fifty-six minutes after the aircraft crashed into the South Tower, it collapsed, beginning with the southeast corner of the 80th floor, whose collapse triggered the progressive collapse of the entire east side of the building. As supports gave way, the collapse began to accelerate. The upper sections fell east and south, damaging the Bankers Trust Building, and the lower sections fell north and west, damaging the Marriott Hotel.

The investigators knew less, however, about the collapse of the North Tower. The Boeing 767 that hit it traveled about 100 miles per hour slower than the one that crashed into the South Tower and severely damaged 36 of the 61 columns on the north

face of the building. Damage was done to all three stairways, and the sprinkler system was knocked out. Parts of the aircraft blew through the building. A massive fire broke out, fueled first by aviation fuel and then by the furniture and paper contained in the offices. Because the aircraft hit high in the building, it bore a lighter load as the fire degraded the steel on the four floors. After nearly two hours of high-temperature fires, the building finally collapsed for the same reasons as the South Tower.

The other buildings in the World Trade Center complex also suffered severe enough damage that they too collapsed. Most mysterious was the burning and eventual collapse that evening of Seven World Trade Center. This building was situated away from the Twin Towers but caught fire nonetheless. Eyewitnesses report that the fuel oil storage unit caught fire at the base of the building. By this time the firefighters were so demoralized by their losses from the collapse of the Twin Towers that the leadership of the Fire Department City of New York (FDNY) refused to risk any more men. Building Seven collapsed from the bottom by early evening. A probable contributing cause was the fire in the fuel storage unit just outside the building. As with the Twin Towers, the fire intensified, fed by furniture and paper in the building, until the structure, undermined, collapsed.

The final report explained the process that contributed to the collapse of the buildings at the World Trade Center complex but left room for further study. Despite earlier criticism of the architectural design and the materials used to build the World Trade Center complex, the committee defended the construction of the buildings while expressing concern about the centralized columns and stairways and recommending that new structures be capable of withstanding the type of airliner crash experienced on September 11.

Stephen E. Atkins

See also: Firefighters at Ground Zero; World Trade Center

Suggested Reading

Bianculli, David. "NOVA: Why the Towers Fell." *Daily News* [New York], April 30, 2002, 91.

Langewiesche, William. *American Ground: Unbuilding the World Trade Center.* New York: North Point, 2002.

Anthrax Attacks

On September 18, 2001, one week after the terrorist attacks of September 11, five letters contaminated with anthrax bacteria were mailed in the United States to five media outlets. Over the next month, two more letters were mailed. All together, the anthrax letters resulted in the deaths of 5 people and the infections of 17 more. The sender mailed the letters from a mailbox in New Jersey.

The letters sent on September 18 were sent to the offices of ABC News, CBS News, NBC News, the *New York Post,* and the *National Enquirer.* After evidence of anthrax was found in the offices, scientists discovered two of the anthrax letters and began analyzing their contents. They found rudimentary anthrax material inside.

Nearly a month later, two more letters were sent, to Democratic senators Tom Daschle and Patrick Leahy at the Senate building in Washington, DC. The postal service misdirected Leahy's letter, but the letter addressed to Daschle was opened by an aide who became infected. Unlike the earlier letters, the second set of letters contained higher-quality, weapons-grade anthrax capable of infecting victims with greater lethality.

In response to the attacks, thousands of people in direct contact with or who were near the envelopes began taking strong doses of Cipro, an antibiotic capable of

On October 23, 2001, the Federal Bureau of Investigation (FBI) released photos of the letters sent to U.S. senator Tom Daschle, broadcaster Tom Brokaw, and the *New York Post* that contained anthrax spores. This envelope, sent to Daschle, was the only one with a return address, which turned out to be false. (Federal Bureau of Investigation)

treating anthrax infections. In addition, the federal government began radiation treatment of all incoming mail to defuse any possible anthrax inside. Post office employees began wearing gloves and masks and warned all Americans to carefully examine their mail and report any suspicious letters or packages. Five people died from the anthrax infection: one employee at the *National Enquirer,* two post office employees, and two other unconnected people whose mail was likely cross-contaminated by the anthrax letters.

In the immediate aftermath of the anthrax attacks, which became popularly known by the name Amerithrax, many speculated that they were connected to Al Qaeda and the September 11 attacks. It was also suggested that Iraq had provided the anthrax spores. Although doctors at the Johns Hopkins Center for Civilian Biodefense Strategies have proposed that one of the 9/11 hijackers may have been infected with cutaneous anthrax when he arrived at a Florida emergency room before the 9/11 attacks presenting a lesion on his leg, no definitive link has been established.

Government officials began an investigation immediately after discovering the anthrax letters. Following a variety of leads, the investigators profiled the suspect as a chemical or biological engineer in the United States who had likely worked previously at government facilities. Some microbiologist experts who examined the anthrax stated that its quality was likely above that of the anthrax found in either U.S. or Russian stockpiles, and thus likely created in recent government anthrax programs.

By April 2005, the Federal Bureau of Investigation (FBI) had identified Bruce Edwards Ivins, a scientist working at the government's biodefense labs at Fort Detrick in Frederick, Maryland, as the primary

suspect in the anthrax attacks. Placed on surveillance beginning in April 2007, Ivins committed suicide on July 27, 2008. On August 6, federal prosecutors named Ivins as the sole perpetrator of the attacks, and on February 19, 2010, the FBI formally closed its investigation. Lingering skepticism, however, has continued to swirl around the conclusions of the FBI's investigation.

Spencer C. Tucker

See also: Federal Bureau of Investigation

Suggested Reading

Coen, Bob, and Eric Nadler. *Dead Silence: Fear and Terror on the Anthrax Trail.* Berkeley: Counterpoint, 2009.

Croddy, Eric A., and James J. Wirtz, eds. *Weapons of Mass Destruction: An Encyclopedia of Worldwide Policy, Technology, and History.* Santa Barbara, CA: ABC-CLIO, 2005.

Atef, Mohammad (1944–2001)

Mohammad Atef was Al Qaeda's head of military operations during the planning and implementation of the September 11, 2001, operation. At that time Atef was number three in the Al Qaeda hierarchy, behind Osama bin Laden and Ayman al-Zawahiri. Atef made decisions about the events of September 11 from the beginning, assisting Khalid Sheikh Mohammed in the final stages of the plot.

Atef converted to Islamist extremism early in his career. Born in 1944 in Menoufya, Egypt, in the Nile Delta, about 35 miles north of Cairo, he was named Sobhi Abu Sitta. After graduating from high school, he served his required two years of military service in the Egyptian Army. Reports that Atef was a policeman in Egypt have been denied by the Egyptian government, but nearly all sources state that he was. In the late 1970s, Atef joined an Egyptian terrorist organization, the Egyptian Islamic Jihad. Evidently a low-ranking member, he didn't meet with its leader, al-Zawahiri, while both were in Egypt. Despite his involvement in this group, he escaped arrest after the crackdown on extremists that followed the assassination of President Anwar Sadat in 1981. In 1983 Atef left Egypt for Afghanistan to fight with the mujahideen against Soviet forces, where he first met al-Zawahiri, who then introduced him to bin Laden. Atef and bin Laden became close friends. Atef also became acquainted with Abdullah Azzam and admired him greatly, but in the subsequent battle between Azzam and al-Zawahiri for bin Laden's support, Atef supported al-Zawahiri. In 1999 Egyptian authorities sentenced Atef to a seven-year prison term in absentia for his membership in the Egyptian Islam Jihad, but Atef never returned to Egypt.

Atef's close personal relationship with bin Laden made him an important member of Al Qaeda. When bin Laden founded Al Qaeda, Atef was a charter member. Ubaidah al-Banshiri was Al Qaeda's head of military operations, and Atef assisted him. He was active in organizing Somali resistance to American military presence in 1992, but some evidence suggests that his stay there was not entirely successful. Atef also served as bin Laden's chief of personal security. Al-Banshiri's death in a boat accident in Africa allowed Atef to replace him in 1996. From then until his death in 2001, Atef was in charge of military operations for Al Qaeda. All military operations came under his oversight, but he remained subordinate to bin Laden even after bin Laden's eldest son married one of Atef's daughters in January 2001.

Atef was aware of the September 11 plot from its beginning. Khalid Sheikh Mohammed outlined the plan to bin Laden and Atef as early as 1996. Bin Laden finally agreed on the basics of the plot in 1998. It was Atef's job to search Al Qaeda's training camps for suitable candidates for a martyrdom mission that required operatives to live unnoticed in the United States. Once the members of the Hamburg Cell were picked and recruited by bin Laden, Atef explained to Mohamed Atta, Ramzi bin al-Shibh, Ziad Jarrah, and Marwan al-Shehhi the outlines of the plot.

Al Qaeda avoided having its leaders at a single site except for particularly special occasions, a policy prompted by fears of American assassination of Al Qaeda's leaders. Bin Laden announced that in case of his death or capture, Atef would succeed him as head of Al Qaeda. Once the United States began military operations against the Taliban and Al Qaeda in Afghanistan, it became even more important for Al Qaeda's leaders to be at separate locations. Atef was at a gathering in Kabul on November 18, 2001, when a Predator unmanned aerial vehicle fired Hellfire missiles, killing Atef and those with him—something for which the United States had been offering a $5 million reward. The loss of Atef was a blow to Al Qaeda, but he was soon replaced as military commander by Abu Zubaydah.

Stephen E. Atkins

See also: Al Qaeda; Atta, Mohamed el-Amir Awad el-Sayed; Bin al-Shibh, Ramzi; Bin Laden, Osama; Hamburg Cell; Jarrah, Ziad Samir; Shehhi, Marwan Yousef Muhammed Rashid Lekrab al-

Suggested Reading

Dawoud, Khaled. "Mohammed Atef; Egyptian Militant Who Rose to the Top of the

al-Qaida Hierarchy." *Guardian* [London], November 19, 2001, 1.

MATP. "Iron Fist Reaches from Far Side of the Globe." *Australian* [Sydney], November 19, 2001, 8.

Atta, Mohamed el-Amir Awad el-Sayed (1968–2001)

Mohamed el-Amir Awad el-Sayed Atta was the commander of the Al Qaeda team that hijacked four American commercial aircraft and used them as guided missiles on September 11, 2001. He had been recruited by Al Qaeda for this mission after being trained by Al Qaeda trainers. Only the most highly motivated individuals were selected for martyrdom missions, and Atta met this requirement.

Atta had a strict family upbringing. He was born on September 1, 1968, in the village of Kafr el-Sheikh in the Egyptian delta. His father was a middle-class lawyer with ties to the fundamentalist Muslim Brotherhood. Atta's family moved to the Abdin District of Cairo in 1978 when Atta was 10. His father, who had a dominating personality, insisted that his children study, not play. Atta's family life allowed him few friends. After attending a local high school, he enrolled in the Cairo University in 1986. As usual in the Egyptian system, Atta's admittance to the university was based on his exam scores, and he was assigned to a specialty—the architecture section of the engineering department. At his graduation in 1990, his grades were not good enough to admit him to graduate school. On the recommendation of his father, he then planned to study town planning in Germany. In the meantime, he worked for a Cairo engineering firm. After learning German at the Goethe Institute in Cairo, Atta traveled to Hamburg, Germany, in July 1992 to begin studying town planning. He applied first to study architecture at the University of Applied Science but, after being turned down, migrated to the Technical University of Hamburg-Harburg to study the preservation of the Islamic quarters of medieval cities in the Middle East. During his coursework, Atta interacted very little with fellow students, earning a reputation as a loner. His classmates also noted his strong religious orientation. He traveled to Turkey and Syria in 1994 to study old Muslim quarters. After receiving a German grant, Atta and two fellow students visited Egypt to study the old section of Cairo, called the Islamic City. They were appalled at what the Egyptian government was doing to this old part of the city. Up to this point in his life, Atta appeared to be an academic preparing for a career as a teacher at a university.

In 1995, however, he became active in Muslim extremist politics. After a pilgrimage to Mecca, he initiated contact with Al Qaeda recruiters. Atta was just the type of individual that Al Qaeda recruiters were looking for—intelligent and dedicated. After his return to Hamburg to continue his studies, he attended the al-Quds Mosque, where his final recruitment to radical Islam took place. There Atta met radical clerics who steered him toward an Al Qaeda recruiter. Muhammad Zammar, a Syrian recruiter for Al Qaeda, convinced Atta to join Al Qaeda. Several of his friends, Ramzi bin al-Shibh, Marwan al-Shehhi, and Ziad Jarrah, also joined Al Qaeda. Atta became the leader of the so-called Hamburg Cell of radical Islamists.

In 1998 Atta left for Kandahar, Afghanistan, to receive military and terrorist training at the Al Qaeda training camp at Khaldan. He so distinguished himself during the training that Al Qaeda leaders decided to recruit him for a future suicide mission. Atta ranked high in all the attributes of an Al Qaeda operative—intelligence, religious devotion, patience, and willingness to sacrifice. Atta, Jarrah, and al-Shehhi met and talked with Osama bin Laden in Kandahar. Bin Laden asked them to pledge loyalty to him and accept a suicide mission. They agreed, and Mohammed Atef, Al Qaeda's military chief, briefed them on the general outlines of the September 11 operation. Then Atta and the others were sent back to Germany to finish their academic training.

Atta was a complex individual, deeply affected psychologically. He had puritanical and authoritarian views toward women and, despite having two sisters and a reportedly normal relationship with his mother, believed women and sexual intercourse were polluting. Only once, in Syria, did a woman attract him—but he complained that the Palestinian woman was too forward. Atta also held strong anti-American views, disturbed by the Americanization of Egyptian society.

After he finished his degree in 1999, Al Qaeda's leaders assigned him his martyrdom mission in the United States, a mission planned by Khalid Sheikh Mohammed. Atta arrived in the United States on June 2, 2000. His orders placed him in charge of a large cell, but he, Jarrah, and al-Shehhi were the only members of his cell who knew the details of his mission. Several times Atta flew back and forth between the United States and Germany and Spain to coordinate the mission. Members of his cell arrived in the United States at various times. Atta and key members of the cell received orders to take pilot lessons to fly large commercial aircraft.

Most of Atta's time was spent in pilot lessons in Florida. Before he could qualify for training on large commercial aircraft, Atta had to learn to fly small planes. Most of his flying instruction took place at Huffman Aviation in Sarasota, Florida. He had an attitude problem that hurt his relations with his instructors, but it did not prevent him from earning his small aircraft license in December 2000. Next, he began to use simulators and manuals to train himself to fly large commercial aircraft.

Atta gathered most of the members of his cell together in Florida for the first time in early June 2001. He organized the cell into four teams, each of which included a trained pilot. Throughout the summer of 2001, each team rode as passengers on test flights in which they studied the efficiency of airline security and strategized about the best time to hijack an aircraft. They discovered that airline security was weakest at Boston's Logan International Airport and decided that the best day for hijacking was Tuesday. They decided that first-class seats would give them better access to cockpits. Although the teams tried to remain inconspicuous, Hollywood actor James Woods reported suspicious behavior by one of the teams on a flight. He reported his suspicions to the pilot and a flight attendant, who passed them on to the Federal Aviation Administration (FAA), but nothing came of his report. Atta selected two airlines— American Airlines and United Airlines— that flew Boeing 757s and 767s, aircraft used for long flights that thus held the most aviation fuel. Furthermore, these aircraft were equipped with up-to-date avionics, making them easier to fly.

Atta called for a leadership meeting in Las Vegas, Nevada, in late June 2001. Atta, Ziad Jarrah, Hani Hanjour, and Nawaf al-Hazmi stayed at the EconoLodge Motel in Las Vegas, where they completed plans for the September 11 operation. Atta and Jarrah used a local Cyberzone Internet Café to send e-mails to Al Qaeda leaders abroad.

Atta then traveled to Spain via Zurich, Switzerland, to update his handlers on his final plans and receive last minute instructions. He met with Al Qaeda representatives in the resort town of Salou on July 8, 2001, receiving his final authorization for the September 11 mission. Atta was given final authority to determine the targets and date of the operation. Several times bin Laden had attempted to push the plan forward, but Atta had refused to carry out the mission before he was ready and was backed by Khalid Sheikh Mohammad in this. Atta flew back to the United States, and, despite an expired visa, had no trouble getting past the Immigration and Naturalization Services (INS) agents at the airport.

Atta issued final instructions about the mission on the night of September 10. One-way tickets for flights on September 11 had been bought with credit cards in late August. Atta had made arrangements to have the cell's excess funds transferred back to Al Qaeda on September 4. He traveled to Portland, Maine, with Abdul Aziz al-Omari, where they stayed at the Comfort Inn in South Portland. They caught a 5:45 a.m. flight out of Portland International Airport, but Atta's luggage arrived too late to make American Airlines Flight 11 from Logan International Airport. At 7:45 a.m., Atta and al-Omari boarded American Airlines Flight 11. Soon afterward, Atta phoned Marwan al-Shehhi, on board United Airlines Flight 175—also at Logan International Airport—to make sure everything was on schedule.

Atta commanded the first team. Approximately 15 minutes after takeoff, his team seized control of the aircraft using box openers as weapons. Atta redirected the aircraft toward New York City and the World Trade Center complex, where it crashed into the North Tower of the World Trade Center at about 8:45 a.m. Other members of the team carried out their attacks successfully except for one flight lost in Pennsylvania.

Stephen E. Atkins

See also: Al Qaeda; American Airlines Flight 11; Bin al-Shibh, Ramzi; Hamburg Cell; Jarrah, Ziad Samir; Mohammed, Khalid Sheikh; Shehhi, Marwan Yousef Muhammed Rashid Lekrab al-; World Trade Center, September 11

B

Beamer, Todd Morgan (1968–2001)

Todd Morgan Beamer was on United Airlines Flight 93 on September 11, 2001, and was one of the passengers who attempted to regain control of the aircraft from the hijackers. Beamer and others burst into the cockpit and contested the hijackers for control of the plane. The fact that the attempt to regain control of the cockpit was unsuccessful does not detract from the effort. Beamer and his fellow passengers kept the hijackers from crashing the airliner into a Washington, DC, building—probably the U.S. Capitol.

Beamer has been described by his wife as an ordinary man. He was born on November 24, 1968, in Flushing, Michigan, near Flint. His father worked for several large corporations, and the family moved several times, ending up in Chicago. Beamer attended a private elementary school in Glen Ellyn—Wheaton Christian Grammar School. For three years he went to Wheaton Christian High School, until his father was transferred to California. In his senior year Beamer attended Los Gatos High School in Los Gatos, California, where he was a starter on the basketball and baseball teams. After graduation from high school, he entered California State University–Fresno, but the aftereffects of a car wreck and his inability to make the nationally ranked baseball team as a walk-on led him to transfer to Wheaton College in Wheaton, Illinois, where he did become a member of the baseball team. After graduating from college with a business degree, he started work on an MBA at DePaul University, which he earned in 1993. He found a job as an account manager for the Oracle Corporation, and over the next eight years he made steady progress up the corporate hierarchy. He worked long hours, and his job required constant travel. On May 14, 1994, Beamer married Lisa Brosious. By September 2001 he and his wife had two young sons, and his wife was five months pregnant. They had just returned from an Oracle Company–sponsored vacation in Rome.

Beamer took Flight 93 on September 11 because he had an important business meeting in San Francisco with high-level representatives of Sony Corporation. Beamer wanted an early-morning flight in order to keep his 1:00 p.m. appointment.

Beamer has become one of the more famous of those who tried to regain control of Flight 93. Soon after the hijackers seized control of the plane at 9:45 a.m., Beamer contacted Lisa Jefferson, the GTE Airfone operator, to inform her that the aircraft had been hijacked. He reported that one passenger had been killed, and that a flight attendant had told him the pilot and copilot had been forced from the cockpit and may have been wounded. From the other passengers Beamer had learned that the hijackers were on a suicide mission. When hijacker Ziad Jarrah turned the aircraft around, Beamer and the others decided to try to regain control by attacking the hijackers. He teamed with Mark Bingham, Thomas Burnett, Jeremy Glick, and others to fight for control of the airliner. Beamer was under no illusions, and he told the Airfone operator that he knew he was going to die and asked her to pray with him. First they recited the Lord's Prayer. Then they recited the 23rd Psalm, and other passengers joined in the prayer. He also asked the operator to relay a message to his wife and their two sons: "Tell her I love her and the boys." Beamer was still on the phone with Lisa Jefferson when his last audible words were heard: "Are you guys ready? Let's roll." By this time all of the hijackers had retreated into the cockpit area. The passengers had coffeepots full of hot water prepared by the flight attendants to use as weapons, and they took a cart of food trays to crash into the cockpit area. A struggle ensued, with the hijackers close to being overpowered. To keep from losing control of the aircraft, hijacker Jarrah crashed it into the ground near Shanksville, Pennsylvania. Beamer has since become famous for the expression, "Let's roll," which became the battle cry of soldiers fighting Al Qaeda in Afghanistan.

Beamer has received several honors since his death. School authorities named a high school in Federal Way, Washington, after him: Todd Beamer High School. His name was given to a post office in Cranbury, New Jersey. His college, Wheaton College, named their student center the Todd M. Beamer Student Center. Finally, his wife, Lisa, wrote a book with coauthor Ken Abraham titled *Let's Roll! Ordinary People, Extraordinary Courage*. She also established a nonprofit foundation in his name in October 2001—The Todd M. Beamer Foundation—to help the families of victims of September 11 with young children.

Stephen E. Atkins

See also: Burnett, Thomas Edward; United Airlines Flight 93

Suggested Reading

Beamer, Lisa, and Ken Abraham. *Let's Roll! Ordinary People, Extraordinary Courage.* Wheaton, IL: Tyndale House, 2002.

Flores, David. "Heroism of Ex-Athletes on Flight 93 Inspiring." *San Antonio Express-News,* September 10, 2002, 7C.

Jefferson, Lisa, and Felicia Middlebrooks. *Called: "Hello, My Name Is Mrs. Jefferson. I Understand Your Plane Is Being Hijacked?"—9:45 AM, Flight 93, September 11, 2001.* Chicago: Northfield Publishing, 2006.

Kelly, Jack. "Flight 93 Uprising Saved Countless Lives in Capital." *Pittsburgh Post-Gazette,* June 18, 2004, A1.

Lane, Charles, Don Phillips, and David Snyder. "A Sky Filled with Chaos, Uncertainty and True Heroism." *Washington Post,* September 17, 2001, A3.

Longman, Jeer. *Among the Heroes: United Flight 93 and the Passengers and Crew Who Fought Back.* New York: HarperCollins, 2002.

McKinnon, Jim. "The Phone Line from Flight 93 Was Still Open When a GTE Operator Heard Todd Beamer Say: 'Are You Guys Ready? Let's Roll.'" *Pittsburgh Post-Gazette,* September 16, 2001, A1.

Bin al-Shibh, Ramzi (1972–)

Ramzi bin al-Shibh was one of the chief planners of the September 11, 2001, attacks in the United States. He was an active member of the Hamburg Cell. Frustrated in his inability to obtain a visa to participate in the September 11 attacks, bin al-Shibh stayed in Hamburg, Germany, where he continued to provide logistical support for the conspirators until the eve of the attack.

Bin al-Shibh was born on May 1, 1972, in Ghayl Bawazir, in the province of Hadramaut, Yemen. His father was a merchant. The family moved to the city of Sana'a in northern Yemen when bin al-Shibh was a small boy. His father died in 1987 when his son was 16. Bin al-Shibh was an enthusiastic child, and from the beginning he was more religious than the rest of his family. After finishing his schooling, he began working as a messenger boy at the International Bank of Yemen. For a time he studied at a business school before deciding to leave Yemen. In 1995, he applied for a U.S. visa, but his application was turned down. Determined to leave Yemen, bin al-Shibh then traveled to Germany, where he claimed to be a Sudanese citizen seeking political asylum using the name Ramzi Omar. German authorities were suspicious of his claim for political asylum, and it was initially turned down. Germany received more than 100,000 political asylum seekers annually, most wanting access to Germany's generous welfare system that would guarantee free health care and money for food and lodging almost indefinitely. Bin al-Shibh spent two years at a special camp, the so-called Container Camp, awaiting his appeal. During the period pending the appeal of his asylum claim, he joined the al-Quds Mosque in Hamburg, where he met Mohammed Atta and other Islamist militants. After his appeal was denied by the German government, bin al-Shibh returned to Yemen in 1997. Shortly thereafter, he returned to Germany, this time using his true name. This time bin al-Shibh enrolled in a school in Hamburg, although academic problems led to his expulsion in September 1998.

Bin al-Shibh was an active member of the Hamburg Cell. There he was known by associates as Omar. He roomed with Atta and Marwan al-Shehhi beginning in 1998. In summer 1998, bin al-Shibh traveled to Afghanistan for special training at one of Al Qaeda's training camps. He was obviously a top student because leaders of Al Qaeda selected him for a special mission. A fellow recruit testified that bin al-Shibh had extensive contact with bin Laden while in Afghanistan. Along with Atta, Ziad Jarrah, and al-Shehhi, he was recruited by bin Laden for a special martyrdom mission. Mohammed Atef, the military commander of Al Qaeda, gave them a briefing on the outlines of the September 11 plot. After returning to Germany, bin al-Shibh joined with Atta and al-Shehhi in working at a warehouse packing computers for shipping.

Bin al-Shibh's personality and abilities made him one of the leaders of the Hamburg Cell. He became one of the chief recruiters for the Hamburg Cell because he was better liked and more influential in the Muslim community than Atta. Bin al-Shibh also traveled extensively throughout Germany, and was able to recruit others for the Hamburg Cell.

Bin al-Shibh also served as the cheerleader for the Hamburg Cell. He gathered cassette tapes of jihad activities in Chechnya, Bosnia, and Kosovo and played them all over Hamburg to Muslim audiences. The longer he was active in the cell, the more militant his beliefs became. He believed that the highest attainment in life was to die for the jihad. Only bin al-Shibh's inability to obtain a visa prevented him from joining Mohamed Atta's suicide team on September 11. Four times he sought a visa—three times in Berlin and once in Yemen. Bin al-Shibh was turned down each time because consular officers believed that, being Yemeni, he might be an unlawful immigrant. He even tried using other people's names, but with no luck. Instead, bin al-Shibh provided logistical support and money from Germany. He kept in close contact with Atta, and served as his banker. He also protected the men of the Hamburg Cell by keeping them registered as students. Bin al-Shibh was the only member of the Hamburg Cell to attend the January 2000 Kuala Lumpur meeting where Al Qaeda midlevel operatives discussed future operations.

Another of bin al-Shibh's responsibilities was recruitment. He recruited Zacarias Moussaoui into Al Qaeda. Bin al-Shibh gave Moussaoui funds for pilot training in the United States. Although Moussaoui was not a part of the Hamburg Cell and the September 11 plot, he was being considered for a future martyrdom mission.

When bin al-Shibh finally learned the date of the attack on the World Trade Center complex, the Pentagon, and the U.S. Capitol or White House in late August 2001, he began to shut down operations in Germany. He was aware that all members and anyone affiliated with the Hamburg Cell would be subject to arrest. In early September bin al-Shibh fled to Pakistan, where he thought he would be safe from American reprisal.

Bin al-Shibh was captured at an apartment complex in Karachi, Pakistan, on September 11, 2002, after a gunfight with Pakistani security forces. On September 16, 2002, the Pakistani government turned bin al-Shibh over to American security officials, who moved him out of Pakistan to a secure interrogation site. Since his arrest, bin al-Shibh has been cooperative in providing intelligence on the nuclear, biological, and chemical capabilities of Al Qaeda, as well as on how the Al Qaeda organization functions. Despite this cooperation, bin al-Shibh has expressed no regrets about his involvement with Al Qaeda; had he not been captured he would likely still be an active participant. In August 2006, bin al-Shibh was transferred to the Guantánamo Bay Detention Camp with 13 other high-profile terrorist suspects. One of five "enemy combatants" originally slated for trial in New York City in 2010 before the controversial plan was dropped and then repeatedly delayed, al-Shibh's trial was recently slated to begin in early 2021. He remains in custody in Guantánamo Bay.

Stephen E. Atkins

See also: Al Qaeda; Atta, Mohamed el-Amir Awad el-Sayed; Guantánamo Bay Detention Camp; Hamburg Cell; Jarrah, Ziad Samir; Mohammed, Khalid Sheikh; Moussaoui, Zacarias; Shehhi, Marwan Yousef Muhammed Rashid Lekrab al-

Suggested Reading

Fouda, Yosri, and Nick Fielding. *Masterminds of Terror: The Truth behind the Most Devastating Terrorist Attack the World Has Ever Seen.* New York: Arcade Publishing, 2003.

McDermott, Terry. *Perfect Soldiers: The 9/11 Hijackers; Who They Were, Why They Did It.* New York: HarperCollins, 2005.

Posner, Gerald. *Why America Slept: The Failure to Prevent 9/11.* New York: Ballantine, 2003.

Bin Laden, Osama (1957–2011)

Besides status as the most notorious terrorist leader in the world, Osama bin Laden's approval of the plan for the September 11, 2001, attacks made him America's public enemy number one. He was born on July 30, 1957, in the Malazz neighborhood of Riyadh, Saudi Arabia, into a wealthy Saudi family. His father, Muhammad bin Oud bin Laden, was from Yemen, and he became fabulously wealthy because of his close contacts with the Saudi regime. He won construction contracts, beginning with road contracts and culminating in the contract to restore and reconstruct the holy sites in Mecca and Medina. He was also strongly anti-Israel.

President Barack Obama and Vice President Joe Biden, along with members of the national security team, receive an update on the mission against Osama bin Laden in the Situation Room of the White House, May 1, 2011. (The White House)

Bin Laden was part of a large extended family. He was the only son of his father's fourth wife. His mother was from Damascus, Syria, and was never one of his father's favorite wives, leading to a divorce. Altogether the father had 21 wives and reportedly had 54 children, of which 24 were sons. Bin Laden was the 17th son, and members of the family have advanced the theory that his position on the fringe of the family rankled him. Bin Laden's family moved several times in Saudi Arabia and ended up in Jeddah, where he attended Jeddah's best school—al-Thagr. Standards were high at this Western-style school, which several sons of Saudi royalty also attended. Even as a boy bin Laden showed such a strong religious streak that it alarmed his family. Bin Laden also had some familiarity with the West through vacations in

Sweden and attendance at a summer class studying English at Oxford University. His father died in the crash of his Cessna aircraft in 1967, leaving an estate of around $11 billion. Bin Laden's inheritance has been described as between $40 million and $50 million. At age 17 he married his mother's 14-year-old cousin. Beginning in 1977, bin Laden studied economics and management in the Management and Economics School at King Abdul Aziz University in Jeddah. Bin Laden was a mediocre student, in part because he neglected his studies to work for the family construction firm. He left school in 1979, and there is considerable disagreement among scholars regarding whether or not he graduated. His initial interest after leaving school was to become involved in the bin Laden family businesses, but he was blocked by his older brothers. By the late 1990s the Saudi Bin-laden Group (SBG) employed 37,000 people and was worth around $5 billion.

As a youngster bin Laden had a solid religious training as a Sunni Muslim but beginning around 1973 he became even more religious. One of his first actions was making contact with the fundamentalist Muslim Brotherhood. There is evidence that he joined the Muslim Brotherhood while in high school. He later admitted that his first interaction with the Muslim Brotherhood was in 1973. At the university, he took courses taught by Muhammad Qutb, the brother of the famous martyred Islamist writer Sayyid Qutb, and he had contact with the advocate of jihad Sheikh Abdullah Yussuf Azzam. Furthermore, two events radicalized bin Laden even more. First was the seizure of the Grand Mosque in Mecca by a group of Islamists under the command of Juhayman ibn-Muhammad-ibn-Sayf al-Taibi. The religious faith and the martyrdom of these Islamists impressed bin Laden. Next, and ultimately more significant, was the Soviet Union's invasion of Afghanistan in late 1979.

Bin Laden's participation in the Afghan-Soviet War was a turning point in his life. His immediate reaction was to go to Afghanistan and join in the fighting. In 1979 he made a quick visit to Pakistan to meet with Afghan leaders Burhanuddin Rabbani and Abdul Rasool Sayyaf. Bin Laden returned to Saudi Arabia, but began planning to help in Afghanistan. He was one of the estimated 10,000 Saudis to flock to the Afghan war. In contrast to most, however, he brought construction machinery with him when he came—bulldozers, loaders, dump trucks, and equipment for building trenches. Soon after arriving in Pakistan, he learned that his organizational

skills were needed more than his skill in combat.

In Pakistan bin Laden renewed his association with Sheikh Abdullah Yussuf Azzam. They had previously met in Jeddah, Saudi Arabia, in summer 1984. Together they formed the Mujahideen Services Bureau (Maktab al-Khidanet, or MAK) in 1984 to recruit and train Afghan fighters. Most of the early expenses of this organization came out of bin Laden's personal finances. Later, funds came from other sources, and in the end several billion dollars flowed through the MAK. Bin Laden used his Saudi contacts in the mid-1980s to bring more heavy construction equipment to protect the Afghans and mujahideen fighters from Soviet artillery and air strikes.

In 1986 bin Laden extended his activities to the battlefield. He joined an Arab mujahideen unit in the field, and participated in the 1987 Battle of the Lion's Den near Jaji. This brief combat experience raised his prestige among Afghan Arab compatriots. Despite his battlefield experience, bin Laden's most significant contribution to the war was in assisting Azzam in radicalizing the Afghan Arab fighters. Bin Laden also met with Ahmed Shah Massoud, the best military leader among the Afghans, but he had closer ties with Gulbuddin Hekmatyar and Abdul Rasool Sayyaf.

By 1987 bin Laden's relationship with Azzam became strained over differences of jihad strategy. Bin Laden had developed ties with Ayman al-Zawahiri, the former head of the Egyptian Islamic Jihad and an open enemy of Azzam. By 1988 bin Laden had broken with Azzam and sided with al-Zawahiri and his Egyptians. Azzam's mysterious assassination on November 24, 1989, cleared the way for bin Laden to play an even greater role in Islamist politics.

Although bin Laden had adopted Azzam's argument in favor of a holy war against the enemies of Islam, he differed from his mentor in his belief that it should be extended to an international holy war to be carried out throughout the world. It was also in fall 1989 that bin Laden first organized the Al Qaeda (the Base) organization. The existence of Al Qaeda was announced at a meeting at which those present were required to sign a loyalty oath (*bayat*).

After the end of the Afghan-Soviet War, bin Laden returned to Saudi Arabia as a war hero. Both the Saudi regime and the general populace acclaimed him. Shortly after his return to Saudi Arabia he approached Prince Turki al-Faisal, head of Saudi intelligence. Bin Laden offered to use Arab irregulars to overthrow the Marxist government of South Yemen, but Turki turned his offer down. Bin Laden settled down in Jeddah working for his family's construction firm until Iraq invaded Kuwait on August 21, 1990. Bin Laden opposed Saddam Hussein's invasion, and he went to the Saudi government offering to lead a mujahideen army against Hussein. But when the Saudi government opted to accept U.S. troops on Saudi soil to regain Kuwait, bin Laden turned against the Saudi regime. Bin Laden was unalterably opposed to the stationing of U.S. troops on Saudi soil, contending that the presence of non-Muslims on holy ground was a sacrilege. His vocal opposition led the Saudi authorities to place him under house arrest for a period of time.

Bin Laden's opposition to the Persian Gulf War led him to leave Saudi Arabia in 1991. To escape possible retaliation from the Saudi security forces, bin Laden and his family moved first to Pakistan and then to Sudan. Bin Laden had been considering a move to Sudan for several years, and he had been buying property in and around Khartoum. This change had both political and religious implications among Muslims. Husan al-Turabi, an Islamist religious and political leader in Sudan, invited bin Laden and his family to stay in Sudan. Bin Laden moved the bulk of his financial assets to Sudan, and there he established a series of businesses, including a road, building company. He acquired a near monopoly of many of Sudan's principal commodity businesses, which ventures only added to his personal fortune.

It was from Sudan that bin Laden launched a propaganda campaign against the Saudi royal family, portraying them as false Muslims. Bin Laden's continuing attacks on the Saudi royal family and religious leadership led to the loss of his Saudi citizenship on April 7, 1994, and to the freezing of his financial assets in Saudi Arabia. This meant bin Laden lost $7 million of his share of the family business. In addition to attacking the Saudi regime, bin Laden made it plain in his publication *Betrayal of Palestine* on December 29, 1994, that he included Israel among the enemies of Islam.

Bin Laden used his secure political base in Sudan to organize the terrorist activities of Al Qaeda. He had established the outline of this organization in 1989, but in Sudan it became a full-fledged terrorist organization. His goal for Al Qaeda was for it to serve as an incitement to Muslims to join a defensive jihad against the West and against tyrannical secular Muslim regimes, and to help train and lead those Muslims who volunteered to participate in the defensive jihad. He established a training camp for Al Qaeda operatives at Soba, north of Khartoum. In 1992 bin Laden sent advisers and military equipment to Somalia to oppose the

American mission there. This mission proved successful for bin Laden and Al Qaeda. The first operations of Al Qaeda were directed against Saudi Arabia and the American forces stationed there. A car bomb exploded in Riyadh on November 13, 1995, killing 5 Americans and 1 Saudi and wounding more than 60 others. This attack was followed by a truck bombing at al-Khobar in Dhahran on June 25, 1996, killing 19 American servicemen and wounding hundreds.

Pressure from the governments of Saudi Arabia and the United States threatened bin Laden's status in Sudan, so he moved his operations to Afghanistan in May 1996. The Sudanese government had no choice but to ask bin Laden to leave, much to his displeasure. Bin Laden left Sudan virtually penniless, as the Sudanese government offered him only pennies on the dollar for all of the property he owned in Sudan. Bin Laden has claimed that his $300 million investment in Sudan was lost. There is some evidence that he hid some of his assets in various companies through partial ownerships.

Afghanistan was a natural haven for bin Laden and Al Qaeda because of the victory of the Islamist Taliban and because of bin Laden's personal relationship with the head of the Taliban, Mohammed Mullah Omar. They had met in Pakistan during the later stages of the Afghan-Soviet War. There are even reports that bin Laden bought Omar a house in Karachi. Although Taliban leaders welcomed bin Laden as a hero of the Muslim world, they were nervous about his terrorist activities and their reflection on the Taliban regime. Responding to this welcome, bin Laden arranged financing from the Arab world for the Taliban regime. In return, the Taliban government allowed bin Laden to organize a series of training camps in Afghanistan to train a cadre of terrorists to carry out operations worldwide. Cementing this alliance, bin Laden's Al Qaeda forces joined Taliban military units fighting the Northern Alliance Army of General Ahmed Shah Massoud.

Once bin Laden had firmly established his organization in Afghanistan, he started an international campaign against those he considered to be enemies of Islam. The top target was the United States. On August 23, 1996, he issued a call for jihad against the Americans for their occupation of Saudi Arabian territory. Then in February 1998 he formed the International Islamic Front for Jihad against Jews and Crusaders. Bin Laden followed this up with the announcement on February 23, 1998, of a global jihad against all enemies of Islam. At the top of this list of enemies of Islam is the United States because bin Laden considered the United States to be "the root of all evil—theologically, politically and morally—and the source of all the misfortunes that have befallen the umma (Muslim world)." In a 1998 interview with an American journalist, bin Laden expressed this viewpoint.

Bin Laden was the political head of Al Qaeda and he was responsible for its operations, but there has always been an on-site command that plans and carries out operations. Because Al Qaeda is an umbrella organization, it is extremely decentralized and has as many as 30 separate extremist groups affiliated with it. Bin Laden's role was to coordinate operations without participating in them. After receiving the go-ahead from bin Laden and Al Qaeda's leadership, the on-site commander made the tactical decisions. Khalid Sheikh Mohammed presented the outline of the plan for the September 11, 2001, operation to bin Laden and the top leaders of Al Qaeda sometime in 1996. Bin Laden approved the plan in principle, but he left the implementation of it to Mohammed and his subordinates. Both bin Laden and Mohammed knew that the failure of the Group Islamique Armé (GIA) to carry out its mission to fly a hijacked aircraft into the Eiffel Tower in December 1994 meant that they needed trained pilots to carry out this mission in the United States.

It is evident that bin Laden was interested in attacking the United States for economic reasons as much as for political ones. Bin Laden's training in economics and business allowed him to see the total picture. In his homage to the 19 martyrs, bin Laden justified the September 11 attack by stating that "it is possible to strike the economic base that is the foundation of the military base, so when their economy is depleted they will be too busy with each other to be able to enslave poor peoples."

After establishing the principles of the plan, the operation proceeded on its own with little or no input from bin Laden. He learned five days before the September 11 attack on what day it would take place. Bin Laden expected a vigorous American response after the end of the attacks in the United States, but he counted on the harshness of the response to mobilize Muslims worldwide against the United States and the West. His anticipation of a vigorous U.S. response proved correct, but the rest of his calculations went awry. Bin Laden was reluctant to assume any responsibility for September 11, but he did praise the hijackers.

The collapse of the Taliban to the Northern Alliance with the assistance of the United States was a major setback for bin Laden. Both the ease and the quickness of the Taliban's fall were unexpected. Bin Laden retreated to the mountain complex of Tora Bora, where he stayed until December 10, 2001, before escaping into northwest Pakistan, where there was strong support for him. Evidently he sustained a wound to his left arm in the American bombing of Tora Bora. Despite efforts by American intelligence in the years since the overthrow of the Taliban, searchers were unable to locate his whereabouts.

In August 2010, unbeknownst to the public at large, American intelligence received information suggesting that bin Laden was living at a compound in Abbottabad, Pakistan, a suburb of the capital, Islamabad. After months of pursuing this lead, and with final approval given by President Barack Obama in late April 2011, U.S. Navy SEALs conducted a raid on the compound on May 1, 2011 (May 2 Pakistani local time). In the ensuing firefight, bin Laden, one of his adult sons, and three others were killed. After photographic and DNA evidence was taken to prove bin Laden's identity, his body was buried at sea.

President Obama's announcement of the events surrounding bin Laden's death prompted spontaneous celebration in the United States and in many locations around the world, although jihadists were quick to promise retribution for bin Laden's killing. Such threats suggest that, despite bin Laden's death, Al Qaeda and similar extremist groups will likely continue to pose a threat to U.S. national security in the future.

Stephen E. Atkins

See also: Al Qaeda; Atta, Mohamed el-Amir Awad el-Sayed; Global War on Terror; Mohammed, Khalid Sheikh; World Trade Center, September 11

Suggested Reading

Anonymous [Michael Scheuer]. *Imperial Hubris: Why the West Is Losing the War on Terror*. Washington, DC: Brassey's, 2004.

Atwan, Abdel Bari. *The Secret History of Al Qaeda*. Berkeley: University of California Press, 2006.

BBC News. "Osama Bin Laden, al-Qaeda leader, dead—Barack Obama." May 2, 2011. https://www.bbc.com/news/world-us-canada-13256676

Bergen, Peter L. *The Osama bin Laden I Know: An Oral History of Al Qaeda's Leader*. New York: Free Press, 2006.

Corbin, Jane. *Al Qaeda: The Terror Network That Threatens the World*. New York: Thunder's Mouth, 2002.

Lawrence, Bruce, ed. *Messages to the World: The Statements of Osama bin Laden*. London: Verso, 2005.

Obama, Barack. "Remarks on the Death of Al Qaida Terrorist Organization Leader Usama bin Laden." May 1, 2011. *Public Papers of the Presidents of the United States: Barack Obama (2011, Book 1)*. Washington, DC: Government Printing Office, 480–482, 2012.

Randal, Jonathan. *Osama: The Making of a Terrorist*. New York: Knopf, 2004.

Robinson, Adam. *Bin Laden: Behind the Mask of the Terrorist*. New York: Arcade, 2001.

Burnett, Thomas Edward (1963–2001)

Thomas Edward "Tom" Burnett was one of the passengers on United Airlines Flight 93 who attempted to retake control of the aircraft on September 11, 2001. The fact that Burnett and his companions did not succeed does not detract from their courage in making the attempt. Burnett was a devoted family man, and his motivation was to survive to return to his family.

Burnett had a typical American upbringing. He was born on May 29, 1963, in Bloomington, Minnesota. His father was a high school English and literature teacher and a Korean War veteran, and his mother was a real estate agent. He had an older and a younger sister. His family was Catholic and Burnett was raised in that faith. Burnett's entire youth was spent in Bloomington, and he attended Ridgeview Elementary School and Olson Middle School before graduating in 1981 with honors from Thomas Jefferson High School. Burnett played football as a quarterback, and in 1980 his team made it to the state semifinals. His prowess as a football player led to several scholarship offers from small colleges. Burnett obtained an appointment to the U.S. Air Force Academy, but after a few weeks there he decided that a military career was not for him. He then attended Saint John's University in Collegeville, Minnesota, for two years, playing football until a shoulder injury caused him to give up the game. After transferring to the Carlson School of Management at the University of Minnesota, he obtained a BS degree in finance. Burnett was also elected president of the Alpha Kappa Psi fraternity in his senior year.

Shortly after graduation, Burnett entered the business world. His first job was with Calicetek, a manufacturer of dental implants. He became sales director and traveled around the United States and the world. In August 1996 he took a job in California with Thoratec Corporation, a company that builds medical devices, headquartered in Pleasanton, California. Starting at the bottom of the corporate ladder, Burnett worked his way up to vice president of the company, eventually becoming its chief financial officer. During this rise up the hierarchy, he earned an MBA from Pepperdine University.

Burnett's job responsibilities called for him to travel around the country. He had married in April 1992, and he and his wife, Deena, had three daughters. Deena had worked as a flight attendant for Delta Airlines, but retired from her job before the birth of their twin daughters. Traveling was tough on Burnett because he liked family life with his wife and daughters. He also was fond of hunting, fishing, and golfing.

On September 11, 2001, Burnett was returning to California from a business trip to New York City. He had called his parents from the New York Marriott Hotel near Times Square on the night of September 10. Wanting to catch an earlier flight, Burnett rushed to Newark International Airport and caught United Airlines Flight 93. Burnett had reserved a first-class seat. There was a 41-minute delay caused by airport congestion.

Nothing about the early flight of United Airlines Flight 93 was out of the ordinary until the hijack team went into action. The team of Ziad Jarrah seized control of the aircraft at approximately 9:28 a.m. Passengers were restricted to the rear of the aircraft. Burnett and others began to make calls to inform authorities that the aircraft had been hijacked. He called his wife at around 9:30 a.m. to tell her of the hijacking. It was a short conversation and Deena had no opportunity to tell him about the other aircraft. He called again and reported that the hijackers had stabbed and killed one of the crew. At this time Deena was able to tell him that the other aircraft had been on suicide missions. Burnett relayed the news to the other passengers. In a third conversation Deena told him about the Pentagon crash. In between calls, Burnett and the other passengers began to discuss regaining control of the cockpit. In the fourth conversation with his wife, Burnett told her they were waiting until the aircraft was over a rural area before taking back the plane. He also

made it plain that they had no choice. Among others, Burnett, Todd Beamer, Mark Bingham, and Jeremy Glick charged the cockpit. They came close to regaining control of the aircraft, but Jarrah crashed the plane in a field near Shanksville, Pennsylvania, killing everybody aboard.

The news of what the passengers on United Airline Flight 93 had tried to do made them national heroes. Jarrah and his team of hijackers had been prevented from crashing the airliner into the U.S. Capitol, or possibly the White House. When family members later listened to the cockpit tapes, they could hear the desperate struggle. All the bodies were obliterated in the crash, and could be identified only by DNA analysis. Medical technicians were able to find and identify some of Burnett's remains for burial at the Fort Snelling National Cemetery on May 24, 2002. Because he had been accepted to the U.S. Air Force Academy, Burnett was eligible to be buried at a national cemetery.

Since Burnett's death, his wife has been active in the families of September 11 movement. She was instrumental in the Federal Bureau of Investigation (FBI) release of the flight records of what happened in the cockpit of United Airlines Flight 93. Knowing that there were unanswered questions, Burnett's wife and parents filed a lawsuit against United Airlines and Argenbright Security Company in August 2002. Then a week later they filed a $1 trillion lawsuit against the financial supporters of terrorist networks; 150 defendants were named in this suit, ranging from individuals to charities. Hundreds of others also signed on to this lawsuit. Most of them knew that no money would be forthcoming, but the families were most interested in exposing the supporters of terrorism. Besides lawsuits, the Burnett family started the Tom Burnett Family Foundation in September 2002, with the goal of educating youths to become active citizens and tomorrow's leaders.

Stephen E. Atkins

See also: Beamer, Todd Morgan; Jarrah, Ziad Samir; United Airlines Flight 93

Suggested Reading

Beamer, Lisa, and Ken Abraham. *Let's Roll! Ordinary People, Extraordinary Courage.* Wheaton, IL: Tyndale House, 2002.

Burnett, Deena, and Anthony Giombetti. *Fighting Back: Living Life beyond Ourselves.* Altamonte Springs, FL: Advantage Books, 2006.

Gordon, Greg. "How We've Changed; 9.11.01–9.11.02." *Star Tribune* [Minneapolis], September 11, 2002, 4S.

Longman, Jere. *Among the Heroes: United Flight 93 and the Passengers and Crew Who Fought Back.* New York: HarperCollins, 2002.

McFeatters, Ann. "Lawsuit Seeks to Cripple Terrorists' Means to Strike." *Pittsburgh Post-Gazette,* August 16, 2002, A1.

McManis, Sam. "Passenger's Act of Courage No Surprise." *San Francisco Chronicle,* September 14, 2001, A10.

Von Sternberg, Bob. "Flight 93 Hero Buried at Fort Snelling." *Star Tribune* [Minneapolis], May 25, 2002, 1A.

Bush, George W. (1946–)

President George W. Bush had been president less than nine months when the events of September 11, 2001, transformed his administration. Bush had won the presidency in one of the closest races in American history in November 2000, but he came into office determined to repudiate the policies of former president Bill Clinton.

President Clinton had pursued an aggressive but lackluster campaign against Osama bin Laden and Al Qaeda. Various efforts had been approved to either assassinate or capture bin Laden, but nothing had come of them. The new Bush administration wanted to reexamine all of Clinton's activities, and members of the Bush administration had priorities that ranged from building a "Star Wars" missile defense shield to fighting domestic crime. Before the attacks, counterterrorism was something of a priority for the Bush administration but was nowhere near the top of the agenda. Several on the administration team had complained openly about overemphasis on bin Laden and Al Qaeda by the Clinton administration. Attorney General John Ashcroft made it plain that he wanted to focus attention on organized crime families and on the trade in street drugs. Counterterrorism also assumed a lower priority for the Justice Department and the Federal Bureau of Investigation (FBI).

Of the government agencies, only the Central Intelligence Agency (CIA) tried to warn President Bush about the danger of terrorism. George Tenet, the director of the CIA, gave Bush daily intelligence briefings in which he frequently warned Bush about the danger of Osama bin Laden and Al Qaeda. Bush developed a good personal relationship with Tenet, but he listened only, and took no action. In an interview with Bob Woodward after September 11, Bush acknowledged that he knew bin Laden and Al Qaeda were a menace, but that he had felt no sense of urgency before September 11. Bush was waiting for a comprehensive plan that would bring bin Laden to justice, and he was willing to sign off on such a plan.

All of this changed on the morning of September 11. President Bush was in

After departing Offutt Air Force Base in Nebraska, President George W. Bush confers with Vice President Dick Cheney from Air Force One during his flight to Andrews Air Force Base Sept. 11, 2001. (White House)

Sarasota, Florida, scheduled to attend a media event at the Emma E. Booker Elementary School in Sarasota, Florida. After an early-morning jog, Bush left for the school. He was in the classroom when American Airlines Flight 11 crashed into the North Tower of the World Trade Center. His chief adviser, Karl Rove, informed Bush of the crash, but he decided to continue with the program at the elementary school. Bush did contact the White House, where National Security Advisor Condoleezza Rice gave him more details about what was happening in New York City. After consulting with Chief of Staff Andrew H. Card Jr., Bush returned to the classroom. Shortly after his advisers learned of the crash into the South Tower they informed Bush. The first crash could have been an accident, but the second meant that

the United States was under attack. After contacting Vice President Dick Cheney and the head of the FBI, Robert Mueller, Bush wanted to return to Washington, DC, although his advisers opposed a return. It was at this time that Bush authorized Vice President Cheney to order the U.S. Air Force to shoot down any hijacked commercial aircraft. Advisers began to look for a safe place for the president.

By 9:55 a.m. Air Force One was in the air with President Bush and his entourage. The vice president suggested that Bush fly to Offutt Air Force Base near Omaha, Nebraska. Offutt Air Force Base was the headquarters of the Strategic Air Command, and had all the facilities necessary for the president to keep up with what was going on. After a brief stop at Barksdale Air Force Base in Louisiana, where Bush made a brief public statement, Air Force One proceeded to Offutt Air Force Base. It arrived at Offutt Air Force Base at 2:50 p.m. After communicating with other government leaders, President Bush insisted, despite opposition from the Secret Service, that he return to Washington, DC. Winning the argument, Bush and his advisers arrived in Washington, DC, at 7:00 p.m.

President Bush took charge after September 11. He asserted himself by making it clear that the country was embarking upon a war with few restraints. He focused on results, and put pressure on the CIA and FBI to produce results. His relationship with Tenet became even closer because the CIA was the only agency that had information on Osama bin Laden and Al Qaeda. The CIA had contacts in Afghanistan, whereas the U.S. military had no assets there. By presidential authority the CIA was given complete freedom to conduct covert operations. President Bush was determined to end bin Laden's sanctuary in Afghanistan, even if it meant overthrowing the Taliban regime. Soon American support started flowing to the Northern Alliance.

President Bush had two foreign policy options in his administration after September 11. One was the traditional international diplomacy using the United Nations (UN). Two groups in government supported this option—the U.S. State Department, headed by Secretary of State Colin Powell, and the CIA leadership. The other option was advocated by a small group of neoconservatives whose goal was to use America's preeminent military power to transform the world order—in particular, the Middle East. Vice President Cheney, Assistant Secretary of Defense Paul Wolfowitz, and Defense Policy Advisory Committee chairman Richard Perl were the leaders advancing these views.

After much soul-searching, Bush accepted the neoconservative position; the invasion of Iraq was a product of this conversion. Once this decision was made, intelligence operations directed at Al Qaeda and other terrorist groups were redirected toward Iraq. Foreign language experts and special operatives were reassigned, and antiterrorism intelligence programs were terminated. The main thrust of Bush and the Bush administration was now the overthrow of Saddam Hussein, and the hunt for bin Laden and other Al Qaeda leaders had less urgency. Hussein was deposed and captured in 2003; in 2006, he was convicted of crimes against humanity by an Iraqi court, and executed by hanging.

While Bush was praised for his leadership in the immediate aftermath of 9/11, his administration has since been criticized for its failure to capture bin Laden, its use of interrogation techniques, and its handling of the Iraq War.

Stephen E. Atkins

See also: Al Qaeda; Bin Laden, Osama; Bush Administration; Bush Doctrine; ENDURING FREEDOM, Operation; Global War on Terror; IRAQI FREEDOM, Operation

Suggested Reading

Aust, Stefan, et al. *Inside 9/11: What Really Happened.* New York: St. Martin's, 2001.

Hersh, Seymour M. *Chain of Command: The Road from 9/11 to Abu Ghraib.* New York: HarperCollins, 2004.

Kessler, Ronald. *The CIA at War: Inside the Secret Campaign against Terror.* New York: St. Martin's Griffin, 2003.

Risen, James. *State of War: The Secret History of the CIA and the Bush Administration.* New York: Free Press, 2006.

Woodward, Bob. *Bush at War.* New York: Simon and Schuster, 2002.

Bush Administration

President George W. Bush showed considerable interest in the activities of Osama bin Laden and Al Qaeda during the early days of his administration; the rest of his administration less so. They had criticized the Bill Clinton administration for its failure to end the Al Qaeda threat, but most high officials in the Bush administration had other priorities. These were missile defense, military reform, China, and Iraq. Most of these priorities were intended to enhance the ambitions of President Bush and his chief administrators. Even those who knew something about Afghanistan—and they were few indeed—had ties to Pakistan. Pakistan was a supporter of the Taliban, who in turn were protecting bin Laden. Briefings about the importance of terrorism and bin Laden given by the existing Clinton administration to the incoming Bush administration were ignored.

Perhaps the least enthusiastic member of the Bush administration was Attorney General John Ashcroft. Ashcroft had higher priorities for the Department of Justice—guns, drugs, and civil rights. He made counterterrorism a third-tier issue. Requests for increased funding for counterterrorism were turned down. Efforts to talk to Ashcroft about counterterrorism were futile. A Federal Bureau of Investigation (FBI) request for an increase to its counterterrorism budget by $58 million had been turned down by Ashcroft on September 10, 2001. This proposal had called for 149 new counterterrorism field agents, 200 additional analysts, and 54 extra translators. Ashcroft's refusal to consider counterterrorism as a priority changed dramatically after September 11.

Secretary of Defense Donald Rumsfeld was no more enthusiastic about bin Laden and Al Qaeda than Ashcroft. Rumsfeld had been briefed on counterterrorism activities in the Defense Department by outgoing Secretary of Defense Cohen, but he has since stated that he remembered little of this briefing. Responsibility for counterterrorism in the Defense Department was given to the Assistant Secretary of Defense for Special Operations and Low-Intensity Conflict (SOLIC). This post had not been filled by September 11, 2001. Rumsfeld's major concern upon taking office had been the building of a missile defense system and development of an advanced weapons system. For this reason a request to allocate $800 million more to counterterrorism was turned down by Rumsfeld, and the funds were diverted to missile defense. Counterterrorism was simply not a part of Rumsfeld's agenda. This is also why a weapon useful against Al Qaeda, the Predator unmanned aircraft and its Hellfire missile system, was allowed to languish behind other projects.

Another leading figure in the Bush administration who showed little interest in Osama bin Laden and Al Qaeda prior to September 11 was Condoleezza Rice. In an article in *Foreign Affairs* published before she took office, Rice criticized the Clinton administration for focusing on terrorism rather than on the few great powers whom she considered dangerous to peace. It was her thesis that American power and prestige had been frittered away by the concentration on issues like terrorism. She carried these ideas into her role as national security adviser to President Bush. Richard Clarke, the holdover counterterrorism expert, tried to persuade Rice of the danger posed by bin Laden and Al Qaeda in a January 2001 memorandum, but Rice took no action. In a meeting on July 10, 2001, George Tenet, the head of the Central Intelligence Agency

(CIA), warned Rice of the strong likelihood of an Al Qaeda strike against the United States, possibly within the United States. Rice listened to Tenet's arguments, but several times afterward when Tenet brought up the subject she was unable to recall either the meeting or the subject of the meeting. It was only in October 2006 that this meeting and its subject matter surfaced in Bob Woodward's book *State of Denial*. Even then Rice stated that she had difficulty remembering the meeting.

Bush's neoconservative advisers were much more attracted to overthrowing Saddam Hussein in Iraq than to Osama bin Laden and Al Qaeda. Paul Wolfowitz, the deputy secretary of defense, complained that too much attention had been devoted to the activities of bin Laden. In his view, bin Laden was overrated as a threat. Bin Laden was far down on the neoconservatives' list of priorities. Only President Bush showed much curiosity about bin Laden and Al Qaeda, ordering intelligence reports sent to him daily about Al Qaeda's activities.

Opposition to Clinton administration policies also extended to economic matters. The previous administration had attempted to control the flow of money to Osama bin Laden. Efforts were made to embarrass those countries with loose banking regulations into tightening them up. More than 30 countries were participating in this effort when the Bush administration assumed office. The Clinton administration had also proposed the creation of the National Terrorist Asset Tracking Center as part of this campaign. Paul O'Neill, the new secretary of the treasury, disapproved of any attempt to interfere in the banking industry, even as regards banks and financial institutions that were supporting terrorist activities. Consequently, O'Neill shut down anti–money-laundering operations, and the National Terrorist Asset Tracking Center was dismantled because of lack of funding.

After September 11, 2001, the Bush administration made a complete reversal, and resources now poured into counterintelligence. President Bush gave the CIA complete authority to carry out covert operations against terrorists and terrorist organizations. Once it became apparent that the Taliban regime would not give up Osama bin Laden, an American-sponsored war was unleashed to overthrow it. But soon the earlier desire to overthrow Saddam Hussein in Iraq became paramount, and this diverted the attention of the Bush administration away from bin Laden and Al Qaeda.

Since leaving office, the use of "enhanced interrogation techniques" in the Iraq War has come under fire, as has the invasion of Iraq. Near the end of the administration, in the fall of 2008, the United States experienced an economic recession, which Bush called an "ugly way to end the presidency."

Stephen E. Atkins

See also: Al Qaeda; Bin Laden, Osama; Bush, George W.

Suggested Reading

Benjamin, David, and Steven Simon. *The Age of Sacred Terrorism*. New York: Random House, 2002.

Bush, George W. *Decision Points*. New York: Crown Publishing Group, 2010.

Coll, Steve. *Ghost Wars: The Secret History of the CIA, Afghanistan, and bin Laden, from the Soviet Invasion to September 10, 2001*. New York: Penguin, 2004.

Naftali, Timothy. *Blind Spot: The Secret History of American Counterterrorism*. New York: Basic Books, 2005.

Risen, James. *State of War: The Secret History of the CIA and the Bush Administration*. New York: Free Press, 2006.

Bush Doctrine

The Bush Doctrine is the foreign/national security policy articulated by President George W. Bush in a series of speeches following the September 11, 2001, terrorist attacks on the United States. The Bush Doctrine identified three threats against U.S. interests: terrorist organizations, weak states that harbor and assist such terrorist organizations, and so-called rogue states. The centerpiece of the Bush Doctrine was that the United States had the right to use preemptive military force against any state that is seen as hostile or that makes moves to acquire weapons of mass destruction, be they nuclear, biological, or chemical. In addition, the United States would "make no distinction between the terrorists who commit these acts and those who harbor them."

The Bush Doctrine represented a major shift in American foreign policy from the policies of deterrence and containment that characterized the Cold War and the brief period between the collapse of the Soviet Union in 1991 and the events of 2001. This new foreign policy and security strategy emphasized the strategic doctrine of preemption. The right of self-defense would be extended to use of preemptive attacks against potential enemies, attacking them before they were deemed capable of launching strikes against the United States. Under the doctrine, furthermore, the United States reserved the right to pursue unilateral military action if multilateral solutions cannot be found. The Bush Doctrine also represented the realities of international politics in the post–Cold War period; that is, that the United States was the sole superpower and that it aimed to ensure American hegemony.

A secondary goal of the Bush Doctrine was the promotion of freedom and democracy around the world, a precept that dates to at least the days of President Woodrow Wilson. In his speech to the graduating class at West Point on June 1, 2002, Bush declared that "America has no empire to extend or utopia to establish. We wish for others only what we wish for ourselves—safety from violence, the rewards of liberty, and the hope for a better life."

The immediate application of the Bush Doctrine was the invasion of Afghanistan in early October 2001 (Operation ENDURING FREEDOM). Although the Taliban-controlled government of Afghanistan offered to hand over Al Qaeda leader Osama bin Laden if it was shown tangible proof that he was responsible for the September 11 attacks and also offered to extradite bin Laden to Pakistan where he would be tried under Islamic law, its refusal to extradite him to the United States with no preconditions was considered justification for the invasion.

The administration also applied the Bush Doctrine as justification for the Iraq War, beginning in March 2003 (Operation IRAQI FREEDOM). The Bush administration did not wish to wait for conclusive proof of Saddam Hussein's weapons of mass destruction (WMDs), so in a series of speeches, administration officials laid out the argument for invading Iraq. To wait any longer was to run the risk of having Hussein employ or transfer the alleged WMDs. Thus, despite the lack of any evidence of an operational relationship between Iraq and Al Qaeda, the United States, supported by Britain and a few other nations, launched an invasion of Iraq.

The use of the Bush Doctrine as justification for the invasion of Iraq led to increasing friction between the United States and its allies, as the Bush Doctrine repudiated the core idea of the United Nations (UN) Charter. The charter prohibits any use of international force that is not undertaken in self-defense after the occurrence of an armed attack across an international boundary or pursuant to a decision by the UN Security Council. Even more vexing, the distinct limitations and pitfalls of the Bush Doctrine were abundantly evident in the inability of the United States to quell sectarian violence and political turmoil in Iraq. The doctrine did not place parameters on the extent of American commitments, and it viewed the consequences of preemptory military strikes as a mere afterthought.

Keith A. Leitich

See also: Bush, George W.; Bush Administration; ENDURING FREEDOM, Operation; Global War on Terror; IRAQI FREEDOM, Operation

Suggested Reading

Buckley, Mary E., and Robert Singh. *The Bush Doctrine and the War on Terrorism: Global Responses, Global Consequences.* London: Routledge, 2006.

Dolan, Chris J. *In War We Trust: The Bush Doctrine and the Pursuit of Just War.* Burlington, VT: Ashgate, 2005.

Gurtov, Melvin. *Superpower on Crusade: The Bush Doctrine in U.S. Foreign Policy.* Boulder, CO: Lynne Rienner, 2006.

Heisbourg, François. "Work in Progress: The Bush Doctrine and Its Consequences." *Washington Quarterly* 6(22) (Spring 2003): 75–88.

Jervis, Robert. *American Foreign Policy in a New Era.* New York: Routledge, 2005.

Schlesinger, Arthur M. *War and the American Presidency.* New York: Norton, 2004.

C

Cantor Fitzgerald

The huge financial brokerage firm Cantor Fitzgerald suffered the largest number of casualties of any company in the World Trade Center complex on September 11. About 1,000 employees worked for Cantor Fitzgerald on the eve of September 11. The company was housed in the North Tower of the World Trade Center complex between the 101st and 105th floors. Employees for the firm handled transactions worth about $200 billion of securities a day, and in the neighborhood of $30 trillion a year. For all intents and purposes it served as the New York Stock Exchange's handler of bonds. Bernie Cantor had founded the firm, and besides a shrewd businessman, he had been a collector of Rodin sculptures. There were some 80 pieces of Rodin's sculpture on display in the North Tower. After Cantor's death, Howard Lutnick became the company's chairman, and he held that position on September 11, 2001.

The September 11 attack on the World Trade Center complex hit Cantor Fitzgerald particularly hard. Shortly after American Airlines Flight 11 hit the North Tower near the 93rd floor, it became apparent that those on the upper floors had little if any chance of escape. Because the roof was locked and the stairwells were blocked, those in the floors above the 93rd floor had no recourse but to resign themselves to their fate. It became more apparent what their fate would be when the South Tower collapsed. As the fire and smoke threatened them, some began jumping to their deaths rather than burn to death. Some of the jumpers were holding hands as they fell. Others called their loved ones to tell them of the hopelessness of their situation. In the end, Cantor Fitzgerald lost 658 employees, including the brother of the company's chairman. Several of the survivors were badly burnt, and one, Renee Barrett-Arjune, died of burns in October.

The members of Cantor Fitzgerald who survived had luck on their side. Lutnick was taking his young son to his first day of kindergarten. Others were on vacation or preparing for vacations. Some had gone to lower floors on individual tasks, thus saving their lives. Lutnick arrived at the World Trade Center complex at about the time that the South Tower fell, and he ran to save his life like so many others.

In the aftermath of the attack, Cantor Fitzgerald was on the verge of ruin. It had lost nearly two-thirds of its employees, its offices were gone, and its computer system was down. There was pressure to reopen the bond market earlier than the September 17 reopening of the New York Stock Exchange. The decision to reopen the bond market on September 15 threatened to bankrupt Cantor Fitzgerald because its competitors were eager to take away its business. Its only hope was that the London office, which was much smaller than the New York office, could absorb the New York office's business as well as conduct its own. Despite immense difficulties, Cantor Fitzgerald did manage to open its doors on Monday, September 17, saving the firm.

In the meantime, family members of those missing began to show up demanding services. At first they were concerned about finding out what had happened to their loved ones. Then grief took over, rendering family members almost helpless. Grief counselors were called in to help the families cope. Finally, family members reconciled themselves to their loss and began to consider financial matters, such as insurance, death certificates, bonuses, and salaries.

Following September 11, Lutnick became a controversial figure. To save his company, he stopped paying salaries for the deceased employees after September 11. In the place of salaries, Lutnick promised the families 25 percent of the profits of Cantor Fitzgerald. The problem was that earning that profit took time, and the national media started attacking Lutnick for financially mistreating the bereaved families. It became especially vicious on Bill O'Reilly's TV show *The O'Reilly Factor* on Fox News. After Lutnick announced his plan to give 25 percent of profits for the next 5 years, health insurance for 10 years, and $45 million in bonuses for the families, some but not all of the pressure came off. There were still attacks on him from the media. In the end, Lutnick's efforts to assist the families of lost members of Cantor Fitzgerald have proven beneficial. As of 2020, Cantor Fitzgerald had paid more than $180 million to the families, and its Relief Foundation has assisted victims of natural disasters such as Hurricane Katrina, Superstorm Sandy, and the Haiti earthquake.

Cantor Fitzgerald has also prospered financially. Lutnick decided to concentrate on core issues, and to transform more of his functions to an electronic trading company system, eSpeed. Much of 2002 was spent rebuilding technology and the company's infrastructure. He has also been involved in litigation over attempts of other companies to take over some of his business in the aftermath of September 11.

Cantor Fitzgerald settled a lawsuit against American Airlines in 2013 for $135 million for damages as a result of negligence on the airline's part for the hijacking of Flight 11.

Stephen E. Atkins

See also: World Trade Center, September 11

Suggested Reading

Atlas, Riva D. "Firm That Was Hit Hard on 9/11 Grows Anew." *New York Times,* September 10, 2004, C4.

Bandur, Heather. "Firm Rises from the Ashes; Being 'Ruthless' Helped CEA Rebuild after Tragedy." *Houston Chronicle,* September 15, 2002, 2.

Barbash, Tom. *On Top of the World: The Remarkable Story of Howard Lutnick, Cantor Fitzgerald, and the Twin Towers Attack.* London: Headline, 2002.

Cantor Fitzgerald Relief Fund. https://www.cantorrelief.org/about/

Henriques, Diana B. "The Bond Trader: From Devastation to Determination." *New York Times,* September 10, 2002, C1.

Ringshaw, Grant. "Counting the Cost at Cantor." *Sunday Telegraph* [London], September 7, 2003, 3.

Talanova, Julia. "Cantor Fitzgerald, American Airlines Settle 9/11 Lawsuit for $135 Million." *CNN,* December 17, 2003. https://www.cnn.com/2013/12/17/us/new-york-cantor-fitzgerald-american-settlement/index.html

Casualties of September II

The explosion of the crashing aircraft, the fire, and the final collapse of the Twin Towers produced massive casualties. The goal of the hijackers was for casualties to be in

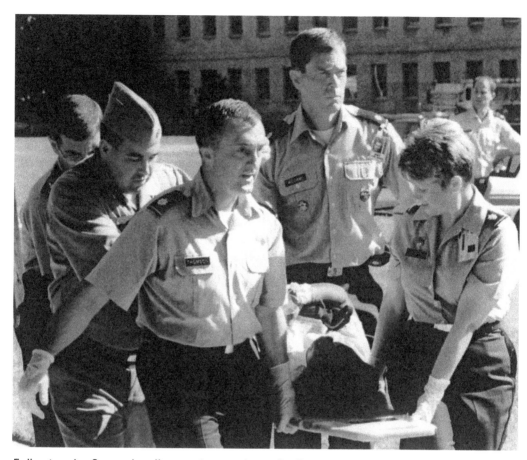

Following the September II terrorist attack on the Pentagon, four soldiers and a sailor help carry an injured worker to a waiting ambulance. (U.S. Army)

the hundred thousands range. It was known that there were around 150,000 people at any one time during the day at the World Trade Center complex. This total included around 50,000 people who worked in the complex, and about 100,000 daily tourists who shopped at the many stores there. The World Trade Center complex was a popular place to visit and shop.

Casualties would have been much higher except for the evacuation supervised by the Fire Department City of New York (FDNY) firefighters, New York City and Port Authority police, and security people for the various companies. Their efforts saved countless lives, but they came at a high cost.

The collapse of the Twin Towers caught firefighters, police, and Port Authority police by surprise. In the South Tower there were only seconds to respond to a call to evacuate. The North Tower took longer to fall, but communications were so poor that information about the collapse of the South Tower and a recall order were difficult to spread. The FDNY took the brunt of the casualties with 343. Employees of the Port Authority of New York and New Jersey suffered 74 dead, and the New York City police lost 37.

Only 18 survivors of the collapse were recovered on September 11, 2001. Rescuers found 2 policemen early on the first day.

Later the same day, 16 others were found. Twelve firemen, 1 policeman, and 1 civilian office worker were saved from the ruins of the North Tower. Finally, late in the day, 2 Port Authority employees were rescued from the North Tower. There were no survivors from the collapse of the South Tower.

The losses on September 11, 2001, were devastating to all these agencies. All of those looking for remains developed a special attitude toward the fallen. Port Authority police lieutenant William Keegan Jr. described it as a sacred trust that impacted psychologically those at Ground Zero.

The various New York agencies were fiercely protective of the remains of their own fallen. FDNY firefighters, New York City police, and Port Authority police wanted only their representatives to handle the bodies, or body parts. For example, once a firefighter's body was found, the body was placed in a body bag and put on an orange plastic stretcher. An American flag was then placed over the body bag. The firefighters would then have a chaplain lead them in prayer. After acknowledging the sacrifice by saluting the fallen firefighter, six firefighters would carry the stretcher several blocks to the morgue. Along the way people would stop working and take off their hard hats to show respect. The New York City police and Port Authority police treated their fallen comrades in much the same way. There has been criticism, however, that civilian remains were not treated with commensurate respect and that their remains were sometimes handled more carelessly.

Early estimates of total casualties at the World Trade Center complex ranged from thousands to as many as tens of thousands. It may be that an accurate figure will never be determined, but as of February 2005

there had been 2,749 death certificates issued by the City of New York as a result of the World Trade Center attack. Of the total of 2,749, it has been determined that 2,117 (77 percent) were males and 632 (23 percent) were females. Only 1,585 (58 percent) had been forensically identified from recovered physical remains when the identification process stopped in February 2005. Median age of the victims was 39 years with the range from 2 to 85. A total of 62 countries were represented among the dead at the World Trade Center complex. Although the overwhelming majority of the dead were American citizens, a significant number of the dead were noncitizens—exactly how many will probably never be known.

Identification of the dead has been difficult. Most of the identifications have been made from body parts, because only 293 whole bodies have been found. More than 21,000 body parts have been located and sent to the morgue for identification. More than 800 victims were identified by DNA alone. But even identification by means of DNA was difficult because the high-temperature fire and changes in temperature caused DNA tissues to deteriorate. Fierce fires and pressure from collapsing buildings made it difficult for scientists to extract usable DNA. This fact meant that the doctors had to experiment with ways to preserve tissue for DNA analysis.

The official date for closure on identifying victims of September 11 was in the middle of February 2005. The New York City medical examiner's office began notifying families that they had been unable to identify their loved ones. In an attempt to identify victims in the future, nearly 10,000 unidentified parts have been freeze-dried and vacuum-sealed for preservation and placed in a memorial.

Although official identification opera-tions have ceased, body parts continue to be found. More than 750 remains, most less than 1/16th of an inch in length, have been found at the former Deutsche Bank build-ing, while approximately 300 were discov-ered near or under a haul road along West Street. In June 2010, 72 human remains were uncovered after sifting through 800 cubic yards of Ground Zero debris. Conclu-sive identification, however, remains difficult.

Stephen E. Atkins

See also: World Trade Center, September 11

Suggested Reading

Abel, David. "Effort to ID Sept. 11 Remains Ends." *Boston Globe,* February 24, 2005, A2.

Ausmus, David W. *In the Midst of Chaos: My 30 Days at Ground Zero.* Victoria, British Columbia: Trafford, 2004.

Keegan, William, Jr., with Bart Davis. *Clo-sure: The Untold Story of the Ground Zero Recovery Mission.* New York: Touchstone Books, 2006.

Littwin, Mike. "Father of Fallen Firefighter Wages War against Complacency." *Rocky Mountain News* [Denver], September 11, 2006, 25.

Robowsky, Shiya. "Challenges in Identifica-tion: The World Trade Center Dean." In *On the Ground after September 11: Mental Health Responses and Practical Knowledge Gained,* edited by Yael Dan-ieli and Robert L. Dingman. New York: Haworth Maltreatment and Trauma Press, 2005.

Smith, Dennis. *Report from Ground Zero.* New York: Viking, 2002.

Von Essen, Thomas, with Matt Murray. *Strong of Heart: Life and Death in the Fire Department of New York City.* New York: ReganBooks, 2002.

Central Intelligence Agency

The Central Intelligence Agency (CIA) rec-ord prior to September 11 was emblematic of the pressures placed upon it in a chang-ing world. Its central problem was the tran-sition from the Cold War to international terrorism, and then to stateless terrorism that could strike the United States at any time. Surveillance against terrorism in the continental United States was the responsi-bility of the Federal Bureau of Investigation (FBI), but the CIA had responsibility for international intelligence gathering. In any case, its record was found to be lacking.

The leaders of the CIA had over the years limited human intelligence assets. In the early and mid-1990s the CIA had reduced its human intelligence capability through a staff reduction of 20 percent. By the late 1990s the agency lacked the agents, the lan-guage skills, and the organizational flexibil-ity to spot a conspiracy in the making. Instead, the CIA depended on intelligence reports from friendly intelligence services and political departments. Even when it had a human intelligence source, the CIA was slow to react to warnings coming from that source. A case in point is that the CIA had an aggressive agent in Germany monitoring the activities of the Hamburg Cell, but no additional resources were placed at his disposal.

Bureaucracy often threatened the effi-ciency of CIA operations. Its agents were reluctant to share information with the FBI for fear of losing control of the case. Part of this fear was an incompatibility of function between the two institutions. The FBI had the task of bringing lawbreakers to justice. They approached a case by accumulating evidence that could stand up in a court of law. CIA agents were less interested in prosecuting than intelligence gathering. They wanted to follow the leads to see where they would go. This meant that the CIA was unwilling to share crucial information because such sharing might compromise intelligence sources.

The decision by John Deutch, director of the CIA from 1995 to 1996, to call for prior approval from CIA headquarters before recruiting any person with a criminal or human rights problem as an intelligence asset made it difficult for the CIA to recruit intelligence agents. This decision came after a controversy involving the CIA's employment of a paid informant in Guatemala who had been involved in the murders of an American innkeeper and the Guatemalan husband of an American lawyer. Hundreds of paid informants were dismissed from the rolls of the CIA. Almost all of the human intelligence assets in the Middle East were terminated in this purge. This restriction was still in place on September 11, 2001.

The CIA had been monitoring the activities of Osama bin Laden and Al Qaeda through its Counterterrorism Center. CIA agents had been able to recruit 30 Afghans operating under the codeword GE/SENIORS to monitor bin Laden's activities in Afghanistan since 1998. They each received $10,000 a month for this mission. Numerous times during the Bill Clinton administration analysts in the Counterterrorism Center and its Alec Station unit proposed operations to neutralize bin Laden using Afghan agents or missile attacks, but none of these operations received approval. Part of the problem was that bin Laden was so elusive, traveling at irregular times. There was also the fear of collateral damage that would outrage domestic and international public opinion. The Clinton administration became paralyzed by indecision caused by its lack of confidence in CIA intelligence and the ongoing political difficulties of President Clinton's Monica Lewinsky scandal.

George Tenet, who succeeded Deutch, was able to make the transition from the Clinton administration to the George W. Bush administration. He had been constantly warning both administrations about the danger of bin Laden and Al Qaeda. Although the Clinton administration came to recognize the truth of the terrorism threat, the Bush administration was slow to accept it until September 11, 2001. Tenet had been able to establish a good working relationship with President Bush, but he was unable to get him to act quickly on Al Qaeda. After September 11, however, the Bush administration left nothing to chance in fighting terrorism. According to Seymour Hersh in *Chain of Command,* it unleashed the CIA to undertake covert action against terrorists with no restrictions but deniability for the president. The support for the Northern Alliance led to the overthrow of the Taliban regime in Afghanistan and ended safe sanctuary for bin Laden and the other leaders of Al Qaeda. But bin Laden and most of Al Qaeda's and the Taliban's leaders were able to escape. Part of the reason for the escape was the reluctance of the Bush administration to commit American forces until it was too late.

In the middle of the hunt for bin Laden and the wiping out of Al Qaeda's leadership, the Bush administration decided that Saddam Hussein and his weapons of mass destruction were greater threats. Even prior to September 11 it was known in the CIA that the Bush administration was eager to overthrow Saddam Hussein. Their reasoning was that deposing Hussein and establishing a favorable government in Iraq would produce a base of support in the Middle East for the United States, because it was apparent that there was no solution to the Israeli-Palestinian conflict.

Extreme pressure from the neoconservatives in the Bush administration, led by Vice President Dick Cheney, for the CIA to produce intelligence justification to go to war with Iraq resulted in widespread dissatisfaction among CIA analysts. Many of them believed that an Iraqi war would hinder the hunt for bin Laden and other Al Qaeda leaders. They believed that the United States should concentrate exclusively on Afghanistan and the Al Qaeda network. Those analysts who were too vocal with their dissatisfaction were fired, transferred, or severely criticized. Despite warnings from these CIA analysts about the lack of concrete intelligence, Tenet assured President Bush and his advisers that Iraq had weapons of mass destruction. The failure to find these weapons of mass destruction ended Bush's confidence in Tenet. In the meantime, the rank-and-file of the CIA had become critics of the Bush administration. They issued a series of intelligence reports that contradicted or were critical of the premises of the Bush administration's occupation of Iraq. Many of these reports were leaked to the news media.

After Tenet's resignation, Bush appointed former Florida congressman Porter Goss to head the CIA. He had worked for the CIA in the 1960s, but most of his knowledge of the CIA came from his seven years as chairman of the House Permanent Select Committee on Intelligence. President Bush gave Goss a mandate to bring the CIA back to Bush's political team. A short time after Goss came into Langley headquarters, senior CIA officials began to leave in droves. In April 2005 the CIA inspector general's report surfaced that presented detailed criticism of the performance of more than a dozen former and current CIA officials. Goss quashed the recommendation that there be accountability boards to recommend personnel actions against those charged in the report. Despite this action, the clash between Goss's team and CIA veterans reached epic proportions. In the long run, however, it was Goss's inability to work with his nominal boss, John Negroponte, the director of national intelligence, that led to his demise. President Bush asked for and received Goss's resignation on May 5, 2006. His successor was U.S. Air Force four-star general Michael Hayden, the former head of the National Security Agency (NSA) and the number two person under Negroponte. In February 2009, following Barack Obama's inauguration as president, Hayden was replaced by Leon Panetta.

The CIA played the central role in gathering the intelligence that led to the raid on the Abbottabad compound that resulted in bin Laden's death on May 1, 2011 (May 2 Pakistani local time). Beginning in August 2010, CIA operatives spent months tracking a lead that eventually allowed them to positively identify one of bin Laden's couriers, who in turn led them to suspect the compound, located in a suburb of the Pakistani capital of Islamabad, as bin Laden's likely hiding place. With Obama's final approval in late April 2011 and under the direction of Panetta, the CIA organized and oversaw the raid on the compound, which was carried out by elements of the U.S. Navy SEALs.

Stephen E. Atkins

See also: Al Qaeda; Bin Laden, Osama

Suggested Reading

Dreyfuss, Robert. "The Yes-Man: President Bush Sent Porter Goss to the CIA to Keep the Agency in Line; What He's Really Doing Is Wrecking It." *American Prospect,* November 2005, 18.

Drumheller, Tyler, and Elaine Monaghan. *On the Brink: An Insider's Account of How the White House Compromised American Intelligence.* New York: Carroll and Graf, 2006.

Hersh, Seymour M. *Chain of Command: The Road from 9/11 to Abu Ghraib.* New York: HarperCollins, 2004.

Joint Inquiry into Intelligence Community Activities before and after the Terrorist Attacks of September 11, 2001. *Hearings before the Select Committee on Intelligence U.S. Senate and the Permanent Select Committee on Intelligence House of Representatives.* 2 vols. Washington, DC: U.S. Government Printing Office, 2004.

Miller, John, Michael Stone, and Chris Mitchell. *The Cell: Inside the 9/11 Plot and Why the FBI and CIA Failed to Stop It.* New York: Hyperion, 2002.

Naftali, Timothy. *Blind Spot: The Secret History of American Counterterrorism.* New York: Basic Books, 2005.

Risen, James. *State of War: The Secret History of the CIA and the Bush Administration.* New York: Free Press, 2006.

Tenet, George, and Bill Harlow. *At the Center of the Storm: My Years at the CIA.* New York: HarperCollins, 2007.

Clarke, Richard A. (1950–)

Richard A. Clarke was the chief counterterrorism adviser on the U.S. National Security Council on September 11, 2001. He was a career specialist in intelligence and counterterrorism. He was one of the few carryovers from the Bill Clinton administration that the George W. Bush administration had retained, but he had difficulty in making the case that Al Qaeda was a major danger to the United States.

His entire career was in government service. He was born in 1950 in Boston, Massachusetts. His father was a blue-collar factory worker at a Boston chocolate factory, and his mother was a nurse. After a divorce, Clarke was raised by his mother. He won a competitive exam to attend the prestigious Boston Latin School, where he graduated in 1969. His undergraduate degree was earned from the University of Pennsylvania in 1972. He then attended the Massachusetts Institute of Technology (MIT), where he earned a degree in management. His first job, beginning in 1973, was with the U.S. Department of Defense as a defense analyst counting Soviet nuclear warheads. After a series of appointments, he was promoted in 1985 to assistant secretary of state for intelligence in the Reagan administration. By this time Steve Coll asserts that he had earned a reputation as being a "blunt instrument, a bully, and occasionally abusive." He continued to work with the George H. W. Bush administration and helped on security affairs during the 1990–1991 Persian Gulf War. In 1992 James Baker, the secretary of state, fired him for his apparent defense of Israel's transfer of U.S. technology to the People's Republic of China. Clarke then moved to the National Security Council in the White House, where he began to specialize in counterterrorism. Clarke was also held over in the Clinton administration, continuing as a member of the National Security Council from 1992 to 2003.

Clarke's preoccupation was with counterintelligence. Among his contentions was that Osama bin Laden's Al Qaeda was a growing threat to the United States. President Clinton agreed with this assessment, but he was engaged in a series of controversies that distracted him and his administration. Clarke lobbied for a Counterterrorism

Security Group to be chaired by a new national security official, the National Coordinator for Infrastructure Protection and Counterterrorism. President Clinton approved this office by signing Presidential Decision Directive 62 on May 22, 1998.

Clarke presided over a working group that included the counterterrorism heads of the Central Intelligence Agency (CIA), Federal Bureau of Investigation (FBI), Joint Chiefs of Staff (JCS), the Defense Department, the Justice Department, and the State Department. But the National Coordinator for Infrastructure Protection and Counterterrorism had a limited staff of 12 and no budget; moreover, operational decision making could come only from the departments and agencies of the intelligence community. As Clarke has pointed out, he had the "appearance of responsibility for counterterrorism, but none of the tools or authority to get the job done." Nevertheless, Clarke was in the middle of several counterterrorism operations. He was involved in the decision making about the CIA's snatch operation against Osama bin Laden in 1998. An Afghan team was to capture bin Laden at his residence at Tarnak Farms near Kandahar. This raid was called off because there was a lack of confidence that it would succeed by CIA leadership, the White House, and Clarke.

Clarke continued his position on the National Security Council during the early years of the Bush administration. He proposed a plan to combat Al Qaeda that included covert aid to the Afghan leader of the Northern Alliance, Ahmad Shah Massoud, spy flights of the new Predator, and ways to eliminate bin Laden as a threat to the United States, but there was little enthusiasm for this report by the Bush administration. Becoming frustrated, Clarke decided to resign from government work in November 2001. In the interval, the events of September 11, 2001, transpired, changing the American political landscape. On September 12, President Bush instructed him to try to find evidence that Saddam Hussein was connected to September 11. Clarke sent a report to the White House stating categorically that Hussein had nothing to do with these terrorist attacks, but there is no evidence indicating whether President Bush read the report. The report was sent back to be updated and resubmitted, but nothing came of it.

Clarke left government service in 2003. He then became an outspoken critic of the Bush administration and its policies prior to September 11. This led the White House to engage in a character assassination campaign against him. Clarke testified for 20 hours during the 9/11 Commission hearings. He made national headlines for his apology that the government had failed to prevent the September 11 attacks. In March 2004, in the middle of the 9/11 Commission hearings, Clarke published his book *Against All Enemies: Inside America's War on Terror,* which gives his side of the controversy.

In his book Clarke was especially critical of the Bush administration's invasion of Iraq. Most of his criticism stems from his belief that, by redirecting attention away from bin Laden and Al Qaeda, the Bush administration has allowed Al Qaeda to reconstitute itself into an ongoing threat to the United States. In his eyes the invasion of Afghanistan was so half-hearted in its commitment of American forces that bin Laden and nearly all of the Al Qaeda and Taliban leaders easily escaped. By not committing the necessary resources to rebuild Afghanistan, Clarke wrote, the Bush administration has allowed both Al Qaeda and the Taliban to threaten the pro–American Afghanistan state, all to depose Saddam Hussein.

Also in 2004, Clarke released *Defeating the Jihadists: A Blueprint for Action,* in which he outlined his idea for a more effective counterterrorism strategy. His other works include *Your Government Failed You: Breaking the Cycle of National Security Disasters* (2008) and *Cyber War: The Next Threat to National Security and What to Do About It* (2010), as well as two novels.

Stephen E. Atkins

See also: Bush, George W.; Bush Administration

Suggested Reading

Benjamin, Daniel, and Steven Simon. *The Age of Sacred Terror.* New York: Random House, 2002.

Clarke, Richard A. *Against All Enemies: Inside America's War on Terror.* New York: Free Press, 2004.

Coll, Steve. *Ghost Wars: The Secret History of the CIA, Afghanistan, and Bin Laden, from the Soviet Invasion to September 10, 2001.* New York: Penguin, 2004.

Naftali, Timothy. *Blind Spot: The Secret History of American Counterterrorism.* Basic Books, 2005.

Cleanup Operations at Ground Zero

Almost immediately after the attacks on the World Trade Center, cleanup operations started at Ground Zero. The collapse of the Twin Towers meant that there was little chance of survivors, but the effort had to be made. Fire Department City of New York (FDNY) firefighters, New York City police, Port Authority police, and others from federal agencies began looking for survivors. Only a handful of survivors were found the first day and none thereafter. For the first few days there was chaos as the bucket brigades were ineffectual and barely scratched the surface of the debris. The problem was that the debris from the buildings had fallen into four different sectors that were almost cut off from each other. At first, heavy equipment could not get into the site because of the fallen pedestrian bridge on West Street, so the only debris that was recovered on the first couple of days was by hand.

There was also a cloud of accumulated dust and fumes hanging over the scene of destruction. This air was toxic because, according to the Environmental Protection Agency (EPA), "Ground Zero inhalation tests of ambient air showed WTC dust consisted predominantly (95 percent) of coarse particles and pulverized cement, with glass fibers, asbestos, lead, polycyclic aromatic hydrocarbons (PAHS), polychlorinated biphenyls (PCB), and polychlorinated furans and dioxins." Thousands of police, firefighters, paramedics, and construction workers worked at the site for several months and breathed this air. Many of them began the hacking cough that soon earned the name "the World Trade Center cough."

Search and rescue teams started clearing the site and recovering as many body parts as possible. Four temporary tent morgues were set up on the site at the World Trade Center complex. Later, body parts were taken to a centralized morgue. It was a slow, grueling job recovering bodies and body parts, and it sometimes turned out to be dangerous. Fortunately, there were few major injuries at the site.

Complicating the early days of the rescue and recovery work were calls from family members stating that their loved ones were still alive. Firefighters and police followed up on these calls in the first days after

Fresh Kills landfill on Staten Island, New York, on October 16, 2001. Although Fresh Kills was officially shut down in March 2001, it acted as the emergency disposal site for debris from the World Trade Center following the September 11 terrorist attacks. (Andrea Booher/FEMA News Photo)

September 11, 2001. Then they realized that the calls had been triggered by the backed up communication system. So many cell phone calls had been made on September 11 that the overloaded communication system could not transmit them all. These messages were stored and sent later, when the communication system went back on line. Families then received messages that their loved ones had made before they died on September 11, confusing them and everyone else.

Within days, more than 1,000 construction workers began clearing debris alongside the emergency workers. Four companies participated in the cleanup: Bovis Company, Turner Construction Company, Tully Construction Company, and AMEC Construction Management. They used more than 150 pieces of heavy equipment, including 20 cranes and the Caterpillar 345 Ultra High Excavator for difficult jobs. Work was slow because of frequent interruptions to recover bodies and body parts of victims.

The construction workers received instructions not to be involved in body removal. After ascertaining that there were no bodies or body parts in a particular area, they loaded debris onto semis and dump trucks and took it to a wash and inspection station for inspection by Federal Bureau of Investigation (FBI) and Secret Service agents and then washed it down. The debris was then hauled down to a pier for loading onto a barge. This barge carried it to the Fresh Kills Landfill on Staten Island. There the debris was searched again before being added to the landfill.

As the debris removal picked up steam, another serious problem surfaced. In the construction of the World Trade Center complex, a wall had been built to keep out water from the Hudson River. This wall had been built because half of the 16-acre site had extended Manhattan Island 700 feet into the river. The problem was that this wall had been weakened in the collapse of the buildings. This wall had to be reinforced, or Hudson River water would have flooded much of lower Manhattan, causing a catastrophe greater than the World Trade Center attack. So a delicate balance had to be maintained between debris removal and bringing in material to reinforce the wall. This balancing act was successful, so no flooding took place.

Soon after the arrival of the construction workers, a controversy developed over the number of firefighters who were to remain working at Ground Zero. This issue had great importance to the firefighters because they were interested in finding bodies and body parts. The construction workers were more concerned about cleaning up the debris. What made the firefighters particularly assertive about finding any remains was that many of the missing victims were Catholic. Unless there was a body part, the Catholic Church refused to perform a funeral mass. Ultimately a compromise was worked out, with a significant number of firefighters staying at the World Trade Center site until the last part of the debris was removed in May 2002.

Another significant problem was that decision making for the World Trade Center site was by committee. Representatives from 26 federal, state, regional, and city agencies made the major decisions. New York City's Department of Design and Construction had been given overall control of the site, but it had only one representative on the committee. A representative from each agency had an equal vote on decisions, but decisions were not made by majority rule. Some agencies had more clout than others, and this clash of interests and opinions made for chaotic decision making.

Throughout the cleanup the presence of fire made work difficult. These fires were entirely under the pile and the workers rarely saw them. Only when the piles were penetrated did the fires' cherry red glow become visible. The fires received their oxygen from tunnels and underground areas, and they burned at a temperature from 1,000 to 1,800 degrees. At times the workers stood in areas where their boots began to melt. Attempts to attack the fires by pouring water on them were ineffective because of the densely packed debris. Water hit the fires and produced steam and smoke, making for two more hazards.

Another hazard of the cleanup was unexploded ammunition. Evidently there had been 1,700 live rounds scattered around World Trade Center Building Six. This ammunition had belonged to the U.S. Customs Service. Although there were no fatalities caused by this loose ammunition, there was one slight injury when a workman set off a round accidentally.

One issue that was unknown by anyone at the site was the gold and silver bullion stored at the World Trade Center complex and owned by Scotiabank. There was $110,000,000 worth of gold bars and $120,000,000 of silver bars in a vault under World Trade Center Building Four. A Port Authority police officer located the vault on October 17, 2001. Scotiabank officials were then notified of the finding of the vault. During a four-day period, all of the gold and silver bars were moved under the authority of the Port Authority police. It took 133 trucks to complete the transfer.

By mid-November a new threat to the site appeared in the form of Freon gas. Underneath the former North Tower was the main chiller plant, which had refrigeration units capable of holding 24,000 pounds of Freon gas. If the units had leaked, the gas would have filled voids in the underground before rising to the surface to kill as many as hundreds of workers. Another danger was that the Freon gas might come into contact with open flames, producing poison gas resembling the mustard gas used in World War I. In this case the casualties could be in the thousands. There was also an increasing danger that one of the large construction machines might puncture the Freon gas storage unit. A special team went underground to explore the condition of the chiller plant. This team discovered that the Freon gas had already vented, and the danger had passed without casualties.

One ongoing problem on the cleanup site was the failure of the firefighters, police, and workers to wear their personal protective equipment. This failure was particularly noticeable in the failure to use respirators, despite safety officials' attempts to persuade those working in the debris to wear them. The most stubborn were the firefighters. Their reasoning was that they needed to be able to smell to find the dead bodies. This safety deficiency was reported to the New York City's Department of Design and Construction and to the committee of 26 representatives of the agencies time and again, but nothing was done. The federal Occupational Safety and Health Administration (OSHA) and other safety officials had no authority to enforce safety rules.

The cleanup at Ground Zero officially ended on May 30, 2002, with a ceremony. The "Last Piece of Steel" was to be ceremoniously carried by truck escorted by an honor guard and signaled by the beat of a single drum. In a meeting it was determined that the Port Authority police would guard and be in charge of the "Last Piece of Steel." Plans came from the mayor's office that the honor guard would be composed of 15 members of each group that had worked at Ground Zero. Those groups interested in the proceedings, however, decided to ignore this limit, and the honor guard consisted of all personnel still working at the site in May 2002. Family members of the victims of September 11 were also invited to participate. The ceremony went off without any difficulty, and crowds lined the way, clapping in rhythm to the drum beat.

Since the end of the cleanup at Ground Zero, numerous workers at the site have been experiencing health problems. Of the approximately 30,000 people who worked at Ground Zero, more than 14,000 have instituted health claims. A study of 5,000 cleanup workers and first responders conducted by the FDNY's Office of Medical Affairs in April 2010 found that all had suffered impaired lung function. Other studies have demonstrated that respiratory illness rates among these groups have risen more than 200 percent, while the incidence of cancer has also increased. Although it is difficult to definitively attribute deaths to 9/11-related health issues, recent reports suggest that the deaths of more than 50 first responders and cleanup workers can be linked to exposure to toxins at Ground Zero. The most famous case was the death in January 2006 of New York Police Department Detective James Zadroga, at age 34, from a lung disease directly related to his more than 450 hours working at Ground Zero.

Many of the sufferers of the Ground Zero cleanup have resorted to lawsuits. A total of 10,563 individuals involved in rescue, recovery, and cleanup operations sued the city of New York for failing to provide adequate health protections, such as respirators. In November 2010, more than 10,000 of them agreed to a $625 million settlement. Numerous others, potentially intimidated by the legal process, may be suffering in silence. The issue has been complicated by the fact that a number of cleanup personnel were undocumented immigrants. In March 2010, more than 200 such workers pushed for continued health care and legal immigrant status. The death toll is rising for those who helped in the cleanup; tumors and lung-scarring diseases have been known to emerge between 5 and 20 years after a toxic exposure.

Ten years after 9/11, President Barack Obama signed the Zadroga 9/11 Health and Compensation Act of 2010, which reactivated the Victim Compensation Fund for those who suffered physical harm during the cleanup. It was reauthorized in 2015, and (after some debate) again in 2019. The 2019 extension allows claims until October 2090 and appropriates "such funds as may be necessary to pay all approved claims."

See also: Firefighters at Ground Zero; Health Effects of September 11; World Trade Center, September 11

Suggested Reading

Ausmus, David W. *In the Midst of Chaos: My 30 Days at Ground Zero.* Victoria, British Columbia: Trafford, 2004.

Butler, Gregory A. *Lost Towers: Inside the World Trade Center Cleanup.* New York: iUniverse, 2006.

Daily News Staff. "The Making of a Health Disaster; Officials Failed to Act on Ground Zero Perils." *Daily News* [New York], July 25, 2006, 24.

DiManno, Rosie. "Toll from 9/11 Climbs, Albeit Too Quietly." *Toronto Star,* January 13, 2006, A2.

Keegan, William, Jr., with Bart Davis. *Closure: The Untold Story of the Ground Zero Recovery Mission.* New York: Touchstone Books, 2006.

Moore, Robert F., Thomas Zambito, and Corky Siemaszko. "Stricken 9/11 Heroes in Fight of Their Lives." *Daily News* [New York], April 16, 2006, 16.

Schapiro, Rich. "WTC Air Doomed Ex-Cop." *Daily News* [New York], April 12, 2006, 7.

September 11th Victim Compensation Fund. "About the Victim Compensation Fund." https://www.vcf.gov/about

Smith, Dennis. *Report from Ground Zero.* New York: Viking, 2002.

Von Essen, Thomas, with Matt Murray. *Strong of Heart: Life and Death in the Fire Department of New York City.* New York: ReganBooks, 2002.

Conspiracy Theories

From the day after the attacks on September 11, 2001, conspiracy theories appeared and began to spread. A disaster of such magnitude, with some mysterious circumstances surrounding it, promotes such theories. The conspiracy theorists started with a hypothesis challenging the official version and began searching for information to support their theories. Any data that did not conform to their preconceived ideas were discounted, particularly if the data came from government sources, the mainstream media, or social scientists.

Conspiracy theories appear at every important event in U.S. history. Marcus LiBrizzi, an English professor at the University of Maine at Machias and an authority on conspiracy theories, however, was shocked at how soon conspiracy theories about 9/11 appeared, because normally it takes a decade or so before conspiracy theories develop enough material to be articulated and to surface.

In the case of September 11, there are four major types of conspiracy theories. The first is a belief that the U.S. government, while it did not actively assist in or perpetrate the attacks, has worked to cover up its own gross negligence and incompetence in the matter. The second theory is that the government knew about the attacks and intentionally allowed them to happen in order to suit its own political, military, and economic agendas. The third theory is that the U.S. government, not Al Qaeda, committed the attacks. (There is disagreement, however, as to how the government accomplished this. Some believe that bombs were planted in the World Trade Center and Pentagon, arguing that burning jet fuel alone could not have caused the extensive damage. Others subscribe to a more extreme "no plane" explanation, contending that the four aircraft were either passengerless remote-controlled devices or missiles surrounded by holograms of planes.) A fourth vein of conspiracy theorists assert that a foreign government or organization, such as Israel or a powerful drug cartel, carried out the attacks.

The leadership of the September 11 conspiracy theories is a diverse group. The movement's most vocal theorists are David Ray Griffin, a retired professor of postmodern theology; James H. Fetzer, a professor at the University of Minnesota–Duluth; Steven F. Jones, a retired physicist from Brigham Young University; and Jim Marrs, a freelance writer who specializes in conspiracy theories. All of them joined Fetzer's Scholars for 9/11 Truth to coordinate the investigations of the events surrounding 9/11. Soon, however, differences over the interpretation of 9/11 developed between Fetzer and Jones. Jones left the Scholars for 9/11 Truth to form the Scholars for 9/11 Truth and Justice.

One particularly radical conspiracy theorist is A. K. Dewdney, a professor emeritus of computer science at the University of Waterloo in Ontario, Canada. His theory, which he calls "Operation Pearl," makes September 11 a U.S. government conspiracy. In his thesis, the first three passenger aircraft landed at Harrisburg International Airport, Harrisburg, Pennsylvania, where the passengers disembarked. Three remote-controlled aircraft then were launched against the World Trade Center complex and the Pentagon. Passengers were then packed into the United Airlines Flight 93 aircraft, which was then shot down over Shanksville, Pennsylvania. The three empty aircraft were flown over the ocean and disposed of in a watery grave.

Dewdney's thesis lacks credibility for a number of reasons. First, there were too many passengers to cram into one aircraft. Second, two videos show and numerous witnesses saw both American Airlines Flight 11 and United Airlines Flight 175 crash into the World Trade Center's twin towers. Third, seven witnesses saw a commercial aircraft crash into the Pentagon. Fourth, and most important, it is unlikely that the U.S. government could carry out such an involved conspiracy without being caught.

Conspiracy theories have also been proposed by non–U.S. academics and leaders. One such individual is French left-wing activist Thierry Meyssan. His book *L'Effroyable Imposture: 11 Septembre 2001* (*The Frightening Fraud: September 11, 2001*) charged that it was a plot by the American government to discredit its enemies and to increase the U.S. defense budget. This book appeared in 2002 and became an immediate best seller. Among his assertions was that the damage to the Pentagon in Washington, DC, could not have been caused by a Boeing 757 but was instead a missile strike or a truck bombing made to appear as a plane crash. He also challenged eyewitness testimony. His thesis was that the September 11 attacks were part of a military conspiracy in the United States to impose a military regime. Media in both France and the United States have attacked the book for its bizarre claims. Shortly after the publication of his book, the U.S. Department of Defense declared Meyssan persona non grata. This status meant that Meyssan would be unable to enter the United States for any reason. The U.S. government followed in July 2005 with a document from the U.S. Department of State classifying him as a major source of anti-American propaganda in the world.

The number of individuals who believe in 9/11 conspiracy theories is, perhaps not surprisingly, highest in Islamic nations, even those that are close American allies, such as Egypt and Pakistan. On September 23, 2010, Iranian president Mahmoud Ahmadinejad delivered a speech before the United Nations (UN) in which he claimed that while most American politicians advanced the idea that September 11 had been carried out by Al Qaeda, most Americans and citizens of other nations believed that the terrorist attacks were in fact orchestrated by the U.S. government for economic and political gain. Although opinion polls have made it clear that Ahmadinejad's appraisal of Americans' opinions was incorrect, his comments underscored the fact that there is ongoing disagreement about the events of September 11.

Although critics have dismissed them as unfounded, conspiracy theories and theorists nevertheless remain an important facet of the ongoing discussions about September 11. And, while the vast majority of Americans blame Al Qaeda for the attacks, a number of national polls indicate that as many as one-third believe the U.S. government either allowed the attacks to happen or actually carried them out.

When President Barack Obama announced on May 1, 2011, that U.S. intelligence had tracked Osama bin Laden to a large compound in Abbottabad, Pakistan, where U.S. Navy SEALs had killed him during a raid and then buried his body at sea, conspiracy theories were quick to emerge. Despite assuring the public that photographic and DNA evidence had been taken that proved the body to be bin Laden's, the Obama administration's reluctance to share this evidence, in combination with the quick disposal of the body (both of which, it claims, have been done to avoid angering Muslims around the world), have led to speculation that bin Laden was in fact not killed in the raid. Some have suggested that someone else other than bin Laden was killed, while others have denounced the claim as a calculated attempt by Obama to ensure his reelection.

Stephen E. Atkins

See also: Al Qaeda; Bin Laden, Osama

Suggested Reading

Dunbar, David, and Brad Reagan. *Debunking 9/11 Myths: Why Conspiracy Theories Can't Stand Up to the Facts.* New York: Hearst Books, 2006.

Gurwitz, Jonathan. "Conspiracy Theories Only Flourish in the Darkness." *San Antonio Express-News,* May 24, 2006, 7B.

Henley, John. "US Invented Air Attack on Pentagon, Claims French Book." *Guardian,* April 1, 2002, 1.

D

Department of Design and Construction

The Department of Design and Construction (DDC) of New York City had the overall responsibility for the cleanup of the World Trade Center complex after September 11, 2001. Before September 11, the DDC was an obscure department in New York City government. Mayor Rudolph Giuliani had created the DDC in 1996 to oversee the work of building and repairing the municipal infrastructure. By New York City standards the DDC was a small department, with only 1,300 employees. But it had a $3.7 billion design and construction budget. Despite this budget, it was so obscure in the city's administrative hierarchy that the department was not even mentioned in the city's official emergency-response plan.

What made the DDC unique was that its head, Kenneth Holden, and his chief lieutenant, Michael Burton, took charge of the World Trade Center site immediately after the Twin Towers collapsed and began directing operations. Without authority and without permission, they began to recruit engineers and schedule heavy equipment at the site. Holden was familiar with the construction companies in the New York City area, and he bypassed ordinary bidding procedures to employ four companies: AMEC, Bovis, Tully, and Turner. He made the decision based on personal and corporate reputations. These companies earned immense profits in the cleanup, but they were also at risk financially because the companies never received adequate insurance for the job. Holden and Burton were so successful in mobilizing resources that Mayor Giuliani assigned the DDC to oversee operations at the World Trade Center complex site.

The first task of the DDC was to survey the site. At the first survey of Ground Zero, Holden and Burton escorted representatives from the construction firms and Richard Tomasetti from the well-respected engineering firm of Thornton-Tomasetti. After this initial survey, six engineers spent two weeks mapping the debris pile. They divided the pile into four quadrants. One quadrant each was assigned to AMEC, Bovis, Tully, and Turner. Except for Tully each of the construction companies was a multinational corporation in the high-rise construction business, and they had little equipment at their disposal. Tully was a family-owned New York paving contractor with little experience in building construction, but it had all the necessary trucks and heavy equipment. All of the companies had experience dealing with the DDC. Within a few weeks there were 3,000 construction workers at the World Trade Center site.

Burton also hired a New Jersey outfit, Weeks Marine, to supply barges to haul the debris from the World Trade Center complex. Until this decision, the trucks hauling the debris were overwhelming the city's transportation system. Marty Corcoran, a marine-construction engineer, persuaded Burton to award the job to Weeks Marine. This decision simplified the debris removal.

Running a complex operation like the cleanup at Ground Zero was a thankless task. Holden's job was to find resources for the cleanup, defend the DDC from political attacks, and allow Burton to do his job. Burton had the responsibility of overseeing the practical details of the cleanup. Together they were an effective team, but they were not without their critics. Both Holden and Burton were hard drivers, and their goal was to clear the debris as soon as possible. There was also the task of meeting with all the representatives of interested parties and coordinating activities. To expedite decision making there were twice-a-day meetings in which each interested party had to appear, because decisions were made and orders given out verbally.

The firefighters were unhappy about the fast pace of the debris removal. They blamed Holden, Burton, and the DDC in general for disrespect for the dead. Holden soon became known as the "Trade Center Czar." This resentment led in part to the riot by firefighters on November 2, 2001. In a meeting on November 12, 2001, families of lost firefighters attacked Burton for the rapid pace of debris removal.

Unhappiness over the pace of debris removal continued until the end of the cleanup in May 2002. Some of the responsibility for the cleanup shifted to private companies beginning in December 2001, but the DDC continued to play a major role in decision making. After May 2002, Holden was reappointed to the DDC, but Burton left for another position. Their personal relationship had never been a happy one, and the tensions of the months after September 11 only intensified the strain of their working together.

Stephen E. Atkins

See also: Cleanup Operations at Ground Zero; Firefighters at Ground Zero; Giuliani, Rudolph William Louis "Rudy," III; Health Effects of September 11

Suggested Reading

Cardwell, Diane. "Workers and Residents Are Safe, Officials Say." *New York Times,* November 2, 2001, B10.

Gittrich, Greg. "Last Hard Days at WTC: Crews Ponder Toll as They Search Few Remaining Piles." *Daily News* [New York], May 10, 2002, 8.

Glanz, James. "Ground-Penetrating Radar to Aid in Cleanup." *New York Times,* December 5, 2001, B8.

Glanz, James, and Kenneth Chang. "Engineers Seek to Test Steel before It Is Melted for Reuse." *New York Times,* September 29, 2001, B9.

Glanz, James, and Eric Lipton. "City Had Been Warned of Fuel Tank at 7 World Trade Center." *New York Times,* December 20, 2001, B1.

Langewiesche, William. *American Ground: Unbuilding the World Trade Center.* New York: North Point, 2002.

Overbye, Dennis. "Experts' Eyes Focus on 'the Bathtub' as Debris Is Cleared." *New York Times,* December 4, 2001, F3.

Department of Homeland Security

The Department of Homeland Security (DHS) is a federal cabinet-level agency established on November 25, 2002, with the passage of the Homeland Security Act of 2002. Created in the aftermath of the September 11, 2001, terrorist attacks, the DHS marked the largest restructuring of the federal government since the end of World War II. The DHS commenced operations on January 24, 2003, and brought together approximately 180,000 federal employees and 22 agencies into a cabinet-level department. The DHS was created to prevent terrorist attacks within the United States, reduce the vulnerability of the United States to terrorism, and minimize the damage from, and speed the recovery after, terrorist attacks.

Homeland security within the United States was traditionally viewed as a state concern, interpreted by the Constitution as related to public health and safety. The federal government historically focused on national security while leaving local and state governments responsible for these types of domestic concerns. However, as federal power has increased in relation to the states, so has the role of the federal government in homeland security matters.

Until the war years of the 20th century, the federal government largely took a secondary role to state governments in homeland security issues. One notable exception to this trend rests with the U.S. Army Corps of Engineers. This organization was tasked with providing flood protection for the nation through such legislation as the Flood Control Act of 1936, in addition to a range of other disaster-related roles. During the Cold War, homeland security took on a truly national role with the creation of the Office of Civil and Defense Mobilization in the early 1950s. Commonly referred to as the Civil Defense Agency, this body gave the federal government a major role in preparing the domestic population for nuclear attack. Other notable federal interventions into domestic homeland security include the Office of Emergency Preparedness, established in 1961, and the Federal Emergency Management Agency (FEMA), established in 1979.

With the end of the Cold War, the federal government increasingly focused on homeland security. The rising threat of weapons of mass destruction (WMDs) and terrorism prompted the national government to take on an even greater role in homeland security. The Presidential Decision Directive/National Security Council (PDD/NSC) document 39 of June 21, 1995, and PDD/NSC 63 of May 22, 1998, both reflected the increased federal focus in protecting domestic populations and resources from terrorist attacks. The National Defense Panel of 1997 called for the federal government to reform homeland security. The panel's recommendations included the need to incorporate all levels of government into managing the consequences of an attack with WMDs or through terrorist activities. Similar findings were made by the Hart-Rudman Commission (also known as the U.S. Commission on National Security/ Twenty-First Century) in January 2001. The commission recommended a cabinet-level agency to combat terrorism.

After the September 11, 2001, terrorist attacks, the George W. Bush administration undertook significant reforms to promulgate the earlier recommendations. Bush established the Office of Homeland Security (OHS) under the direction of former Pennsylvania governor Tom Ridge on October 8, 2001, through Executive Order 13228. The goals of the OHS involved coordinating homeland security efforts among the various federal, state, and local government agencies, and the development of a comprehensive homeland security strategy. However, the new body had no real budgetary or oversight authority, and its ability to accomplish its goals was limited. The principal strategy for the DHS was developed in the July 2002 National Strategy for Homeland Security White Paper and the earlier October 24, 2001, USA PATRIOT Act. Legislative authority was granted for the formation of the DHS on November 25, 2002, through the Homeland Security Act.

Headquartered in Washington, DC, the DHS became the 15th cabinet department within the federal government. It was tasked to serve as the coordinating body for the

87,000 different jurisdictions within the United States. The DHS consists of four major directorates: Border and Transportation Security, Emergency Preparedness and Response, Science and Technology, and Information Analysis and Infrastructure Protection.

In the area of border and transportation security, the U.S. Customs and Border Protection Agency and the U.S. Immigration and Customs Enforcement service were established. Other agencies transferred into this directorate include the Federal Protective Service, Animal and Plant Health Inspection Service, Transportation Security Administration, and the Federal Law Enforcement Training Center. The Emergency Preparedness and Response section was created when the Homeland Security Act transferred the following agencies into the DHS: FEMA; the Strategic National Stockpile, Office of Emergency Preparedness, Metropolitan Medical Response System, and the National Disaster Medical System, all transferred from the Department of Health and Human Services; Domestic Emergency Support Team, from the Department of Justice; National Domestic Preparedness Office, from the Federal Bureau of Investigation (FBI); and the Integrated Hazard Information System, from the National Oceanic and Atmospheric Administration (NOAA). In addition, the Department of Energy's Nuclear Incident Response Team can operate from the DHS during emergencies. To facilitate Information Analysis and Infrastructure Protection, the act transferred to the DHS the Critical Infrastructure Assurance Office, from the Department of Commerce; Federal Computer Incident Response Center; the National Communications System, from the Department of Defense; the National Infrastructure Protection Center,

from the FBI; and the National Infrastructure Simulation and Analysis Center, including the energy security and assurance program, from the Department of Energy. To deal with science and technology issues, the Homeland Security Act transferred from the Department of Energy various programs relating to the nonproliferation of chemical, biological, and nuclear weapons and research; the Environmental Measurements Laboratory; and the Lawrence Livermore National Laboratory. All functions relating to the Department of Defense's National Bio-Weapons Defense Analysis Center and the Plum Island Animal Disease Center were also transferred to the DHS.

In addition, the U.S. Coast Guard and the U.S. Secret Service were transferred into the DHS. The Coast Guard is the primary agency for maritime safety and security. In addition, the Coast Guard's long history of interdiction and antismuggling operations bolstered the ability of the DHS to protect the nation's maritime boundaries. The Secret Service is the lead agency in protecting senior executive personnel and the U.S. currency and financial infrastructure. Under the DHS, the U.S. Citizenship and Immigration Services was formed to replace the Immigration and Naturalization Services (INS). A fifth directorate, Management, is responsible for budget, facilities, and human resource issues.

In addition to the key directorates and agencies, the DHS operates a number of other offices. The Office of State and Local Government Coordination serves as the primary point of contact for programs and for exchanging information between the DHS and local and state agencies. The Office for Domestic Preparedness assists state and local authorities to prevent, plan for, and respond to acts of terrorism. The

Office of the Private Sector facilitates communication between the DHS and the business community. The Privacy Office of the DHS minimizes the dangers to, and safeguards, the rights to privacy of U.S. citizens in the mission of homeland security. The Office for Civil Rights and Civil Liberties provides policy and legal guidance on civil rights and civil liberties issues. These agencies were created to allay the fears and concerns of civil libertarians and ensure that the DHS does not violate citizens' civil liberties. The National Infrastructure Advisory Council provides advice to security agencies on protecting critical information systems. The Interagency Coordinating Council on Emergency Preparedness and Individuals with Disabilities ensures the consideration of disabled citizens in disaster planning.

The DHS relies on other branches of government to fulfill its mission of protecting the U.S. homeland. Tasked with a largely preventive role, investigative responsibility continues to primarily rest with local, state, and federal law enforcement agencies, including the FBI. While the DHS employs many of its own analysts, the majority of its intelligence-collection efforts are conducted outside of the department by other members of the intelligence community. Some called for the DHS to incorporate the FBI and the Central Intelligence Agency (CIA) into a single intelligence clearinghouse within the department. However, the two were left as autonomous entities. In order to aid states, the DHS provides funding in the form of grants and targeted expenditures to states, localities, and private bodies, including research centers.

The military also maintains a role in homeland security, chiefly through its Northern Command. The Northern Command plays a role in homeland defense as well as domestic airway security. The military currently maintains the largest capability for chemical, biological, and nuclear incident response, as well as personnel augmentation during domestic emergencies, most notably through federalization of the National Guard. One example of this type of federalization occurred with the deployment of the National Guard to bolster airport security following the September 11, 2001, terrorist attacks.

Former governor of Pennsylvania Tom Ridge was appointed the first secretary of homeland security and oversaw the creation of the OHS and its conversion into a cabinet-level department. By 2004 the DHS had grown to 183,000 employees with an annual budget of $36.5 billion. Ridge resigned on November 30, 2004, to pursue a career in private industry. He was replaced by Michael Chertoff on February 15, 2005. By 2008 the DHS had more than 207,000 employees, and its yearly budget was approximately $45 billion. On January 21, 2009, Janet Napolitano became the third secretary of Homeland Security, assuming her duties as a cabinet member of the Barack Obama administration. By 2020, the DHS had expanded to 240,000 employees and operated with a budget of more than $50 billion.

Tom Lansford

See also: Bush, George W.; Bush Administration; Federal Emergency Management Agency; Office of Emergency Management

Suggested Reading

Daalder, Ivo H., et al. *Assessing the Department of Homeland Security.* Washington, DC: Brookings Institution, 2002.

Kettl, Donald F. *The Department of Homeland Security's First Year: A Report Card.* New York: Century Fund, 2004.

White, Jonathan. *Defending the Homeland: Domestic Intelligence, Law Enforcement, and Security.* Belmont, CA: Wadsworth, 2003.

Disaster Mortuary Operation Response Team

The most difficult problem facing the authorities after the recovery of remains of victims of the September 11, 2001, attacks was identifying the victims. It was a horrendous business at all three sites—the World Trade Center complex, the Pentagon, and the United Airlines Flight 93 crash site. Into this void stepped the Disaster Mortuary Operation Response Team (DMORT) movement. Teams from DMORT were to assist local authorities in the handling and identification of bodies or body parts. In New York City, the Office of the Chief Medical Examiner (OCME) was in charge overall.

In the early 1980s the National Funeral Directors Association saw the need for a rapid deployment of mortuary operations in the event of large-scale disasters. To correspond to this need the association formed the Disaster Mortuary Operation Response Team concept. It was a multidisciplinary, nonprofit organization of forensic practitioners capable of responding in the event of a massive loss of life due to a disaster. In 1996 Congress passed the Family Assistance Act, which augmented the mission of the DMORT. On the eve of September 11, 2001, DMORT had two specialized Disaster Portable Morgue Units (DPMUs) stationed at the Federal Emergency Management Agency (FEMA) Logistic Centers in Rockwell, Maryland, and in San Jose, California. These DMORT teams had all the specialists necessary to handle a disaster with huge

loss of life: medical examiners, forensic pathologists, forensic anthropologists, fingerprint specialists, forensic orthodontists, DNA specialists, mental health specialists, and an administrative staff to coordinate their activities.

DMORT teams operated at all of the September 11, 2001, sites. This meant that the two teams of specialists had to be subdivided into three parts. Reduction in the number of specialists at any one site led the DMORT teams to draw on local medical volunteers. There was no lack of competent medical personnel ready to volunteer their services.

Because of the nature of the crashes and collapsing buildings, most of the identification of victims has come from recovered body parts. Morgue workers systematically processed each body part individually. It was then catalogued and assigned a number, photographed, X-rayed, and examined further for some kind of identifying characteristic. For those that could not be identified from dental records or some distinguishing characteristic other than DNA, analysis was necessary. This process meant taking DNA samples from family members. DNA analysis allowed an amazing number of victims to be identified, especially at the United Airlines Flight 93 crash site near Shanksville, Pennsylvania. Ultimately, everyone on that plane was identified from body parts at this site. It was much more difficult at the other sites. It was especially difficult at the World Trade Center because the high-temperature fire and changes of temperature caused the DNA to deteriorate, making identification sometimes impossible.

The huge number of deaths at the World Trade Center and the nature of the deaths made it impossible to identify all of the victims. There were more complete bodies found there, but others were so affected by the combination of high-temperature fires and the weight of the collapsing buildings that they simply disappeared. Even with the help of non-DMORT forensic help in New York City, the task verged on the impossible. Because of the heavy demands on the DNA-processing centers around the country, some of the identification took longer than usual and upset some of the families of the victims, but there was no way to rush the process. Once an identification was made, the families were contacted and given various options on what to do with the remains. Some families wanted to wait and see if more remains could be identified, but other families wanted closure and accepted the identified remains for burial services. Remains that nobody claimed were disposed of in a dignified way.

One of the problems with the slow identification process was the difficulty that it caused for families who needed death certificates to file legal papers for life insurance and other important legal documents. This fact was more of a problem in Pennsylvania than in New York City, because officials there issued an affidavit that expedited death certificates. Two enterprising men from Pennsylvania offered a solution by calling for an Action of Declaratory Judgment that the court accepted after receiving corroborating evidence that there were no survivors on United Airlines Flight 93. It took only a month after September 11, 2001, for the death certificates to be issued.

Stephen E. Atkins

See also: Casualties of September 11; Pentagon Attack; United Airlines Flight 93; World Trade Center, September 11

Suggested Reading

Hannah, Lawrence. "Sifting through Ground Zero." *Dominion Post* [Wellington, New Zealand], September 14, 2002, 14.

Jones, Adrian. "The Days of the Remains." In *On the Ground after September 11: Mental Health Responses and Practical Knowledge Gained,* edited by Yael Danieli and Robert L. Dingman. New York: Haworth Maltreatment and Trauma Press, 2005.

Kashurba, Glenn J. *Quiet Courage: The Definitive Account of Flight 93 and Its Aftermath.* Somerset, PA: SAJ Publishing, 2006.

Dog Rescue and Recovery Teams

Dogs were the unsung heroes of the rescue and recovery at the World Trade Center complex site after September 11, 2001. More than 300 dogs worked at the World Trade Center site, of which between 50 and 60 were police dogs. Different types of dogs performed the invaluable service of locating survivors and then locating bodies and body parts. The dogs were divided into two types: search-and-rescue dogs and cadaver-sniffing dogs. The two types were trained differently. Search-and-rescue dogs reacted negatively to finding bodies or body parts. A cadaver-sniffing dog's job was to find remains. In the early days a search-and-rescue dog and a cadaver-sniffing dog would work as a team. Later, when it became apparent that there were no more survivors, the cadaver-sniffing dogs took over.

Regardless of the type of dog, the dogs and their handlers climbed up and down over the debris. Some of the dogs had to wear booties to protect their paws from sharp objects and the heat coming from the debris pile. This duty was exhausting, and the dogs often took naps in stretchers, in the beds of trucks, or on a pile of firefighting equipment. There was even a hospital trailer to treat the dogs for injuries. Cleanliness

A member of the French Urban Search and Rescue Task Force works with his Alsatian to uncover survivors at the site of the collapsed World Trade Center after the 9/11 attacks. (Andrea Booher/FEMA News Photo)

was important, and a bath improved the morale of the dog.

The cadaver-sniffing dogs were experts at finding bodies or body parts. A handler and the dog would traverse back and forth over the debris until the dog would stop and sniff. The dog would start pawing the ground. If a cadaver-sniffing dog got excited, digging and barking, there was a good chance a body or body part was nearby. The handler would then notify the firefighters, who would begin digging until the body or body part could be found. Since the dogs could detect any decomposing flesh, one time a dog smelled a side of beef from one of the restaurants in the World Trade Center. Sometimes, to keep up the morale of the dogs, a police officer would hide in the rubble so the dogs would hit upon a live person. This action helped both search-and-rescue and cadaver-sniffing dogs from becoming too depressed.

Some of the dogs became celebrities. One such dog was a golden retriever named Bear. His fame came from finding the most bodies in the rubble, including that of Fire Chief Peter Ganci. He was featured in the *Guinness Book of World Records* as "the most celebrated dog in the world." He worked with his human partner, Scott Shields, who worked for a private safety firm. Not long after working at the World Trade Center site, Bear started having health problems. He developed cancer, arthritis, and other ailments associated with his work at the site; his veterinarian fees were $3,000. Bear was 12 years old when he died on September 23, 2002.

Besides assisting in finding remains, dogs also provided another service. Fourteen certified teams of trauma-response dogs had come from around the country to serve at Ground Zero. A donor had provided airline tickets for these teams to come from as far away as Oregon. These affectionate dogs gave assistance to distraught workers who needed reassurance.

Stephen E. Atkins

See also: Cleanup Operations at Ground Zero

Suggested Reading

Ausmus, David W. *In the Midst of Chaos: My 30 Days at Ground Zero.* Victoria, British Columbia: Trafford, 2004.

Bode, Nicole. "Human Pals Mourn WTC Hero Pooch." *Daily News* [New York], October 28, 2002, 18.

Fink, Mitchell, and Lois Mathias. *Never Forget: An Oral History of September 11, 2001.* New York: HarperCollins, 2002.

Huntley, Sarah. "Dog Handler Recounts Search at Ground Zero." *Rocky Mountain News* [Denver], September 23, 2002, 6A.

E

Economic Impact of September 11

The financial impact of September 11, 2001, was devastating to New York City and to the commercial airline industry. It was this economic damage as much as the physical damage that had appealed to Osama bin Laden. He wanted to attack the United States at its source of strength and cause it economic distress. Bin Laden was partially successful, as property losses, particularly in New York City, were high. Southern Manhattan was the center of the New York City government and international finance, and both were paralyzed. Office buildings were empty, and the subways stopped running. The tens of thousands of people who lived below Canal Street were prevented from going there. All schools and bridges were closed. But where the economic impact was greatest and most long lasting was with the airline industry.

It took the American airline industry nearly five years to recover from September 11. Both American and United airlines lost two aircraft to the hijackers, but insurance covered most of those losses. What hurt the airlines was the loss of customers, many of whom were afraid to fly. Airports had been shut down around the country. Even 10 days after September 11 the New York City airports were running 80 percent of their flights but with only 35 percent of passenger seats filled. Lost revenue from the three New York Airports was around $250 million a day.

Compounding the problem was the rocketing cost of oil and the higher aviation premiums from insurers. In the period from September 11, 2001, to September 2004, the airline industry lost $23 billion. In October 2001 airline passenger traffic dropped 23.2 percent in comparison to October 2000. An infusion of $1.5 million of federal aid helped the airline industry, but a series of bankruptcies occurred in the next few years. Only gradually have the airlines begun to creep back to financial health.

New York City had a massive loss of jobs and buildings. Job loss has been estimated at 143,000 a month, with lost wages of $2.8 billion. Nearly 70 percent of the jobs lost and 86 percent of the wages lost were to persons with well-paying positions in finance, insurance, and banking. Building loss has been assessed at $34 billion, with only about half of the building loss insured at value. It has been estimated that the city lost $60 billion in revenue, with $82 million coming from lost parking ticket revenue alone.

The shortest-lasting economic impact was on the stock market. On September 11, 2001, the hijacked aircraft crashed into the World Trade Center complex before the opening of the stock market. Damage to communications, evacuation orders, and rescue efforts led to the closing of the market for the next four days. When the stock market reopened on Monday, September 17, there was an immediate sell-off. On September 10, the Standard & Poor's 500 Index had closed at 1,092.54, and when trading closed on September 17 the index was at 891.10. By September 24, however, the stock market was climbing again. On October 11, the index closed at 1,097.43.

The American economy rebounded from the September 11 attacks within months. One reason that these attacks did not have a more lasting impact was that they were concentrated by geography and industry. Whereas New York City, and to a lesser extent Washington, DC, suffered economic dislocation from unemployment and property damage, the rest of the country was left relatively untouched.

Stephen E. Atkins

See also: World Trade Center, September 11

Suggested Reading

Griffiths, Katherine. "US Airline Industry in Tailspin to Disaster." *Independent* [London], September 10, 2004, 46.

Kawar, Mark. "9/11 Shock Didn't Bring Bears to Stock Market." *Omaha World Herald,* September 17, 2002, 1D.

Polgreen, Lydia. "Study Confirms 9/11 Impact on New York City Economy." *New York Times,* June 30, 2004, B6.

Zuckerman, Sam. "9/11 before and after: It's the Rebound, Stupid." *San Francisco Chronicle,* December 30, 2001, D7.

Soldiers from the 101st Airborne Division out of Fort Campbell, Kentucky, check local residents for possible weapons or contraband in the vicinity of Narizah, Afghanistan, on July 23, 2002. Shortly after the September 11, 2001, terrorist attacks, the United States and its allies launched Operation ENDURING FREEDOM with the aim of toppling the Taliban regime in Afghanistan that had provided aid to Al Qaeda. (U.S. Department of Defense)

ENDURING FREEDOM, Operation

ENDURING FREEDOM was the code name given to the U.S.-led invasion of Afghanistan that began on October 7, 2001. The purpose of the invasion was to topple the Taliban government and kill or capture members of the Al Qaeda terrorist group, which had just carried out the terrorist attacks of September 11, 2001. The Taliban had sheltered Al Qaeda and its leader, Osama bin Laden, on Afghan territory and provided the terrorists with bases, training facilities, and quite possibly financial support.

The United States faced major problems in planning a war against the Taliban and Al Qaeda. Prime among these were logistical concerns, for Afghanistan is a landlocked country distant from U.S. basing facilities. American planners decided that an alliance would have to be forged with the Afghan United Front (also known as the

Northern Alliance), an anti-Taliban opposition force within Afghanistan. The Northern Alliance would do the bulk of the fighting but would receive U.S. air support, along with assistance, advice, and cash from U.S. special operations forces.

The war began with American air strikes from land-based B-52 and B-1 bombers, carrier-based F-14 Tomcat and F-18 Hornet aircraft, and Tomahawk cruise missiles. These attacks were intended to knock out the Taliban's antiaircraft defenses and communications infrastructure. However, desperately poor Afghanistan had a very limited infrastructure to bomb, and the initial air attacks had only minimal impact. Al Qaeda training camps were also targeted, although they were quickly abandoned once the bombing campaign began. U.S. special operations forces arrived in Afghanistan on October 15, at which time they made contact with the leaders of the Northern Alliance.

The first phase of the ground campaign was focused on the struggle for the northern city of Mazar-e Sharif, which fell to the Northern Alliance forces led by generals Abdul Dostum and Ustad Atta Mohammed on November 10, 2001. The fighting around Mazar-e Sharif was intense, but U.S. air strikes, directed by special operations forces on the ground, did much to break Taliban and Al Qaeda resistance.

As the fighting progressed, the Taliban and Al Qaeda improved both their tactics and combat effectiveness. Camouflage and concealment techniques were also enhanced, helping to counter American air power. However, the Taliban's limited appeal to the population meant that the regime could not withstand the impact of a sustained assault. The repressive rule of the Taliban ensured that the Taliban never widened its base of support beyond the Pashtun ethnic group from which they originated.

Northern Alliance forces captured the Afghan capital of Kabul without a fight on November 13. On November 26 a besieged garrison of 5,000 Taliban and Al Qaeda soldiers surrendered at Kunduz after heavy bombardment by American B-52s. Meanwhile, an uprising by captured Taliban fighters held in the Qala-e-Gangi fortress near Mazar-e Sharif prison was suppressed with great brutality in late November.

The scene of the fighting then shifted to the city of Kandahar in southern Afghanistan. Because the Taliban had originated in Kandahar in the early 1990s, they were expected to put up a stiff fight for the city. Kandahar was attacked by Northern Alliance forces led by generals Hamid Karzai and Guyl Agha Shirzai, with U.S. special operations forces coordinating the offensive. The Taliban deserted Kandahar on December 6, and Taliban leader Mohammed Mullah Omar and the surviving Taliban elements went into hiding in the remote mountain regions of Afghanistan and Pakistan. The fall of Kandahar marked the end of Taliban rule in Afghanistan, only nine weeks after the beginning of the bombing campaign. On December 22, 2001, an interim administration, chaired by Hamid Karzai, took office.

Despite the rapid and efficient progress of Operation ENDURING FREEDOM, Taliban and Al Qaeda elements remained at large in Afghanistan, and the operation failed to capture or kill either Osama bin Laden or Omar. Bin Laden was believed to be hiding in mountain dugouts and bunkers located in the White Mountains near Tora Bora. A 16-day offensive in early December 2001 failed to find bin Laden. For this offensive, the United States once again relied on Northern Alliance ground troops supported by U.S. special operations forces and American air power. Later there would be charges that this offensive was mishandled, and an opportunity to take bin Laden was lost. Bin Laden escaped, probably into Pakistan through the porous border that separates Afghanistan from Pakistan.

Despite the failure to capture or kill bin Laden, the United States could point to notable success in the so-called War on Terror by the end of 2001. The Taliban had been deposed and Al Qaeda was on the run, with many of its members and leaders having been killed or captured. This occurred despite the fact that the United States deployed only about 3,000 service personnel, most of them special operations forces, to Afghanistan by the end of the year. The U.S. death toll was remarkably light, with only two deaths attributed to enemy action. Estimates of Afghan fatalities are approximate at best. As many as 4,000 Taliban soldiers may have been killed during the campaign. Afghan civilian deaths have been estimated at between 1,000 and 1,300, with several thousand refugees dying from disease and/or exposure. Another 500,000 Afghans were made refugees or displaced persons during the fighting.

The United States attempted a different approach in March 2002, when Al Qaeda positions were located in the Shahi-Kot Valley near Gardez. On this occasion, U.S. ground troops from the 10th Mountain Division and the 101st Airborne Division led the way, along with special operations forces from Australia, Canada, and Germany, and Afghan government troops, in an offensive code-named Operation ANACONDA. Taliban reinforcements rushed to join the Al Qaeda fighters, but both were routed from the valley with heavy losses.

After 2002 the Taliban and Al Qaeda remnants maintained a steadily increasing insurgency in Afghanistan. Troops from the United States and allied countries, mainly from North Atlantic Treaty Organization (NATO) member states, remained in Afghanistan operating under the banner of Operation ENDURING FREEDOM until December 2014.

President Barack Obama announced the end of Operation ENDURING FREEDOM on December 28, 2014, and ongoing U.S. military operations in Afghanistan that continue to the present day do so under the name Operation FREEDOM'S SENTINEL, shifting from large-scale military operations to an emphasis on counter-terrorism with support and training for allied Afghan security forces.

Paul W. Doerr

See also: Al Qaeda; Bin Laden, Osama; Bush, George W.; Bush Doctrine; Global War on Terror; Taliban

Suggested Reading

Biddle, Stephen. *Afghanistan and the Future of Warfare: Implications for Army and Defense Policy.* Carlisle, PA: Strategic Studies Institute, 2002.

Hanson, Victor Davis. *Between War and Peace: Lessons from Afghanistan to Iraq.* New York: Random House, 2004.

Kagan, Frederick. *Finding the Target: The Transformation of American Military Policy.* New York: Encounter Books, 2006.

Maley, William. *The Afghanistan Wars.* New York: Palgrave Macmillan, 2002.

F

Fahrenheit 9/11

Fahrenheit 9/11 is an award-winning documentary by the filmmaker Michael Moore. It is highly controversial because of its pronounced bias against President George W. Bush and his policies. The documentary opened in movie theaters across the United States on June 25, 2004, and it received mixed reviews, which often reflected the political persuasion and beliefs of the reviewers. Moore had a reputation for making documentaries that evinced a liberal bias, and this documentary fits into that category as well.

The film highlights President George W. Bush's conduct before and after the events of September 11, 2001. Moore is particularly harsh toward President Bush's passivity and apparent lack of action against the threat of terrorism before September 11. In his documentary, Moore reported that Bush spent 42 percent of his time on vacation in the period leading up to September 11. Moore also spotlighted the close personal and business relationship between President Bush (and his family) and the Saudi regime. This relationship led to the evacuation of Osama bin Laden's family from the United States just after September 11 in such haste there was no time for debriefing by law enforcement and intelligence officials. Moore was also highly critical of the rationale for the invasion of Iraq. Finally, Moore criticized the national media for cheering on the Bush administration's war against terror and the invasion of Iraq.

Even before its appearance in movie theaters, the documentary was so controversial that it had trouble finding a distributor. Harvey Weinstein, the CEO of Miramax Films, had provided most of the $6 million financial support for the documentary. Miramax is a subsidiary of Walt Disney Company, and Michael Eisner, then the CEO of Walt Disney Company, refused to allow Miramax to distribute the film. This decision was made by Eisner despite the fact that he had not yet seen the documentary. Moore claimed that Eisner had been concerned about retaliation from Florida governor Jeb Bush, the brother of George W. Bush, concerning Disney's real estate holdings and other interests in Florida. In the trade journals it was already common knowledge that *Fahrenheit 9/11* was going to be a hot property and that it would draw interest from a number of distributors. Weinstein discussed the issue with Eisner, but he lost the argument and the documentary was ultimately not distributed by Miramax. Moore then turned to a second distributor, Lions Gate Entertainment Corporation, which was a Canadian distributor based in Vancouver, British Columbia. To handle such a large booking Lions Gate had to conclude a secondary partnership with IFC Films and Fellowship Adventure Group.

The documentary has been fabulously successful financially. During its opening weekend (July 25–27, 2004), it generated box office revenues of $23.9 million in the United States and Canada despite opening in only about 40 percent of the theaters normally available for top-flight movies. In less than a year the documentary had grossed over $120 million in the United States and over $220 million worldwide. Because of its anti-Bush theme and opposition to the Iraq War, the documentary was an international best seller. Moore decided to release the documentary in a DVD format, which was made available in stores on October 5, 2004. Around 2 million copies of the DVD were sold on the first day.

Besides producing controversy, the documentary has also received some critical acclaim. In April 2004 the documentary was entered to compete for the prestigious Palme d'Or (Golden Palm) Award at the 57th Cannes Film Festival. It was received with great fanfare at its first showing. The nine-person panel for the award had four Americans and only one Frenchman on it. They voted for *Fahrenheit 9/11* as the winner of the 2004 Palme d'Or award.

Supporters of President Bush and the conservative movement tried in various ways to block the release of the documentary. They were worried that the documentary might have a negative effect on the 2004 reelection campaign of President Bush. Organizations such as Patriotic Americans Boycotting Anti-American Hollywood (PABAAH) launched an anti-Moore campaign. Subsequently, some Bush supporters held an anti-Moore film festival, called the American Film Renaissance, in Texas, showing films that attacked Moore and his views regarding the Bush administration. The key feature was Michael Wilson's film *Michael Moore Hates America*. To counter the charges from conservatives that he distorted facts in his documentary, Moore hired a staff of researchers and two lawyers to check the facts and claims in *Fahrenheit 9/11*. There appeared to have been a backlash against this anti-Moore

campaign and the documentary continued to be shown in theaters, attracting more viewers and making more money.

Stephen E. Atkins

See also: Bush, George W.; Bush Administration

Suggested Reading

Booth, William. "*Fahrenheit 9/11* Too Hot for Disney?" *Washington Post,* May 6, 2004, C1.

Denby, David. "Michael Moore's Viciously Funny Attack on the Bush Administration." *New Yorker,* June 28, 2004, 108.

Donegan, Lawrence, and Paul Harris. "American Right Vows to Settle Score as Bush's Nemesis Turns Up the Heat." *Observer* [London], June 27, 2004, 18.

Goldstein, Patrick. "Eisner Fumbles PR Stunt—and Show Biz Politics." *Gazette* [Montreal], May 14, 2004, D1.

Scott, A. O. "Moore's *Fahrenheit 9/11* Wins Top Honors at Cannes." *New York Times,* May 23, 2004, 6.

Smith, Gavin. "Michael Moore Gives Much More." *New Statesman,* July 19, 2004, 1.

Wendy Stueck, "Lions Gate Hits Jackpot with Fahrenheit 9/11 Distribution," *Globe and Mail* [Canada], June 29, 2004, B1.

Families of Victims of September II

Soon after September 11, 2001, the families of the victims began to organize into support groups. At first the families underwent a period of mourning. Many of the families did not even have the opportunity to give their loved ones a proper burial and achieve closure. Next, the families had to deal with the real-world repercussions of their loss in the form of financial liabilities and uncertainty. Government programs were available,

JOHN CHARLES JENKINS   EDWARD R. HENNESSY, JR.

PAUL DALE   BERRY BERENSON PERKINS   ROBERT JAY

MORALES PUOPOLO   LAURIE ANN NEIRA   BAR

The 9/11 Memorial at World Trade Center Ground Zero, as seen on July 11, 2015. The memorial was dedicated on the 10th anniversary of the September 11, 2001 attacks. The pools with water-falls cover the footprints of the twin towers; they are surrounded by parapets with the names of 2,983 victims. (Frederic Prochasson/Dreamstime.com)

but dealing with government bureaucracy was confusing and troubling for many of the survivors. Some family members were unable to cope without help. Various organizations and support groups were formed to help the families cope with their losses and to teach them how to handle their new responsibilities. Later, these organizations set up a formidable lobbying group to compel Congress and the George W. Bush administration to examine how the events of September 11 could have happened and how they could have been prevented. The group's other endeavors include the Building Bridges Project, launched in 2004, and the Living Memorial Project, launched in 2006.

The largest and one of the most active groups in the families of victims of 9/11 movement is known as the Voices of

September 11th. It is a nonprofit, nonpartisan organization founded by Mary Fetchet and Beverly Eckert in October 2001. Fetchet, a clinical social worker from New Canaan, Connecticut, lost her 24-year-old son in the collapse of the South Tower of the World Trade Center complex on September 11, and Eckert lost her husband. Headquarters for the Voices of September 11th is in New Canaan, with a satellite office in New Brunswick, New Jersey. They began by setting up an Internet clearinghouse for disseminating information about all aspects of September 11 for the families of the victims. The goal of the Voices of September 11th group has been to serve as an advocate for the 9/11 families. As one of the largest of the support groups for the 9/11 families, with around 11,000 members, it has proven to be a potent lobbying force. Fetchet and her colleagues in other groups fought hard for the creation of the 9/11 Commission. Fetchet has testified before several committees of Congress on the need to investigate what happened on September 11 and to understand why it happened. The group now assists other communities affected by mass violence and natural disasters.

Another leading 9/11 family group was the Families of September 11 (FOS11), a nonprofit organization founded in October 2001 by Donald W. Goodrich and Carie Lemarck. Both founders lost relatives on September 11. The primary goals of FOS11 were to support the families of the victims of September 11 by providing information on topics relevant to their situation and to engage in lobbying efforts on issues relating to the domestic and international efforts to combat terrorism. Representatives from FOS11 were active in lobbying for the creation of the 9/11 Commission, and they campaigned for the Congressional implementation of the 9/11 Commission's recommendations.

The World Trade Center United Family Group, or WTC United, was another important member of the families of 9/11 movement. This nonprofit organization was established shortly after September 11. Its goal was to ensure that the memories and the legacies of the victims of 9/11 are protected. Members were also active in lobbying the U.S. Congress on issues important to them and worked for the 9/11 Memorial to be built on the former World Trade Center complex site.

A major source of contention was the proposed memorial to the victims of September 11. The 9/11 families wanted the memorial to be built first, but the decision to build the One World Trade Center building (formerly known as Freedom Tower) first was made by Governor George Pataki for financial and political reasons. Although the major decision had been made by Governor Pataki, the details of the decision became a source of contention between the mayor's office and representatives of the families. Other issues have also caused friction.

Where the families of 9/11 movement made the biggest impact was in the creation of the 9/11 Commission and the passage by Congress of most of that commission's recommendations. For almost two years representatives from the various groups formed by 9/11 families lobbied the halls of Congress and the White House for the establishment of such a commission. The Bush administration tried to stonewall the request, but eventually President Bush gave in and agreed to cooperate. Bush's selection of Henry Kissinger to be the co-chair of the commission was unsatisfactory to the families because of his business dealings with prominent Saudi families, including Osama bin Laden's family. The newly formed Family Steering Committee made it a condition of its support for the commission that members of the committee disclose their business ties, and Kissinger consequently resigned from the commission. Throughout the remainder of the activities of the 9/11 Commission, there was constant agitation by the Family Steering Committee and its subgroup, the Jersey Girls. Their biggest concern was that nobody was being held accountable for what had happened on September 11. Regardless, the Family Steering Committee and the other groups lobbied Congress for passage of the necessary legislation to implement the 9/11 Committee's recommendations. Victims' families were also instrumental in pushing for other 9/11-related legislation such as the James

Zadroga 9/11 Health and Compensation Act, which was signed into law on January 2, 2011, and reauthorized in 2015 and 2019.

The fact that the families of victims of September 11 have been represented by such a variety of organizations means that there is no consensus on certain controversial topics. For instance, plans in 2010 to build Park51, an Islamic community center and prayer space near the site of the World Trade Center sparked intense debate among victims' families. Some individuals and groups, including the 9/11 Families for a Safe & Strong America, opposed the building, which has been referred to in the media as the Ground Zero Mosque. They argued that constructing the building so close to Ground Zero is insensitive to those who lost their lives in the September 11 attacks at the hands of radical Islamic terrorists. Other family members of victims, however, supported the project, countering that opponents are motivated by intolerance and baseless fear and hatred. A temporary Islamic center opened in the space in September 2011; in 2014, it was announced as a museum, prayer space, and condos. A condominium building opened in 2019.

Stephen E. Atkins

See National Commission on Terrorist Attacks upon the United States

Suggested Reading

Braun, Bob. "Kean Feels the Wrath of Irate 9/11 Families." *Star-Ledger,* February 12, 2004, 1.

Chaddock, Gail Russell. "A Key Force behind the 9/11 Commission." *Christian Science Monitor,* March 25, 2004, 3.

Kean, Thomas H., Lee H. Hamilton, and Benjamin Rhodes. *Without Precedent: The Inside Story of the 9/11 Commission.* New York: Knopf, 2006.

Zremski, Jerry. "Families of 9/11 Victims Urge Action on Report." *Buffalo News,* August 16, 2004, A1.

Federal Aviation Administration

The Federal Aviation Administration (FAA) has the authority and the responsibility to regulate and monitor all U.S. civil aviation. All functions of the Civil Aeronautics Administration (CAA) and the Civil Aviation Board (CAB) had been transferred to the FAA by the Federal Aviation Act of 1958. The FAA has a mandate to both regulate and promote civil aviation in a manner to best foster its development and safety. The FAA's dual responsibility—both to promote development and to provide safety—consists of two competing functions that were never reconciled. The FAA did not receive any Congressional guidelines on how to reconcile these competing functions, so market forces came to dominate the process. In time, the commercial airline industry was regulating the FAA. Even when Congress passed the 1996 Reauthorization Act under Title IV and tried to eliminate the word "promotion" from the description of the FAA's mandate by designating "assigning, maintaining, and enhancing safety and security as the highest priorities in air commerce," this congressional mandate was implemented in only a cursory fashion. Before September 11, 2001, the FAA had other concerns that its leadership considered more pressing than international terrorism: safety, consumer service, capacity, and economic issues. Its mission was made doubly difficult by the fact that it lacked both the funding and personnel to enforce its regulations.

The FAA also had to face a powerful aviation lobby that wanted as few restrictions on their operations as possible. By 2000, the airline industry was spending $46,020,819 annually on lobbyists. The airline industry also gave large amounts of money to politicians running for Congress, mostly to Republicans. This lobby was particularly powerful on issues relating to regulation that might cost the airline industry money. In the 1960s the FAA had tried to introduce armed federal marshals on flights, but the pilots and the airlines feared the possibility of a shootout more than they feared the prospects of a hijacking. It took a series of aircraft hijackings in the late 1960s and early 1970s to persuade the federal government and the airline industry to set up a screening system for passengers and luggage, which went into effect on January 5, 1973. The FAA was less successful in getting airlines to install bulletproof cockpit doors. Moreover, there were numerous unclassified reports from various government agencies outlining the vulnerabilities of the American domestic commercial aviation system. The findings of these reports had been publicized in the mass media, and the problems they underlined were well known within the aviation industry.

The commercial airlines tended to ignore warnings from American authorities. American intelligence warned the FAA and the airlines—Trans World Airlines, Pan American Airlines, and Delta—of the danger of a terrorist attack on aircrafts flying from Germany to the United States. Nothing was done by the airlines to institute special screening procedures for those flights. The result was the explosion of a luggage bomb that caused the downing of Pan Am Flight 103 over Lockerbie, Scotland, killing 259 crew and passengers and 11 people on the ground. After an exhaustive investigation, it was concluded that agents from Libya had planted the bomb.

By this time, there was a screening process at each airport in the United States, but it was so ineffective as to be considered almost a joke. Several times there had been tests of the security system and the system had failed miserably each time. But any efforts to upgrade the system were fought bitterly by the airline industry, because delays in the processing of passengers and luggage cost them money.

The FAA had a counterintelligence unit, but it had difficulty obtaining information from other government agencies. Its 40-person unit operated 24 hours per day collecting information to the extent that the Federal Bureau of Investigation (FBI), Central Intelligence Agency (CIA), and the State Department shared their intelligence with it. These agencies gave out only general information. The FAA had a no-fly list, but none of the September 11 hijackers were on it. In fact, the list had fewer than 20 names. The CIA had a list of suspected terrorists, but it was not shared with the FAA because the list was classified. Although the State Department had a watch list with 61,000 names on it, neither the FAA nor the airlines had access to the list. What is more significant is that the FAA did not want or ask for access to the watch list because the airlines would have been unwilling to check it because of cost and time constraints.

The FAA was completely unaware of any hijacking plots, but civil aviation security officials knew about Osama bin Laden and Al Qaeda's interest in plots aimed at civil aviation. They had intelligence dating from the 1990s that Al Qaeda affiliates were interested in hijackings and the possible use of aircraft as a weapon. Moreover, FAA intelligence analysts were aware of the increased intelligence activity forecasting possible terrorist acts in the summer of

2001. The FAA issued a series of alerts to air carriers about possible terrorist activity directed toward civil aviation operations. However, most of the FAA's concern was related to explosives being smuggled into aircraft. This had also been the main area of focus for the Commission on Aviation Safety and Security, also known as the Gore Commission, which President Bill Clinton had authorized in 1996. That commission had been reluctant, however, to assume the role and duties of screening airport passengers and luggage because it would have meant hiring 50,000 new federal employees at a cost of several billion dollars at a time when the Clinton administration and Congress were busy cutting the number of federal employees and the federal budget.

The FAA starts its check on airline passengers with a process known as prescreening. Passenger prescreening begins with the ticketing process and concludes with the passenger check-in at the airport ticket counter. Prescreening occurs when passenger names are checked against the FAA's list of individuals known to pose a threat to commercial aviation. On September 11, 2001, there were only 12 names on the list, and none of the names of the 9/11 hijackers were on it. This meant that none of the 9/11 hijackers were subjected to extra security measures at the airport. The hijackers did have to go through the Computer-Assisted Passenger Prescreening System (CAPPS) for examination of luggage for explosives. They all passed the CAPPS inspection because explosives were not part of their plot.

The checkpoint screening system failed miserably on September 11, 2001. Numerous studies had noted various weaknesses in the checkpoint screening system. The FAA had attempted since 1996 to set certification requirements for screening contractors, but

these requirements had not been implemented by September 11, 2001. Counteracting these security efforts were FAA's instructions to checkpoint supervisors "to use common sense about what items should not be allowed on an aircraft." This loose definition of what was allowed created confusion among the screeners. Among the items that the 19 hijackers carried through the checkpoint system were chemical sprays, utility knives, and box cutters. Even though utility knives were permissible under FAA regulations, box cutters and chemical sprays were not. Several of the hijackers set off alarms at security checkpoints; however, all of them were allowed to board their planes.

Two of the hijacked airliners had departed from Logan International Airport. Logan International Airport had long been known as one of the least secure airports in the United States. As the 18th-busiest airport in the country, it had the 5th-highest number of security breaches from 1991 to 2000. The Massachusetts Port Authority (Massport) ran the airport, and it had more security violations than any other airport authority in the United States. All of this was well known before September 11, but nothing was done to rectify the situation. Even an April 2001 memorandum from Massport's director of security, Joe Lawless, on the need for Logan International Airport to address its known security vulnerabilities was ignored. Lawless had been a career law enforcement officer, who had worked as a state trooper and then provided security for former Massachusetts governor William F. Weld. He had tried to institute mandatory criminal background checks on airline employees and subcontractors after discovering that the airline checks had failed to detect the criminal records of some employees. His reward for trying to improve security was to become a designated scapegoat for what happened at Logan International Airport on September 11, and he was subsequently demoted to a lower-level job.

Once the 9/11 terrorists had passed through the screening process and boarded, there were no impediments to a successful hijacking. Because these flights were domestic, federal marshals were not flying on them. Airlines had fought against having air marshals on domestic flights because of the expense and lost revenue of giving up a first-class seat. Cockpit doors had not been hardened; thus the hijackers would have had little difficulty breaking down the door of the cockpit. Although the cockpit doors were locked during the flight, the door was designed to withstand only 150 pounds of pressure.

Besides breaking down the cockpit door, there were two other ways for the hijackers to gain access to the cockpit. All flight attendants were required to carry keys to the cockpit at all times during the flight in case of an emergency. All it would take for a hijacker to gain control of a key was to assault the flight attendant and take the key away from him or her. The other way to gain access to the cockpit was to create such a disturbance that would ensure that the pilot or copilot would open the cockpit door, as required by regulations. Then the hijacker could overpower the pilot and walk into the cockpit without resistance.

The policy of the airlines at the time of the terrorist attacks was for flight crews not to fight against hijackers and to dissuade passengers from interfering. This policy was known as the "Common Strategy," and its premise was to placate the hijackers and get the plane on the ground where law enforcement teams could storm the aircraft. The safety of the aircraft and its passengers was paramount. What this policy

failed to take into account was a suicide mission.

The FAA also had a mandate to notify the North American Aerospace Defense Command (NORAD) in the event of a hijacking of an aircraft. In the event of a hijacking, a chain of command, which had been established expressly for this purpose, would have to be followed. Commercial pilots were to notify air traffic controllers by radio or a code 7500 transponder message. FAA controllers were then required to report the hijacking up a complicated and time-consuming multilayered chain of command, beginning with the Pentagon's National Military Command Center (NMCC). Then the NMCC was to request approval of military assistance to the aircraft involved in the hijacking from the secretary of defense. Only after receiving the necessary approval from the secretary of defense would NORAD issue orders for jets to scramble toward the hijacked aircraft. A flight of jets had orders to locate the aircraft and monitor it from a distance of five miles. This standard operating procedure (SOP) had no provision for encountering a hijacked airplane on a suicide mission. It would take a presidential order for the military jets to fire and shoot down an American commercial aircraft.

The FAA's response after the hijackings on September 11 was confused, and there was little reliance on the SOP upon contact with NORAD. The response on the ground was incredulous, confused, and unhurried. Nobody knew what to do. Never having experienced such a situation, the system failed to do anything useful.

As news of the hijackings of the four airliners spread, there were fears and rumors that other aircraft had been hijacked. One such erroneous report was disseminated by the Boston office of the FAA, which reported that a fifth aircraft had gone missing. This missing aircraft, according to the report, was Delta Flight 89. But Delta Flight 89 had not been hijacked and landed safely in Cleveland, Ohio, at about 9:47 a.m. This misinformation only added to the confusion of an already chaotic situation. Ultimately, 3,949 commercial aircraft landed at the closest available airport on orders from the FAA.

There were other irregularities in the immediate aftermath of the attacks. When the Herndon office of the FAA received a request at 9:07 a.m. on September 11 from the Boston Center to warn all pilots about possible cockpit invasions, the Herndon FAA did not send out the warning. Questioned about this by the 9/11 Commission, FAA personnel stated that it was not the FAA's responsibility to relay such a message.

The FAA ended up losing control of aviation security to the new Transportation Security Administration (TSA), but the airline industry's lobbyists made sure that the airline industry survived intact. These lobbyists were so successful that Congress passed and President George W. Bush signed the Air Transportation Safety and System Stabilization Act, which gave the airline industry $5 billion in grants and $10 billion in secured loans. Title IV of the Act offered 9/11 victims compensation of $1.6 million each in taxpayer money if they signed a waiver forgoing their right to sue the airlines for additional compensation. Title V of the law required the federal government to take over the responsibility and the cost of aviation security. After taking the money, airlines began to downsize, laying off about 20 percent of their staff in the next few years. The airlines also began cutting service to dozens of cities around the United States.

Stephen E. Atkins

See also: American Airlines Flight 11; American Airlines Flight 77; United Airlines Flight 93; United Airlines Flight 175

Suggested Reading

Murphy, Sean P. "In Letter before Attacks, FAA Urged Easing Background Checks." *Boston Globe,* December 12, 2001, B4.

Murphy, Sean P. "Logan Security Head Issued Warning: April Memo Noted Terrorist Activity." *Boston Globe,* April 7, 2002, 1.

Murphy, Tom. *Reclaiming the Sky: 9/11 and the Untold Story of the Men and Women Who Kept America Flying.* New York: AMACOM, 2007.

Naftali, Timothy. *Blind Spot: The Secret History of American Counterterrorism.* New York: Basic Books, 2005.

Thomas, Andrew R. *Aviation Insecurity: The New Challenges of Air Travel.* Amherst, NY: Prometheus Books, 2003.

Trento, Susan B., and Joseph J. Trento. *Unsafe at Any Altitude: Failed Terrorism Investigations, Scapegoating 9/11, and the Shocking Truth about Aviation Security Today.* Hanover, NH: Steerforth, 2006.

Federal Bureau of Investigation

The record of the Federal Bureau of Investigation (FBI) prior to September 11, 2001, has been controversial. Numerous times there were solid leads that might have led FBI agents to the Islamist extremists planning the attack, but the FBI failed to take advantage of those leads. Part of the difficulty was that the FBI had an "arrest and convict" mentality before 9/11. Its unofficial golden rule was that, whenever there was a possibility that intelligence gathering would conflict with the making of legal cases, intelligence gathering lost out.

Since the mid-1990s, the FBI has had expanded powers to investigate potential and actual terrorists. A 1995 presidential directive gave the FBI the lead authority in both investigating and preventing acts of terrorism wherever in the world American lives or American interests were threatened. Much like the Central Intelligence Agency (CIA), the FBI was reluctant to share its intelligence information with other law enforcement agencies. The FBI used Rule 6E of the Federal Rules of Criminal Procedure, which states that information arising from grand jury testimony is secret, as an excuse never to give out investigative information. Another barrier to the free flow of information was the Foreign Intelligence Surveillance Act (FISA) court created in 1979, which served as the arbiter of information that could be shared between government agencies. Like the CIA and the National Security Agency (NSA), the FBI avoided the FISA court by simply not asking for permission to share.

The FBI created two units at its headquarters to handle and respond to the growing threat of terrorism in the United States and abroad. One was the Radical Fundamentalist Unit (RFU). The mission of this unit was to research radical fundamentalist activities at mosques and gather intelligence for possible court cases if there was evidence of law breaking. The other was the Usama bin Ladin Unit (UBLU). This unit was more localized, and its mission was to follow the activities of Al Qaeda members in the United States. Both units had a mandate to monitor the activities of possible agents and to prepare court cases against those agents in cases where laws were broken. There was significant overlap between the two units because of the nature of their assignments. Coordination between the two units was always a problem, even though both units resided at FBI headquarters. Another difficulty was that assignment to

either unit was not considered a good career move within the FBI, so qualified agents left as soon as possible. Consequently, there was a lack of experienced intelligence gatherers in both units.

The FBI had internal communication problems as well. It had finally developed its own computer system in the mid-1990s, but the system had never worked properly or adequately. At the time of the attacks of September 11, it was a system on which nothing more than the simplest searches could be performed. The system also did not provide access to the Internet. Old-time FBI agents refused to use it. It was a system that had been modeled after the FBI's court-case system, and it was never designed to improve communications between regional field offices and FBI headquarters. People who have used the FBI computer system said to John Schwartz that the "bureau has often intentionally disregarded industry standards, in part because of fears that such systems might be more vulnerable to hackers."

Before September 11, 2001, the FBI had already begun to consider implementing a new computer system. It ultimately adopted a computer system with the name of Trilogy, but the system never became operational despite $626 million in expenditures. In a state of constant upgrades and rebuilding, the Virtual Case File System was eventually abandoned in January 2005.

The FBI's internal system for handling communications created additional obstacles in carrying out its mission. It had a system of assigning communications and memos (called "leads") to individuals at FBI headquarters for further investigation. The problem was that the lead system had been overwhelmed. In mid-2002 the Joint Committee on Intelligence of the U.S. Congress found that the FBI's Counterterrorism

Division had 68,000 outstanding unassigned leads dating back to 1995. The Phoenix Memo, an attempt by FBI field agent Kenneth Williams in July 2001 to warn FBI headquarters of a suspiciously large number of Middle Eastern men studying to become commercial pilots, was a victim of this system.

But of all the reasons why the FBI failed to uncover the September 11 conspiracy, the most compelling one is that the FBI underestimated the terrorist threat. Efforts to assess the counterterrorism efforts of the FBI were met with defensiveness rather than cooperation. When Richard Clarke, the National Security Council's counterterrorism expert, quizzed FBI agents in late 1999 about their counterterrorism activities, he received assurances that the FBI had things under control, even though this was not the case. Dale Watson, the FBI's antiterrorism unit chief, tried to get FBI field offices to concentrate on counterterrorism, but he ended up concluding that too few FBI agents were working on terrorism cases, or even knew what to do with regard to terrorism. His efforts proved futile, as shown by the fact that there were fewer FBI agents assigned to counterterrorism activities on September 10, 2001, than there had been in 1998.

Since September 11, the FBI has been busy reforming its practices to avoid the intelligence lapses that occurred in the days, months, and years leading up to the terrorist attacks. Intelligence gathering is now a top priority for the Bureau. In fact, the FBI is now being criticized for concentrating its efforts and resources so much on gathering intelligence to prevent terrorist activities that it is neglecting its traditional job of crime fighting.

See also: Anthrax Attacks

Suggested Reading

Freeh, Louis J., and Howard Means. *My FBI: Bringing Down the Mafia, Investigating Bill Clinton, and Fighting the War on Terror.* New York: St. Martin's, 2005.

Graham, Bob. *Intelligence Matters: The CIA, the FBI, Saudi Arabia, and the Failure of America's War on Terror.* New York: Random House, 2004.

Joint Inquiry into Intelligence Community Activities before and after the Terrorist Attacks of September 11, 2001. *Hearings before the Select Committee on Intelligence U.S. Senate and the Permanent Select Committee on Intelligence House of Representatives.* 2 vols. Washington, DC: U.S. Government Printing Office, 2004.

Lance, Peter. *1000 Years for Revenge: International Terrorism and the FBI; The Untold Story.* New York: ReganBooks, 2003.

Miller, John, Michael Stone, and Chris Mitchell. *The Cell: Inside the 9/11 Plot and Why the FBI and CIA Failed to Stop It.* New York: Hyperion, 2002.

Posner, Gerald. *Why America Slept: The Failure to Prevent 9/11.* New York: Ballantine, 2003.

Schwartz, John. "[FBI] Computer System That Makes Data Secure, but Hard to Find." *New York Times,* June 8, 2002, A10.

Federal Emergency Management Agency

The Federal Emergency Management Agency (FEMA) has had a mixed record in dealing with the aftermath of September 11, 2001. The legislative mandate for FEMA was to provide direct assistance to those who had been impacted by a natural or a man-made disaster. In September 2001 it was a large agency, with 2,600 employees and nearly 4,000 standby reservists. On September 11, 2001, Joe M. Allbaugh was

Federal Emergency Management Agency director Joe Allbaugh meets with rescue team members at the site of the World Trade Center attack in New York City on September 24, 2001. (FEMA)

the director of FEMA. Allbaugh was a Texan with close ties to President George W. Bush.

Where FEMA excelled was in its prompt response to the disaster. Emergency services personnel from 18 states responded almost immediately to the sites of the attacks. FEMA sent 28 urban search-and-rescue task forces to the sites of the disasters. Each task force had 62 members. The urban search-and-rescue task forces sent to the World Trade Center complex site to locate survivors worked 24-hour days, with the personnel working two 12-hour shifts. Conditions were horrible, and the dust from the debris made the task extremely difficult for the searchers. They employed portable cameras to spot survivors, sniffer dogs to smell for

survivors, and sensitive life-detector sensors to look for signs of life. Despite these heroic efforts, few survivors were found because of the horrendous impact of the collapse of the Twin Towers. As it became apparent that there would be no more survivors, FEMA started pulling out its search-and-rescue teams. The last to leave was an Oakland, California, unit, which left on October 6, 2001. A spokesperson for FEMA stated that the site had been turned over to the Fire Department City of New York (FDNY) and the Army Corps of Engineers.

FEMA also sent in Critical Incident Stress Management (CISM) teams to help the workers at the site of the attacks. These teams had psychologists, psychiatrists, social workers, and professional counselors whose mission was the prevention and miti-gation of disabling stress among the person-nel working at the World Trade Center site. There were nearly as many members of these CISM teams as there were workers at the site. This caused some difficulty because members of these teams were so eager to help that they became intrusive. They soon earned the nickname "therapy dogs" from workers at the site. Members of these teams undoubtedly helped some of those working at the site, but others resented their constant interference with the urgent job at hand.

FEMA's biggest failure was in its handling of the September 11 disaster relief funds. September 11 had caused the loss of 75,000 jobs and $4.5 billion in lost income. Despite promises of quick financial relief for those who had lost their jobs, FEMA's administrators changed the rules in the aftermath of September 11, making it more difficult for people to qualify for financial relief. Thousands of people were denied housing aid after FEMA decided to limit benefits to those who could prove that their lost income was a "direct result" of the attacks rather than merely the "result" of the attacks, which had been the previous standard. This seemingly minor change in language led to FEMA's rejection of the claims of 70 percent of the people applying for relief under the mortgage and rental pro-gram after losing their jobs. Between Sep-tember 11, 2001, and April 2002, less than $65 million was paid out by FEMA to help families in the disaster area pay their bills, avoid eviction, and buy food.

Decisions on accepting or rejecting claims were made by FEMA agency evaluators (two-thirds of whom were temporary work-ers) at processing centers in Texas, Mary-land, and Virginia. These evaluators had little or no knowledge of New York City or its culture, institutions, or geography.

Moreover, the application form had not been changed to make it possible for evaluators to determine whether job losses were directly related to the disaster, and all the forms were printed exclusively in English. It was only on November 14, 2001, that the application form was revised and issued in six lan-guages, but even the new forms did not explain how FEMA defined "direct result."

Furthermore, some odd decisions were made by the FEMA evaluators. One appli-cant provided the name of the restaurant where he had worked in the World Trade Center and his supervisor's telephone num-ber, as required by the application. His application was denied because the evalua-tor was unable to make contact by telephone with the restaurant, which had of course been destroyed on September 11.

As bad as the situation was in New York City, it was even worse in Virginia. Thou-sands of workers had lost jobs by the closing of Reagan National Airport in Washington, DC, in September, but the evaluators were slow to recognize this fact. Only a handful of applications from those workers had been approved by April 2002.

Criticisms of FEMA reached the halls of Congress. Under pressure from politicians, FEMA reevaluated its program in late June 2002 and eased its eligibility criteria. But the bad feelings were hard to overcome.

The immediate result of the change in direction was that FEMA approved more applications. Between September 2001 and June 2002, FEMA sent $20.6 million to 3,585 households. After June 2002, FEMA dispersed $25.3 million to 3,053 households in less than two months. This relaxation of eligibility rules helped the financial situa-tion for people in New York and Virginia, but there was still widespread distrust of FEMA.

Stephen E. Atkins

See also: Department of Homeland Security; World Trade Center, September 11

Suggested Reading

Chen, David W. "More Get 9/11 Aid, but Distrust of U.S. Effort Lingers." *New York Times,* August 27, 2002, B1.

Henriques, Diana B., and David Barstow. "Change in Rules Barred Many from September 11 Disaster Relief." *New York Times,* April 26, 2002, A1.

Keegan, William, Jr., with Bart Davis. *Closure: The Untold Story of the Ground Zero Recovery Mission.* New York: Touchstone Books, 2006.

Mitchell, Kirsten B. "Government Trying to Decide FEMA's Fate." *Tampa Tribune,* August 7, 2002, 1.

Firefighter Riot on November 2, 2001

The firefighters of the Fire Department City of New York (FDNY) were possessive of their dead after the September 11, 2001, attacks on the World Trade Center complex. After all, the firefighters had just lost 343 members of a close-knit fraternity of brothers. They had made a special ceremony of the recovery of their fallen comrades. In some cases, these efforts caused resentment among members of the New York Police Department (NYPD), Port Authority police, and the 3,000 or so construction workers. Tempers flared on several occasions between firefighters and others.

Work at the World Trade Center site was always chaotic, so Mayor Rudolph Giuliani proposed that the number of firefighters, police, and Port Authority police be reduced to 25 representatives each on the grounds of safety. At that time, around 100 firefighters were active in helping locate bodies and body parts. The firefighters, unlike the NYPD police and the Port Authority police, were furious at this announcement. They charged that the Giuliani administration wanted to accelerate the disposal of debris at the expense of finding the remains of the victims. Complaints made their way up the ladder to the management of both firefighter unions. Union leaders decided to organize a demonstration at Ground Zero on November 2, 2001. This demonstration was scheduled seven weeks and three days after September 11.

The heads of the Department of Design and Construction (DDC) found themselves in the middle of the controversy. Kenneth Holden and Michael Burton, the two top officials at DDC, agreed that there were safety issues involved with having so many people at the site, but they also knew that Giuliani's decision would cause political trouble. Holden was a veteran civil service administrator and to buck Giuliani would have been a career breaker. Both leaders wanted to clear the debris out of the World Trade Center site as soon as possible, but not at the expense of finding the remains of the victims.

Union leaders assured the Giuliani administration that the demonstration would be orderly, but tensions were so high that the situation soon developed into a confrontation between the firefighters and the police. Around 500 firefighters joined the demonstration at the beginning, but during the course of the demonstration another 500 showed up. Since there was no love lost between the NYPD and the FDNY, pushing and shoving soon turned into an attempt by the firefighters to break police lines. The police responded by meeting force with force. Soon police began arresting the most violent of the demonstrators. Twelve firefighters were arrested, including the two heads of the firefighter unions. These arrests further infuriated the firefighters.

The Giuliani administration, including Mayor Giuliani and the fire commissioner, Thomas Von Essen, knew that they had a serious public relations problem. Giuliani was furious at the riot. At first, the mayor wanted to arrest some of the construction workers for supporting the demonstration, but cooler heads soon prevailed. Then, on the evening of November 12, 2001, the families of the dead firefighters vented their frustrations at the inability of the search-and-rescue teams to find bodies, and they expressed their concern about the rapid pace of the cleanup at Ground Zero. It was an emotional meeting in which the widows attacked the leaders of the DDC in a variety of ways and for a variety of reasons. They accused the medical examiner and Burton of lying. The mayor came away from this meeting relatively unscathed, but he was aware that things had to be calmed down.

Mayor Giuliani decided to compromise. He authorized first 50 and then 75 firefighters to remain at the site to help recover human remains. These concessions, including the release of the 12 arrested demonstrators without charges, did little to reconcile the firefighters with the Giuliani administration. Strong feelings remained after the Giuliani administration stepped down on January 1, 2002. Some of the distrust on the part of the firefighters carried over to the new mayor and his administration.

Stephen E. Atkins

See also: Department of Design and Construction; Firefighters at Ground Zero; Giuliani, Rudolph William Louis "Rudy," III

Suggested Reading

Becker, Maki. "Widows Vent to Mayor in Secret Talks." *Daily News* [New York], November 13, 2001, 5.

Langewiesche, William. *American Ground: Unbuilding the World Trade Center.* New York: North Point, 2002.

Lombardi, Frank, and Dave Goldiner. "City Adds Bravest at WTC, Hikes Number of Firefighters to 75 from 50 after Protests." *Daily News* [New York], November 17, 2001, 17.

Lombardi, Frank, and Michele McPhee. "Bravest vs. Finest in Melee at WTC." *Daily News* [New York], November 3, 2001, 3.

Steinhauer, Jennifer. "Mayor Criticizes Firefighters over Stand on Staffing at Trade Center Site." *New York Times,* November 9, 2001, D5.

Firefighters at Ground Zero

Firefighters from the Fire Department City of New York (FDNY) immediately responded to the first airliner crashing into the North Tower of the World Trade Center. American Airlines Flight 11 crashed into the tower at 8:46:40 a.m. The FDNY units were in the middle of a shift change. This meant that the maximum number of firefighters (those whose shifts had just ended and those whose shifts were just starting) were able to respond to the emergency. Engine Company 10 and Ladder Company 10 were the first to respond because their firehouse was located across Liberty Street from the World Trade Center. Other fire stations also reacted quickly. Within 30 minutes more than 100 fire trucks had appeared at the World Trade Center complex. Firefighters were on duty fighting the fire and handling survivors when United Airlines Flight 175 hit the South Tower of the World Trade Center at 9:03:11 a.m. Firefighters continued fighting the fire and trying to save survivors until both towers collapsed. One of the problems the firefighters had to overcome was

This bronze memorial is dedicated to the 343 New York City firefighters (and one volunteer firefighter) who died on September 11, 2001. It can be found at FDNY Engine 10 Ladder 10, directly across from the World Trade Center site. (Dreamstime.com)

climbing up between 60 and 80 floors while hauling the self-contained breathing apparatus (SCBA), with the pants, jacket, and helmet weighing an additional 70 pounds.

The FDNY is huge. In the five boroughs of New York City there were 2,629 fire officers, 8,599 firefighters, 3,000 emergency technicians and paramedics, and 2,000 civilians. They were organized into 203 engine companies, 143 ladder companies, 5 rescue companies, 7 investigative squads, 3 marine companies, and a hazardous materials (hazmat) company. These units were stationed in 225 firehouses scattered throughout the five boroughs. This demonstrates the extent of the manpower that responded to the crisis on September 11. Some reports have estimated that somewhere around

10,000 firefighters made it to the World Trade Center on September 11.

Two factors hindered the efforts of firefighters to be more effective. One was the failure of the communication systems. Radios did not work, and other communication systems were overwhelmed by the traffic. Almost as serious was the lack of coordination between the firefighters and the police. Distrust between the two agencies had a lengthy history, as firefighters believed that the police department was favored over the fire department by New York politicians. These feelings of hostility were reciprocated by the police, even though both departments had traditionally recruited from the same segments of the population— Irish and Italians.

An example of the way this discord influenced operations on September 11 was the helicopter rescue issue. In the 1993 World Trade Center bombing, police helicopters rescued people from the rooftop by helicopter. Afterward the FDNY's Chiefs Association claimed that this was grandstanding and complained to the mayor. After some infighting, the fire and police departments reached a compromise. Police helicopters would thereafter attempt rooftop rescues only when requested by a fire chief.

At the same time the roof exits on both towers at the World Trade Center had been securely locked by the Port Authority, ostensibly to prevent vandals, daredevils, and suicidal people from gaining access to the rooftop. New York City building code regulations did call for access to rooftops in emergencies, but the World Trade Center complex was exempt from the code. The FDNY had agreed with this decision.

On September 11 the rooftop doors remained shut, dooming those unable to climb down the staircases. The rooftop doors could be opened by using the computers on the 22nd floor, but this system failed because of the explosion and fire. Moreover, the firefighters were unable to communicate with the police helicopters because of the collapse of the communication systems. Police helicopters flew over the towers, but there was no authorization to rescue people from the rooftops even if they had been able to make it to the rooftops of either tower.

The firefighters never had a chance to put out the fire because it was a high-rise fire. A high-rise fire can only be extinguished from inside the building because no ladder truck and no stream of water can reach that high, making it the most dangerous type of fire to fight. In many cases, the only hope is that the building remains standing and the fire burns itself out.

A characteristic of the Twin Towers was that there were large open areas of 20,000 to 30,000 square feet on each floor. This made firefighting almost impossible, but the firefighters tried their best anyway. Half of the firefighters tried to fight the fire and the other half were busy evacuating people from the burning buildings. The fire chiefs had become concerned about the possibility of the towers collapsing, but too many people were in distress to pull the firefighters out. Consequently, losses among the firefighters when the towers collapsed were horrific. The final tally of firefighters killed on September 11 was 343. Among the dead were the first deputy fire commissioner, the chief of the department, 23 station chiefs, 21 captains, 46 lieutenants, 249 firefighters, 1 fire marshal, 2 paramedics, and 1 chaplain. Others were injured, and some of the surviving firefighters have had serious health problems since. New York firefighters have always had a reputation for bravery, and September 11 was no exception. It was part of a long history of fighting dangerous and deadly fires.

After it became apparent that there would be no more survivors, the firefighters began searching for bodies and body parts. Even the recovery of a small part of a body meant that DNA analysis would allow the deceased to be identified. The firefighters had a code that they did not leave comrades behind. They worked diligently to recover whatever body parts could be found, but particular emphasis was put on finding the remains of firefighters. When the mayor's office announced that the number of firefighters, police, and Port Authority personnel at the site would be reduced in early November 2001, the firefighters protested to the point of almost rioting at the World Trade Center site. They felt that moving the debris had become more important to the city government than finding the remains of the victims. Bad feelings developed between the firefighters and Mayor Rudy Giuliani. Only after a direct appeal by relatives who had lost firefighters in the attacks did the mayor back down and allow more firefighters to search for body remains.

The efforts and sacrifices of the New York City firefighters have been recognized. On June 10, 2006, a bronze memorial was dedicated to the memory of the dead firefighters with names listed on the memorial according to rank. It begins with First Deputy Commissioner William F. Feehan and ends with paramedic Ricardo J. Quinn.

The toll on the New York City firefighters was extreme. Besides the heavy loss of experienced personnel and the loss of 91 vehicles, there were still 415 members of the department on medical leave or light duty six months after September 11. Stress-related problems have been particularly severe. To replace the lost firefighters the department lowered entrance requirements for its recruits. One firefighter said, "It is going to take us a couple of generations, at least, to get the Fire Department back to where it was prior to 9/11."

Stephen E. Atkins

See also: Fire House 40/35; Health Effects of September 11

Suggested Reading

Aust, Stefan, et al. *Inside 9/11: What Really Happened.* New York: St. Martin's, 2001.

Baker, Al. "The True Toll on Firefighters Is Still Untold." *New York Times,* March 10, 2002, 41.

Bernstein, Richard. *Out of the Blue: The Story of September 11, 2001, from Jihad to Ground Zero.* New York: Times Books, 2002.

Dunlap, David W. "A 'Silent Roll Call' of 9/11's Firefighter Heroes." *New York Times,* June 10, 2006, 1.

Dwyer, Jim, and Kevin Flynn. *102 Minutes: The Untold Story of the Fight to Survive inside the Twin Towers.* New York: Times Books, 2005.

Halberstam, David. *Firehouse.* New York: Hyperion, 2002.

Lance, Peter. *1000 Years for Revenge: International Terrorism and the FBI; The Untold Story.* New York: ReganBooks, 2003.

Smith, Dennis. *Report from Ground Zero.* New York: Viking, 2002.

Von Essen, Thomas, with Matt Murray. *Strong of Heart: Life and Death in the Fire Department of New York City.* New York: ReganBooks, 2002.

Fire House 40/35

Firefighters from Fire House 40/35 in mid-Manhattan responded to the September 11, 2001, attacks, and in the process of handling evacuations and firefighting, 12 of the 13 of those responding died. All of the firefighters died in the collapse of the South Tower of the World Trade Center complex. Like many firefighters in New York City, most of the men of the 40/35 came from firefighting families. They had a strong commitment to their jobs and to their unit.

Fire House 40/35 was considered to be one of the better firefighting units in New York City. The strength of the unit was 50 men working in shifts—11 at any given time. There were 8 officers in 40/35—2 captains and 6 lieutenants. This house contained both an engine (Engine 40) unit and a ladder (Ladder 35) unit for both rescue and firefighting operations. There was a lively rivalry between the two units as to whose role was more important.

September 11 started out peacefully enough at Fire House 40/35, but after the news of the aircraft crashes into the Twin Towers of the World Trade Center complex, everything changed in an instant. Captain Frank Callahan was the shift commander at the time of the attack. A veteran of almost 28 years in the fire department, he was an old-school firefighter, and he held the men under his command to the highest standards of performance. Callahan had assumed command of Ladder 35 in July 1998. After hearing about the second crash, into the South Tower, Fire House 40/35 mobilized and headed for the scene of the emergency at 9:08 a.m. They arrived and immediately began evacuating personnel and fighting the fire in the South Tower; it suddenly collapsed on top of them. Of the 13 firefighters on the scene, only Kevin Shea survived, but he was badly injured. Shea had been blown out of danger, suffering a concussion, a broken neck, and other serious injuries. He was found by Todd Maisel, a photographer for the *New York Daily News.*

Eleven of the 12 bodies of members of Fire House 40/35 were gradually recovered. The first to be found was the body of Bruce Gary, which was found under four stories of rubble some three weeks after September 11. Beside him was a medical bag that he must have been carrying and the bodies of several firefighters and civilians. On January 1, 2002, Michael D'Auria's body was located. In early February 2002, two other bodies—belonging to Mike Boyle and David Arce—were found. They had been lifelong friends. Then, on March 21, 2002, searchers found the bodies of Lieutenant John Gintly, Michael Lynch, and Vince Morello. Ultimately, the only body not recovered was that of Steve Mercado.

The loss of so many men from a single firehouse was devastating. Even before most of the bodies had been found, the families had held ceremonies honoring the deceased. Because the families of the firefighters were so close, there was a strong support system. Nevertheless, some of the wives had severe adjustment problems. The families achieved closure, but the loss of their husbands left the wives raising their families as single parents.

Stephen E. Atkins

See also: Firefighters at Ground Zero

Suggested Reading

Brice, Charles. "Inside Story of New York's Heroes." *Advertiser* [New York], September 7, 2002, W11.

Halberstam, David. *Firehouse.* New York: Hyperion, 2002.

G

Giuliani, Rudolph William Louis "Rudy," III (1944–)

Mayor Rudolph William Louis "Rudy" Giuliani III achieved worldwide fame for his role in the aftermath of the September 11, 2001, attack. He was born on May 28, 1944, in Brooklyn, New York, to a working-class family. Giuliani attended and, in 1961 graduated from, Bishop Loughlin Memorial High School in Brooklyn. His collegiate years were spent at Manhattan College in the Bronx where he graduated in 1965. Next, Giuliani obtained a law degree from New York University Law School in 1968. His first job was clerking for Judge Lloyd Mac-Mahon, U.S. district judge for the Southern District of New York.

The bulk of Giuliani's career has been spent in government service. His first position was with the Office of the U.S. Attorney in 1970. After a stint as the chief of the narcotics unit and executive U.S. attorney, he left for Washington, DC, in 1975 to become the associate deputy attorney general and chief of staff to the deputy attorney general. Giuliani briefly left government service in 1977 to practice law at the Patterson, Belknap, Webb and Tyler law firm. Then, in 1981 the Ronald Reagan administration recruited Giuliani to the office of associate attorney general. Giuliani then was appointed the U.S. attorney for the Southern District of New York and earned a reputation for tackling high-profile cases, including those of Wall Street icons Ivan Boesky and Michael Milken.

Giuliani's law-and-order reputation led to his running for the post of New York City mayor. His first attempt as the Republican candidate was unsuccessful; he lost to David Dinkins in 1989 in a close race. His second attempt in 1993 led to his election as mayor after a campaign featuring attacks on crime and rising taxes. Giuliani won reelection in 1997 by a large margin. His law-and-order campaign led to a reduction in crime in New York City. New York City's limit on mayoral terms meant that Giuliani could not run for a third term as mayor, but he was still mayor in September 2001.

Giuliani's career received a boost because of his role in the management of New York City in the aftermath of the September 11, 2001, attacks on the World Trade Center. His response immediately after the assault on the Twin Towers was to coordinate the response of various city departments, and he made quick contact with state and federal authorities. Giuliani made contact with President George W. Bush and received assurances of federal aid. In the next new few weeks Giuliani held meetings several times a day to coordinate aid and relief. He also worked closely with the fire commissioner, Thomas Von Essen, and the police commissioner, Bernard Kerik, on the activities at the World Trade Center site. Von Essen described the mayor's style as barking, pleading, commiserating, and questioning. At every meeting Giuliani demanded measurable progress on the situation from his subordinates. He was also present and often talked at ceremonies honoring the dead. Giuliani did run into some difficulty trying to reduce the number of firefighters at the World Trade Center site, and he had to back down in a confrontation that took place in early November 2001. This conflict with the firefighters made him furious, but he realized that he had a growing public relations problem unless he compromised.

Because the scheduled date of the mayoral primary was September 11, this primary had to be rescheduled. Few people could make it to the polls on September 11 because the city had been closed down. Giuliani first sought an emergency override of the term-limit law, but this attempt ran into political opposition, as did his effort to have his term of office extended four months. He left the mayoral office on December 31, 2001.

Giuliani left public life with a national reputation. *Time* magazine named Giuliani its Person of the Year for 2001. Shortly after leaving office, Giuliani founded a security consulting business, and he purchased the accounting firm Ernst & Young's investment banking unit, which he named Giuliani Capital Advisors LLC. He also traveled around the country making speeches. He campaigned vigorously for the reelection of President George W. Bush. Bush responded by inviting Giuliani to replace Tom Ridge as secretary of homeland security, but Giuliani turned down the offer. Then in March 2005, Giuliani joined the firm of Bracewell & Patterson LLP, which was promptly renamed Bracewell & Giuliani LLP. Giuliani has maintained his political contacts in the Republican Party, and he has constantly been advanced as a candidate for national office. In the meantime, he was appointed to Congress's Iraq Study Group (ISG). This group had the mission to assess the military situation in Iraq under the sponsorship of the U.S. Institute of Peace.

Giuliani's role has a hero of September 11 has been challenged in recent years. Much of the criticism has come from family members of the victims of September 11. The most vocal have been the families of firefighters. They have criticized Giuliani for separating the police and firefighter command posts on the morning of September 11 and for not holding emergency drills to check on communication equipment prior to the attacks. Another criticism has been the ineffectiveness of the Office of Emergency Management because of its locations in the World Trade Center complex.

In 2007 Giuliani announced his intention to seek the 2008 Republican presidential nomination. He ran a lackluster campaign trying to capitalize on his 9/11 reputation. Because of his previous positions on gun control and abortion, he had trouble convincing social conservatives in the Republican Party to support him. After low vote totals in the primaries, Giuliani dropped out of the presidential race on January 31, 2008. Declining to run for political offices in 2010 and 2012, Giuliani supported Donald Trump in the 2016 presidential election, and in 2018 became one of President Trump's personal lawyers.

Stephen E. Atkins

See also: Kerik, Bernard Bailey; Office of Emergency Management; World Trade Center, September 11

Suggested Reading

Barrett, Wayne, and Dan Collins. "The Real Rudy: The Image of Rudy Giuliani as the Hero of September 11 Has Never Been Seriously Challenged. That Changes Now." *American Prospect* 17 (September 1, 2006).

Newfield, Jack. *The Full Rudy: The Man, the Myth, the Mania*. New York: Thunder's Mouth, 2003.

Polner, Robert. *America's Mayor: The Hidden History of Rudy Giuliani's New York*. New York: Soft Skull, 2005.

Siegel, Fred. *The Prince of the City: Giuliani, New York, and the Genius of American Life*. New York: Encounter Books, 2005.

Von Essen, Thomas, with Matt Murray. *Strong of Heart: Life and Death in the Fire Department of New York*. New York: ReganBooks, 2002.

Global War on Terror

"Global War on Terror" is the term used to describe the military, political, diplomatic, and economic measures employed by the United States and other allied governments against organizations, countries, or individuals that are committing terrorist acts; that might be inclined to engage in terrorism; or that support those who do commit such acts. The Global War on Terror is an amorphous concept and a somewhat indistinct term, yet its use emphasizes the difficulty in classifying the type of nontraditional warfare being waged against U.S. and Western interests by various terrorist groups that do not represent any nation. The term was coined by President George W. Bush in a September 20, 2001, televised address to a joint session of the U.S. Congress, and has been presented in official White House pronouncements, fact sheets, State of the Union messages, and such National Security Council (NSC) position papers as the National Security Strategy (March 2006) and the National Strategy for Combating Terrorism (February 2003 and September 2006 editions). Since 2001, the Global War on Terror has been directed primarily at Islamic terrorist groups but has also been expanded to include actions against all types of terrorism. During the Bush administration, Secretary of Defense Robert Gates also called it the "Long War."

As with the Cold War, the Global War on Terror is being waged on numerous fronts, against many individuals and nations, and involves both military and nonmilitary tactics. President George W. Bush's September 20, 2001, announcement of the Global War on Terror was in response to the September 11, 2001, terror attacks against the United States, which led to the deaths of some 3,000 civilians, mostly Americans but representing civilians of 90 different countries.

Although the war constitutes a global effort, stretching into Asia, Africa, Europe, and the Americas, the Middle East remains a focal point of the effort. The ongoing conflict and the manner in which it has been waged have been the source of much debate. There is no widely agreed-upon estimate regarding the number of casualties during the Global War on Terror because it includes the invasion of Afghanistan in 2001 and the war in Iraq, as well as many acts of terrorism around the world. Some estimates, which include the U.S.-led coalition invasion of Afghanistan in 2001 and the invasion of Iraq in March 2003, claim that well over 2 million people have died in the struggle.

Following the September 11, 2001, terror attacks, the United States responded quickly and with overwhelming force against the organizations and governments that supported the terrorists. Evidence gathered by the U.S. government pointed to the Al Qaeda terrorist organization. Al Qaeda at the time was being given aid and shelter by the Taliban regime in Afghanistan. On September 20, 2001, President George W. Bush announced to a joint session of Congress that the Global War on Terror would not end simply with the defeat of Al Qaeda or the overthrow of the Taliban, but only when every terrorist group and terrorist-affiliated government with a global reach had been defeated. These broad aims implied attacks on countries known to support terrorism, such as Iran and Syria. Bush further assured the American people that every means of intelligence, tool of diplomacy, financial pressure, and weapon of war would be used to defeat terrorism. He told the American people to expect a lengthy campaign. Bush also issued an ultimatum to every other nation, stating that each had to choose whether they were with the United States or against it. There would be no middle ground. Clearly Bush's pronouncements were far-reaching, yet the enemies were difficult to identify and find.

Less than 24 hours after the September 11 attacks, the North Atlantic Treaty Organization (NATO) declared the terrorist attacks of 9/11 to be against all member nations, the first time the organization had made such a pronouncement since its inception in 1949.

On October 7, 2001, U.S. and coalition (chiefly British) forces invaded Afghanistan to capture Osama bin Laden, the head of Al Qaeda, to destroy his organization, and to overthrow the Taliban government that supported him. Eventually Canada, Australia, France, and Germany, among other nations, joined that effort. However, when a U.S.-led coalition invaded Iraq in March 2003, there was considerable international opposition to this campaign being included under the rubric of the Global War on Terror. One problem for national leaders who supported President Bush's policies was that many of their citizens did not believe that the overthrow of Iraqi dictator Saddam Hussein was really part of the Global War on Terror and questioned other reasons stated by the Bush

administration to justify the U.S.-led invasion. International opinion polls have shown that support for the War on Terror has consistently declined since 2003, likely the result of opposition to the Bush administration's preemptive invasion of Iraq in 2003 and later revelations that Iraq possessed neither ties to Al Qaeda nor weapons of mass destruction.

The Global War on Terror has also been a sporadic and clandestine war since its inception in September 2001. U.S. forces were sent to Yemen and the Horn of Africa in order to disrupt terrorist activities, while Operation ACTIVE ENDEAVOR was a naval operation intended to prevent terror attacks and limit the movement of terrorists in the Mediterranean. Terrorist attacks in Pakistan, Indonesia, and the Philippines led to the insertion of coalition forces into those countries as well and concerns about the situation in other Southeast Asian countries. In the United States, Congress has also passed legislation intended to help increase the effectiveness of law enforcement agencies in their search for terrorist activities. In the process, however, critics claim that Americans' civil liberties have been steadily eroded, and government admissions that the Federal Bureau of Investigation (FBI) and other agencies have engaged in wiretapping of international phone calls without requisite court orders and probable cause have caused a storm of controversy, as have the methods used to question foreign nationals.

The Bush administration also greatly increased the role of the federal government in an attempt to fight terrorism at home and abroad. Among the many new government bureaucracies formed is the Department of Homeland Security, a cabinet-level agency that counts at least 210,000 employees. The increase in the size of the government, combined with huge military expenditures—most of which went to the Iraq War—has added to the massive U.S. budget deficits.

Proponents of the Global War on Terror believe that proactive measures must be taken against terrorist organizations to effectively defeat global terrorism. They believe that in order to meet the diverse security challenges of the 21st century, a larger, global military presence is needed. Without such a force, they argue, terrorist organizations will continue to launch strikes against innocent civilians. Many of the people argue that the United States, Great Britain, Spain, and other countries, which have been the victims of large-scale attacks, must go on the offensive against such rogue groups and that not doing so will only embolden the attackers and invite more attacks. Allowing such organizations to gain more strength may allow them to achieve their goal of imposing militant Islamist rule.

Critics of the Global War on Terror claim that there is no tangible enemy to defeat, as there is no single group whose defeat will bring about an end to the conflict. Thus, it is virtually impossible to know if progress is being made. They also argue that "terrorism," a tactic whose goal is to instill fear into people through violent actions, can never be truly defeated. There are also those who argue against the justification for preemptive strikes, because such action invites counterresponses and brings about the deaths of many innocent people. Many believe that the Iraqi military posed no imminent threat to the United States when coalition forces entered Iraq in 2003, but the resultant war was disastrous for both the Iraqi and American peoples. Civil rights activists contend that measures meant to crack down on terrorist activities have infringed on the rights of American citizens as well as the rights of foreign detainees.

Furthermore, critics argue that the war and the amount of spending apportioned to military endeavors negatively affects the national and world economies. Others argue that the United States should be spending time and resources on resolving the Arab-Israeli problem and trying to eradicate the desperate conditions that feed terrorism. As support for the Global War on Terror effort has diminished, the debate over its effectiveness has grown. Terrorist attacks have continued, and the deliberation over the best way to ensure the safety of civilian populations around the world likewise continues.

The Barack Obama administration chose not to use the terms "Global War on Terror" or "Long War," instead using the phrase "Overseas Contingency Operations." White House press secretary Robert Gibbs explained that the name change was made "in order to denote a reaching out to many moderate parts of the world that we believe can be important in a battle against extremists." However, the term "Global War on Terror" is still widely used in the media and in public discourse.

On May 1, 2011 (May 2 Pakistani local time), the Global War on Terror reached a milestone with the death of bin Laden. After intelligence information suggested that bin Laden was in Abbottabad, Pakistan, U.S. Navy SEALs raided a compound at which he was staying, killing bin Laden and four others in the ensuing firefight. President Obama addressed the nation to announce bin Laden's death, declaring that "justice has been done," but admonishing Americans to "remain vigilant at home and abroad." Threats made by Al Qaeda and other extremist groups to seek revenge for bin Laden's killing underscored Obama's assessment that the Global War on Terror remains far from over.

Gregory W. Morgan

See also: Al Qaeda; Bin Laden, Osama; Bush, George W.; Bush Doctrine; ENDURING FREEDOM, Operation; IRAQI FREEDOM, Operation; London Underground Bombings; Madrid Bombings; Taliban

Suggested Reading

Bacevich, Andrew J. *The New American Militarism: How Americans Are Seduced by War.* New York: Oxford University Press, 2005.

Mahajan, Rahul. *The New Crusade: America's War on Terrorism.* New York: Monthly Review, 2002.

Woodward, Bob. *Bush at War.* New York: Simon and Schuster, 2002.

Guantánamo Bay Detention Camp

The Guantánamo Bay Detention Camp is situated on the Cuban mainland. Guantánamo Bay is an area of 45 square miles that has been occupied by the United States since 1903. U.S. president Theodore Roosevelt signed an agreement with the Cuban government leasing the bay for 2,000 gold coins per year on February 16, 1903. The original intent of the base was to serve as a coaling station for the U.S. Navy. A subsequent lease was signed on July 2, 1906, on the same terms. A new lease was negotiated between the Cuban government and Franklin Delano Roosevelt in 1934. Shortly after the Cuban Revolution in 1959, the Castro government demanded that the Guantánamo Bay area be returned to Cuban sovereignty, but the American government refused, citing that both parties had to agree to the modification or abrogation of the agreement. The United States sends a check to the Cuban government for the lease amount every year, but the Cuban government has refused to cash the checks.

An Afghan detainee being escorted to a security cell at the U.S. detention facility at Guantánamo Bay, Cuba, May 9, 2003. Guantánamo has held suspected Al Qaeda members since 2001, and has been widely criticized by human rights organizations for holding the prisoners without formal charge. (U.S. Department of Defense)

In its invasion of Afghanistan, the U.S. military captured a large number of Al Qaeda fighters. What to do with these and other prisoners captured in Afghanistan became a national problem. The George W. Bush administration determined that those captured were enemy combatants, not prisoners of war. This decision came after lawyers from the White House, the Pentagon, and the Justice Department had issued a series of secret memorandums that maintained the prisoners had no rights under federal law or the Geneva Conventions. In this ruling enemy combatants were not covered by the Geneva Conventions for treatment as prisoners of war, and they could be held indefinitely without charge. A number of conservative lawyers in the Justice Department's Office of Legal Counsel (OLC) provided the legal opinions for this decision, which the Bush administration issued on January 22, 2002. Finally, after considering several sites to hold these prisoners, the U.S. military decided to build a prison at Guantánamo Bay, Cuba: the Guantánamo Bay Detention Camp. Camp X-Ray was the first facility, and the first 110 prisoners arrived there on January 11, 2002. These prisoners were held in wire cages. Later, Camp Delta was constructed; neither camp was up to standards for prison inmates in the United States. At their peak, the camps held 680 prisoners.

The Bush administration picked the Guantánamo Bay area for a specific reason. If the prisoners were held on U.S. soil, then the prisoners might claim access to legal representation and American courts. Guantánamo Bay had a unique legal situation because the land is leased from Cuba and not technically on American soil. Because the United States has no diplomatic relationship with Cuba, the prisoners can have no access to the Cuban legal system. The prisoners reside in legal limbo with few if any legal rights.

The camp is run by the military. At the beginning, command responsibility for the base was divided between Major General Michael Dunlavey, an army reservist, and Brigadier General Rick Baccus, of the Rhode Island National Guard. Dunlavey maintained a hard-line attitude toward the detainees, but Baccus was more concerned about their possible mistreatment. They quarreled over interrogation techniques and other issues. This situation changed when U.S. Army major general Geoffrey Miller replaced them and assumed command at Guantánamo in November 2003. Miller had no experience running a prison camp, and he was soon criticized for allowing harsh interrogation techniques. Miller was later transferred to Iraq where he took over responsibility for military prisons there.

After Camp Delta was built, the detainees lived in better but still restrictive conditions. At Camp X-Ray, the original camp, the detainees lived behind razor wire in cells open to the elements and with buckets in place of toilets. At Camp Delta the detainees were held in trailer-like structures made from old shipping containers that had been cut in half lengthwise with the two pieces stuck together end to end. Cells were small, six feet eight inches by eight feet, with metal beds fixed to the steel mesh walls. Toilets were squatting-style flush on the floor, and sinks were low to the ground so that detainees could wash their feet before Muslim prayer. There was no air-conditioning for the detainees, only a ventilation system that was supposed to be turned on at 85 degrees but rarely was. Later, a medium-security facility opened up, and it gave much greater freedom and better living conditions to the detainees.

The Bush administration gave the Central Intelligence Agency (CIA) responsibility for interrogations. Because these enemy combatants had no legal standing in American courts, they were treated as merely sources of intelligence. President Bush had determined this stance after deciding that Al Qaeda was a national security issue, not a law enforcement issue. Consequently, the Federal Bureau of Investigation (FBI) was completely left out of the loop. But this did not mean that the FBI gave up; for various reasons, FBI personnel did interrogate the detainees on occasion.

To encourage cooperation, levels of treatment for detainees were determined by the degree of the detainee's cooperation. Level one was for cooperating prisoners, and they received special privileges. Level two included more moderately cooperative detainees, and they received a few privileges like a drinking cup and access to the library. Level three was for the detainees who absolutely refused to cooperate. They were given only the basics—a blanket, a prayer mat and cap, a Quran, and a toothbrush.

The CIA determined that the most important Al Qaeda prisoners should not be held at the Guantánamo Bay Detention Camp. There were simply too many American officials from too many agencies trying to interrogate the prisoners. Moreover, it was too public. CIA leaders wanted a secret location where there would be no interference in the interrogations. Several secret interrogation sites were set up in friendly countries where the CIA could do what they wanted without interference.

Soon after the prisoners had been transferred to the Guantánamo Bay Detention Camp, reports began to surface about mistreatment of the detainees. A CIA analyst visited the camp in the late spring of 2002, and he was aghast at the treatment of the prisoners. Because he spoke Arabic, he was able to talk to the detainees. In his report this analyst claimed that half of the detainees did not belong there. This report traveled around the Bush administration, but nothing was done about it. The American public was still upset over September 11, and public reports about mistreatment of those held at Guantánamo Bay garnered little sympathy.

The Bush administration decided in the summer of 2006 to transfer the top captured Al Qaeda leaders to the Guantánamo Bay Detention Camp. In September 2006, the transfer of these 14 detainees was complete. Then, beginning in March 2007, court proceedings were started to determine their status. In the most important case, that of Khalid Sheikh Mohammed, the accused made a total confession of all his activities both inside and outside Al Qaeda. Among these were the planning for the September 11 attacks and the execution of journalist Daniel Pearl. His justification was that he was at war against the United States. Proceedings against the other detainees continued in the spring of 2007.

Meanwhile, growing public criticism in the United States and elsewhere about the status of the detainees led to a series of court cases in the United States in 2007 and 2008 that tried to establish a legal basis for them. Finally, in June 2008 the U.S. Supreme Court ruled that Guantánamo detainees were indeed subject to protection under the U.S. Constitution. By that time the situation in Cuba had become a public relations fiasco for the Bush administration. In October 2008 a federal court judge ordered the release of five Algerians being held at Guantánamo because the government had shown insufficient evidence for their continued incarceration. More detainees were likely to be reevaluated, which would result in their potential release or a trial. Experts have recommended exactly such a process, which they termed R2T2: (1) review, (2) release or transfer, and (3) try. In January 2009 President Barack Obama firmly declared that his administration would close the prison at Guantánamo but conceded that doing so presented unique challenges and would take some time.

Since 2008, discussions have taken place with other countries, including Italy, Ireland, Saudi Arabia, and Bermuda, that have agreed to take prisoners. On May 20, 2009, however, the Senate passed an amendment to the 2009 Supplemental Appropriations Act that blocked funds necessary for the release or transfer of Guantánamo detainees. On December 15, 2009, Obama issued a presidential memorandum calling for the federalization of the Thomson Correctional Center, a state prison in Illinois, that, once properly prepared, would be used to hold detainees from Guantánamo. As of November 2010, 174 prisoners remained at Guantánamo. By 2017, that number had declined to 41 as detainees were released or transferred to other countries. President Donald Trump signed an order in January 2018 to keep the Guantánamo Bay Detention Camp open indefinitely.

Stephen E. Atkins

See also: Bush Administration

Suggested Reading

Epstein, Edward. "Guantanamo Is a Miniature America." *San Francisco Chronicle,* January 20, 2002, A6.

Hansen, Jonathan M. "Making the Law in Cuba." *New York Times,* April 20, 2004, A19.

Hersh, Seymour M. *Chain of Command: The Road from 9/11 to Abu Ghraib.* New York: HarperCollins, 2004.

Saar, Erik, and Viveca Novak. *Inside the Wire: A Military Intelligence Soldier's Eyewitness Account of Life at Guantanamo.* New York: Penguin, 2005.

Yoo, John. *War by Other Means: An Insider's Account of the War on Terror.* New York: Atlantic Monthly Press, 2006.

H

Hamburg Cell

A group of radical Islamists formed a terrorist cell affiliated with Al Qaeda in Hamburg, Germany. This cell began when Mohamed Atta, Ramzi bin al-Shibh, and Marwan al-Shehhi began rooming together on November 1, 1998, in an apartment on 54 Marienstrasse in Hamburg. They were members of a study group at the al-Quds Mosque run by Mohammad Belfas, a middle-aged postal employee in Hamburg originally from Indonesia. Both in the study group and at the apartment they began talking about ways to advance the Islamist cause. Soon the original three attracted others of a like mind. The nine members of this cell were Mohamed Atta, Said Bahaji, Mohammad Belfas, Ramzi bin al-Shibh, Zakariya Essabor, Marwan al-Shehhi, Ziad Jarrah, Mounir el Motassadez, and Abdelghani Mzoudi. At first Belfas was the leader of the group, but he was soon replaced by Atta and left the cell. Atta then became the formal leader of the Hamburg Cell, but bin al-Shibh was its most influential member because he was better liked in the Muslim community than the dour Atta.

At first the members of the Hamburg Cell wanted to join the Chechen rebels in Chechnya in fighting against the Russians. Before this move could take place, the leaders of the cell met with Mohamedou Ould Slahi, an Al Qaeda operative in Duisburg, Germany, who advised that they undertake military and terrorist training in Afghanistan first. Atta, bin al-Shibh, Jarrah, and al-Shehhi traveled to Kandahar, Afghanistan, where they underwent extensive training in terrorist methods. They also met with Osama bin Laden, at which time Atta, Jarrah, and al-Shehhi were recruited for a special martyrdom mission to the United States.

Bin al-Shibh was to have been a part of this mission, but he was never able to obtain a visa to travel to the United States. Instead, bin al-Shibh stayed in Hamburg, serving as the contact person between the Hamburg Cell and Al Qaeda. He also served as the banker for the September 11, 2001, plot.

The most dedicated members of the Hamburg Cell participated in the September 11 plot. Other members of the group, however, provided moral and technical support. Mamoun Darkanza was the money man for the Hamburg Cell. What made those in the Hamburg Cell so important was that they were fluent in English, well-educated, and accustomed to the Western lifestyle, so they could fit in without arousing suspicion in any of the Western countries. They also had the capability to learn how to pilot a large aircraft with some training.

Bin al-Shibh shut down the Hamburg Cell as soon as he learned the date of the attacks. He made certain that anyone connected with the Hamburg Cell was forewarned so that they could protect themselves. Bin al-Shibh destroyed as much material as possible before leaving for Pakistan. Only later did German and American authorities learn of the full extent of the operations of the Hamburg Cell.

German authorities had been aware of the existence of the Hamburg Cell, but German law prevented action against the cell's members unless a German law was violated. This restriction did not prevent a veteran Central Intelligence Agency (CIA) officer attached to the American consulate in Hamburg, Thomas Volz, from attempting to persuade the German authorities to take action against the Islamist extremists in the Hamburg Cell. Volz had become suspicious of several members of the Hamburg Cell and their connections with other Muslim terrorists. He hounded the German authorities to do something until his actions alienated them to the point that they almost had him deported from Germany.

After the September 11 attacks, German authorities began a serious investigation of the Hamburg Cell and its surviving members. By this time there was little to examine or do except to arrest whoever had been affiliated with it. German authorities learned the extent to which Al Qaeda had been able to establish contacts in Germany and elsewhere in Europe.

Stephen E. Atkins

See also: Atta, Mohamed el-Amir Awad el-Sayed; Bin al-Shibh, Ramzi; World Trade Center, September 11

Suggested Reading

Bernstein, Richard. *Out of the Blue: The Story of September 11, 2001, from Jihad to Ground Zero.* New York: Times Books, 2002.

McDermott, Terry. *Perfect Soldiers: The 9/11 Hijackers; Who They Were, Why They Did It.* New York: HarperCollins, 2005.

Posner, Gerald. *Why America Slept: The Failure to Prevent 9/11.* New York: Ballantine, 2003.

Sageman, Marc. *Understanding Terror Networks.* Philadelphia: University of Pennsylvania Press, 2004.

Hanjour, Hani Saleh Husan (1972–2001)

Hani Saleh Husan Hanjour was the leader and probable pilot of the terrorist group that seized the American Airlines Flight 77 and crashed it into the Pentagon on September 11, 2001. He was a last-minute recruit because the September 11 conspirators needed one more pilot. Although Hanjour was a terrible pilot, he had enough skill to guide an airliner into a stationary target.

Hanjour had advantages in life, but he lacked the abilities to capitalize on them. He was born on August 30, 1972, in Taif, Saudi Arabia. His father was a successful food-supply businessman in Taif. Hanjour was a devout Muslim, and it colored all of his conduct. Because he was an indifferent student, Hanjour was only persuaded to stay in school by his older brother. This older brother, who was living in Tucson, Arizona, encouraged him to come to the United States. Hanjour arrived in the United States on October 3, 1991. He stayed in Tucson, where he studied English at the University of Arizona. After completing the English program in three months, Hanjour returned to Taif. He spent the next five years working at his family's food-supply business. In 1996 he briefly visited Afghanistan. Following this visit, Hanjour decided to move back to the United States. He stayed for a time with an Arab American family in Hollywood, Florida. Then in April 1996, Hanjour moved in with a family in Oakland, California. This time he attended Holy Names College and attended a course in intensive English. Hanjour decided to become a pilot and fly for Saudi Airlines. Hanjour also enrolled in a class at Sierra Academy of Aeronautics, but he withdrew because of the cost. After leaving

Oakland in April 1996, he moved to Phoenix, Arizona. This time he paid for lessons at CRM Flight Cockpit Resource Management in Scottsdale, Arizona, but his academic performance there was disappointing. His instructors found him to be a terrible pilot, and it took him a long time to master the essentials of flying. While in Phoenix, he roomed with Bandar al-Hazmi. In January 1998, Hanjour took flying lessons at Arizona Aviation, and after a three-year struggle, he earned his commercial pilot rating in April 1999. Hanjour was unable to find a job as a pilot. His Federal Aviation Administration (FAA) license expired in 1999 when he failed to take a mandatory medical test.

Frustrated in his job hunting, Hanjour traveled to Afghanistan. He arrived there just as Khalid Sheikh Mohammed's men were looking for another pilot for the September 11 plot. Hanjour was made to order. After his recruitment by Al Qaeda, he returned to the United States. In September 2000, when he moved to San Diego, California, Hanjour met up with Nawaf al-Hazmi. Hanjour returned to Phoenix to continue his pilot training at the Jet Tech Flight School. He was so inept as a flyer and his English was so bad that the instructors contacted the FAA to check on whether his commercial license was valid. The FAA confirmed that his commercial license was indeed valid. Hanjour spent most of his time at Jet Tech on the Boeing 737 simulator. Next he moved to Paterson, New Jersey, in the early spring of 2001. There he met several times with other members of the September 11 conspiracy. On September 11, 2001, Hanjour was the hijackers' pilot of American Airlines Flight 77. Despite his lack of ability, he managed to fly that aircraft into the Pentagon.

Stephen E. Atkins

See also: American Airlines Flight 77; Mohammed, Khalid Sheikh; Pentagon Attack; Pilot Training for September 11

Suggested Reading

Graham, Bob. *Intelligence Matters: The CIA, the FBI, Saudi Arabia, and the Failure of America's War on Terror.* New York: Random House, 2004.

McDermott, Terry. *Perfect Soldiers: The 9/11 Hijackers; Who They Were, Why They Did It.* New York: HarperCollins, 2005.

Health Effects of September 11

The collapse of the Twin Towers and Building Seven of the World Trade Center complex on September 11, 2001, produced thousands of tons of airborne debris that enveloped Lower Manhattan in a thick cloud of contaminants. Studies performed since the attacks have suggested that those exposed to this polluted air—particularly first responders and cleanup workers—are at serious risk of developing a number of potentially life-threatening medical conditions.

The toxic cloud produced by the collapse of buildings 1, 2, and 7 of the World Trade Center contained an estimated 2,500 contaminants. These included pulverized concrete, glass, silica, lead, mercury, and asbestos, as well as high levels of dioxin and polycyclic aromatic hydrocarbons (PAHs) produced by fires at Ground Zero. Many of these pollutants are known to cause respiratory illness, while others are carcinogenic or linked to deterioration of the kidneys, liver, or other organ systems.

A number of studies have been conducted in an effort to gauge the long-term health effects of exposure to this toxic cloud. A Pennsylvania State University/Monmouth

A rescue worker reaches into a New York Police car covered with debris, while New York City fire fighters spray water on smoldering ruins in background. The dust and chemicals released into the air as the buildings collapsed have caused health problems for decades. (Library of Congress)

University study found that rates of respiratory illness among those surveyed had risen by more than 200 percent in the year and a half following the attacks. This trend was confirmed by Dr. David J. Prezant, chief medical officer for the Fire Department City of New York (FDNY) Office of Medical Affairs, in a report published in April 2010. Prezant surveyed 5,000 rescue workers, noting that all had suffered impaired lung function, with 30 percent reporting persistent symptoms and 20 percent on "persistent respiratory disability." Doctors have noticed an increase in other illnesses, as well. One study found that more than 75 rescue and recovery workers had contracted blood cell cancers, which researchers believe were caused by carcinogens in the dust cloud. According to a 2008 report by New York City's Department of Health, as many as 70,000 individuals are at risk of developing lasting health complications. As of 2020, the World Trade Health Program lists aerodigestive disorders (such as asthma, lung diseases, and chronic obstructive pulmonary disease) as well as many types of cancers, mental health conditions, and musculoskeletal diseases as associated health conditions.

A number of institutions are conducting ongoing monitoring programs, including the World Trade Center Worker and Volunteer Medical Screening Program at Mount Sinai Medical Center. The Columbia University Center for Children's Health is also following children whose mothers were exposed to the 9/11 dust cloud to gauge its impact on fetal development. Several health registries have been created in order to assist researchers in identifying and tracking those affected by the dust cloud. The largest of these is the 9/11 Health Registry, which includes more than 70,000 people. Established in 2002 by the Agency for Toxic Substances and Disease Registry and the New York City Department of Health and Mental Hygiene, the registry coordinates its efforts with the National Institute for Occupational Safety and Health (OSHA). For those with 9/11-related health problems living in the New York City area, low- and no-cost screening and treatment programs are available at a number of area hospitals that have been designated WTC Centers of Excellence. The WTC National Responder Health Program provides similar care for those living outside New York City.

Political action at both the local and federal levels has also been taken in response to 9/11 health concerns. In 2006, President George W. Bush appointed John Howard, director of OSHA, to the newly created position of WTC health czar. In that position until 2008, Howard was responsible for developing and overseeing the implementation of the World Trade Center Medical Monitoring and Treatment Program. In June 2007, New York City mayor Michael Bloomberg appointed Jeffrey Hon as World Trade Center health coordinator, tasked with facilitating information-sharing among patients, researchers, and other interested groups.

On February 4, 2009, New York Democratic Congressman Carolyn Maloney introduced HR 847, also known as the James Zadroga 9/11 Health and Compensation Act. The bill was named for New York City police officer James Zadroga, who died on January 5, 2006, from respiratory illness most likely caused by exposure to the dust cloud. The bill, which was signed into law by President Barack Obama on January 2, 2011, and reauthorized in 2015 and 2019, provides billions of dollars in medical care to those whose health has been impacted by the destruction of the World Trade Center.

Perhaps more disturbing than the long-term health effects of 9/11 is the possibility that local and federal officials mismanaged cleanup operations and intentionally downplayed the risks of reopening the area around Ground Zero so soon after the collapse of the World Trade Center. Then-mayor of New York City Rudy Giuliani gave the locally run Department of Design and Construction oversight of cleanup operations, sidestepping federal agencies that customarily handle such tasks, including the Federal Emergency Management Agency (FEMA), the Army Corps of Engineers, and OSHA. Giuliani has been accused of ignoring federal safety requirements, including providing respirators for cleanup workers. A total of 10,563 workers sued the city of New York for negligence during cleanup operations. In November 2010, more than 10,000 of them agreed to a $625 million settlement.

Allegations of misconduct have also been leveled against Bush and other top Washington officials, including Christine Todd Whitman, then-head of the Environmental Protection Agency (EPA). In a September 18, 2001, statement, Whitman assured New York residents that the air around Ground Zero was safe and that returning to work posed no health risks. A report issued by the EPA's Office of the Inspector General in August 2003, however, asserted that Bush and the White House Council on Environmental Quality had pressured the EPA to omit all negative or cautionary statements from its reports on air quality. Critics claim that the health of New York City residents was jeopardized in an effort to minimize the economic impact of the 9/11 attacks.

Spencer C. Tucker

See also: Cleanup Operations at Ground Zero; Department of Design and Construction; Federal Emergency Management Agency; Firefighters at Ground Zero; New York City Police Department; Occupational Safety and Health Agency; Office of Emergency Management

Suggested Reading

Barry, Ellen. "Lost in the Dust of 9/11." *Los Angeles Times,* October 14, 2006.

DePalma, Anthony. *City of Dust: Illness, Arrogance, and 9/11.* Upper Saddle River, NJ: FT Press, 2010.

Edelman, Susan. "Charting Post-9/11 Deaths." *New York Post,* January 6, 2008.

Garrett, Laurie. "EPA Misled Public on 9/11 Pollution." *Newsday,* August 23, 2003.

Lioy, Paul J. *Dust: The Inside Story of Its Role in the September 11th Aftermath.* Lanham, MD: Rowman and Littlefield, 2010.

World Trade Center Health Program. https://www.cdc.gov/wtc/conditions.html

International Reactions to September 11

Although the terrorist attacks on September 11, 2001, targeted the United States, many other countries throughout the world were also affected. In addition to the 2,657 Americans killed, 316 foreign nationals from more than 90 different countries also died in the attacks, including 67 Britons, 28 South Koreans, 26 Japanese, and 25 Canadians. The shock and horror engendered by the attacks were truly international in scope.

Most public reaction and media coverage outside the United States was extremely sympathetic. The French national newspaper, *Le Monde,* declared *"Nous sommes tous Américains"* ("We are all Americans"). The British *Mirror* labeled the attacks a "War on the World." The Spanish paper *El Correo* ran a single-word headline: *"Muerte"* ("Murder"). Most world leaders were also quick to condemn the terrorists. Russian president Vladimir Putin urged that "the entire international community should unite in the struggle against terrorism," adding that the attacks were "a blatant challenge to humanity." Japanese prime minister Junichiro Koizumi said that "this outrageous and vicious act of violence against the United States is unforgivable." German chancellor Gerhard Schrüder told reporters that "they were not only attacks on the people in the United States, our friends in America, but also against the entire civilized world, against our own freedom, against our own values, values which we share with the American people."

Perhaps even more moving was the spontaneous outpouring of sympathy from average people around the globe. Tens of thousands of people left flowers, cards, and other personal mementos at U.S. consulates and embassies in many countries. Vigils and prayers were held throughout the world in a wide range of faiths. Thousands turned out in the streets of major capitals to protest the attacks, nearly 200,000 in Berlin alone. Ireland proclaimed a day of national mourning, while in Britain the American national anthem played at the changing of the guard in front of Buckingham Palace. With many international flights grounded for days after September 11, volunteers in 15 Canadian cities took care of 33,000 stranded passengers-mostly Americans—who had been aboard 255 planes diverted from U.S. airports.

Sympathy came from unlikely places. Libyan leader Muammar Qaddafi, himself linked to terrorism, called the attacks "horrifying" and counseled Muslims that "irrespective of the conflict with America it is a human duty to show sympathy with the American people." Iranian president Mohammed Khatami expressed his "deep regret and sympathy with the victims," while a visibly shocked Palestinian president Yasser Arafat denounced the attacks, repeating how "unbelievable" they were. Even the Democratic People's Republic of Korea (DPRK, North Korea), a rogue nation considered by many a sponsor of international terrorism, offered Americans sympathy following such a great "tragedy." In fact, few people demonstrated anything but sympathy for those who suffered in the attacks.

Sympathy for the United States and the victims of September 11 continued when in October 2001 the United States led an invasion of Afghanistan to destroy Al Qaeda training camps, hunt its elusive leader Osama bin Laden, and overthrow the oppressive Taliban regime that had given refuge to the organization responsible for the carnage. On September 12 the North Atlantic Treaty Organization (NATO) had invoked Article 5 of its charter, which pledged mutual assistance in the war against Al Qaeda. This was the first time in NATO's 52-year history that Article 5 was invoked.

Pakistan offered bases from which to plan operations in Afghanistan and support in tracking down Al Qaeda and Taliban fighters. Simultaneously, British prime minister Tony Blair pursued multilateral antiterrorist planning within the European Union (EU). French president Jacques Chirac promised to stand with the United States, "fighting shoulder to shoulder" against terrorism. Many governments quickly arrested suspected terrorists operating in their countries. They also developed and implemented legislation aimed at combating terrorist organizations. While such measures were not without their critics, much of the world adopted more stringent security measures in the first few months after September 11.

This general outpouring of sympathy did not, however, translate into open-ended support for American foreign policy or its Global War on Terror. Many criticized U.S. president George W. Bush's worldview when he said a few days after September 11 that "you're either with us or with the terrorists." Some saw the Global War on Terror as a cover for extending U.S. power abroad, particularly when the Bush administration erroneously began to link September 11 terrorists with Iraq. Bush's controversial "Axis of Evil" reference, in which he grouped Iraq, Iran, and North Korea in his State of the Union address on January 29, 2002, struck many listeners as inflammatory and off the mark.

Reports by organizations such as Amnesty International would condemn the United States for the treatment of suspected terrorist prisoners in camps at Guantánamo Bay, Cuba, where detainees from the conflict in Afghanistan were held. More than anything, international sympathy for the United States was largely undermined by Bush's decision to invade Iraq in March 2003 despite the fact that its major allies and the United Nations (UN) refused to support such action. Thus, the legacy of September 11 turned from one of sympathy and commonality to one of suspicion and condemnation.

Arne Kislenko

See also: Bin Laden, Osama; ENDURING FREEDOM, Operation; Global War on Terror; Guantánamo Bay Detention Camp; Taliban

Suggested Reading

Goh, Evelyn. "Hegemonic Constraints: The Implications of 11 September for American Power." *Australian Journal of International Affairs* 57(1) (April 2003): 77–97.

Hirsh, Michael. "Bush and the World." *Foreign Affairs* 82(5) (September–October 2002): 18–43.

Scheuer, Michael. *Imperial Hubris: Why the West Is Losing the War on Terror.* Washington, DC: Potomac Books, 2004.

IRAQI FREEDOM, Operation

Those who take the long view of history may be inclined to blame British prime minister David Lloyd George as much as U.S. president George W. Bush for the war in Iraq. British and French actions after World War I to fill the Middle Eastern void

U.S. marines on a foot patrol in Baghdad prepare to rush a house believed to contain a weapons cache during Operation IRAQI FREEDOM, April 18, 2003. (U.S. Department of Defense)

left by the collapse of the Ottoman Empire created modern Iraq and other Arab nations without regard for traditional ethnic and religious boundaries. Conditions in the European-created, artificial country of Iraq (especially the long-held animosity between the country's three major ethnic and religious populations of Kurds, Sunni, and Shia) made it a perfect breeding ground for such strong-arm dictators as Saddam Hussein to seize and hold power over a divided population, while incubating simmering ethnic and religious rivalries.

Iraq, compared with Afghanistan, the other major theater of combat operations for President Bush's Global War on Terror, played out with mixed success in two very different campaigns: a stunning conventional assault that rapidly destroyed the Iraqi army, captured Baghdad, ousted Saddam Hussein, and paved the way for a

U.S.-led occupation of the country, and a smoldering insurgency conducted by Al Qaeda fighters and both Sunni and Shia faction Iraqi militia groups that began shortly after Hussein's defeat.

Although the two Iraq campaigns bear a superficial similarity to what transpired in Afghanistan (large-scale conventional combat operations to defeat the enemy's main forces followed by an insurgency), the Iraq War and occupation have shown striking differences in scope, intensity, and even in the justification U.S. leaders gave for invading the country. While Operation ENDURING FREEDOM was launched to strike directly at those presumed responsible for masterminding the September 11, 2001, terror attacks and the Afghan Taliban regime that harbored them, no such justification can be claimed for the Bush administration's decision to launch the March 2003 invasion of

Iraq. Despite Iraqi president Saddam Hussein's track record of general support for terrorist organizations hostile to the United States and the West, no direct link to Al Qaeda has ever been proven. And while U.S. strategy regarding Afghanistan might be classified as *reactive,* the decision of America's leaders to invade Iraq can only be termed *proactive,* a surprising and controversial preemptive action.

In the wake of the 1990–1991 Persian Gulf War, Hussein used chemical weapons on Iraq's Kurdish minority. Subsequently, Hussein was often vilified for using chemical weapons on "his own people," but he did not consider the Kurds to be "his people"; his loyalty lay only with his Baathist Party cronies and his own tribe. What is perhaps surprising about his use of chemical weapons is that he did not use them more extensively. Iraqi officials were recalcitrant to inspections by the United Nations (UN) and failed, by late 2002, to produce an adequate accounting of the disposition of the weapons of mass destruction the country was known to possess (and use) in 1991. Furthermore, the Iraqis failed to provide a full and open disclosure of the status of the country's suspected nuclear weapons program. If Iraq had added nuclear weapons to its 1991 chemical arsenal, as was charged by Iraqi émigrés (such as Khidhir Hamza, self-proclaimed "Saddam's Bombmaker," who toured U.S. college campuses in the autumn of 2002 trumpeting his "insider" knowledge of Iraq's alleged nuclear program), it would be foolish to ignore the threat such weapons posed. By failing to cooperate promptly, fully, and openly with UN weapons inspectors, Hussein had almost literally signed his own death warrant.

Opting for a preemptive strategy instead of risking a potential repeat of the September 11 terror attacks—with the added specter of chemical, biological, or nuclear weapons— Bush and his advisers (principally Vice President Dick Cheney and Deputy Secretary of Defense Paul Wolfowitz, described as "a major architect of Bush's Iraq policy . . . and its most passionate and compelling advocate") decided to act, unilaterally if necessary. Armed chiefly with what would later be exposed as an egregiously inaccurate Central Intelligence Agency (CIA) report about Iraq's possession of nuclear and other weapons of mass destruction, Bush obtained a legal justification for invading Iraq when the Senate approved the joint resolution titled "Authorization for Use of Military Force against Iraq Resolution of 2002" in October 2002. In February 2003 Secretary of State Colin Powell addressed the UN Security Council with information based largely on the same flawed CIA report, but action was blocked by France, Germany, and Russia. Although the three powers bolstered their opposition with claims that military action against Iraq would threaten "international security," their true motives were suspect to some who supported military action (France and Germany, for example, already had made billions of dollars by illegally circumventing the UN Oil-for-Food Programme with Iraq). Regardless of their motives, all three countries had a vested interest in maintaining the status quo in Iraq and little motivation to participate in an American-led preemptive strike. Although Britain joined Bush's "coalition of the willing" (from 2003, 75 countries contributed troops, matériel, or services to the U.S.-led effort), the absence of France and Germany left his administration open to strong criticism for stubbornly proceeding without broad-based European support.

Bush's proactive rather than reactive strategy was heavily criticized by administration opponents as a sea-change departure from that of past U.S. presidents and slammed for its unilateralism. Yet, as historian John Lewis Gaddis points out in *Surprise, Security, and the American Experience,* it was not without historical precedent. He cites the preemptive, unilateral actions of presidents John Adams, James K. Polk, William McKinley, Woodrow Wilson, and even Franklin D. Roosevelt. Yet, with U.S. ground forces already stretched thin by Operation ENDURING FREEDOM, mounting a major, preemptive invasion of Iraq was considered by many—particularly U.S. military leaders—as risky. Military drawdowns during Bill Clinton's presidency, for example, had reduced U.S. Army active duty strength from 780,000 to about 480,000.

Even in the years before the 2003 Iraq invasion, U.S. Army chief of staff General Eric Shinseki had clashed with Secretary of Defense Donald Rumsfeld over Department of Defense proposals to reduce army end strength even further. Rumsfeld had taken office in 2001, firmly convinced that technology could replace large numbers of ground combat forces, and he doggedly clung to that conviction. Moreover, Rumsfeld, who had previously served as president Gerald Ford's secretary of defense in 1975–1977, often acted as if he were unaware of how profoundly the 1986 Goldwater-Nichols Act had affected U.S. military culture by eliminating much of the petty, interservice bickering that he had earlier witnessed. Shinseki further provoked Rumsfeld's ire when he told the Senate Armed Services Committee on the eve of the Iraq invasion that an occupation of that country would require "several hundred thousand" troops, an estimate that, in hindsight, seemed prescient indeed, but which was sharply criticized in 2003 by Rumsfeld and Paul Wolfowitz as "wildly off the mark."

On March 20, 2003, U.S. and British forces (plus smaller contingents from Australia and Poland) invaded Iraq in Operation IRAQI FREEDOM. The 297,000-strong force faced an Iraqi army numbering approximately 375,000, plus an unknown number of poorly trained citizens' militia. U.S. combat strength was about half of that deployed during the 1990–1991 Persian Gulf War. With U.S. Central Command general Tommy Franks in overall command, the U.S. ground forces prosecuting the invasion were led by U.S. V Corps commander Lieutenant General William Scott Wallace.

Preceded by a shock-and-awe air campaign reminiscent of the one that blasted Hussein's forces and Iraqi infrastructure in the Persian Gulf War, ground forces (including U.S. marines and British combat units) executed another "desert blitzkrieg" that quickly smashed the Iraqi army. Despite the failure of the Turkish government at the last minute to allow the United States to mount a major invasion of northern Iraq from its soil, two ground prongs struck north from Kuwait, while Special Forces and airborne forces worked with the Kurds in the north in a limited second front. The ground advance north was rapid. Baghdad fell on April 10, and Hussein went into hiding. (He was captured in December 2003, brought to trial, found guilty, and executed on December 30, 2006.)

President Bush declared "mission accomplished" and the end of major combat operations while aboard the U.S. aircraft carrier *Abraham Lincoln* on May 1, 2003. Subsequent events during the postinvasion occupation of Iraq would prove Bush's dramatic statement to be wildly premature: although only 139 U.S. personnel and 33 British soldiers died during the invasion, thousands more were killed during the insurgency that accompanied occupation, particularly during the 2007 U.S. troop surge mounted in an effort to stabilize the country. By late 2008, the American public's support for the war in Iraq had plummeted. Throughout that same year, the American and Iraqi governments negotiated the U.S.-Iraq Status of Forces Agreement, which outlined a clear timetable for the withdrawal of U.S. troops. Under this agreement, the last U.S. combat troops left Iraq on August 19, 2010, although some 50,000 support personnel will remain in the country until the end of 2011. On September 1, 2010, the name Operation NEW DAWN was adopted to emphasize this major turning point.

Jerry D. Morelock

See also: Bush, George W.; Bush Doctrine; Global War on Terror

Suggested Reading

Atkinson, Rick. *In the Company of Soldiers: A Chronicle of Combat.* New York: Holt, 2005.

Cavaleri, David. *Easier Said Than Done: Making the Transition between Combat Operations and Stability Operations.* Fort Leavenworth, KS: Combat Studies Institute Press, 2005.

DiMarco, Louis A. *Traditions, Changes and Challenges: Military Operations and the Middle Eastern City.* Fort Leavenworth, KS: Combat Studies Institute Press, 2004.

Franks, Tommy, with Malcolm McConnell. *American Soldier.* New York: Regan-Books, 2004.

Gaddis, John Lewis. *Surprise, Security and the American Experience.* Cambridge: Harvard University Press, 2005.

Gordon, Michael R., and General Bernard E. Trainor. *Cobra II: The Inside Story of the Invasion and Occupation of Iraq.* New York: Pantheon Books, 2006.

Murray, Williamson, and Robert H. Scales Jr. *The Iraq War: A Military History.* Cambridge, MA: Belknap, 2005.

Ricks, Thomas E. *Fiasco: The American Military Adventure in Iraq.* New York: Penguin, 2006.

Sanchez, Ricardo S., and Donald T. Phillips. *Wiser in Battle: A Soldier's Story.* New York: Harper, 2008.

Woodward, Bob. *Bush at War.* New York: Simon and Schuster, 2002.

Woodward, Bob. *Plan of Attack.* New York: Simon and Schuster, 2004.

Woodward, Bob. *State of Denial: Bush at War, Part III.* New York: Simon and Schuster, 2006.

Zinmeister, Karl. *Boots on the Ground: A Month with the 82d Airborne Division in the Battle for Iraq.* New York: St. Martin's, 2004.

Zinmeister, Karl. *Dawn over Baghdad: How the U.S. Military Is Using Bullets and Ballots to Remake Iraq.* New York: Encounter Books, 2004.

J

Jarrah, Ziad Samir (1975–2001)

Ziad Samir Jarrah was among the 19 suicide hijackers on September 11, 2001. He had been recruited by Ramzi bin al-Shibh at al-Quds Mosque. Less religious than the other members of the Hamburg Cell, Jarrah still joined the September 11 conspiracy. He was the hijackers' pilot on United Airlines Flight 93.

Jarrah was born on May 11, 1975, in Beirut, Lebanon, into a wealthy and influential family. His father held a high-ranking post in the Lebanese social security system, and his mother taught school. Members of his family were secular Muslims who paid little attention to religion. Although the family lived in a prosperous area of Beirut, the Lebanese civil war that began in 1975 made this Sunni neighborhood less than secure. Jarrah attended the best private Christian schools in Beirut, but he was never more than an indifferent student. His family claimed that he was more interested in girls than his studies. He flunked his high school finals and only graduated two years later. After finishing his schooling, the family sent him to study biochemistry in Greifswald, Germany, in the spring of 1996. His parents subsidized his education by sending him at least $2,000 a month. In Germany, Jarrah met Aysel Sengün, a young Turkish student studying dental medicine, and they became a couple.

Jarrah was a happy-go-lucky person until he returned to Lebanon for a winter break in 1997. He returned with a much more serious outlook on life, and he began to have trouble with his girlfriend. Jarrah wanted her to conform to a more traditional Muslim form of behavior. Searching for a career, Jarrah decided to study aeronautical engineering at Hamburg University of Applied Science. Jarrah joined the al-Quds Mosque in Hamburg, and he became a militant Islamist. Bin al-Shibh was his chief contact at the al-Quds Mosque, and Jarrah had little contact with Mohamed Atta. Jarrah was never an active member of the Hamburg Cell, but he shared most of its orientation. As religion became a more important part of his life, his relationship with his girlfriend deteriorated to the point that she was unable to understand him. They still intended to be married at a future time, however.

Jarrah was a follower, not a leader, among the members of the Hamburg Cell. In some respects, he was the weak link among the members of the plot. He was intelligent enough to pass the qualifying tests as a pilot, but he lacked some of the other characteristics of a dedicated terrorist, such as ruthlessness. An American psychological profile pointed out character flaws: "indecisive and impulsive as well as immature, unstable, and unprofessional." Nevertheless, he trained at an Al Qaeda camp beginning in November 1999 along with Mohamed Atta. He was with Atta and Marwan al-Shehhi when they met and talked with Osama bin Laden in Kandahar. It was at this time that bin Laden asked them to swear allegiance to him and to be part of a suicide mission. Jarrah agreed with the others to do both. He then received a briefing from Mohammad Atef, the military chief of Al Qaeda, on the general outlines of the September 11 operation. Jarrah returned to Germany with the others to prepare for their mission.

Jarrah entered the United States on June 27, 2000, on a Delta flight from Munich. He trained at the Florida Flight Training Center in Venice, Florida. His flight instructor considered him an average pilot who needed more training to become a proficient pilot. Jarrah left the school without a commercial pilot's license. In an October 2000 note Jarrah wrote about his longing for paradise.

In January 2001 Jarrah returned to Germany. In April 2001, Jarrah was back in the United States, living in Hollywood, Florida. While there, Jarrah took martial arts lessons at the U.S. 1 Fitness Club, working with Bert Rodriguez. Rodriguez held eight black belts in the martial arts, and he considered Jarrah a good student. Jarrah made one last trip to Germany to see his girlfriend, leaving on July 25 and returning on August 4. While still in Germany, Jarrah was notified that he had qualified for a commercial license to fly single-engine aircraft. After his return from Germany, Jarrah began to study the manuals on flying Boeing 757 and 767 aircraft. Later in August 2001, Jarrah moved to an apartment in Lauderdale-by-the-Sea. In the weeks before September 11, Jarrah lived with Ahmed al-Haznawi. Throughout late August and September, Jarrah traveled frequently from south Florida to the Washington, DC, area. On September 7, 2001, Jarrah made a flight from Fort Lauderdale to Newark, New Jersey, on Continental Airlines with al-Haznawi. Jarrah reappeared in the Washington, DC, area when he received a speeding ticket on Interstate 95 in Maryland. Jarrah and two of his fellow conspirators checked in at the Newark Airport Marriott soon after midnight on September 11. Before boarding United Airlines, Jarrah made a last phone call to Aysel Sengün in Germany.

Jarrah was the leader and pilot of the hijack team of United Airlines Flight 93. Team members had some trouble passing through security at Dulles International Airport, but they all made it. Once in the air, the hijackers seized control of the aircraft and Jarrah assumed the role of pilot. He began turning the aircraft around to head to the Washington, DC, area. There were only three hijackers to control the crew and passengers. Soon passengers learned through cell phone calls that the aircraft was to be used as a flying bomb. They revolted and attempted to regain control of the plane. When it became apparent that the hijackers were about to be overpowered by the passengers, Jarrah crashed the aircraft into the ground near Shanksville, Pennsylvania, following instructions to destroy the aircraft if the mission did not have a chance of success.

Stephen E. Atkins

See also: Atta, Mohamed el-Amir Awad el-Sayed; Hamburg Cell; United Airlines Flight 93

Suggested Reading

Bernstein, Richard. *Out of the Blue: The Story of September 11, 2001, from Jihad to Ground Zero.* New York: Times Books, 2002.

Longman, Jere. *Among the Heroes: United Flight 93 and the Passengers and Crew Who Fought Back.* New York: Perennial, 2003.

McDermott, Terry. *Perfect Soldiers: The 9/11 Hijackers; Who They Were, Why They Did It.* New York: HarperCollins, 2005.

Judge, Mychal (1933–2001)

Father Mychal Judge was a Franciscan priest serving as the chaplain for the Fire Department City of New York (FDNY) who died serving others on September 11, 2001. He was born on May 11, 1933, in Brooklyn, New York, into an Irish immigrant family from County Leitrim. His birth name was Robert Emmett Judge. When he was only six years old, his father died from a lingering illness. Judge took jobs as a boy to help support his mother and two sisters. Judge entered the Franciscan order in 1954, and he attended St. Bonaventure College, graduating in 1957. He was ordained a priest in 1961. His assignment was to serve as the pastor of St. Joseph's parish in East Rutherford, New Jersey, and then at St. Joseph's parish in West Milford, New Jersey. Judge showed an early interest in firefighting. After other assignments at Siena College in Loudonville, New York, and St. Francis of Assisi, he became a fire chaplain in 1992.

Father Judge took his responsibilities as fire chaplain seriously. He always carried a pager and responded to calls throughout the city regardless of the time and circumstances. At the scene of fires he was seen counseling people in need, and he was active in consoling family members at the hospital. Judge also performed masses at FDNY ceremonies. He became a beloved figure in the FDNY. Part of his popularity was that although he talked about his love for Jesus, he was never judgmental or unfairly critical of anyone. Father Judge had been an alcoholic, but he had avoided drink for more than 20 years as an active member of Alcoholics Anonymous (AA).

On two occasions before his death, Father Judge received national attention. The first was his support for the victims of AIDS. Long before it was acceptable to give help to AIDS victims, Father Judge was active, even though he had opposition from within the Catholic Church. Judge was open about his homosexuality, but few if any of the firefighters he served cared. Many members of the church hierarchy, however, were uncomfortable with Father Judge because he was gay.

Father Judge's second venture onto the national headlines was his role in comforting the families of the victims of TWA Flight 800 off Long Island, New York, in 1996. This aircraft had exploded in midair, killing all of the 230 crew and passengers. Despite lengthy investigations, the exact nature of the explosion is still a subject of dispute. After conducting masses for the victims, he spent time counseling the families regardless of their denominations.

Father Judge was serving as the chaplain to the FDNY on September 11, 2001. He was a gregarious man who enjoyed being a chaplain and loved publicity. As soon as he heard about the World Trade Center incident, Father Judge dashed to the World Trade Center to render aid to the victims. He began giving last rites to the dying. While giving the last rites to a firefighter named Daniel Suhr, Father Judge was struck by falling debris. Shortly afterward, Father Judge entered the lobby of the North Tower of the World Trade Center. Debris from the collapse of the South Tower of the World Trade Center hit him, killing him instantly. His body was removed later by the firefighters with great dignity. A picture of firefighters and a policeman carrying his body out has received the title "American Pieta." They respected his courage in administering the last rites for the victims of September 11 in the face of danger. Father Judge was buried on September 15, 2001, at Holy Sepulchre Cemetery in Totowa, New Jersey. His life is chronicled in two books: Michael Ford's *Father Mychal Judge: An Authentic American Hero* (2002) and Michael Daly's *The Book of Mychal: The Surprising Life and Heroic Death of Father Mychal Judge* (2008).

Since his death, Father Judge has become a controversial figure because there is a growing campaign to make him a saint. For a candidate to qualify for sainthood, five years must have passed since his or her death, and at least two miracles must be attributed to the candidate. His conduct at the World Trade Center has led to a growing mythology. Several people have claimed that their prayers to Father Judge produced miracles. The archdiocese of New York has left it up to the Franciscan order to advance his sainthood, but the leaders of the order say they will not because although he was a good friar he should not be set apart from others. The fact that Father Judge was gay is a complicating factor.

Stephen E. Atkins

See also: Firefighters at Ground Zero; World Trade Center, September 11

Suggested Reading

Brazao, Dale, and Kevin Coombs. "Father Mike Died Doing His Duty; Father Mike Loved Life, Loved Souls." *Toronto Star,* September 16, 2001, A1.

Jones, Charisse. "The Making of St. Mychal." *USA Today,* February 20, 2003, 1A.

Smith, Dennis. *Report from Ground Zero.* New York: Viking, 2002.

Von Essen, Thomas, with Matt Murray. *Strong of Heart: Life and Death in the Fire Department of New York.* New York: ReganBooks, 2002.

Wakin, Daniel J. "Killed on 9/11, Fire Chaplain Becomes Larger Than Life." *New York Times,* September 27, 2002, A1.

Justification for the September 11 Suicide Mission

The most difficult aspect of the September 11 attacks for Americans to understand was the use of suicide as a weapon. Nineteen young men bonded together to hijack four American commercial aircraft and crash them into preselected targets. They had no regard for their safety or for anybody else's. Each had received at least basic training at Al Qaeda camps to prepare for such a mission. An important part of this training was religious instruction that prepared them for what they called a martyrdom mission.

The religious justification for suicide missions is controversial among Muslim religious authorities. Both opponents and proponents refer to the religious teachings of the Prophet Mohammad as stated in the Quran or to the sayings of the Prophet in the hadiths. Personal suicide is not a part of Muslim religious practice, and this is reflected in the low personal suicide rate in the Muslim world. On the other hand, suicide undertaken as part of jihad, or holy war, is where it becomes controversial.

Jihad has two meanings in Muslim theology. Foremost, jihad means a personal struggle to adhere to the precepts of being a Muslim. The other meaning of jihad is war against the enemies of Islam. Again there are two meanings to this concept. There is jihad that aggressively wages war for the faith. This was the type of jihad that the Muslim successors to the Prophet Mohammad waged in the expansionary period of Islam's history. Then there is defensive jihad, which exists when the Islamic world is attacked by outsiders. According to this concept, it is the obligation of every able-bodied Muslim to participate in a war against an invader. Islamist groups consider the presence of Israel in the Middle East as part of an invasion of the Muslim world. Because the United States is an ally of Israel and has a presence in the Middle East, it is also considered a partner in this invasion. Al Qaeda and other Islamist groups maintain that the war against Israel and the

United States is a continuation of the war between the West and the Muslim world that dates back to the Crusades in the Middle Ages.

Suicide as a political weapon has a history in the Muslim world. The most famous historical cases of suicide used as a political weapon were those carried out by the assassins of the Ismaeli Shiite sect of Hassan ibn Sabbah, who established the Ismaeli Assassins in the Middle Ages (1034–1255); they carried out suicide missions against Muslim Sunnis and Christian Crusaders. After the collapse of this sect, there were sporadic suicide missions, mostly against European colonial targets. Only in the early 1980s did the use of suicide as a weapon reappear in the Middle East. It has appeared elsewhere mostly in association with the Tamil Tigers in Sri Lanka. The first incident of a suicide mission in the Middle East in modern times was by the Shiite Amal organization when a suicide bomber drove a car with explosives into the Iraqi embassy in Beirut on December 15, 1981, killing 61 people. Hezbollah (the Party of God) in Lebanon borrowed this tactic and has used it with lethal effect against American and Israeli targets. Later, both the Palestinian Islamic Jihad and Hamas began depending on suicide bombers for use against the Israelis. The military wing of Fatah, the al-Aqsa Martyrs Brigades, has also resorted to the use of suicide bombers.

Noting the effectiveness of suicide bombers, Al Qaeda's leadership adopted the practice. Suicide bombing is considered an effective weapon in a war in which one side is so much stronger militarily than the other. Besides its lethal impact, a suicide bombing has the element of surprise. The suicide bomber is able to get close to the target before he or she detonates the bomb. Al Qaeda leaders claim that it is the most successful tactic in inflicting damage and at the same time the least costly in terms of loss of its operatives. This belief is reinforced by the fact that suicide attacks claim 10 to 15 times the casualties of any other terrorist operation.

At training camps in Afghanistan, candidates were appraised for the characteristics necessary to recruit for a martyrdom mission. Candidates had to be religious and of strong character. The members of the Hamburg Cell were ideal candidates for the September 11 mission because of their strong religious views, language expertise, and ability to adapt to Western society without arousing suspicion. Once a candidate had been selected, he underwent specialized training for the mission. For those on the September 11 mission, this meant concentrating on hijacking a commercial aircraft in flight. Those selected to be pilots were given leadership training and sent to the United States for pilot training. Other candidates received different training for different missions.

Stephen E. Atkins

See also: Al Qaeda; Hamburg Cell

Suggested Reading

Atwan, Abdel Bari. *The Secret History of Al Qaeda.* Berkeley: University of California Press, 2006.

Pape, Robert A. *Dying to Win: The Strategic Logic of Suicide Terrorism.* New York: Random House, 2005.

Rubin, Barry, and Judith Colp Rubin, eds. *Anti-American Terrorism and the Middle East: A Documentary Reader.* New York: Oxford University Press, 2002.

K

Kerik, Bernard Bailey (1955–)

Bernard Bailey Kerik was the police commissioner of the City of New York on September 11, 2001. He was a longtime political ally of Mayor Rudolph Giuliani. His actions at the World Trade Center on September 11 elevated him, along with Giuliani, to the national limelight.

Kerik had an unusual background. He was born on September 4, 1955, in Paterson, New Jersey. His mother was a prostitute, and his father deserted him when he was only two years old. He was raised by a violent stepfather with a criminal record. He had trouble in school, often getting into fights. Kerik finally dropped out of high school. He later earned a GED and a mail-order bachelor's degree from Empire State College. In his autobiography Kerik states that his violent tendencies were leading to a life of crime until he joined the U.S. Army. Kerik became a military policeman, serving in Korea and then with the 18th Airborne Corps at Fort Bragg, North Carolina. His passion was martial arts, and he earned a black belt at age 18. After leaving the army, he worked at security assignments for the Saudi royal family between 1982 and 1984. Returning to the United States, Kerik joined the Passaic County Sheriff's Office, where he held a number of jobs.

Kerik's career took off when he took a job with the New York City Police Department (NYPD). His first assignment was working undercover for the anticrime and narcotics units in Harlem, Spanish Harlem, and Washington Heights. His successes led to his selection for the U.S. Justice Department's New York Drug Enforcement Task Force. During his duty as a uniformed and plainclothes officer, Kerik earned 30 medals for meritorious and heroic service, including the department's Medal for Valor. On January 1, 1998, he was appointed commissioner of the New York City Department of Correction. Kerik earned praise for improving the safety of the city's jail system, and improving the morale of the guards. Kerik became the 40th police commissioner of the City of New York on August 21, 2000, appointed by Mayor Rudolph Giuliani. Kerik had responsibility for a uniformed force of more than 41,000 officers, and a civilian force of more than 14,500. He had a reputation as "a tough-talking, sometimes coarse, law enforcer who rarely stood on ceremony," and as one interested in shaking up the status quo. He was considered a tough boss who was willing to fire subordinates whom he considered to be slackers. Kerik was also known to be reluctant to cooperate with the Federal Bureau of Investigation (FBI).

Kerik was in charge of the NYPD on September 11. He was taking a shower in his office at 1 Police Plaza when he was informed about the aircraft that hit the North Tower. He immediately headed for the World Trade Center, where he took charge of police operations. Kerik was there when the second aircraft crashed into the South Tower. By this time Mayor Giuliani had made an appearance at the World Trade Center. Communications equipment failed, and coordination between police and firefighters was lacking. Both Giuliani and Kerik survived the collapse of the towers, but they were at risk from falling debris. They made it out of the area and established a new communication center.

Over the next few months Kerik worked to rebuild the NYPD. The loss of 27 police officers on September 11 was debilitating to the department. Kerik spent the next four months working to build the department back to pre–September 11 standards and to improve morale. Mayor Giuliani and Kerik worked hand in hand to restore New York City to normalcy. They both received considerable media attention for their efforts.

Kerik retired from the police commissioner's job at the end of Mayor Giuliani's tenure in office. He worked for a while as a partner in Giuliani's consulting firm, Giuliani Partners, until President George W. Bush sent him to Iraq to create an Iraqi police force after the invasion. Kerik's role there turned out to be controversial: his stay was short, and he was not effective. Returning to the United States, he served on the board of directors of Taser International, manufacturer of stun guns used by police departments. He used his stock options as a director to sell $5.8 million of Taser stock.

Kerik's performance on September 11, 2001, came under scrutiny by the 9/11 Commission. Commissioners criticized Kerik and the NYPD for their performance on September 11. They cited the long-running rivalry between the police and firefighters for having led to failures in command and control and for communication problems. Kerik countered by calling the criticism Monday morning quarterbacking.

Kerik tried to stay out of the limelight until President George W. Bush nominated him for the position of secretary of Homeland Security on December 3, 2004. Rudolph

Giuliani had pressed the White House to select Kerik for this post. A problem arose in the failure of the Bush administration to have Kerik vetted properly; when they did review his background, they found financial and moral problems. His financial picture was clouded by suspicions of illegality. On the moral side, there was evidence of adultery involving more than one woman. When it became apparent that Kerik could not survive the confirmation process, he withdrew from consideration as secretary of Homeland Security, citing an illegal immigrant nanny he had hired for whom he failed to pay taxes. Soon afterward Kerik also quit the Giuliani Partnership.

Since 2004 Kerik has been in and out of legal trouble. Federal and state authorities began to investigate his various financial transactions. After leaving Giuliani Partners, he formed his own security firm, the Kerik Group. In July 2006 he pleaded guilty to conflict-of-interest charges for accepting $165,000 in gifts from a mob-linked construction firm that was seeking business with the city. Kerik was ordered to pay $221,000 in fines and fees and faced a misdemeanor charge for failing to inform city ethics regulators about a $28,000 loan from a real estate developer in 2002. In September 2006 Kerik became embroiled in an illegal wiretapping case involving a woman who wanted evidence of her husband's adultery. Federal authorities also investigated him for violating federal tax laws, and on November 8, 2007, Kerik was charged with conspiracy, tax fraud, and making false statements. In the next two years, additional indictments were added, while others were dropped. Kerik pled guilty on November 5, 2009, and in February 2010 was sentenced to four years in prison and restitution payments of nearly $188,000. He was released from the Federal

Correctional Institution, Cumberland, in Cumberland, Maryland, in October 2013.

On February 18, 2020, Kerik was granted a presidential pardon by Donald Trump.

Stephen E. Atkins

See also: Giuliani, Rudolph William Louis "Rudy," III; World Trade Center, September 11

Suggested Reading

Allen, Mike, and Peter Baker. "On Kerik Nomination, White House Missed Red Flags." *Washington Post,* December 15, 2004, A4.

Buettner, Russ, and William K. Rashbaum. "Kerik Is Again a Figure in an Official Investigation." *New York Times,* September 28, 2006, B6.

Buffa, Dennis, Murray Weiss, and Todd Venezia. "Bernie—From a Hero to a Zero." *New York Post,* July 1, 2006, 8.

Bumiller, Elisabeth, and Erick Lipton. "Kerik's Position Was Untenable, Bush Aide Says." *New York Times,* December 12, 2004, 1.

de Borchgrave, Arnaud. "Bernard Kerik, a Life." *Pittsburgh Tribune Review,* December 8, 2004, 1.

Flynn, Kevin, et al. "A Street Cop's Rise from High School Dropout to Cabinet Nominee." *New York Times,* December 3, 2004, A26.

Gaskell, Stephanie, Jennifer Fermino, and Andy Soltis. "Heroes Rage at WTC Probe." *New York Post,* May 19, 2004, 6.

Solomon, John, and Matthew Mosk. "Ex-Partner of Giuliani May Face Charges." *Washington Post,* March 31, 2007, A1.

L

London Underground Bombings

On July 7, 2005, four suicide bombers coordinated a series of attacks on the city of London's public transportation system during the morning rush hour. Three of the bombings took place in the London Underground, and the fourth occurred on a double-decker bus. Fifty-six people were killed, including the four suicide bombers, later identified as Mohammad Sidique Khan, Shehzad Tanweer, Hasib Hussain, and Germaine Lindsay. The explosions also left more than 700 people wounded. Subsequent investigations discovered that the bombers were Islamic foreign-born immigrants living in London at the time.

The suicide bomb attacks on the London public transportation system shocked the country of Great Britain, which had yet to experience attacks by Islamic terrorists. The bombings occurred at a strategic time. The previous day, the International Olympic Committee (IOC) announced London as the site of the 2012 Summer Olympics, and the same day, world leaders met in the United Kingdom for the beginning of the G8 summit. In addition, Great Britain had recently begun the trial of a fundamentalist Islamic cleric and assumed the rotating presidency of the Council of the European Union (EU).

Following the blasts, authorities investigating the bombings received mixed reports as to the nature and cause of the explosions. Initial reports suggested that the explosions may have resulted from power grid overloads, but further evidence quickly pointed to intentional attacks. Investigations by the British intelligence branch MI5 discovered several locations in Leeds where the terrorists had created the bombs. Police raided the locations on July 12 and 13, seizing bomb-related materials. Further investigations led to arrests in March and May 2007 of a number of individuals with possible connections to the bombings, although most were later released.

On September 1, 2005, Al Jazeera released a videotaped statement made by Khan before the attacks. Another prerecorded message from Tanweer was broadcast on July 6, 2006. In the videos, which both appear to have been edited to also include remarks by Al Qaeda member Ayman al-Zawahiri, the bombers assert that attacks would continue until Britain stopped its support of the United States, Israel, and the wars in Afghanistan and Iraq. It remains unclear whether the suicide bombers acted alone or as part of a terrorist cell affiliated with Al Qaeda. On July 9, Abu Hafs al-Masri Brigades, an extremist group with ties to Al Qaeda, claimed responsibility for the attacks, although these claims have not been verified.

On July 21, 2005, terrorists attempted to detonate four more bombs on the London public transportation system. In each case, the detonators failed to ignite the bomb material, leading to no casualties. Authorities investigating the explosions tracked the men responsible for the attempted bombings and arrested all four within a week of the bombings. It remains unclear, however, whether the July 21 bombings were the work of the same terrorist cell that conducted the July 7 attacks.

In October 2010 a coroner's inquest into the bombings began, aimed at addressing the many lingering questions and concerns related to the attacks, including whether the attack might have been prevented. It determined that 52 victims had been unlawfully killed, but that the city's capability and funding of emergency medical care should be reviewed.

Spencer C. Tucker

See also: Al Qaeda; Global War on Terror; IRAQI FREEDOM, Operation

Suggested Reading

BBC News UK. "7/7 Inquest: Emergency Delays 'Did Not Cause Deaths.'" May 6, 2011. https://www.bbc.co.uk/news/uk-133 07382

Intelligence and Security Committee. *Report into the London Terrorist Attacks on 7 July 2005.* Presented in Parliament, May 2006.

Muir, Hugh, and Rosie Cowan. "Four Bombs in 50 Minutes: Britain Suffers Its Worst-Ever Terror Attack." *Guardian,* July 8, 2005.

"Tube Bombs 'Almost Simultaneous.'" BBC News, July 9, 2005.

M

Madrid Bombings

The terrorist bombing attacks in Madrid, Spain, on March 11, 2004, were also referred to as 3/11. The attacks were launched in the morning against the city's commuter train system, killing an announced 191 people and wounding 1,755 others. Later estimates, after reexamination of the remains of the victims, reduced the death toll to 190. The victims included citizens of 17 countries.

The attacks took place during the morning rush hour on four commuter trains traveling between Alcala des Henares and the Atocha Station in Madrid in an obvious effort to inflict the greatest amount of casualties possible. Thirteen bombs, hidden in backpacks, were placed on the trains, and 10 of these exploded within a two-minute period beginning at 7:37 a.m. Two of the three additional bombs were detonated by a police bomb squad, as was a suspicious package found near the Atocha Station. An additional unexploded bomb was brought intact to a police facility and later dismantled. This unexploded bomb provided evidence for the investigation and subsequent trial of the terrorists.

In the immediate aftermath of the attacks, the Spanish government blamed the attacks on Euskadi Ta Askatasuna (ETA), the Basque separatist movement that had launched terrorist attacks in the past. Investigators quickly absolved ETA of the attacks, however, and the blame shifted to the terrorist group Al Qaeda, which had perpetrated the September 11, 2001, attacks against the United States. Spanish authorities have claimed that the attackers were a loosely knit group of radical Muslims primarily from Morocco, Syria, and Algeria. A number of Spanish nationals were also involved, mainly by selling the explosives to the terrorists.

The Partido Popular (Popular Party, PP), which then formed the government of Spain, was defeated in national elections held three days later, replaced in power by the left-leaning Partido Socialista Obrero Españo (Spanish Socialist Workers' Party, PSOE). While Al Qaeda later claimed that the attacks had led to the electoral defeat, most experts agree that the PP government's clumsy handling of the aftermath of the attacks was the primary factor in the PSOE victory in the election. The PP had held only a narrow and shrinking lead in the polls prior to the attacks. The government's early declaration that the attacks were the work of the ETA had been seen by many as influenced by electoral considerations, and when the claim was quickly shown to be untrue, the government's credibility was badly damaged.

The PSOE had strongly opposed Spain's participation in the U.S.-led invasion of Iraq, which the PP had supported. Shortly after the elections the new government under Prime Minister José Luis Rodríguez Zapatero withdrew Spanish troops from the coalition in Iraq, adding some weight to the Al Qaeda assertion that its attacks had directly affected Spanish foreign policy. The precipitous Spanish troop withdrawal also led to considerable tension in U.S.-Spanish relations. As late as the 2008 U.S.

presidential elections, Republican candidate John McCain said that he would not meet with Spanish prime minister Zapatero.

A few weeks after the attacks, on April 2, 2004, an additional explosive device was found on the tracks of a high-speed rail line. The explosives had been prepared for detonation but were not connected to any detonating device. Following this further discovery, new investigations were launched, and Spanish police tracked down suspects in an area south of Madrid. During the raid to apprehend them, an explosion, apparently caused by a suicide bomb, killed seven suspects. Security officials believe that between five and eight suspects managed to escape the police that day. They have not yet been apprehended.

In all, 29 suspects—20 Moroccans and 9 Spaniards—were apprehended and charged for involvement in the attacks. Their trial began on February 15, 2007, and lasted four and a half months. The verdict, handed down on October 31, 2007, found 21 guilty of various crimes, ranging from forgery to murder. Two of the convicted terrorists were sentenced to prison terms that added up to 42,924 years, but Spanish law limits actual imprisonment to 40 years.

The court sentences did not mention any direct links between the convicted terrorists and Al Qaeda, however. While Al Qaeda may have inspired the Madrid terrorists and a connection cannot be ruled out, no irrefutable evidence has been found to connect it with the planning, financing, or execution of the Madrid attacks.

Nevertheless, the Madrid attacks may well have been the first major success for an Al Qaeda–type terrorist organization in Europe. The attacks did lead to greater cooperation between West European security services in an attempt to prevent further attacks. Yet on July 7, 2005, London suffered multiple terrorist bombings that also appear to have been independent from but inspired by Al Qaeda.

Elliot P. Chodoff

See also: Al Qaeda; Global War on Terror; IRAQI FREEDOM, Operation

Suggested Reading

Jane's Intelligence Review, August 2004. Coulsdon, Surrey, UK: Jane's, 2004.

Puniyani, Ram. *Terrorism: Facts versus Myths.* New Delhi: Pharos Media, 2007.

Von Hippel, Karin. *Europe Confronts Terrorism.* New York: Palgrave Macmillan, 2005.

Mohammed, Khalid Sheikh (1965–)

Khalid Sheikh Mohammed was the operational chief for the planning for the September 11, 2001, operation. He had been active in extremist Islamist activities with his nephew Ramzi Yousef before and after the 1993 World Trade Center bombing, but it was his role as instigator of the September 11 plot that made him notorious. Until his capture in Pakistan, he rivaled Osama bin Laden as public enemy number one in the United States.

Mohammed came from a family with strong religious and political views. He was born on April 24, 1965, in the Fahaheel neighborhood of Budu Camp, Kuwait. His father was a Muslim cleric from the Pakistani province of Baluchistan. Because of the citizenship rules of Kuwait, the family remained as guest workers instead of Kuwaiti citizens. The young Mohammed grew up in Kuwait resenting his inferior status. Mohammed was a good student and excelled in science. His father died before he graduated high school, and his elder brothers assumed responsibility for his care. Because both brothers had strong political views, they guided his political orientation, which eventually led him to join the Muslim Brotherhood at age 16. He graduated from Fahaheel Secondary School in 1983, and his brothers decided to send Mohammed to the United States to further his education. Mohammed traveled to the United States in 1983 to study mechanical engineering at Chowan College, a Baptist school in Murfreesboro, North Carolina. After a short stay there, Mohammed transferred to North Carolina Agricultural and Technical State University in Greensboro (now University of North Carolina at Greensboro). At both schools, Mohammed remained aloof from American students and American society. Most of his contacts were with other students from Arab countries.

After graduating in 1986 with a degree in mechanical engineering, Mohammed traveled to Pakistan to join the mujahideen in fighting Soviets in Afghanistan. His older brother Zahed Sheikh Mohammed was head of a Kuwaiti charity, the Committee for Islamic Appeal (Lajnat al Dawa al Islamia [LDI]), in Peshawar, Pakistan. His brother Abed worked for Abdul Rasool Sayyaf's newspaper in Peshawar. For a time Mohammed taught engineering at a local university. The three brothers worked together with Abdullah Azzam, Sayyaf, and Gulbaddin Hekmatyar to determine the strategy of the Afghan resistance. Mohammed's war experiences in Afghanistan changed his life, especially after he lost his brother Abed in the fighting late during the war, at the Battle of Jalalabad. Mohammed became secretary to the Afghan warlord Sayyaf and, through him, made the acquaintance of Osama bin Laden and other Islamist leaders.

After the end of the Afghan-Soviet War in 1989, Mohammed stayed in Pakistan, where

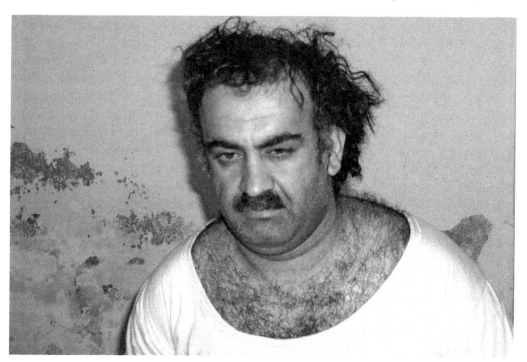

Khalid Shaikh Mohammed, upon his capture in Pakistan on March 1, 2003. (Taken by U.S. forces when KSM was captured.)

he devoted his activities to operations run against the West. When the political situation in Afghanistan deteriorated for Islamist militants, Mohammed looked elsewhere for employment. The conflict in Bosnia attracted him, and he fought with the mujahideen there in 1992. During these years, Mohammed held a number of jobs before ultimately working for the Qatari government as an engineer in its electricity headquarters.

Mohammed's first involvement in a major terrorist operation was with his nephew, Ramzi Yousef. His role in the planning of the February 26, 1993, bombing of the World Trade Center in New York City is still mostly conjecture, but it is known that he sent Yousef $660 to help build the bomb. This bombing, however, proved a disappointment: although it caused many casualties, it failed to cause the collapse of the Twin Towers or kill the hoped-for thousands. After Yousef returned to Karachi, Pakistan, he met with Mohammed. It was at one of these meetings in 1993 that Yousef and his friend, Abdul Hakim Murad, suggested a way to attack the United States. Murad, who had earned a commercial pilot license at an American commercial pilot school, proposed packing a small airplane full of explosives and dive-bombing into the Pentagon or the headquarters of the Central Intelligence Agency. Mohammed quizzed Murad about details of pilot training and the ways that such an operation might be carried out. Nothing was done at that time, but Mohammed later used this information in the September 11 plot.

Later in 1993 Mohammed contacted Hambali, the operation chief of the Indonesian Islamist terrorist group Jemaah Islamiyah. Mohammed and Yousef traveled to the Philippines to work on a plan, Operation BOJINKA, that envisaged the bombing of a dozen U.S. commercial aircraft over the Pacific during a two-day period. He also worked with Yousef to plan the assassination of Pope John Paul II during his visit to the Philippines, but a chemical mishap caused by Yousef ended this attempt. Mohammed returned to Pakistan, where he kept in touch with Yousef. Only after Yousef was captured in 1995 did Mohammed begin to make separate plans for terrorist operations, one of which was the use of commercial aircraft as terrorist weapons. However, he needed allies before undertaking such a massive operation.

American intelligence was slow to realize the importance of Mohammed in the terrorist world even as he traveled throughout the Muslim world making contacts. Evidence obtained in Yousef's apartment in Manila indicated Mohammed's association with Yousef, but nothing else was known. Beginning in 1993, Mohammed lived in Doha, Qatar, working at the Ministry of Electricity and Water. In his spare time, Mohammed raised money for terrorist groups. Enough evidence about his participation in Yousef 's activities existed that a New York grand jury issued a secret indictment against him in January 1996. Although American authorities tried to persuade Qatari officials to extradite Mohammed, the Qatari government was reluctant to do so. Efforts to mount a seizure operation were hindered by a lack of commitment on the part of the American military, the Central Intelligence Agency (CIA), and the Federal Bureau of Investigation (FBI). Eventually a half-hearted effort was made by the FBI, but Mohammed was long gone, warned by his friend Abdullah ibn Khalid, the minister of religious affairs in Qatar, that the Americans were looking for him.

Mohammed began cooperating with Al Qaeda in 1996. Bin Laden invited him to join Al Qaeda's military committee under Mohammad Atef. Mohammed was to swear loyalty (*bayat*) to bin Laden and to Al Qaeda, bringing with him connections to the Middle East and South Asia, as well as plans to attack the United States. He met with bin Laden and Atef, Al Qaeda's military commander, at bin Laden's Tora Bora mountain refuge in 1996, where Mohammed presented to them a variety of terrorist schemes, the most promising of which was the use of commercial airliners as flying bombs to use against targets in the United States. Yet, though bin Laden asked Mohammed to join Al Qaeda, Mohammed turned him down, wishing to retain his autonomy. Despite this, Mohammed developed a close working relationship with Al Qaeda. Mohammed needed Al Qaeda to supply money and martyrs for his operations even as he supplied the planning, but bin Laden was noncommittal about the plan until 1998, when he proposed that the four leaders of the plane hijackings should be two Saudis (Khalid al-Mihdhar and Nawaf al-Hazmi) and two Yemenis (Walid Mohammed bin Attash and Abu Bara al-Yemeni). This plan, however, fell apart when the two Yemenis were unable to obtain American visas. At this time no need existed for pilots—something that soon changed. This change of plans led to the later recruitment of Mohamed Atta, Ziad Jarrah, and Marwan al-Shehhi from the Hamburg Cell. American intelligence had no idea of the extent of Mohammed's growing contacts with Al Qaeda, but the FBI was offering a $2 million reward for his capture because of his role in the Manila plot.

Shortly after his 1996 meeting with bin Laden, Mohammed began recruiting operatives for a future suicide mission. His liaison with Al Qaeda's leadership was Ramzi bin al-Shibh. He briefed bin Laden and the leadership of Al Qaeda orally on his final plan for a suicide mission using commercial aircraft sometime in 1998 or 1999. By this time, Mohammed, who had sworn a loyalty oath to bin Laden, had been integrated into Al Qaeda's leadership hierarchy. Recruits for the mission were trained at the Afghan al-Matar Training Complex, where Abu Turab al-Urduni, a Jordanian trainer, taught them how to hijack planes, disarm air marshals, and use explosives. Mohammed confessed in a June 2002 interview with the Muslim journalist Yosri Fouda that the operation in the United States had been planned two-and-a-half years before it took place.

Mohammed's original plan included the hijacking of 10 aircraft and the destruction of 10 targets but was ultimately reduced to 4 targets. Once the operatives were selected and Mohamed Atta had been picked and briefed as mission leader, Mohammed watched from behind the scenes.

After September 11, Mohammed knew that he was a marked man. He eluded capture for nearly two-and-a-half years. Considerable investigation was required by American authorities before they realized just how important Mohammed was to the planning of September 11, but once his importance was realized, his capture was only a matter of time. On March 1, 2003, a joint team of Pakistani and American agents arrested Mohammed in Rawalpindi, Pakistan, seizing his computer, cell phones, and documents. For more than two-and-a-half years, American authorities held him at a remote prison site in Pakistan, where he was interrogated about his role in Al Qaeda and in the September 11 attacks. In September 2006 Mohammed was transferred to the Guantánamo Bay Detention Camp. In early March 2007 the Bush administration announced that he and others would appear before military courts which would determine whether or not they were enemy combatants; enemy combatants would appear before a military tribunal. Before the proceedings, it was reported that Mohammed had been increasingly forthcoming about his role in the September 11 plot. His confessions included myriad plots—most of which were never carried out or were failures. At his hearing at the Combatant Status Review Tribunal Hearing on March 10, 2007, Mohammed stated that he had been the organizer of the September 11 plot, justifying it as part of a war between the Islamist world and the United States. Mohammed also confessed to complicity in many other plots, among which were the 1993 World Trade Center bombing and the killing of the Jewish journalist Daniel Pearl in Pakistan—in which he claimed personal involvement only, stating that it was not related to his Al Qaeda activities. Although his open confession of participation in these terrorist acts equated to a guilty plea, Mohammed simultaneously claimed that he had been tortured.

In February 2008, military prosecutors charged Mohammed and five other Guantánamo prisoners with war crimes and murder for their roles in the September 11 attacks and said they would seek the death penalty for the six men. During his arraignment hearing before a military tribunal in Guantánamo Bay in June 2008, Mohammed declared he wanted to be put to death and viewed as a martyr. In November 2009, the Barack Obama administration announced that Mohammed and four co-conspirators would face a civilian trial in New York City. However, after that news set off a firestorm of controversy, those plans were dropped, but the case continues to progress through the legal system. In August 2019, Judge W. Shane Cohen set a tentative date of January 11, 2021, for the trial to begin. In the meantime, Mohammed is being held indefinitely under the laws of war.

Stephen E. Atkins

See also: Atta, Mohamed el-Amir Awad el-Sayed; Bin al-Shibh, Ramzi; Bin Laden, Osama; Guantánamo Bay Detention Camp; World Trade Center, September 11; World Trade Center Bombing (1993); Yousef, Ramzi Ahmed

Suggested Reading

Eggen, Dan. "9/11 Report Says Plotter Saw Self as Superterrorist." *Washington Post,* July 27, 2004, A1.

Fouda, Yosri, and Nick Fielding. *Masterminds of Terror: The Truth behind the Most Devastating Terrorist Attack the World Has Ever Seen.* New York: Arcade Publishing, 2003.

Lance, Peter. *1000 Years for Revenge: International Terrorism and the FBI; The Untold Story.* New York: ReganBooks, 2003.

McDermott, Terry. *Perfect Soldiers: The 9/11 Hijackers; Who They Were, Why They Did It.* New York: HarperCollins, 2005.

Richey, Warren. "The Self-Portrait of an Al Qaeda Leader." *Christian Science Monitor,* March 16, 2007, 1.

Soltis, Andy. "'I Did 9/11 from A to Z'—Qaeda Big's Evil Boasts & Slay-Plot Shockers at Gitmo Trial." *New York Post,* March 15, 2007, 8.

Moussaoui, Zacarias (1968–)

Zacarias Moussaoui has become infamous as the so-called 20th member of the suicide hijacking mission of September 11, 2001. He was born on May 30, 1968, in St.-Jean-de-Luz, near Narbonne, France, to Moroccan parents. His father was a successful tiler, and his mother worked in a variety of menial jobs until finding a position in the French postal system. Moussaoui's parents divorced when he was only three years old, and his mother raised him along with his older brother and two older sisters. She continued to bring up her children in France, but their upbringing was secular. During Moussaoui's youth, his family moved around France—first to a resort in the Dordogne and then to Mulhouse in Alsace before finally settling down in Narbonne. While in Mulhouse, the children spent a year in an orphanage run by the local Social Services Department. Moussaoui and his mother did not get along and had frequent and furious arguments. Things became so serious that Moussaoui left home in 1986. A good student, he easily passed his vocational baccalaureate. After passing entrance exams, he opted to study mechanical and electrical engineering at a school in Perpignon. His French girlfriend, Fanny, followed him, and they lived together. Moussaoui transferred to the University of Montpellier's Economic and Social Administration program, but he had begun to tire of school when the Persian Gulf War broke out in 1991.

The plight of Iraqi civilians and Palestinians concerned Moussaoui, and he became increasingly interested in politics. He had experienced racism in France, and his sympathy for Muslim causes was increasing. While at the University of Montpellier, he came into contact with Muslim students advocating extremist Islamist views. He made a six-month visit to London in 1992, but his stay in England proved disillusioning when he found British society intolerant and class-ridden. This experience, however, did not prevent him from returning to England, where he stayed for the next three years. He attended the South Bank University in

London, studying international business. Moussaoui earned his degree in 1995, and he moved back to Montpellier. Some time during his stay in England, Moussaoui was converted to the Wahhabi strain of Islam by the militant Islamic teacher Abu Qatada, who ran a religious community, the Four Feathers, near Baker Street in London. His behavior during visits to France and Morocco alarmed his family. Soon after his conversion, Moussaoui was convinced to join Al Qaeda by recruiters.

Between 1995 and 2001, Moussaoui's association with Al Qaeda became even closer. He received training in Afghanistan at Al Qaeda's Khaldan camp in 1998, at the same time as Mohamed Atta. Moussaoui's trainers found him enthusiastic but questioned his stability. Moussaoui was finally recruited for a future suicide mission, but little evidence exists to show that it was the September 11 plot. The Al Qaeda leadership had other plans for him, and he wanted to work on a Boeing 747 simulator, unlike the hijackers of the September 11 bombings, who trained exclusively on 757 and 767 simulators. Moussaoui's friend, Hussein al-Attas, described him "as the kind of man who believed it was acceptable to kill civilians who harmed Muslims and that he approved of the 'martyrs' who did just that."

Moussaoui entered the United States in hopes of becoming a pilot. He arrived at Chicago's O'Hare Airport on February 23, 2001, with a 90-day visa. Within days of his arrival, he began learning to fly small aircraft at the Airman Flight School in Norman, Oklahoma. He became frustrated by his lack of progress after failing the written examination, for which he blamed inexperienced instructors at the school. After looking at other pilot schools, Moussaoui contacted the Pan Am International

Flight Academy in Eagan, Minnesota, near Minneapolis, hoping to learn how to fly the huge Boeing 747-400. After only a few days of training in mid-August, the school's instructors became suspicious of Moussaoui, who showed more interest in flying than in taking off or landing. He also inquired about the protocols used for communicating with flight towers, asked about cockpit doors, and wondered how much damage a fully loaded 747 could do. After a meeting of the instructors, one volunteered to contact a friend in the Minneapolis Federal Bureau of Investigation (FBI) field office. Instead the call went to FBI special agent Harry Samit, a U.S. Navy aviation veteran and small-engine pilot who was immediately suspicious of Moussaoui.

The Minneapolis FBI field office was part of the Joint Terrorism Task Force (JTTF) system, and a brief investigation showed that Moussaoui's visa was "out of status," having expired on May 22, 2001. This led the Immigration and Naturalization Services (INS) agent in the JTTF to authorize the arrest of Moussaoui on August 16, 2001. Moussaoui refused to allow the FBI agents to search his belongings but agreed to allow them to be taken to the local INS building. Because of Moussaoui's French citizenship, the FBI requested information concerning him from French authorities, who deemed Moussaoui dangerous and conveyed this to the FBI office in Minneapolis.

The Minneapolis FBI agents wanted a search warrant to examine Moussaoui's belongings—in particular, his laptop—but ran into difficulties at FBI headquarters in Washington, DC. Two types of search warrants are possible—standard criminal search warrants and Foreign Intelligence Surveillance Act (FISA) search warrants, which are issued by a secret Foreign Intelligence Surveillance Court (FISC). FBI headquarters found insufficient cause for a criminal warrant. The agents' request for a FISA court warrant was denied because Moussaoui was not affiliated with a recognized terrorist group, even though he had contacts with Chechen rebels and close ties to Al Qaeda.

The political climate changed after September 11, and Moussaoui became a key target for retribution. American federal prosecutors charged Moussaoui with capital crimes, accusing him of six acts: (1) preparing acts of terrorism, (2) conspiracy to hijack an aircraft, (3) destruction of an aircraft, (4) use of weapons of mass destruction, (5) murder of American officials, and (6) destruction of property—even though Moussaoui had been in jail for 25 days when the events of September 11 occurred. Moreover, doubt still lingered about Moussaoui's role in the September 11 plot. The FBI had difficulty in proving that, had Moussaoui cooperated, the September 11 attacks could have been prevented.

Nevertheless, Attorney General John Ashcroft insisted that the Justice Department seek the death penalty. Opposition to this position arose within the Justice Department, because a death sentence would make plea bargaining impossible. Although Moussaoui had information about Al Qaeda, no attempt was made to extract it from him.

The trial in 2006 was a national event. Moussaoui's irrational behavior and sudden guilty plea created even more controversy. It became apparent that Moussaoui *wanted* to be martyred. During the sentencing, prosecutors argued for the death sentence, but a dubious jury handed him six life sentences without chance of parole instead, reflecting Moussaoui's role as an Al Qaeda operative who intended to commit acts of terror rather than any action he might have taken. Moussaoui is now serving his sentence at a federal maximum-security prison.

Stephen E. Atkins

See also: Al Qaeda; Federal Bureau of Investigation

Suggested Reading

Graham, Bob. *Intelligence Matters: The CIA, the FBI, Saudi Arabia, and the Failure of America's War on Terror.* New York: Random House, 2004.

Hersh, Seymour M. *Chain of Command: The Road from 9/11 to Abu Ghraib.* New York: HarperCollins, 2004.

Hersh, Seymour M. "The Twentieth Man: Has the Justice Department Mishandled the Case against Zacharias?" *New Yorker,* September 30, 2002, 56.

Joint Inquiry into Intelligence Community Activities before and after the Terrorist Attacks of September 11, 2001. *Hearings before the Select Committee on Intelligence U.S. Senate and the Permanent Select Committee on Intelligence House of Representatives,* Vol. 2. Washington, DC: U.S. Government Printing Office, 2004.

Moussaoui, Abd Samar, with Florence Bouquillat. *Zacarias, My Brother: The Making of a Terrorist.* New York: Seven Stories, 2003.

N

National Commission on Terrorist Attacks upon the United States

The creation of an independent commission to inquire into all aspects of the 9/11 attacks was prompted because of the stark limitations of earlier congressional inquiries. Congress's Joint Inquiry on Intelligence had outlined serious deficiencies in governmental intelligence-gathering and interagency cooperation, but the White House had refused to turn over documents to the investigators, citing constitutional separation of powers. Senator John McCain described the process as "slow-walked and stonewalled." A more in-depth inquiry into the policy miscalculations of the George W. Bush and Bill Clinton administrations engendered partisanship and found Republicans and Democrats attacking the other party's administration. The best way to mitigate such issues was to create an independent, bipartisan commission having unlimited access to all documents and officials.

However, conflicting interests caused delays in forming such a commission. The Bush administration was reluctant to support such a commission, fearing that it would concentrate chiefly on mistakes made during the Bush administration. Democrats feared a witch hunt for errors made during the Clinton administration. Intense pressure from the families of those killed during the attacks finally forced the creation of the commission. The survivors of the dead made it plain to all involved that they wanted an immediate investigation of the events surrounding September 11, but it was not until 14 months after the attacks that the 9/11 Commission was announced. The National Commission on Terrorist Attacks upon the United States, or the 9/11 Commission, received a mandate from the president of the United States and the U.S. Congress to investigate the facts and circumstances of the attacks on the United States that occurred on September 11, 2001. Legislative authority for this commission was given by Public Law 107-306, signed by President Bush on November 27, 2002. The five Republicans and five Democrats selected for this commission were a matter of some controversy. President Bush selected Henry Kissinger, once Richard Nixon's secretary of state, to chair the committee, and Senator Tom Daschle appointed George Mitchell, former Senate majority leader and chief negotiator of the Northern Ireland Peace Accords, as vice chair.

These appointees soon encountered political difficulties. The families of the victims confronted Kissinger about his consulting firm's clients, some of whom were suspected to be Saudis and even, possibly, the bin Laden family. Responding to pressure, the Senate Ethics Committee ruled that the members of the commission had to abide by congressional rules on the disclosure of possible conflicts of interest, which meant that Kissinger had to disclose his entire client list. He was unwilling to do so and resigned from the commission. Mitchell encountered the same problem with the client list of his law firm, so he, too, resigned from the commission. President Bush then turned to the well-respected former governor of New Jersey Thomas H. Kean and former Indiana congressman Lee H. Hamilton. Neither Kean nor Hamilton had prior dealings with each other, but they soon began to work well together.

The final members of the commission were Thomas H. Kean (chair), Lee H. Hamilton (vice chair), Richard Ben-Veniste, Fred F. Fielding, Slade Gorton, Max Cleland, John F. Lehman, Timothy J. Roemer, and James R. Thompson. Midway through the commission's deliberations, Cleland left the commission for a government job and was replaced by Bob Kerrey. In the interests of bipartisanship, Kean made Hamilton cochair.

The families of the victims maintained the momentum behind the creation of the 9/11 Commission, championing its subpoena powers by lobbying members of Congress and even the White House. These representatives formed the 12-member Family Steering Committee (FSC). Members of the FSC came mainly from four organizations: Families of September 11, Voices of September 11th, the Skyscraper Safety Campaign, and September 11th Advocates. Soon after the creation of the 9/11 Commission, representatives from the FSC met with Kean and Hamilton to express their desire for the commission to move swiftly and aggressively. They presented to Kean and Hamilton a document titled *September 11 Inquiry: Questions to Be Answered,* which consisted of 57 questions about 9/11 that reflected their greatest desire: accountability.

Almost immediately the 9/11 Commission began to work with Philip Zelikow, who had a reputation as a presidential historian and who was the director of the Miller Center of Public Affairs at the University of Virginia. Zelikow's Republican connections included work on the National Security Council of President George H. W.

Bush and on the transition team of the National Security Council of President George W. Bush. His coauthorship of a book with Condoleezza Rice on German unification, as well as his relationship with Stephen Hadley, the national security adviser, made Democratic commissioners leery of him. Members of the FSC were also unhappy with his selection and petitioned to have him removed. Both Kean and Hamilton, however, had confidence in his integrity, and he stayed. Zelikow became the mainstay of the 9/11 investigation, supervising the 80-person staff and playing a major decision-making role.

Much criticism was also directed at the composition of the 9/11 Commission staff, at least half of which was drawn from the agencies the commission was tasked to investigate. This raised worries that evidence would be looked at in lights that would exonerate the agencies and people implicated. Some critics have maintained that the evidence was cherry-picked to produce a portrayal that sat well with investigators. Again members of the FSC complained, but to no avail. Even Kean and Hamilton expected the 9/11 Commission to fail in its mission, realizing that the odds of its success were low because the political stakes were so high. Republican and Democratic members lined up together to find fault as part of a commission expected to operate on a rigid, unrealistic timeline with inadequate funds.

Although the 9/11 Commission had broad subpoena powers, it used these judiciously and only against those unwilling or unable to produce necessary documents. The most notorious offenders were the Federal Aviation Administration (FAA) and the North American Aerospace Defense Command (NORAD), both of which were so reluctant to produce documents regarding the events of September 11 that the commission was forced to subpoena documents from them. Both agencies complied with the subpoenas—which also acted as a warning to the White House to produce its own documents when required.

In its analysis of the failures to detect the September 11 conspiracy, the 9/11 Commission listed four contributing factors: (1) a "failure of imagination" to even conceive of the possibility of such an operation, (2) a "failure of capabilities" that allowed Al Qaeda to operate in the United States despite agencies designed to prevent just such activity, (3) a "failure of management" by national security leaders whose agencies neither shared information nor collaborated in their activities, and (4) a "failure of policy" by both the Clinton and Bush administrations to prioritize counterterrorism.

The 9/11 Commission not only criticized the failures leading to September 11 but also made a series of recommendations. Among these recommendations were a National Counterterrorism Center, a national intelligence director, the reform of congressional oversight of national security, reform within the Federal Bureau of Investigation (FBI), more transparent levels of information sharing between government agencies, and smoother transitions between presidential administrations. It did recognize, however, that not all of its recommendations would find approval both in the White House and in Congress.

In the course of the commission's investigations, members of the commission and its staff reviewed 2.5 million documents and interviewed more than 1,200 individuals in 10 countries. Nineteen days of public hearings and the testimony of 160 witnesses informed its investigation, but from the beginning, the commission was under pressure to achieve its objectives in a short time. Its request for an extension was greeted with little enthusiasm because the report would be produced too near to the 2004 presidential election. An extension of two months was granted, but still too little time remained to answer all the questions posed.

Despite its attempts at thoroughness, the 9/11 Commission has been subjected to severe criticism both from the inside and the outside. One of the criticisms has to do with the Able Danger controversy. Then-congressman Curt Weldon charged that the commission ignored Able Danger and its alleged identification of Mohamed Atta before September 11, but Kean and Hamilton have replied that Able Danger was brought to the commission's attention late in its deliberations. Both the commissioners and the staff concluded that none of the Able Danger materials indicated any knowledge of Atta—despite the meeting of the commission's executive director, Philip Zelikow, with Lieutenant Colonel Anthony Shaffer at Bagram Air Base in Afghanistan in late 2003, at which time Shaffer informed Zelikow of the findings of Able Danger.

Stephen E. Atkins

See also: American Airlines Flight 11; American Airlines Flight 77; Atta, Mohamed el-Amir Awad el-Sayed; Pentagon Attack; United Airlines Flight 93; United Airlines Flight 175; World Trade Center, September 11

Suggested Reading

Kean, Thomas H., Lee H. Hamilton, and Benjamin Rhodes. *Without Precedent: The Inside Story of the 9/11 Commission.* New York: Knopf, 2006.

May, Ernest R., ed. *The 9/11 Report with Related Documents.* Boston: Bedford, 2007.

Strasser, Steven ed. *The 9/11 Investigations: Staff Reports of the 9/11 Commission;*

Excerpts from the House-Senate Joint Inquiry Report on 9/11; Testimony from 14 Key Witnesses, Including Richard Clarke, George Tenet, and Condoleezza Rice. New York: PublicAffairs, 2004.

National Security Agency

The National Security Agency (NSA) is the U.S. government's electronic intelligence-gathering service. When President Harry Truman created this agency to consolidate the government's code-breaking activities, the NSA's mandate included the surveillance of both domestic and international communications, something that changed when Congress passed the Foreign Intelligence Surveillance Act (FISA) in 1978, requiring search warrants from the FISA court before granting NSA domestic wiretaps in cases of national security. Until September 11, 2001, the primary mission of the NSA was the surveillance of international communications.

The head of the NSA at the time of the 9/11 attacks was U.S. Air Force general Michael Hayden, who was director of the NSA from March 1999 to April 2005—at the time, the longest tenure in the history of the agency. Officially, his boss was George Tenet, head of the Central Intelligence Agency (CIA), but in reality the NSA was an independent agency answering to the president more than to the CIA.

Exploiting the capabilities of today's supercomputers, the NSA has learned to deal with a massive amount of intelligence-related information. International intelligence-gathering has been hidden under the code name Echelon. As reported by James Risen, the NSA has recruited personnel who were "technicians, math and linguistic geeks, and military and civilians who were bureaucratic conformists." In 1990, in its greatest success, it stole every Soviet code machine and manual.

The NSA began to target the communications of Al Qaeda leaders in the late 1990s. At that time, Al Qaeda leaders used communication systems that the NSA could monitor by using satellites and other signals technologies, as it did with transmissions from an Al Qaeda logistics center in Yemen in 1998. After word leaked out in an article in the *Washington Times* that the NSA had this capability, Al Qaeda leaders stopped using satellite cell phones and e-mail. Since then, all of Al Qaeda's communication has been in code. A problem developed in the late 1990s that affected the NSA's ability to handle its normal volume of data: the NSA's computer system, which was becoming outdated, crashed for four days in January 2000. The required upgrades cost $1 billion and were not totally in place by September 11, 2001. Even today, the NSA's attempts to overhaul its badly dated computer system have not been successful.

As the volume of Al Qaeda traffic went up, ominous conversations about "Zero Hour" made NSA and CIA analysts nervous. George Tenet, director of the CIA, warned the Bush administration that something big was going to happen—perhaps even in the United States. He communicated this to Condoleezza Rice in a meeting on July 10, 2001, but nothing came of it. Later, General Hayden was forced to explain before congressional committees why a key intercept on September 10, 2001, regarding something big scheduled for September 11, was not translated until September 12.

Within weeks of September 11, the NSA received permission from the George W. Bush administration to start the controversial "terrorist surveillance program." Although domestic surveillance does not fall under the NSA's purview, the program allowed for warrantless wiretapping and electronic surveillance of communications involving U.S. citizens as long as two conditions were met. First, at least one side of the phone call, e-mail, or text message had to be from outside the United States and, second, there had to be probable cause to believe that members of Al Qaeda or another terrorist organization were involved in the communication. These covert wiretaps were exposed to the public in a December 16, 2005, article in the *New York Times,* igniting a firestorm of controversy. Supporters argue that the president has the executive authority to override FISA regulations, while detractors maintain that the program is illegal under FISA and a violation of citizens' Fourth Amendment rights. Critics have also accused the NSA of using the program to engage in large-scale domestic surveillance unrelated to terrorism.

In the August 2006 case *ACLU v. NSA,* a U.S. district court judge ruled that the NSA's warrantless wiretapping was both illegal and unconstitutional. The U.S. Sixth Circuit Court of Appeals, however, overturned the decision on July 6, 2007. Earlier that year, on January 17, 2007, Bush's attorney general, Alberto Gonzales, announced that surveillance would only be conducted with FISA warrants. Many, however, assumed that warrantless wiretaps were still being conducted. Gonzales' replacement, Eric Holder, and other members of the Barack Obama administration have defended the legality of the warrantless wiretaps, continuing the controversy. Because of the clandestine nature of the program, it remains difficult to ascertain its full scope.

Although carried out predominantly by the CIA, it appears that the NSA assisted with the intelligence gathering that led to the May 1, 2011 (May 2 Pakistani local time), raid on the Abbottabad compound where Osama bin Laden was shot and killed by U.S. special forces.

Stephen E. Atkins

See also: Al Qaeda; Central Intelligence Agency

Suggested Reading

Barr, Bob. "Privacy . . . Now the Guard? Approve a Rollback of Bush's Power." *Atlanta Journal-Constitution,* May 2, 2007, 15A.

Gorman, Siobhan. "Management Shortcomings Seen at NSA." *Baltimore Sun,* May 6, 2007, 1A.

Graham, Bob. *Intelligence Matters: The CIA, the FBI, Saudi Arabia, and the Failure of America's War on Terror.* New York: Random House, 2004.

Risen, James. *State of War: The Secret History of the CIA and the Bush Administration.* New York: Free Press, 2006.

Woodward, Bob. *State of Denial.* New York: Simon and Schuster, 2006.

Naudet Documentary on 9/11

The Naudet brothers' documentary film on the events of September 11, 2001, was an accidental product, but it is the most accurate portrayal of the events of that day. Jules and Gédéon Naudet, who were filming a documentary about a rookie firefighter's experiences in the Fire Department City of New York (FDNY), were on location filming with Engine 7 Company, Ladder 1 Company, of the FDNY on the morning of September 11. Jules Naudet was riding with Battalion Chief Joseph Pfeifer to check out a gas leak when American Airlines Flight 11 flew overhead. Naudet turned his camera in time to record the aircraft crashing into the North Tower. Pfeifer allowed Naudet to record the rescue operations until it became too dangerous.

Meanwhile Gédéon was back at the firehouse filming the reactions of the firefighters as they prepared to head to the World Trade Center complex. He then followed the firefighters to the World Trade Center complex to film their ordeal. The Naudets were filming when the Twin Towers collapsed. Together they filmed 180 minutes, much of it considered too graphic for public consumption. The footage includes jumpers landing, a screaming woman burning from aviation fuel that poured down an elevator shaft, and the removal of Father Mychal Judge's body. Naudet and Gédéon received permission to film both the rescue attempts and the subsequent hunt for bodies.

The Naudet brothers turned their footage into a documentary with the assistance of retired New York City firefighter James Hanlon as codirector. CBS aired the film, titled simply *9/11,* and narrated by actor Robert De Niro, commercial-free on March 10, 2002. It has since been shown by CBS several times. Normally the film would have had to be edited because of the use of profanity by the participants, but a federal appeals court granted a temporary halt to the Federal Communications Commission's enforcement of its indecency rules. The film has been studied by law enforcement authorities trying to understand the sequence of events of September 11.

Stephen E. Atkins

See also: Firefighters at Ground Zero; Judge, Mychal

Suggested Reading

Gough, Paul J. "9/11 Documentary Update Exposes CBS to Indecency Laws." *Ottawa Citizen* [Canada], August 11, 2006, D7.

Peck, Renee. "On Sept. 11, Two French Filmmakers Were Shooting a Documentary about New York City Firefighters When the Unthinkable Happened." *Times-Picayune* [New Orleans], March 9, 2002, 1.

Top, David Usborne. "The Brothers Who Made Ground Zero, the Movie." *Independent* [London], February 8, 2002, 7.

New York City Police Department

The New York City Police Department (NYPD) responded en masse to the attacks of September 11, 2001. Police worked to rescue and evacuate those trapped in the World Trade Center complex and in doing so suffered their greatest casualties. They also tried to control traffic around the complex, with mixed levels of success. One major problem was the lack of coordination between the police and the firefighters, two departments that have traditionally had poor relations. Both police and firefighters tended to act independently, without coordinating with the other agency. Much of the bad feelings arose from the Fire Department City of New York (FDNY) belief that the NYPD was a political favorite, receiving more funds and personnel. Whatever the reason, the hostility between the two departments hindered operations at the World Trade Center complex on September 11.

Failures in the communication system also hindered the activities of the police. The radios refused to work around the World Trade Center, and what communication systems did work were soon overwhelmed by traffic. Police and others had to use cell phones to call family members and establish communications.

Casualties, lower among police than among the firefighters, were nevertheless high. Police lost 23 officers, including 1 woman. This loss paled beside that of the firefighters of the FDNY, but police losses were severe enough to cause a crisis of

New York City Police Department personnel at the site of the World Trade Center, October 19, 2001. (Andrea Booher/FEMA News Photo)

confidence. A demoralized police force had to be returned to normal police duties, a task that was the responsibility of Police Commissioner Bernard Kerik—who was generally successful. Kerik left office in January 2002, leaving much still to be done to reestablish the morale of the members of the NYPD. Later, when the 9/11 Commission questioned New York firefighters and police about their conduct on September 11, Kerik and the police became defensive, charging that the commission was unfairly second-guessing their actions.

Stephen E. Atkins

See also: Firefighters at Ground Zero; Health Effects of September 11; Kerik, Bernard Bailey

Suggested Reading

Lance, Peter. *1000 Years for Revenge: International Terrorism and the FBI; The Untold Story.* New York: ReganBooks, 2003.

O'Shaughnessy, Patrice. "Painful Days for Cops Who Won't Give Up." *Daily News* [New York], December 16, 2001, 28.

Smith, Dennis. *Report from Ground Zero.* New York: Viking, 2002.

Nineteen Martyrs

In parts of the Muslim world, the participants in the attacks on September 11, 2001, have been characterized as the Nineteen Martyrs. These 19 young men are revered in some areas of the Middle East, where it is believed that by giving up their lives they weakened the power of the hated United States. Yet several of the participants' families have denied that their sons were capable of such an act, and some of the families accuse the Central Intelligence Agency (CIA) of having them killed. Moreover, the identities of all but the leaders of the operation are in doubt. Reports have surfaced that some of them had entered the United States on false passports, and their names may never be known. Regardless, the 19 hijackers sought and found martyrdom, their apparent motivation the threat they believed the United States posed to Islam. They differed in the intensity of their religious beliefs, but they were united in their worldview, believing that the West had been corrupted by greed, sin, and selfishness. In contrast, they believed the Islamic world to be an oasis of faith threatened by the West— in particular, the United States. Fifteen of the 19 hailed from Saudi Arabia. They were sons of well-to-do families, and most were well educated. Their fathers' occupations ranged from supermarket owners to tribal princes.

The members of the September 11 plot arrived in the United States at different times. Mohamed Atta and the other designated pilots arrived earliest for their pilot training and served as mentors of the later arrivals. Those later arrivals entered the United States from Dubai between March and June 2001, traveling in small groups and landing at four different airports to allay suspicion. Although they arrived in the United States knowing they were part of a martyrdom mission, for reasons of operational security they were not given the details of their mission. The plan called for more than 20 hijackers, but at least 6 of the men selected for the mission were unable to

obtain visas to enter the United States. In all, the 19 terrorists entered and reentered the United States 33 times—most of that activity on the part of the 4 pilots. They flew back to Europe to consult with Al Qaeda leaders on the progress of the mission, as well as on personal business.

The leader of the 19 was Atta, who was assisted by Marwan al-Shehhi, Hani Hanjour, and Ziad Jarrah. These individuals were also the pilots of the four hijacked aircraft: Atta of American Airlines Flight 11, al-Shehhi of United Airlines Flight 175, Hanjour of American Airlines Flight 77, and Jarrah of United Airlines Flight 93. The pilots bought tickets for flights on Boeing 757s and 767s, because learning to fly these more modern models was much easier than learning to fly older aircraft. The pilots trained on simulators. Takeoffs and landings were difficult, but actually flying was relatively easy. The flight control systems made the aircraft responsive and made normal flight easy. The leadership of the plot took at least 12 intercontinental flights to check on security and plan for takeovers.

The secondary leaders of the plot were Nawaf al-Hazmi and Khalid al-Mihdhar. They had originally been selected to be pilots, but their lack of English and limited education made them poor choices. Their responsibilities then became providing logistical support. The remainder of the hijackers were muscle men sent over to the United States later, most of them from Saudi Arabia.

The 13 muscle men had been trained to hijack aircraft and provide physical support for the pilots. At Al Qaeda camps in Afghanistan, they were trained in hand-to-hand combat and taught how to assault a commercial airliner's cockpit area, giving no quarter to crew or passengers.

Each of the muscle men was assigned to a team. American Airlines Flight 11 carried

Abdul Aziz al-Omari, Wail al-Shehri, Waleed al-Shehri, and Satam al-Suqami. The team on United Airlines Flight 175 was assigned Fayez Rashid Banihammad, Ahmed al-Ghamdi, Hamza al-Ghamdi, and Mohammad al-Shehri. American Airlines Flight 77 carried Salem al-Hazmi and Majed Moqued. The United Airlines Flight 93 team received Saeed al-Ghamdi, Ahmed al-Haznawi, and Ahmed al-Nami.

In the week before September 11, the hijackers moved around the eastern coast trying to avoid suspicion. They enrolled at local gyms to stay physically fit. In the meantime, Atta and the other leaders were traveling the country on commercial airliners noting weaknesses in security. Atta's choice of Tuesday, September 11, 2001, was based on their research that led them to consider that date the best for a successful hijacking.

Because the 19 knew their mission to be one of martyrdom, each selected a name that honored an important person or event from the Golden Age of Islam, the decades that followed the death of the Prophet Muhammad. Each name was recognizable in the Muslim world and chosen for maximum mass appeal. Several made videotapes of their confessions of faith before leaving the Middle East. After their deaths, these videotapes were broadcast over the Internet. The mission and the publicity surrounding the 19 martyrs themselves made them popular figures throughout much of the Muslim world.

On the morning of September 11, each team proceeded to its assigned airport, passing through security with only minimal interference. Each team member carried box cutters, utility knives, and chemical sprays. Both box cutters and chemical sprays were prohibited items. Teams had been divided into two groups: cockpit assault and passenger security. Two members of each team,

including the designated pilot, were assigned to the cockpit assault unit and had seats near the cockpit door in the first-class section. The others were seated at the rear of the first-class section to provide security from the crew and the passengers, keeping them from interfering in the hijacking. Anyone who stood in their way was to be either killed or incapacitated.

The goal of the hijackers was to seize control of the aircraft within 15 minutes after takeoff. This goal was accomplished on American Airlines Flight 11, American Airlines Flight 77, and United Airlines Flight 175, but not on United Airlines Flight 93. Delay in seizing the aircraft, exacerbated by the time it took to reverse the aircraft's course, allowed the passengers and crew to organize resistance against the terrorists. This aircraft crashed rather than completing its mission. In the eyes of Osama bin Laden and Al Qaeda's leadership, the mission was still a success. Some in the Muslim world perceived the events of September 11 as a just response to what they considered the many transgressions of the United States against the Muslim world. Many others, however, denounced the hijackings.

Stephen E. Atkins

See also: American Airlines Flight 11; American Airlines Flight 77; Atta, Mohamed el-Amir Awad el-Sayed; United Airlines Flight 93; United Airlines Flight 175; World Trade Center

Suggested Reading

McDermott, Terry. *Perfect Soldiers: The 9/11 Hijackers; Who They Were, Why They Did It.* New York: HarperCollins, 2005.

Strasser, Steven. *The 9/11 Investigations: Staff Reports of the 9/11 Commission; Excerpts from the House-Senate Joint Inquiry Report on 9/11; Testimony from 14*

Key Witnesses, Including Richard Clarke, George Tenet, and Condoleezza Rice. New York: PublicAffairs, 2004.

North American Aerospace Defense Command

The North American Aerospace Defense Command (NORAD) has the military responsibility to defend the continental United States from enemy attacks, but on September 11, 2001, it failed. NORAD's mission includes defending the United States from foreign bombers or ballistic missiles; defending against civilian aircraft was not a part of this mission. On September 11, NORAD's radars were mostly directed outward to detect attacks from abroad. Because the Federal Aviation Administration (FAA) was responsible for domestic aviation, NORAD depended on information from the FAA, but the FAA was not a part of the infrastructure of defense against foreign attack. This gap in responsibility meant that both NORAD and the FAA lacked protocols for dealing with a scenario such as that surrounding the events of September 11.

The lack of protocols did not mean that no Standard Operating Procedures (SOP) existed between the FAA and NORAD. In the event of a hijacking the FAA was responsible for informing the Pentagon's National Military Command Center (NMCC), which would then seek approval from the secretary of defense for military assistance in the hijacking. Upon the secretary's approval, NORAD would receive orders from NMCC to scramble a flight of jets to find the aircraft and monitor it from a distance of five miles, at no time interfering with the hijacking. No guidelines were in place for dealing with a hijacking meant to end in a suicidal crash. Only a presidential

order could be given to shoot down an American commercial aircraft—an order that had to be relayed through the chain of command.

Because of a lack of coordination and information between NORAD and the FAA, the actions of NORAD turned into a morass of errors on September 11. On that date NORAD had 14 National Guard jets on standby throughout the country. Complicating the situation, NORAD was conducting three war games on September 11. One of the war games was with the Northeast Air Defense Sector (NEADS), which reduced the number of fighter jet flights available. FAA officials disregarded SOP and contacted NORAD directly. NEADS scrambled two F-15s from Otis Air National Guard Base in Massachusetts at 8:46 a.m., but the pilots had only a vague notion of their mission. They were vectored toward military-controlled airspace off Long Island. Within seconds of their takeoff, American Airlines Flight 11 crashed into the North Tower of the World Trade Center complex. Eight minutes before the F-15s arrived in New York City at 9:10 a.m., United Airlines Flight 175 crashed into the South Tower of the World Trade complex. The jets' slowness in arriving indicates that they had not traveled at their maximum speed. Even if they had arrived sooner, they had no orders to intercept the hijacked aircraft, so it is uncertain just what they could have done to prevent the second crash. Much the same can be said about the two jets of the 177th Flight Wing of the New Jersey Air National Guard in Atlantic City, New Jersey, which, though available, were never called to assist.

By 9:00 a.m. it had become apparent that the hijacking plot involved more commercial airliners. At 9:24 a flight of F-16s of the

National Guard's 119th Fighter Wing was scrambled from Langley Air Force Base in Virginia, tasked with protecting the Washington, DC, area after a report that American Airlines Flight 11 was heading in that direction. Flight 11, however, had crashed into the North Tower 40 minutes before. Lacking accurate information, the pilots of the F-15s and F-16s tried to keep visual contact with possible hijacked aircraft. Again, exactly what these pilots would have done if ordered to intercept a hijacked aircraft is unknown. Their orders were to "identify type and tail numbers of the hijacked aircraft"—nothing more.

Orders to intercept and possibly shoot down a hijacked aircraft had to be authorized by President George W. Bush. President Bush was in Sarasota, Florida, and Vice President Dick Cheney was in Washington, DC. Cheney contacted President Bush and received authorization from him to shoot down hijacked aircraft shortly after 10:00 a.m. This order did not reach NORAD until 10:31—much too late to do anything, as American Airlines Flight 77 had already crashed into the Pentagon at 9:37. It was known by the FAA at this time, however, that hijackers had seized United Airlines Flight 93, and that this airliner might be headed toward the Washington, DC, area. For some reason, this information was not transmitted by the FAA to the NMCC, which did not learn that United Airlines Flight 93 had been hijacked until after it had crashed, when they were informed at last by the Secret Service.

The shoot-down order authorization was sent to NORAD at 10:31 a.m., but the 9/11 Commission reported that this order never reached the F-15 or F-16 pilots. It was a moot point, because by the time this order would have reached the pilots, it was already too late. United Airlines Flight 93 had crashed near Shanksville, Pennsylvania, at 10:03 a.m. Shooting down an American commercial airliner would have been a traumatic experience for the pilots, even with a presidential order authorizing it. It is doubtful whether the pilots would have done so, especially if over heavily populated areas.

The confusion on September 11 extended into NORAD's record-keeping about the events of that day. So many contradictory accounts came out of NORAD that the 9/11 Commission staff had difficulty determining just what had happened. NORAD's leadership has been particularly defensive about its conduct on September 11, and so many discrepancies have appeared in its records that conspiracy theorists have used NORAD as an example of government complicity in the attacks. In fact, NORAD depended on the FAA for information, some of which proved to be both inaccurate and belated. As the 9/11 Commission pointed out, the military had "nine minutes' notice that American Airlines Flight 11 had been hijacked; two minutes' notice that an unidentified aircraft, American 77, was headed toward Washington, and no notice at all about United Airlines 175 or 93." The military, which depends heavily on contingency plans, had no contingency plan available to help NORAD handle hijackers determined to use commercial aircraft on suicide missions. Because NORAD was operating in the dark, it failed as much as any other agency in the government on that fateful day.

Stephen E. Atkins

See also: American Airlines Flight 11; American Airlines Flight 77; National Commission on Terrorist Attacks upon the United States; United Airlines Flight 93; United Airlines Flight 175

Suggested Reading

Kashurba, Glenn J. *Quiet Courage: The Definitive Account of Flight 93 and Its Aftermath.* Somerset, PA: SAJ Publishing, 2006.

Kean, Thomas H., Lee H. Hamilton, and Benjamin Rhodes. *Without Precedent: The Inside Story of the 9/11 Commission.* New York: Knopf, 2006.

Lance, Peter. *Triple Cross: How Bin Laden's Master Spy Penetrated the CIA, the Green Berets, and the FBI—and Why Patrick Fitzgerald Failed to Stop Him.* New York: ReganBooks, 2006.

Occupational Safety and Health Agency

The federal Occupational Safety and Health Agency (OSHA) arrived at the site of the World Trade Center complex on September 12, 2001. The OSHA office in World Trade Center Building Six had been destroyed along with the rest of the buildings in the complex. OSHA employees faced many of the dangers of the others at the World Trade Center complex, but all were successfully evacuated. Much like others at the site, OSHA employees had helped the injured to treatment centers and searched for survivors. When the Twin Towers collapsed, they, too, had to run for their lives. Official OSHA activity began on September 12, 2001.

OSHA monitors workplace safety. Individuals working on the debris pile at the World Trade Center site performed dangerous jobs. Sharp metal objects, unstable footing, dust, smoke, and fires all posed a danger to rescuers. OSHA officials had consulting powers but not enforcement powers; they could point out dangerous situations but had no authority to do anything but verbalize their concerns. Nevertheless, 1,000 OSHA agents appeared at the World Trade Center site during the cleanup.

OSHA also provided equipment support, distributing more than 113,000 respirators from September 13, 2001, to February 6, 2002, of which 4,000 were made available during the first few weeks after the attacks. But OSHA workers had difficulty convincing those working at the site to use the respirators. OSHA agents found that the firefighters were the most reluctant to use the respirators (although they were not alone), objecting that their sense of smell was vital to locating some remains. OSHA reported that fewer than 45 percent of Ground Zero workers wore respirators.

OSHA's main responsibility was monitoring air samples. Its agents took 3,600 bulk and air samples looking for metals, asbestos, silica, and other airborne compounds. Despite these efforts, the air around the World Trade Center site remained toxic. Most OSHA tests check for the existence of individual compounds, but the air at the World Trade Center was a chemical soup.

Stephen E. Atkins

See also: Cleanup Operations at Ground Zero; Firefighters at Ground Zero; Health Effects of September 11

Suggested Reading

Rayman, Graham. "9/11 Five Years Later; Still More Blame amid Lasting Pain." *Newsday* [New York], September 9, 2006, A6.

Stranahan, Susan Q. "The Health of Ground Zero." *Milwaukee Journal Sentinel,* January 24, 2002, 11A.

Office of Emergency Management

The Office of Emergency Management (OEM) is New York City's disaster management team, but during and after the

September 11, 2001, attacks on the World Trade Center it ceased to function effectively—not because of lack of planning or preparedness, but because its headquarters was located in the World Trade Center complex and neutralized by the attacks.

A similar type of organization, intended to handle emergencies after aircraft crashes, had been set up by the mayor of New York City, David N. Dinkins, in 1990 under the name Aviation Emergency Preparedness Working Group (AEPWG). Representatives from the Fire Department City of New York (FDNY), the New York City Police Department (NYPD), the Emergency Medical Services, and other agencies served in this group. A report from the AEPWG recommended that the various agencies practice working together and stated that they needed a single radio frequency that commanders of the agencies could share during emergencies. After several drills, the group was disbanded in 1994 when Rudolph W. Giuliani became the new mayor and established the Office of Emergency Management.

The OEM was to serve as the command-and-control center during large-scale emergencies. Its offices were on the 23rd floor in Seven World Trade Center, a 47-story building on the north side of the complex. This post had been made bomb-resistant and bulletproof and had been reinforced to be able to withstand hurricanes. It also had a reserve of 30 days' worth of food and water. The OEM operated on a 24-hour schedule and was responsible for coordinating the 68 city, state, and federal agencies, as well as the city's fire and police departments. Personnel monitored all emergency radio frequencies, and the center had a state-of-the-art communication system.

Despite support from the mayor's office, the OEM never had enough political clout to force cooperation between the FDNY and the NYPD, even though this lack of cooperation had been one of the reasons for founding the OEM. Despite the reminder of the 1993 World Trade bombing, the rivalry and distrust between the two departments remained high. Instead of bickering, they refused to communicate, exacerbating the situation by using different radio frequencies. This utter inability to communicate interdepartmentally greatly hindered evacuation operations on September 11.

The airliner crashes into the Twin Towers destroyed the ability of the OEM to operate. When the first aircraft hit the North Tower, it rendered the elaborate communications system at the OEM's headquarters in Seven World Trade Center useless. Throughout the course of the evacuations and the final collapse of the Twin Towers, OEM was effectively out of the loop. Cut off from the OEM, firefighters and police operated without coordination. Moreover, the damage to the Twin Towers extended to Seven World Trade Center, requiring the offices of the OEM to be evacuated. Later that evening, Seven World Trade Center collapsed as well.

As soon as possible, the OEM reestablished its command-and-control headquarters in a warehouse at one of the harbor piers in Manhattan. By setting up its bank of computers and establishing communications with other government agencies, the OEM was able to participate in the decision making during the World Trade Center cleanup, readying itself for any future emergencies.

After September 11, controversy arose over who had located the OEM in the World Trade Center complex. The director of OEM, Jerome M. Hauer, had recommended a site in Brooklyn, but Giuliani wanted it in

Manhattan. Hauer, with the advice of the mayor's aides, selected the World Trade Center complex. Fingerpointing about the decision has led to bitter exchanges among those who were in power at the time.

Stephen E. Atkins

See also: Department of Homeland Security; Giuliani, Rudolph William Louis "Rudy," III; World Trade Center, September 11

Suggested Reading

Ausmus, David W. *In the Midst of Chaos: My 30 Days at Ground Zero.* Victoria, British Columbia: Trafford, 2004.

Bell, J. Bowyer. *Murders on the Nile: The World Trade Center and Global Terror.* San Francisco: Encounter Books, 2003.

Dwyer, Jim, and Kevin Flynn. *102 Minutes: The Untold Story of the Fight to Survive inside the Twin Towers.* New York: Times Books, 2005.

P

Pentagon Attack

The attack on September 11, 2001, damaged the west side of the Pentagon and caused heavy loss of life. The building was built between 1941 and 1943, during World War II. As the headquarters of the United States Department of Defense, the Pentagon was an obvious target in any type of hostilities, including terrorist acts. It is considered the world's largest office building. The building is huge, covering 29 acres. Ten numbered corridors provide 17.5 miles of hallways. Although the building was constructed to house as many as 50,000 military and civilian personnel, on September 11, 2001, it had approximately 18,000 employees as well as about 2,000 nondefense support personnel working there. Its unique construction incorporates five concentric rings named A, B, C, D, and E, from the inner ring facing the courtyard (A) to the outermost ring (E).

Five terrorists seized American Airlines Flight 77 as it traveled from Dulles International Airport (outside Washington, DC) to Los Angeles, California, and they crashed it into the Pentagon. The five hijackers—Hani Hanjour, Nawaf al-Hazmi, Salem al-Hazmi, Khalid al-Mihdhar, and Majed Moqued—had little trouble passing through the Dulles checkpoint with weapons that they subsequently used to take over the aircraft. Once seated in the first-class section, they seized control of the aircraft shortly after takeoff. As air traffic controllers at Dulles tried to regain contact with the airliner, the hijackers redirected the aircraft toward the Washington, DC, area. A request was made to a

Smoke rises from the Pentagon minutes after a hijacked jetliner crashed into the building at approximately 9:30 a.m. on September 11, 2001. (United States Marine Corps)

U.S. Air Force transport for a visual sighting, and the pilot replied that he had the airliner in sight. An air traffic controller asked the C-130 pilot, Lieutenant Colonel Steve O'Brien, to monitor the airliner. He reported that the airliner was moving low and fast, and then he watched it crash into the west side of the Pentagon. The flight hit at first-floor level and penetrated three of the five rings of that section of the Pentagon.

The personnel at the Pentagon had no warning of the approaching aircraft. Many of the Pentagon workers were watching news footage on TV of the attacks on the World Trade Center complex. Several of the survivors remarked later that they talked about how vulnerable the Pentagon was to a similar type of attack. Suddenly there was a tremendous explosion. Those not killed or injured in the original explosion had to face fire and reduced visibility from the smoke. Most of those working in the Pentagon were evacuated, but those trapped in the west side of the building were unable to escape.

The key to survival was finding a safe route out of the building. Most of the rescues of the trapped or incapacitated took place in the first half-hour after the attack. Both military personnel and civilians aided hundreds of individuals badly shaken or injured. This help enabled many people to escape the building, keeping the casualty rate relatively low. Once firefighters and other professional rescue workers arrived, they began to discourage active participation by nonprofessionals because it was simply too dangerous entering a building where there were still fires and structural collapses.

Firefighting teams from the Arlington County Fire Department and other area fire departments responded to the emergency as soon as they heard the news. News of the attack came to the Arlington County Emergency Communications Center (ECC), which began broadcasting the news of the attack to various agencies and fire departments. On arriving at the Pentagon, the firefighters began fighting the fire and rescuing some of those who were trapped. Many of those rescued were severely burned. Although firefighting at the Pentagon was much easier than at the World Trade Center complex because of the Pentagon's fewer number of floors, difficulties were caused by the high-temperature fire from burning aviation fuel. It took firefighters nearly five hours to put out the fire feeding on the aviation fuel and the burning building. As soon as the fire and smoke subsided, a general search for survivors took place. There were no survivors found. Because many of the offices on the west side were undergoing renovation, the number of casualties was lower than it would have been if the offices had been occupied. The blast and fire killed 128 Pentagon personnel as well as the crew and passengers of Flight 77.

The evacuation process and firefighting were interrupted several times because of warnings about possible other airliner attacks. Most serious of these warnings concerned United Airlines Flight 93 approaching the Washington, DC, area. At each warning the Pentagon had to be evacuated. Despite these interruptions, by the end of the day on September 12 the fires had been contained.

It took 10 days after the attack for all human remains to be removed from the Pentagon. A body-recovery team of one or more Federal Bureau of Investigation (FBI) agents, one or two Federal Emergency Management Agency (FEMA) representatives, a photographer, and a four-body carrier unit from the 3rd Infantry Regiment (Old Guard) looked for remains. Each body or body part was photographed at the site. Later, cadaver-sniffing dogs were brought in to help the body-recovery teams.

Stephen E. Atkins

See also: American Airlines Flight 77 Pentagon Attack

Suggested Reading

Bernstein, Richard. *Out of the Blue: The Story of September 11, 2001, from Jihad to Ground Zero.* New York: Times Books, 2002.

Goldberg, Alfred, et al. *Pentagon 9/11.* Washington, DC: Historical Office, Office of the Secretary of Defense, 2007.

Hedges, Michael. "Workers at Pentagon Recount Horrific Scene." *Houston Chronicle,* September 12, 2001, A22.

Pilot Training for September 11

The key to the terrorist conspiracy of September 11 was pilot training. Khalid Sheikh Mohammed's original plan, as presented to Osama bin Laden and the other leaders of Al Qaeda in mid-1996, envisaged the use of aircraft as flying bombs. Mohammed's nephew, Ramzi Yousef, had proved in the 1993 World Trade Center bombing in New York City that no bomb delivered by conventional means could cause enough damage to destroy a complex as large as the World Trade Center. The use of an aircraft as a flying bomb meant that the aircraft had to be large enough to carry a huge load of aviation fuel. The only candidates for such a mission were the aircraft flown by commercial airlines. Mohammed and his planners knew that seizing a commercial aircraft was possible, but the big problem was flying the aircraft to the target. Al Qaeda knew that it could recruit intelligent, educated, and highly motivated suicide bombers, but training a handful of them to fly commercial aircraft was beyond them. Al Qaeda was forced to send a select group of Al Qaeda operatives to the United States and enroll them into commercial pilot training schools. Such training was expensive—about $30,000 per person—but Al Qaeda had the necessary funds available. An additional risk that nevertheless had to be taken was the exposure of operatives to the attention of American authorities both on entry into the United States and during their stay in the country.

The United States has a thriving commercial pilot training industry. In 2000 around 3,000 commercial flight schools operated under the auspices of the National Air Transportation Association (NATS). These schools were located around the country, often in remote areas, operating from local airstrips and often training their students in airplane hangers—about 70,000 students annually, before September 11, 2001. Local interest in pilot training is steady, but some of the more ambitious schools actively recruited students from foreign countries. These schools had an agreement with the Immigration and Naturalization Services (INS) that allowed foreign students to enter the United States on the highly coveted I-20M immigration forms designed to help foreign students acquire visas to enter the United States as vocational students. Foreign students have flocked to the United States because a commercial pilot license in Europe or the Middle East would cost as much as $100,000 to earn, in contrast to $30,000 in the United States. In Florida's 220 commercial pilot training schools in 2000, 27 percent of the students were international students.

It was easy for Al Qaeda to send a handful of its operatives to receive commercial pilot training. These operatives trained in at least 10 schools—from the Sorbi Flying Club in San Diego, California, to the Freeway Airport in Bowie, Maryland. After investigating the Airmen Flight School in Norman, Oklahoma, in July 2000 and finding it unsatisfactory, Mohamed Atta and Marwan al-Shehhi trained together at two Florida schools—Huffman Aviation in Venice, Florida, and Jones Aviation Flying Service at the Sarasota-Bradenton International Airport. After rejection by a flight instructor at the Jones Aviation Flying Service, they received most of their pilot training from Huffman Aviation. After Atta and al-Shehhi received their commercial pilot licenses in December 2000, they began renting small aircraft to fly up and down the East Coast. It was on one such trip, on December 26, 2000, that Atta abandoned his rented aircraft on the taxiway at a Miami Airport after its engine sputtered before takeoff. The Federal Aviation Administration (FAA) complained about this but did nothing about it. In January 2001, Atta and al-Shehhi took even more flying lessons at the flight school at Gwinnet County Airport, near Atlanta, Georgia.

The other pilots trained at different schools. Several of them raised the suspicions of their flight instructors because of their apparent indifference to takeoffs and landings. All they seemed to be interested in was flying aircraft. This apparent disinterest made these pilots-in-training poor candidates for commercial pilots. Only one of the hijackers, Hani Hanjour, had ambitions to be a commercial pilot, but he was so poor a pilot that no commercial aviation company would hire him. Frustrated in his ambition to be a pilot, he joined the ranks of the hijackers.

The pilot flight schools have fallen on hard times after September 11, hurt by a combination of security-related red tape, diminished enrollment, and the stigma of association with the 9/11 hijackers. Florida and its pilot schools have suffered the most, but the hard times have affected the entire industry.

Stephen E. Atkins

See also: Atta, Mohamed el-Amir Awad el-Sayed; Hanjour, Hani Saleh Husan; Shehhi, Marwan Yousef Muhammed Rashid Lekrab al-

Suggested Reading

Fainaru, Steve, and Peter Whoriskey. "Hijack Suspects Tried Many Flight Schools." *Washington Post,* September 19, 2001, A15.

Hirschman, David. "I Didn't See Evil." *Atlanta Journal-Constitution,* January 27, 2002, 1A.

Klein, Barry, Thomas C. Tobin, and Kathryn Wexler. "Florida Flight Schools Decry Rush to Regulate after Attacks." *St. Petersburg Times,* September 24, 2001, 1A.

Sharockman, Aaron. "9/11 Hijackers Practiced Here." *St. Petersburg Times,* March 31, 2006, 1A.

R

Rescorla, Cyril Richard
(1939–2001)

One of the heroes of September 11, 2001, was Cyril Richard "Rick" Rescorla. He was the vice president of security for Morgan Stanley in the South Tower of the World Trade Center. Part of his job was to conduct security drills for Morgan Stanley. After arriving at his office at 7:00 a.m. on the 44th floor of the South Tower, he was present when American Airlines 11 crashed into the North Tower. Rescorla spent the remainder of his life helping evacuate Morgan Stanley's 2,600 employees from the South Tower.

Most of Rescorla's life was spent in the military. He was born in 1939 in Hayle, Cornwall, England, and raised by his grandparents. His grandfather worked at the local power plant, and his grandmother was a housewife. He had a normal childhood and soon became a competitive rugby player. He did well in school, but the family lacked the funds to send him to a university. As soon as he finished schooling at Penzance County Grammar School at age 18, he joined the British Army in 1957, serving in an intelligence unit. His tour of duty took him to Cyprus where he fought against the Greek terrorist group Ethnikí Orgánosis Kipriakoá Agónos (EOKA). Upon leaving the British Army, he found a job as a colonial policeman in Northern Rhodesia. It was here that Rescorla met Dan Hill, an American veteran of the U.S. Army. They became lifelong friends.

Rescorla decided to immigrate to the United States in 1963. When he arrived, he contacted his friend Dan Hill. Once in the States, he joined the U.S. Army. After attending Officer Candidate School and obtaining a commission as a second lieutenant, he was sent to South Vietnam as a rifle platoon leader. He was assigned to Company B, 1st Battalion, 7th Cavalry, 1st Cavalry Division (Airmobile), where he saw combat in the Ia Drang Valley under Lieutenant Colonel Harold G. Moore. Rescorla became a battlefield legend in his unit for his bravery, and he earned the nickname "Hard Core." When the going got toughest, Rescorla would start singing Cornish songs in a baritone voice, settling everybody down. He earned a Silver Star, Bronze Stars for Valor and Meritorious Service, and a Purple Heart.

After the Vietnam War, Rescorla returned to the States. He attended the University of Oklahoma on the GI Bill. After graduating with bachelor's and master's degrees in literature, he went on to earn a law degree, also at the University of Oklahoma. Shortly after law school, in 1972, he married. In 1967 he became an American citizen. Rescorla briefly taught criminal justice at the University of South Carolina Law School. He also remained first in the Oklahoma National Guard and then in the Army Reserve, from which he retired as a colonel in 1989. Next, he turned to corporate security. His first corporate security job was with Continental Illinois National Bank and Trust Company in Chicago. He then moved to New York City to take a job with Dean Witter at the World Trade Center. After Dean Witter merged with Morgan Stanley, Rescorla was promoted to executive vice president in charge of security.

Rescorla was always concerned about the lack of security at the World Trade Center complex. After studying the security situation at the World Trade Center, Rescorla made a series of recommendations to tighten security, but these recommendations were ignored. He and fellow consultant Dan Hill were particularly concerned about the underground garage entrances, but again their warnings were ignored. They were proved right when the 1993 World Trade Center bombing took place. Rescorla believed that other terrorists would target the World Trade Center complex as well. He even envisaged that terrorists might hijack a cargo plane and load it with explosives, chemicals, or biological weapons before flying the aircraft into the World Trade Center complex or some other monumental building. It was even possible that the aircraft might have a small nuclear weapon. Based on these suspicions, Rescorla recommended that Morgan Stanley move someplace more secure and in a building only several stories high.

When nothing came of his recommendations, Rescorla began tightening security. He conducted fire and evacuation drills every other month. These drills were not popular. Rescorla also implemented a policy of the employees obeying his and his staff's announcements rather than those of the Port Authority.

Rescorla died on September 11, 2001, while evacuating Morgan Stanley staff from the South Tower. Immediately after the first plane plowed into the North Tower, he began evacuating people from the South Tower. Rescorla ignored instructions for everybody to stay where they were, believing that the North Tower might collapse. Soon afterward, another aircraft crashed into the South Tower. Rescorla made it plain to everyone that he would evacuate only when everybody else had been evacuated. He went back into the South Tower to search for stragglers. His actions meant that Morgan Stanley lost only six of its employees on September 11. While he was hunting for stragglers, the tower collapsed, killing him. His body has never been recovered.

Rescorla had earlier told his wife that if she ever wanted a memorial to him, he would be okay with a plaque at a nearby bird sanctuary called the Raptors, to be placed on two American eagle cages. This plaque is his memorial. His wife had the following words engraved on them after his name and dates: "Just like the eagle, you have spread your wings, and soared into eternity."

Stephen E. Atkins

See also: World Trade Center, September 11; World Trade Center Bombing (1993)

Suggested Reading

Bernstein, Richard. *Out of the Blue: The Story of September 11, 2001, from Jihad to Ground Zero.* New York: Times Books, 2002.

Grunwald, Michael. "Tower of Courage; On September 11, Rick Rescorla Died as He Lived: Like a Hero." *Washington Post,* October 28, 2001, F1.

Stewart, James B. *Heart of a Soldier: A Story of Love, Heroism, and September 11th.* New York: Simon and Schuster, 2002.

Yardley, Jonathan. "A Hero's Tale." *Washington Post,* September 8, 2002, T2.

S

Senate Select Committee on Intelligence and the House Permanent Select Committee on Intelligence Joint Inquiry into the Terrorist Attacks of September 11

The Select Committee on Intelligence and the House Permanent Select Committee on Intelligence Joint Inquiry into the Terrorist Attacks of September 11 was the first attempt to study intelligence failures leading up to September 11, 2001. Robert Graham, chair of the Senate Select Committee on Intelligence, and Porter Goss, chair of the House Permanent Select Committee on Intelligence, agreed on the need for a joint committee of the two houses to study intelligence gathering before September 11. For the inquiry to be successful, they agreed that it had to be bipartisan, and it would need to have the full support of the congressional leadership and the White House. Despite assurances of support, the committee ran into opposition from the Central Intelligence Agency (CIA), the Federal Bureau of Investigation (FBI), and the White House. There was also little enthusiasm in Congress; it took Congress five months to announce the inquiry and another four months before the committee began to function.

The Joint Inquiry committee finally received its mandate in early 2002, and the cochairmen Robert Graham and Porter Goss announced its beginning on February 14, 2002. It had a 10-month deadline to accomplish its task of evaluating the intelligence record before September 11, 2001. In the first months, the investigators for the Joint Inquiry began to compile evidence. Hearings began in June 2002. Those hearings in June, July, and the first half of September were held in closed sessions. In the second half of September, there were open hearings. Hearings in October alternated between open and closed. A final report of the Joint Inquiry appeared on December 10, 2002, but only 24 of the more than 800 pages were released to the public.

Eleanor Hill, a lawyer and former Pentagon inspector general, was the staff director for the committee. Hill had not been the first choice of the committee, but its first choice, L. Britt Snider, had run into difficulty because of his friendship with George Tenet, the director of the CIA. Hill was recommended by Sam Nunn, a former Georgia senator, to Senator Richard Shelby (R-Ala.). She was a partner in the law firm King and Spalding when she was offered the job working with the Joint Inquiry committee.

Hill's job was to supervise the creation of a variety of staff reports that pointed out intelligence-gathering deficiencies. Her crew had to comb through the 150,000 pages of documents from the CIA, and a like number of documents from the FBI. Most of the difficulty was in obtaining access to the documents in the first place. Members of the staff also conducted intensive interviews and attended briefings.

Hill reported to the Joint Inquiry committee on all aspects of the intelligence picture before September 11. Among her reports to the committee was one on the FBI's failure to react to the Phoenix Memo and the refusal of FBI headquarters to authorize a search warrant for Zacarias Moussaoui's possessions. She also reported that the intelligence community had received at least 12 reports of possible terrorist attacks before September 11 but that nothing had been done about them.

A controversy developed when closed-session testimony from General Michael Hayden about the National Security Agency (NSA) was leaked. The testimony related to the fact that the NSA had intercepted two Al Qaeda messages on September 10, 2001, indicating that something would happen on September 11, but these fragmentary messages were not translated until September 12, 2001. Despite the classified nature of this material, first the *Washington Times* and then CNN obtained it and publicized it widely. Other newspapers then picked up the story. Vice President Dick Cheney attacked the Joint Inquiry committee as the source of the leak and reprimanded both Goss and Graham by telephone. The leak produced negative publicity for the committee and led Goss and Graham to invite the FBI to investigate. Nothing came of the investigation, but it gave critics of the committee more ammunition. It also further clouded an already tense relationship between the inquiry and the George W. Bush administration.

Cooperation from the CIA and the FBI was minimal. Only four CIA witnesses testified, including George Tenet. None of the key FBI agents appeared before the committee. Senator Shelby complained about the lack of cooperation.

The Bush administration had doubts about the Joint Inquiry committee from the beginning, but it was particularly unhappy with the final report. The administration wanted the final report to be a validation of

its position that there was no way the attacks of September 11 could have been avoided, meaning that no one was responsible. As soon as the White House realized the Joint Inquiry committee did not subscribe to this view, all cooperation ceased.

Officials in the White House worked to block the release of the full report, wanting instead to retroactively classify parts of the material. Consequently, the issuing of the full report was delayed, and significant parts of it were classified as secret and redacted. Most notable of the blacked-out text was the section on Saudi citizens on American soil on September 11. Even the 9/11 Commission had difficulty gaining access to the full report, but in the end the report was released in its entirety.

In the final analysis the failure to obtain key documents made the 37-member Joint Inquiry committee unhappy. The staff had reviewed almost 500,000 pages of documents from intelligence agencies and other sources. Approximately 300 interviews had been conducted, and 600 people had briefed them about intelligence matters. There had been 13 closed sessions and 9 public hearings.

Once the classified report was released on December 20, 2002, the battle began on the classified parts of the report. The first agency to look at the report was the CIA, which classified whole sections of the report—including material that had already appeared in the media. This wholesale reclassification was too much for the Joint Inquiry committee's staff. In a meeting with representatives from the CIA, the FBI, and the NSA, the staff went over the report page by page, reclaiming much of the material. The final obstacle was the White House; its representatives wanted large parts of the report classified. The most notable section blacked out by the White House consisted of 27 pages that dealt with help given to the September 11 conspirators by the Saudi government. White House representatives wanted the changes to the report to be hidden, but the final unclassified version of the report has those areas shaded in black. On July 24, 2003, the final unclassified report appeared.

Although there were gaps in the report because of documents that were never produced, the Joint Inquiry committee did document the failures of U.S. intelligence agencies. Both the CIA and the FBI received special criticism. The staff of the Joint Inquiry committee did uncover new information—the Phoenix Memo, the Moussaoui debacle, warnings about possible use of aircraft as weapons, failures to monitor known Al Qaeda operatives, and lack of coordination between CIA and FBI, to name only a few. Its most important recommendation was for the creation of a cabinet-level position, director of national intelligence, to coordinate all American intelligence agencies and their activities.

Stephen E. Atkins

See also: Central Intelligence Agency; Moussaoui, Zacarias

Suggested Reading

Allen, Mike. "Bush Seeks to Restrict Hill Probes of Sept. 11." *Washington Post,* January 30, 2002, A4.

Gertz, Bill. *Breakdown: The Failure of American Intelligence to Defeat Global Terror.* Rev. ed. New York: Plume Books, 2003.

Lichtblau, Eric. "Report Details FBI's Failure on 2 Hijackers." *New York Times,* June 10, 2005, A1.

Prados, John. "Slow-Walked and Stonewalled." *Bulletin of the Atomic Scientists* 59(2) (March/April 2003): 28–37.

Priest, Dana. "FBI Leak Probe Irks Lawmakers." *Washington Post,* August 2, 2002, A1.

Risen, James. "White House Drags Its Feet on Testifying at 9/11 Panel." *New York Times,* September 13, 2002, A12.

Shehhi, Marwan Yousef Muhammed Rashid Lekrab al- (1978–2001)

Marwan Yousef Muhammed Rashid Lekrab al-Shehhi was one of the key figures in the suicide hijacking of the American aircrafts on September 11, 2001. While attending school in Hamburg, al-Shehhi attended the al-Quds Mosque and joined the Islamist extremists in the Hamburg Cell. His friendship with Mohamed Atta and their sharing of a commitment to Islamist religious views made it easy for al-Shehhi to become a member of the September 11 conspiracy. He was the hijackers' pilot for United Airlines Flight 175 that crashed into the South Tower of the World Trade Center complex on September 11, 2001.

Al-Shehhi was raised in a religious environment. He was born on May 9, 1978, and raised in Ras al-Khaimah in the United Arab Emirates (UAE). Ras al-Khaimah was one of the poorest and most conservative of the emirates. The family was a member of the Shooh Bedouin tribe. His father was the muezzin—the person who called people to pray at the mosques in Ras al-Khaimah. Good grades allowed him to attend the Emirates al-Ain University. After finishing his schooling, al-Shehhi entered the UAE Army. Soon after he entered the military and reached the rank of sergeant, the army awarded him a scholarship to further his education in Germany. His goal was to study marine engineering. The government of the UAE gave him a scholarship of $2,000 monthly with a yearly bonus of $5,000. He entered into a German-language preparatory course in Bonn, which he passed in 1996. Next he enrolled at the University of Bonn, but his father's death in 1997 caused him to fail his coursework when he took an unofficial leave to return to the UAE. Returning to Germany, al-Shehhi passed the next course in 1997. He was an average student with little ambition. One of his teachers called him "aimless and immature."

By the time al-Shehhi returned to Germany, he was becoming increasingly militant in his religious views. Unhappy with the environment in Bonn, he petitioned the UAE Army to allow him to transfer his studies to the Technical University of Hamburg-Harburg. The strict religious environment at the al-Quds Mosque satisfied his new religiosity. His friendship with Atta only increased this tendency.

By this time al-Shehhi's relationship with Atta had solidified, with Atta as the leader and al-Shehhi as a faithful follower. They had different personalities, with al-Shehhi playing the role of the joker and Atta the serious strategist. Despite his easygoing style, al-Shehhi was the acknowledged expert on Islamic scripture. Together with Ramzi Bin al-Shibh, the three were the heart and soul of the Hamburg Cell. The friends constantly debated how they could make a contribution to the Muslim cause. At first, they wanted to fight on the side of the Chechen rebels in Chechnya. But an Al Qaeda recruiter convinced them that joining Al Qaeda would be a better alternative to fighting in Chechnya. Al-Shehhi traveled with his friends to Afghanistan to train at Al Qaeda training camps.

Al-Shehhi left for Afghanistan in the fall of 1998 for training at the Al Qaeda Khalden camp. While in Kandahar, he—along with Mohamed Atta and Ziad Jarrah—met and talked with Osama bin Laden. Al-Shehhi, Atta, and Jarrah were recruited at this conversation for a special future martyrdom mission. Once they accepted the mission, Mohammad Atef outlined the basic outlines of the September 11 plot. Returning to Germany, al-Shehhi joined with Atta and al-Shibh in working at a warehouse, packing crates of computers for shipping. Never excited about his education, al-Shehhi stopped going to class, and the school dropped him as a student in December 2000.

Al-Shehhi became the number-two man behind Atta in the September 11 plot. He arrived in the United States separately from Atta, but they kept in touch. They trained together in Florida. Although al-Shehhi was never a skilled pilot, he was able to pilot United Airlines Flight 175 into the South Tower on September 11, 2001.

Stephen E. Atkins

See also: American Airlines Flight 11; Atta, Mohamed el-Amir Awad el-Sayed; Bin al-Shibh, Ramzi; Hamburg Cell; World Trade Center

Suggested Reading

Aust, Stefan, et al. *Inside 9/11: What Really Happened.* New York: St. Martin's, 2001.

Corbin, Jane. *Al Qaeda: The Terror Network That Threatens the World.* New York: Thunder's Mouth, 2002.

McDermott, Terry. *Perfect Soldiers: The 9/11 Hijackers; Who They Were, Why They Did It.* New York: HarperCollins, 2005.

T

Taliban

The first casualty of the American reaction to the September 11, 2001, attacks was the Taliban regime in Afghanistan. Mohammed Mullah Omar founded the Taliban in the spring of 1994 in reaction to the feuding among Afghan warlords, and he remained its head until the Northern Alliance, with the assistance of the United States and other coalition nations, overthrew the Taliban regime in late 2001. It was Omar's alliance with Osama bin Laden and the sponsorship of Al Qaeda training camps that led to the overthrow of the Taliban.

Omar was born in 1959 into a poor Pashtun family in the small village of Nodeh near Kandahar, Afghanistan. His father was a landless peasant belonging to the Pashtun Hotak tribe of the Ghilzai branch of the Pashtuns. His early death left Omar in the hands of relatives. Omar studied at an Islamic school in Kandahar, but he never graduated from it. This failure to graduate did not prevent him from opening a madrasah (religious school) in Singhesar, a village near Kandahar.

Shortly after fighting broke out between the Soviet army and the Afghans, Omar joined the mujahideen. He served in the ranks of the Younis Khalis' Brigade of the Islamic Party. Omar was in the middle of heavy fighting, and he suffered four wounds, including a shrapnel wound that caused the loss of his right eye. His combat experience and his wound increased his prestige among the Afghan Islamists because it proved that he had suffered for the Muslim cause. After the end of the war in 1989, Omar returned to his religious school.

Omar remained at his school until he became enraged by the conduct of an oppressive warlord who had raped two young women. He gathered a group of religious students (*taliban*), and they hanged the warlord. Pakistani authorities in the Pakistani Inter-Services Intelligence (ISI) noted Omar's growing popularity among the Pashtuns after this act, and they decided to give military aid to Omar and his Taliban forces. In the March 1996 council of Afghanistan's religious leaders at Kandahar, Omar was selected to be the head of the Taliban—commander of the faithful. Using this religious authority, along with financial and military aid from Pakistan and Saudi Arabia, Omar and his Taliban forces were strong enough militarily on September 27, 1996, to seize Kabul and control most of Afghanistan.

After the triumph of the Taliban, Omar's strict interpretation of the Quran led him to impose the most severe religious restrictions on the Afghan population. The Taliban had difficulty ruling Afghanistan because its members preferred to focus on religion rather than politics or ways to run a government. Consequently, it was easy to turn to the Quran to rule. The Taliban regime issued a series of rules. Men were subjected to compulsory praying, and they were required to grow beards and wear turbans. With only a few exceptions, women lost all rights to hold jobs outside the home, and they could appear in public only when completely covered from head to foot and in the company of a male relative. Art, dancing, music, and television were forbidden. All secular education ended immediately, and boys were required to attend religious schools. Schooling for girls ended entirely. Criminals faced execution or mutilation for their crimes following the laws laid down in the Quran.

Omar had his Islamist Taliban regime firmly in control of most of Afghanistan, but his forces were still trying to defeat the anti-Taliban coalition of the Northern Alliance in the northern area of Afghanistan. For this the Taliban needed an ally, and bin Laden and Al Qaeda were available. Bin Laden had settled in Afghanistan in May 1996 after leaving Sudan, and his Al Qaeda network had been placed at the disposal of the Taliban regime. To consolidate his relationship with the Taliban, bin Laden swore an oath of allegiance (*bayat*) to Mullah Omar. Al Qaeda forces fought alongside Taliban forces in the war against the Northern Alliance. In return, the Taliban allowed bin Laden to build training camps to train Al Qaeda operatives.

Omar refused requests by the United States to hand bin Laden over after the September 11, 2001, attacks. In response, the United States and its North Atlantic Treaty Organization (NATO) allies joined with the Northern Alliance in fighting against the Taliban. During the struggle, many local pro-Taliban leaders switched sides. Despite the loss of its most important military leader in the Al Qaeda assassination of General Ahmed Shah Masoud, the Northern Alliance was able to overthrow the Taliban regime. Taliban forces retreated from Kabul on November 12, Jalalabad on November 13, and Kandahar by early December. Omar and his followers fled to neighboring Pakistan, where they found support among various tribal groups. Since that time, the name "Taliban" has been used to refer to both Omar's original group and, more generally, to the other factions fighting alongside the exiled regime.

Although U.S. and coalition forces easily toppled the Taliban regime, they have not been able to eradicate its members or establish lasting stability in the region. Taliban forces continue to engage in an ever-worsening guerrilla war that by October 2010 had claimed the lives of more than 750 U.S. troops and wounded thousands of others. Coalition forces have countered these attacks with targeted missile strikes aimed at Taliban leaders and strongholds and carried out by special operations forces or unmanned Predator drones. Rising numbers of civilian casualties from these airstrikes, as well as the destruction of opium poppy fields (a major funding source for the Taliban but also the economic livelihood for many rural farmers in Afghanistan) has led to a resurgence in support for the Taliban.

In late 2009, President Barack Obama announced that the United States would begin a troop surge in Afghanistan similar to that used in Iraq, with the goal of definitively ending the Taliban and Al Qaeda insurgency. In January 2010, Taliban leaders suggested that the group was ready to break with Al Qaeda in order to bring about peace in Afghanistan. Despite these military and diplomatic measures, both the situation in Afghanistan and the final fate of the Taliban remain uncertain. The Taliban insurgency against Afghan National Security Forces and NATO forces has continued since that time. A peace agreement between the Taliban and the United States was reached in February 2020, but it remains uncertain if this agreement will last.

Stephen E. Atkins

See also: Al Qaeda; Bin Laden, Osama; ENDURING FREEDOM, Operation; Zawahiri, Ayman al-

Suggested Reading

Atwan, Abdel Bari. *The Secret History of Al Qaeda*. Berkeley: University of California Press, 2006.

Gohari, M. J. The *Taliban: Ascent to Power*. Oxford: Oxford University Press, 1999.

Marsden, Peter. The *Taliban: War and Religion in Afghanistan*. Rev. ed. London: Zed Books, 2002.

Rashid, Ahmed. *Taliban: Islam, Oil and the New Great Game in Central Asia*. London: Tauris, 2002.

U

United Airlines Flight 93

United Airlines Flight 93's Boeing 757-222 was the fourth aircraft hijacked by Al Qaeda hijackers on September 11, 2001. It took off from Newark International Airport at 8:43 a.m. bound for San Francisco International Airport. Normal flight time was six hours. The flight was nearly 45 minutes late for its scheduled takeoff time of 8:01 a.m. On board were 2 pilots, Captain Jason M. Dahl and First Officer LeRoy Homer; a crew of 5 flight attendants; and 37 passengers (including the 4 hijackers). The plane held 11,489 gallons of aviation fuel.

The hijack team had little difficulty passing security. Security checkpoints at Newark International Airport were operated by Argenbright Security under contract to United Airlines. Only two of the four hijackers had luggage and only one of them triggered the CAPPS (Computer-Assisted Passenger Prescreening System) process—Ahmed al-Haznawi's luggage was checked for explosives.

This hijack team was the smallest of the four. Ziad Jarrah was the team leader and designated pilot. He sat in first-class seat 1B, nearest the cockpit door. Other members of the team, Saeed al-Ghamdi, Ahmed al-Haznawi, and Ahmed al-Nami, were in seats 3C, 3D, and 6B, respectively. The hijackers seized control of the aircraft at 9:28 a.m., just minutes after the pilot received a warning about possible cockpit invasions on the cockpit computer device ACARS (Aircraft Communications and Reporting System). The cockpit door was no obstacle, taking only about 150 pounds of pressure to knock down. In addition, the flight attendants had keys to the cockpit door—another means of access to the cockpit.

Exactly how the hijackers gained access to the cockpit will never be known, but they took control relatively easily. They probably took a key to the cockpit from the flight attendant in first class. Within minutes of the assault, the hijackers had complete control of the aircraft. Both pilots were down; either killed or seriously incapacitated. Ahmed al-Haznawi, Saeed al-Ghamdi, and Ahmed al-Nami took turns controlling the 33 passengers and 5 flight attendants. Matters were complicated by having about a dozen passengers in the first-class section, with the rest seated in the back of the plane. Unlike the other teams, these hijackers were lenient on passenger discipline. After injuring one of the passengers, the hijackers controlled the others and the crew by threatening them with a bomb. To keep discontent down, they encouraged passengers and crew to contact their families by cell phone. Passengers made more than two dozen phone calls. This relaxed style came back to haunt the hijackers, since passengers who contacted family members learned that three other aircraft had been hijacked and had been turned into flying bombs.

As passengers began to realize there was no possibility of survival, plans circulated among some of the more aggressive men on board to attack the hijackers and regain control of the aircraft. By this time the passengers suspected that the hijackers had no bomb. About a dozen of them had experience in action sports, including football, rugby, and judo. Todd Beamer, Mark Bingham, Tom Burnett, Jeremy Glick, and several others decided to wait until the aircraft cleared populated areas to begin their attack. They were under no illusion about their probable fate, and showed extraordinary courage and compassion for others by waiting for the aircraft to fly over a rural area. They had other allies in CeeCee Ross-Lyles, one of the flight attendants, who was a former police officer; Rich Guadago, an enforcement officer with the California Fish and Wildlife Service; Linda Gronlund, a lawyer who had a brown belt in karate; and William Cashman, a former paratrooper with the 101st Airborne. Finally, Don Greene, vice president of Safe Flight Instrument Group, was a pilot with experience in single-engine aircraft, who could follow instructions to land the aircraft.

The passengers waited for their opportunity. In the meantime, flight attendant Sandy Bradshaw started boiling water to be used against the hijackers. Sometime around 10:00 a.m. the passengers attacked the hijackers using a food tray container to smash into the cockpit area. Earlier the hijackers had all retreated into the cockpit area. A voice recording from the black box (cockpit data recorder) indicated the fierce nature of the struggle. For the next seven minutes the outcome was in doubt.

Jarrah was the pilot, and his contingency plan was to crash the aircraft if it seemed as though the hijackers would lose control of the plane. Evidently this is what happened; the aircraft crashed upside down at a 45-degree angle, creating a crater 30 feet or more in diameter. The plane crashed in a reclaimed mining area, where the ground was relatively soft, and plunged deep into the ground. The fuel tanks exploded, leaving a blackened crater. Smoke from the explosion allowed local volunteer authorities to find the site soon after the crash. The crash was reported by numerous witnesses, and a visual inspection from a passing unarmed Air National Guard C-130H cargo jet on a mission from Washington, DC, to Minnesota confirmed the crash site.

The violence of the crash left no survivors. The black box was excavated 15 feet into the crater, and the cockpit voice recorder was found 25 feet down. Only body parts were recovered. Sixty percent of the recovered remains were identified by a combination of fingerprint verification, dental records, and DNA analysis.

In commercial air disasters the National Transportation Safety Board (NTSB) handles investigations, but because this was a case of air piracy, the Federal Bureau of Investigation (FBI) assumed control although the Bureau of Alcohol, Tobacco, Firearms and Explosives (ATF); the NTSB; and the Pennsylvania State Police also assisted. Nothing could be done at the site, however, without the permission of the FBI. Early in the investigation 2,000 people worked at the site daily.

The probable target of Flight 93 was the U.S. Capitol. Earlier meetings by Al Qaeda leaders had determined that the White House would present navigational problems. They had preferred that the White House be the target, but the Capitol was a target more easily recognized by inexperienced navigators.

Stephen E. Atkins

See also: Beamer, Todd Morgan; Burnett, Thomas Edward; Jarrah, Ziad Samir

Suggested Reading

Aust, Stefan, et al. *Inside 9/11: What Really Happened.* New York: St. Martin's, 2001.

Beamer, Lisa, and Ken Abraham. *Let's Roll! Ordinary People, Extraordinary Courage.* Wheaton, IL: Tyndale House, 2002.

Kashuba, Glenn J. *Quiet Courage: The Definitive Account of Flight 93 and Its Aftermath.* Somerset, PA: SAJ, 2006.

Longman, Jere. *Among the Heroes: United Flight 93 and the Passengers and Crew Who Fought Back.* New York: Perennial, 2003.

9/11 Commission. *The 9/11 Commission Report: Final Report of the National Commission on Terrorist Attack upon the United States.* New York: Norton, 2004.

Trento, Susan B., and Joseph J. Trento. *Unsafe at Any Altitude: Failed Terrorism Investigations, Scapegoating 9/11, and the Shocking Truth about Aviation Security Today.* Hanover, NH: Steerforth, 2006.

United Airlines Flight 175

Terrorists gained control of the Boeing 767-222 of United Airlines Flight 175 on September 11, 2001, and crashed it into the South Tower of the World Trade Center in New York City. Although this flight was scheduled to leave at 7:59 a.m., it left Logan International Airport at 8:15 a.m., with Los Angeles International Airport its destination. The pilot was Captain Victor Saracini, a 51-year-old U.S. Navy veteran pilot, and the first officer was Michael Horrocks. On board with the two pilots were 7 flight attendants and 56 passengers. The plane held 23,980 gallons of aviation fuel. Shortly after takeoff, traffic controllers asked Saracini whether he could see American Airlines Flight 11. After he replied affirmatively, the pilots were ordered to maintain distance from the hijacked aircraft.

Among the 56 passengers on board were 5 members of an Al Qaeda terrorist team. The leader of this hijack team and its pilot was Marwan al-Shehhi. Other members of the team were Fayez Rashid Ahmed Hassan al-Qadi Banihammad, Ahmed al-Ghamdi, Hamza al-Ghamdi, and Mohand al-Shehri. The hijackers had little difficulty passing through security. The security checkpoint at Logan International Airport for United Airlines was staffed by personnel from Huntleigh USA. The hijackers had purchased tickets in the first-class section to be close to the cockpit. Much as in the takeover of American Airlines Flight 11, the terrorists organized themselves into sections: two were near the cockpit (in seats 2A and 2B), pilot al-Shehhi was in seat 6C, and the other two sat near the passenger section (in seats 9C and 9D).

The hijackers seized control of the aircraft sometime around 8:47 a.m. They used knives and mace to subdue the pilots and crew, and then killed the pilots and at least one flight attendant. The hijackers then herded the crew and passengers toward the rear of the aircraft, assuring them everything would be okay. They lulled the passengers into thinking that the plane would land someplace safely and that the hijackers would use them as hostages in negotiations. Not all passengers believed this. One passenger, Peter Hanson, called his father in Easton, Connecticut, and reported the hijackers' takeover. One of the flight attendants also reported the hijacking to the United Airlines office in San Francisco.

Al-Shehhi turned the aircraft around and headed it toward the New York City area; air traffic controllers lost contact with the plane. The passengers became concerned because of the aircraft's jerky movements. At this point some of the passengers considered storming the cockpit to regain control of the plane, but they did not have enough time. At 9:03 a.m. United Airlines Flight 175 slammed into the South Tower of the World Trade Center complex. The aircraft hit between floors 78 and 84. Because the aircraft hit at greater speed than American Airlines Flight 11 had hit the North Tower, the South Tower was more severely damaged than the North Tower had been. Consequently, the South Tower collapsed before the North Tower. There were no survivors on United Flight 175.

Stephen E. Atkins

See also: World Trade Center, September 11

Suggested Reading

Aust, Stefan, et al. *Inside 9/11: What Really Happened.* New York: St. Martin's, 2001.

9/11 Commission. *The 9/11 Commission Report: Final Report of the National Commission on Terrorist Attacks upon the United States.* New York: Norton, 2004.

USA PATRIOT Act

One of the first post–September 11, 2001 legislative outcomes was the adoption of the USA PATRIOT (Uniting and Strengthening America by Providing Appropriate Tools Required to Intercept and Obstruct Terrorism) Act. The intent of this legislation was to plug holes in domestic intelligence gathering considered to have developed over previous decades. The legislation was controversial because it dropped many of the safeguards that Americans had come to expect for protection against government interference in their private affairs.

The USA PATRIOT Act moved through Congress to the White House quickly. In an immediate reaction to the events of September 11, the USA PATRIOT Act was approved in the Senate on October 11, 2001, by a vote of 96 to 1. On October 12, 2001, the House of Representatives approved it with a vote of 337 to 79. The act became law when President George W. Bush signed it on October 26, 2001. Rarely has legislation moved through Congress and been signed into law with such speed. Critics have charged that adoption was too hasty, allowing the Department of Justice under Attorney General John Ashcroft to throw provisions defeated during the Bill Clinton administration into a package passed with few members of Congress thoroughly understanding it.

Provisions of the original act were controversial for greatly expanding the power of government, with few checks and balances. The act expanded the range of crimes that could be tracked by government agencies using electronic surveillance. Federal authorities were granted authority to use roving wiretaps on any phone that a suspected terrorist might be expected to use. Law enforcement officers could now conduct searches of suspects without notifying them until later, a tactic that became known as a sneak-and-peek operation. This particular type of search had previously been used against organized crime figures and major drug dealers. Now Federal Bureau of Investigation (FBI) agents could obtain secret court orders to search such personal records as business, medical, library, and other files without probable cause in potential terrorism cases. The act made it a federal crime to harbor a terrorist. It also increased criminal penalties for a laundry list of offenses, ranging from conspiracy to commit terrorism to interference with a flight crew. Search warrants became easy to obtain in terrorist-related investigations. The attorney general was authorized to detain foreign terrorism suspects for a full week without initiating any type of legal proceeding or having to show cause. Finally, the law provided for new financial and legal tools to end international money laundering. The only restriction on this law was that its surveillance and wiretap provisions were required to be renewed in 2005.

Critics of the USA PATRIOT Act have come from both ends of the political

President George W. Bush signs the USA PATRIOT Act during a ceremony in the White House on October 26, 2001. (The White House)

spectrum. Among the leading critics has been the American Civil Liberties Union (ACLU). A second leading critic has been the oldest conservative grassroots lobbying organization in the country, the American Conservative Union (ACU). The ACLU's opposition is based on the argument that the law violates rights to privacy; in contrast, the ACU's opposition stems from its belief in the need to limit federal authority. Both organizations are hesitant about the use of antiterrorism investigations to charge American citizens with crimes unrelated to terrorism. The USA PATRIOT Act has been used to investigate everything from murder to child pornography. Together the ACLU and ACU have lobbied to amend the USA PATRIOT Act to ensure protection for civil liberties.

Two other critics of the USA PATRIOT Act have been business interests and librarians. Business interests object to the act's anti–money-laundering provisions. These provisions were intended to prevent, detect, and prosecute money laundering and the financing of terrorism, and required banks and other financial institutions to establish programs to monitor financial activities. Fines and prison sentences are the penalties for noncompliance with money-laundering restrictions, and representatives of financial institutions have complained about the cost of compliance.

Librarians have challenged the right of FBI investigators to inspect library records, with the American Library Association (ALA) having initiated several lawsuits against this provision. Besides objecting to the access given the FBI to inspect individuals' library records, librarians also oppose the act's prohibition against informing patrons that their records are the subject of a search. Most court fights to defeat the issuance of National

Security Letters (the subpoenas for records, which do not require a judge's approval) have been unsuccessful, but the public's negative opinion of the practice has deterred the FBI from using it except in rare cases.

Supporters of the USA PATRIOT Act have maintained that its restrictions are necessary to fight the war against terrorism, and favor even greater restrictions if they prevent the conduct of terror operations on American soil. The act is required to be periodically renewed, and supporters consider it a necessity as long as terrorist threats continue.

Despite opposition to several of its provisions, the USA PATRIOT Act was renewed on March 7, 2006. With amendments to address a few objections to it, the act was approved in the Senate by a vote of 95 to 4, and in the House by 280 to 138. One amendment excluded libraries that function in a "traditional capacity" from having to furnish the records sought in a National Security Letter. Another amendment gave persons subpoenaed by the Foreign Intelligence Surveillance Act (FISA) Court the right to challenge the nondisclosure, or gag order, requirement of the subpoena. Finally, two of the act's provisions—the authority of the FBI to conduct roving wiretaps and the power of the government to seize business records with the FISA Court's approval— were constrained by a sunset requirement and were set to expire on December 31, 2009. In February 2010, however, the House of Representatives and Senate approved a one-year extension on these provisions, as well as a third that allowed for surveillance of non-U.S. citizens engaged in terrorism but not part of a recognized terrorist organization. On February 27, President Barack Obama signed the extensions into law. The provisions of the USA PATRIOT Act have been largely re-authorized since then, but it expired on March 15, 2020, when Congress failed to come to an agreement.

Stephen E. Atkins

See also: Bush Administration; Foreign Intelligence Surveillance Act of 1978

Suggested Reading

Babington, Charles. "Congress Votes to Renew Patriot Act, with Changes." *Washington Post,* March 8, 2006, A3.

Baker, Stewart A. *Patriot Debates: Experts Debate the USA Patriot Act.* New York: American Bar Association, 2005.

Ball, Howard, and Mildred Vasan, eds. *The USA PATRIOT Act: A Reference Handbook.* Santa Barbara, CA: ABC-CLIO, 2004.

Etzioni, Amitai. *How Patriotic Is the PATRIOT Act?* New York: Routledge, 2004.

Leone, Richard C., and Greg Anriq, eds. *The War on Our Freedoms: Civil Liberties in the Age of Terrorism.* New York: PublicAffairs, 2003.

Rush, Paul. "Patriot Act Forges Unlikely Alliance." *Insight on the News,* September 29, 2003, 26.

Yoo, John. *War by Other Means: An Insider's Account of the War on Terror.* New York: Atlantic Monthly Press, 2006.

V

Victims' Compensation Fund

The Victims' Compensation Fund (VCF) was a program allowing the government to partially compensate 9/11 victims with a monetary award. It covered both economic and noneconomic damages, and came in the aftermath of a $15 billion allocation from Congress to save the airline industry from bankruptcy. Members of Congress decided that it would not be prudent to assist the airline industry while ignoring the 9/11 families who had lost loved ones. Another reason for the VCF was to protect the airline companies from costly lawsuits. To do this, Congress set a cap of $1.6 million for each family. But this cap was later raised to cope with problems with the cap. In the final analysis the average award was $1.8 million.

The administrator of the Victim's Compensation Fund was attorney Kenneth Feinberg. Feinberg soon became unpopular with 9/11 families for having promised greater awards than were granted and for his slowness in responding to victims' families. Some of this criticism was unjust because he was in charge of a bureaucracy that took time to calculate awards. Feinberg had an aggressive attitude, arguing that the 9/11 families should join the VCF because they could not sue any party other than the planners of the attacks, which enraged some of the families. Feinberg served without pay and was glad to return to private practice at the end of the process.

The victims' families were slow to sign up for the VCF. Part of their hesitation was in gauging whether it was wiser to sign up

for the VCF than to privately pursue action in the courts. It soon became apparent that the families of those who died in the airliners were more likely to succeed in court than were the families of those who died on the ground. Additionally, action in court would be a long-term process with uncertain results, whereas the VCF offered almost immediate financial help with none of the uncertainty of the courts.

The families whose members had held higher-paying jobs were among the most unhappy with the VCF. Many of the victims in the Twin Towers had high-paying jobs, earning more in five years than the amount projected to be awarded to their families— the families of victims of high net worth were initially awarded an amount equivalent to about 10 cents on the dollar of their salaries. Moreover, life insurance and pension payments counted against the final settlement. Finally, the VCF deducted Social Security payments to children in the final settlement. In the end the U.S. government made it plain that it was a take-it-or-leave-it proposition.

Because the Victims' Compensation Fund was financed by U.S. taxpayers, it became controversial. Many people attacked the 9/11 families for being greedy. This backlash caused much anguish among the families of the 9/11 victims. Some of the families became so angry that they attacked the VCF and Feinberg. When it became apparent that lawyers were reluctant to press their claims in court after being pressured by leaders in the legal profession, some of the leaders of the 9/11 families movement began organizing a lobby group. The Jersey Girls—widows of those killed in the North Tower on September 11—were active in this movement.

The work of the Victims' Compensation Fund ended on its deadline of December 22, 2003. It paid out its first claim on August 22, 2002, and its final payment went out in early January 2005. More than $7 billion went to the survivors of 2,880 people who were killed and to 2,680 people who were injured in the attacks or rescue efforts that followed. Families of the people killed collected awards averaging more than $2 million, and the injured drew payouts averaging $400,000. It cost the government $86.9 million to administer the fund. Eighty families opted out of the VCF in order to privately sue the airlines and the Federal Aviation Administration (FAA). Thirteen families chose to simply ignore the VCF altogether—from grief or for other reasons.

The VCF was reinstituted in October 2011 to fulfill the James Zadroga 9/11 Health and Compensation Act to address the continuing health effects on first responders. It was reauthorized in 2015 and permanently authorized in July 2019.

Stephen E. Atkins

See also: Families of Victims of September 11; Health Effects of September 11

Suggested Reading

Breitweiser, Kristen. *Wake-Up Call: The Political Education of a 9/11 Widow.* New York: Warner Books.

Chen, David W. "Victims' Kin Find Fault with Overseer of 9/11 Fund." *New York Times,* November 13, 2002, B1.

Kasindorf, Martin. "Compensation Battles Inflict New Wounds on 9/11 Families." *USA Today,* January 19, 2004, 1A.

Kasindorf, Martin. "9/11 Families Filing Claims as Deadline Nears." *USA Today,* December 19, 2003, 1.

Lee, Christopher. "Report on Sept. 11 Fund Is Released." *Washington Post,* November 18, 2004, A3.

Mueller, Mark. "For Some, 9/11 Fund Is No Compensation." *Star-Ledger* [Newark, NJ], November 21, 2004, 3.

World Trade Center

The World Trade Center was one of the signature complexes in New York City. It was a complex of seven buildings on a 16-acre tract in the lower end of Manhattan on a superblock bounded by Vesey, Liberty, Church, and West Streets, about three blocks north of the New York Stock Exchange. Nelson and David Rockefeller had proposed such a complex in the 1950s as a way to revitalize lower Manhattan. The Port Authority of New York and New Jersey constructed and operated the complex. The U.S. architect was Minoru Yamasaki, assisted by Antonio Brittiochi and the architecture firm of Emery Roth and Sons, which handled the production work; the Worthington, Skilling, Helle, and Jackson firm served as project engineers. Yamasaki designed a complex with twin towers and three lower-rise structures. His design was selected over those of a dozen other American architects. The North Tower had a height of 1,368 feet and the South Tower 1,362 feet, making them the tallest buildings in the world—until Chicago's Sears Tower surpassed them both in 1974.

Construction of the World Trade Center complex took more than a decade to finish. The groundbreaking was on August 5, 1966. One World Trade Center (North Tower complex) was open to its first tenants late in 1970, although its top floors remained uncompleted until 1972. Two World Trade Center (the South Tower complex) was not finished until 1973. The ribbon-cutting ceremony took place on April 4, 1973.

It cost an estimated $1.5 billion to construct the World Trade Center complex. Because the complex was built on six acres of landfill, the foundation for each tower had to be extended more than 70 feet below ground level, to rest on solid bedrock. It took 200,000 tons of steel, and controversy developed over the fireproofing of the steel.

The World Trade Center complex was immense. This complex was in the middle of New York City's financial district. Each of the towers had 110 stories. The complex contained 13.4 million square feet of office space—enough to house 50,000 office employees working for 438 companies from 28 countries. There were 21,800 windows. To provide access to the office space and other operations, each tower had 104 passenger elevators. In each tower there were also three staircases to be used in case of emergencies.

The World Trade Center complex was essentially a commercial site, but it was also a popular tourist destination. Around 140,000 tourists visited the World Trade Center complex daily to take advantage of its many amenities. In comparison, about 50,000 employees worked in the complex on any given workday. The four-star restaurant, Windows on the World, on the 107th floor of the North Tower was popular, not only for its food but also because of the view. The Twin Towers were a major asset to the New York City skyline, but they were also a tempting target.

See also: World Trade Center, September 11

Suggested Reading

Darton, Eric. *Divided We Stand: A Biography of New York City's World Trade Center.* New York: Basic Books, 2001.

Glanz. James, and Eric Lipton. *City in the Sky: The Rise and Fall of the World Trade Center.* New York: Times Books, 2004.

World Trade Center, September II

On September 11, 2001, the day started normally in the World Trade Center. In the Twin Towers the usual number of employees was 14,154. Approximately 14,000 people were present at the time the first commercial aircraft hit the North Tower. American Airlines Flight 11 crashed into the North Tower at 8:46:40 a.m. The aircraft cut a swath through 8 floors—from the 93rd to the 100th—as it hit at about 450 miles an hour.

The force of the impact and the resulting fire from aviation fuel destroyed most elevators and most staircases above the 100th and below the 93rd floors. Nearly 1,000 people were trapped on the upper floors of the North Tower, the majority of whom worked for Cantor Fitzgerald brokerage company. At least 60 people jumped from the North Tower rather than burn to death. One firefighter was killed after being hit by one of the jumpers.

An emergency call went out to the Fire Department City of New York (FDNY). More than 1,000 firefighters from 225 units showed up at the World Trade complex. There were so many vehicles that parking became a problem. Immediately, FDNY commanders realized that they could not extinguish the growing fire in the North Tower, so they concentrated on evacuating people. Because of lack of water, only a few firefighters were engaged in trying to put out the fire. Operators for the 911 system told people to stay put, and assured them that firefighters would be coming to rescue them. To those on the top floors of the North Tower the deteriorating conditions made it imperative that help come soon. Some tried to make it to the roof, but the FDNY had decided after the 1993 World Trade Center bombing to lock the heavy doors leading to the building's sole roof exit. This decision had been made because rooftop rescues by helicopters were a safety risk.

Events at the North Tower caused concern among those in the South Tower. Many of those in the South Tower decided to evacuate the building. Those who tried to evacuate the South Tower were told to return to their offices. This was because the standard firefighting philosophy in high-rise fires was to "stay put, stand by." An announcement broadcast over the intercom at 8:55 a.m. stated that there was no need to evacuate the South Tower. This announcement directly contradicted a decision by Sergeant Al DeVona, ranking Port Authority police officer on the scene, who had ordered that both the North Tower and the South Tower be evacuated within minutes of the first crash. DeVona reordered the evacuations at 8:59 a.m. Captain Anthony Whitaker, commander of the Port Authority Police, confirmed this order shortly thereafter. Faulty communications equipment made these decisions difficult to implement. Because of the communication problems, the 911 operators could not be informed of the deteriorating situation and they continued to give outdated advice to people to stay where they were.

The difficulty in evacuating the towers was compounded by their structural defects. Decisions made during construction made it difficult for people to evacuate, there

The skyline of Manhattan with smoke billowing from the Twin Towers following the September 11th terrorist attack on the World Trade Center, New York City. (Library of Congress)

being only three staircases. Changes in building codes in 1968 had reduced both the number of staircases and the level of fire protection required for high-rise buildings. These changes allowed more rentable space, but meant that the staircases were built for only a few hundred people at a time to walk three or four stories, not for mass evacuation. The location of the three staircases in the center of the building, rather than being dispersed, turned the upper floors of both towers into death traps because the plane crashes in both buildings cut off access to the staircases. With inferior fireproofing, there was nothing to prevent the spread of the fires. The New York City building codes were not to blame because the builder, the Port Authority of New York and New Jersey, as a regional entity was not required to follow building codes.

The Twin Towers had been able to sustain the impact of the two airliners, but the fires endangered the structures. Later reports indicated that the high temperature of the fire, caused by the ignition of the aviation fuel and intensified by the burning office furniture and paper, caused the worst damage. Another factor was that the World Trade Center complex buildings had been constructed with 37 pounds of steel per square foot, in contrast to the normal high-rise buildings of that era, which were built with 75 pounds of steel per square foot. This type of construction saved millions of dollars during construction and increased the square footage of rental space, making the buildings more profitable. Since steel begins to degrade at 300 degrees and continues to degrade by 50 percent at 1,000 degrees, the high-temperature fire, combined with the reduced amount of steel supporting the buildings, led to weakening of the structure of the buildings.

The South Tower collapsed first. United Airlines Flight 175 hit at higher speed than did American Airlines Flight 11. This higher speed and the resulting explosion and fire in the South Tower caused it to collapse in a heap.

Total deaths at the World Trade Center numbered 2,749. Of this total, 147 were passengers and crew of the two aircraft. Another 412 of the dead were rescue workers killed when the two towers collapsed. The remaining 2,190 dead succumbed either to the plane crashes or the collapse of the towers. Without the actions of key individuals and the firefighters, the casualties could have been much higher. Except in the case of those trapped in the Twin Towers above where the planes hit, there was no discernable reason for some people to have died while others survived.

Besides attacking the physical structures of the towers, the hijackers also affected the financial health of the United States. Many companies simply went out of business in New York City. Many others struggled to regain financial viability. Layoffs in the period between September 12 and January 21, 2002, related to September 11 were calculated at 1,054,653. The attack on the airline industry was an indirect financial blow in that it accounted for about 9 percent of the total gross domestic product of the United States, and because around 11 million jobs are directly related to commercial aviation.

Stephen E. Atkins

See also: American Airlines Flight 11; Firefighters at Ground Zero; Giuliani, Rudolph William Louis "Rudy," III; United Airlines Flight 175

Suggested Reading

Bernstein, Richard. *Out of the Blue: The Story of September 11, 2001, from Jihad to Ground Zero.* New York: Times Books, 2002.

Dwyer, Jim. "Errors and Lack of Information in New York's Response to Sept. 11." *New York Times,* May 19, 2004, B8.

Dwyer, Jim, and Kevin Flynn. *102 Minutes: The Untold Story of the Fight to Survive Inside the Twin Towers.* New York: Times Books, 2005.

Smith, Dennis. *Report from Ground Zero.* New York: Viking, 2002.

World Trade Center Bombing (1993)

The first attempt by terrorists to destroy the World Trade Center complex failed in 1993. Islamist terrorists exploded a bomb in the underground garage, level B-2, of One World Trade Center (North Tower) on Friday, February 26, 1993, at 12:18 p.m. They used a yellow Ford Econoline Ryder truck filled with 1,500 pounds of explosives. Their bomb was built from a mix of fuel oil and fertilizer with a nitroglycerin booster.

The conspirators were militant Islamists led by Ramzi Yousef. Yousef confessed to American authorities after his capture that they had selected the World Trade Center complex because it was "an overweening symbol of American arrogance." Other participants were Mohammed Salameh, Nidal Ayyad, Mahmud Abouhalima, and—to a lesser extent—Sheikh Omar Abdel Rahman. Beginning in January 1993, Yousef and his fellow conspirators began to locate and buy the ingredients for the bomb. They needed everything, ranging from a place to work to storage lockers, tools, chemicals, plastic tubs, fertilizer, and lengths of rubber tubing. It took about $20,000 to build the bomb. Yousef wanted more money so that he could build an even bigger bomb. Most of the funds were raised in the United States, but some money came from abroad. Yousef's uncle, Khalid Sheikh Mohammed, had sent him $600 for the bomb. It was Yousef's intention that the explosion would bring down the North Tower of the World Trade Center complex and that the impact on the South Tower of the collapse would bring it down also. This expectation was too high: the North Tower shook in the explosion but withstood its force.

Despite the force of the explosion, casualties were relatively low. The bomb produced a crater 22 feet wide and 5 stories deep. The force of the explosion came close to breaching the so-called bathtub, a structure that prevented water from the Hudson River from pouring into the underground areas of the complex and into the subway system. If this breach had occurred, the resulting catastrophic loss of life would have eclipsed the losses from the later attacks of September 11, 2001. Six people—John DiGiovanni, Bob Kirkpatrick, Steve Knapp, Bill Backo, Wilfredo Mercado, and Monica Rodriguez-Smith—were killed, and more than 1,000 were injured. The Fire Department City of New York (FDNY) responded with 775 firefighters from 135 companies, but they arrived too late to do anything but tend to the wounded and carry away the dead. It took nearly 10 hours to get everyone out because the elevators shorted out in the explosion and power to the staircases failed. Evacuations took place in the dark amid heavy smoke. The towers were repaired and the complex reopened in less than one month. It cost $510 million to repair the damage. The bombing was significant in that it showed how vulnerable the World Trade Center complex was to terrorist attacks.

At first investigators believed that a transformer had blown up, but once they started examining the site, it became obvious that a large bomb had detonated. Within five hours the Federal Bureau of Investigation (FBI) and the New York City Police Department (NYPD) had confirmed that the explosion had been caused by a bomb. The next question was who had done it. There had been 20 calls to the police claiming responsibility, but this was not unusual. The top candidate was Balkan extremists, but the investigation was just beginning.

Within weeks the investigating team of 700 agents had identified or arrested all of the World Trade Center bombers. What broke the case was the discovery of a unique vehicle identification number on the frame of the Ryder van. They learned that Salameh had rented the van. He had reported the van stolen and was trying to recover the $400 deposit. Salameh was arrested while trying to collect the deposit. Investigators then turned to identification of his fellow conspirators, and Yousef was finally identified as the leader of the plot.

By the time authorities had identified Yousef as the leader of the plot and maker of the bomb, he was already in Pakistan planning other operations. Ultimately, a Central Intelligence Agency (CIA) and FBI team captured him in Pakistan, but not before he had initiated several other plots. Yousef had always been a freelancer, but there is evidence that he had connections with Al Qaeda operatives before and after the World Trade Center bombing. After a series of trials, the participants in the bomb plot received life sentences. Yousef was sentenced to 240 years in solitary confinement.

Stephen E. Atkins

See also: Mohammed, Khalid Sheikh; Yousef, Ramzi Ahmed

Suggested Reading

Bell, J. Bowyer. *Murders on the Nile: The World Trade Center and Global Terror.* San Francisco: Encounter Books, 2003.

Caram, Peter. *The 1993 World Trade Center Bombing: Foresight and Warning.* London: Janus Publishing, 2001.

Davis, Mike. *Duda's Wagon: A Brief History of the Car Bomb.* London: Verso, 2007.

Lance, Peter. *1000 Years for Revenge: International Terrorism and the FBI; The Untold Story.* New York: ReganBooks, 2003.

Miller, John, Michael Stone, and Chris Mitchell. *The Cell: Inside the 9/11 Plot and Why the FBI and CIA Failed to Stop It.* New York: Hyperion, 2002.

Reeve, Simon. *The New Jackals: Ramzi Yousef, Osama bin Laden, and the Future of Terrorism.* Boston: Northeastern University Press, 1999.

Y

Yousef, Ramzi Ahmed (1968–)

Ramzi Ahmed Yousef gained fame as the leader of the 1993 bombing of the World Trade Center complex in New York City. For a time Yousef was the most famous terrorist in the world. Bombing the World Trade Center complex made him a hero in Muslim extremist circles. He used his fame to recruit followers and plan other terrorist operations throughout South Asia, especially in the Philippines. Yousef was described by Terry McDermott as a "freelancer, the harbinger of a new type of independent, non–state-sponsored global terrorist."

Yousef's political inclinations and strong scientific abilities prepared him to become a terrorist. He was born on April 27, 1968, in the small town of Fuhayhil, Kuwait, and was given the birth name of Abdul Basit Mahmud Abdul-Karim. His father was an engineer by training from the Baluchistan region of Pakistan who worked for Kuwaiti Airlines. Besides being a Baluchi nationalist, Yousef's father was a devotee of the theology of Wahhabism, a strict form of Muslim religious practice initiated by the conservative 18th-century cleric Muhammad ibn Abd al-Wahhab. (Wahhabism is the form of Sunni Islam practiced in Saudi Arabia.) His mother was a Kuwaiti of Palestinian origin. His uncle was Khalid Sheikh Mohammed of September 11, 2001, fame. Because of his non-Kuwaiti origin, Yousef and his family were treated as second-class citizens in Kuwait, causing him to resent the Kuwaiti regime. One of his childhood friends was Abdul Hakim Murad.

After finishing his local schooling and showing promise in mathematics and science, Yousef decided to study abroad. Beginning in 1986, Yousef took a 12-week course in English at Oxford University. He then attended a small technical school in Wales—the West Glamogan Institute in Swansea. In summer 1988 Yousef traveled to Afghanistan with the intention of fighting with the Afghans against the Soviets, but instead he spent his time in Peshawar at Al Qaeda training camps. It was at a camp that he first met Mahmud Abouhalima. Yousef obtained a Higher National Diploma in computer-aided electrical engineering in 1989. While still at the university, Yousef affiliated with a local cell of the Muslim Brotherhood. Hassan al-Banna (1906–1949) had founded the Muslim Brotherhood in Egypt in 1928 to restore religious and political practices of the time of the Prophet Muhammad. Leaders of the Muslim Brotherhood form the opposition to most of the regimes in the Middle East.

Returning to Kuwait, Yousef landed a job with the Kuwaiti government, working as a communications engineer at the National Computer Center for the Ministry of Planning. This position lasted until Saddam Hussein invaded Kuwait in August 1990. The next year Yousef moved to Quetta, Pakistan, where he married a young Baluchistani woman.

Yousef committed himself to terrorism soon after he left Kuwait. Unlike other terrorists, Yousef was not particularly religious, and his motivation for taking up terrorism was the Palestinian cause—he identified with his Palestinian mother's family. While in Pakistan, Yousef participated in another Al Qaeda training camp, first as a trainee and later as an instructor in the making of bombs. His specialty in camp was making nitroglycerin bombs. At this camp Yousef made contact with terrorists-in-training from South Asia, particularly from the Philippines. One of his connections was with Abdurajak Janjalani, the future founder of the Abu Sayyaf group in the southern Philippines. Yousef briefly visited Basilian Island in the Philippines in 1991 to instruct at a Muslim guerrilla camp.

Yousef decided to turn his attention toward a terrorist act in the United States. He told a friend that he wanted to attack Israel, but because Israel was too tough a target he decided to attack the United States instead. This friend told him that a lot of Jews worked at the World Trade Center complex in New York City. He entered the United States in 1992 with the goal of establishing contact with possible terrorist allies. Yousef lacked a valid visa so he filed a claim for political and religious asylum with the Immigration and Naturalization Services (INS) at the John F. Kennedy International Airport. Confronted with the choice of deportation or arrest, he chose arrest but authorities released him on his own recognizance with instructions to appear for an asylum hearing. His traveling companion, Ahmed Ajaj, was arrested and later deported. Yousef never showed up at the INS hearing scheduled for December 8, 1992, so after that date his stay in the country became technically illegal.

Yousef's first contacts in the United States were with the militant Islamists at the al-Kifah Refugee Center in Brooklyn. There he met with the Egyptian Islamist leader Sheikh Omar Abdel Rahman, formerly the spiritual leader of the Egyptian terrorist organization Jemaah Islamiyah. Although blind since infancy, Abdel Rahman had a considerable following in both the Middle East and United States. He had entered the United States in July 1990, and consolidated political control at the al-Kifah Refugee Center.

Yousef took advantage of the presence of these militants to plot a bombing attack of the World Trade Center complex. According to Terry McDermott, Yousef was able to recruit a team of "largely marginal, unaccomplished men" to build a bomb. His major accomplice was Mahmud Abouhalima. Yousef's intent was to build a bomb big enough to bring down the World Trade Center complex and kill 250,000 Americans.

A major problem for Yousef was his lack of funds to build the size bomb that he wanted. The size of the bomb was determined by the amount of money he had available. Yousef's uncle, Khalid Sheikh Mohammed, sent him $660 from Pakistan to help, but he needed much more money. Ultimately, Yousef had to limit the size of the bomb because he had only $20,000 available. Yousef and his small team of terrorists built a large bomb in an apartment at 40 Pamrapo Avenue in Jersey City, New Jersey. He was able to purchase 1,500 pounds of urea, 130 gallons of nitric acid, and a variety of other chemicals from City Chemical in New Jersey. These ingredients, 100 pounds of aluminum powder, and hydrogen gas tanks made a 1,500-pound bomb.

On the morning of February 26, 1993, the conspirators loaded the bomb into a large, rented Ford Econoline Ryder van. After the van was parked in the underground garage of the World Trade Center under the North Tower, it was detonated at 12:18 p.m. on

February 26, 1993. The explosion killed 6 people and injured more than 1,000. It also produced $510 million in damages. Although the bomb produced a large crater, the World Trade Center complex remained standing. Yousef had hoped that by undermining one of the towers, it would fall and impact the other tower, achieving his goal of killing 250,000 people. By the time of the explosion Yousef was already en route back to Pakistan. Shortly after the detonation, Yousef had an associate send a letter to five American newspapers justifying the bombing. He was bitterly disappointed in the failure of the bomb to do more damage to the World Trade Center, but it did take six lives and caused thousands of injuries.

After leaving the United States, Yousef returned to Quetta, Pakistan, where his family lived. Later he traveled to Karachi, where he had a fateful meeting with his uncle, Khalid Sheikh Mohammed. Yousef had several conversations with his good friend Abdul Hakim Murad, and they discussed ways to attack targets in the United States. Murad, who had a commercial pilot's license and had attended a commercial pilot school in the United States, proposed packing a small airplane full of explosives and dive-bombing into the Pentagon or the headquarters of the Central Intelligence Agency (CIA). Yousef found this idea intriguing enough that he introduced Murad to his uncle. His uncle asked Murad about pilot training and the availability of aircraft. Nothing further happened with this idea at the time, but the idea had been planted in the mind of Khalid Sheikh Mohammed, and he presented a variation of it to Osama bin Laden in 1996.

Yousef kept busy planning terrorist operations in Pakistan. His next target was Pakistani politician Benazir Bhutto. Militant Islamists wanted her assassinated, and he

was offered $68,000 to carry it out. His plan was to assassinate Bhutto with a bomb, but while he was planting the bomb detonator outside Bhutto's residence, it exploded in his face, injuring an eye. Prompt medical attention saved the eye, but the explosion attracted the attention of Pakistani authorities. Knowing that he was vulnerable to both American and Pakistani intelligence services, Yousef realized that he had to leave Pakistan. Before he left, however, Yousef traveled to Mashad, Iran, where he planted a C-4 bomb at a Shiite shrine that killed 26 people and injured another 200.

Yousef's next terrorist act was the bombing of the Israeli embassy in Bangkok, Thailand, in early 1994. He built a bomb and loaded it onto a truck. His designated driver became disoriented by Bangkok traffic and had an accident. Panicking, he abandoned the truck. The police had the truck towed to their headquarters. When they opened the truck, they found a huge bomb and the body of the truck's owner.

After his failure in Bangkok, Yousef decided to continue his career as a terrorist elsewhere, and he picked the Philippines as his new his area of operations. The Philippines was an obvious choice because it was home to a large cadre of militant Islamists, it was cheap, and Yousef already had contacts there. He moved to the Philippines, along with his uncle, Khalid Sheikh Mohammed, in spring 1994. After renewing his close ties with the Abu Sayyaf group, Yousef established his base of operations in Manila at the third-class Manor Hotel. By mid-1994 Yousef began planning several plots: one was to blow up 11 U.S. commercial airliners; another was to assassinate U.S. president Bill Clinton during a visit to the Philippines; and the final plot was to assassinate Pope John Paul II during a papal visit to Manila on January 15, 1995. Yousef and his uncle Khalid Sheikh Mohammed decided that the assassination of Pope John Paul II held the most promise. They settled on using remote-controlled pipe bombs planted along the route to and from the papal ambassador's home where the pope would reside during his stay in Manila. Yousef experimented with a small nitroglycerine bomb that he tested first at a Manila movie theater on December 1, 1994, and then on an American commercial aircraft on December 8, 1994. Both tests were successful, with one of the bombs killing a passenger and almost causing the Boeing 747 to crash.

The bomb designed by Yousef was ingenious. He passed through Manila Airport carrying liquid nitroglycerin in a contact lens case and a nine-volt battery in the heel of each of his shoes. He assembled the bomb in the bathroom, using a Casio watch as a timer. On the first leg of the flight Yousef armed the bomb, and then he left the plane, headed for Cebu City in the southern Philippines. The bomb exploded two hours later, on the next leg of the flight. It tore a hole in the fuselage and damaged the aileron cables that controlled the plane's wing flaps. It took considerable skill for the plane's pilot to land the aircraft at Naha Airport in Okinawa. There was only one victim—a 24-year-old Japanese engineer named Haruki Ikegami. Yousef has been described by Federal Bureau of Investigation (FBI) agents, after they studied his miniature bombs, as "a genius when it came to bomb building."

Yousef's next plan was the assassination of the pope. This plan miscarried in a chemical mishap while Yousef was burning off extra chemicals in his Manila apartment on January 6, 1995. Yousef fled the scene and returned to Pakistan, but Philippine authorities found in his laptop computer the plans for his various plots. Among these plots was the one to fly commercial airliners into the Pentagon, White House, and other prominent targets. They also captured his associate and fellow bomb maker Murad. Under duress Murad identified Yousef and his role in the 1993 World Trade Center bombing. Murad also confessed that it was his idea for an aircraft to dive-bomb into CIA headquarters. This information enabled American and Philippine authorities to place Yousef on an international terrorist list. On the evening of February 7, 1995, Pakistani security forces arrested Yousef in Room 16 at the Su Casa Guest House in Islamabad, Pakistan, after being tipped off to his location by former associate Istaique Parker. Parker turned him in because he did not want to participate in a suicide mission and because of the appeal of the $2 million reward that was offered. Pakistani prime minister Bhutto authorized turning Yousef over to American authorities, who transported him to the United States to stand trial for the World Trade Center bombing.

Yousef stood trial for both the World Trade Center bombing and for conspiracy to plant bombs on U.S. commercial airlines. His first trial was for the charge of conspiring to plant bombs on U.S. commercial airlines. After deciding to plead his case without a lawyer, Yousef was convicted by a jury on September 5, 1996, and was sentenced to life imprisonment in solitary confinement without possibility of parole. In the second and more publicized trial, for the World Trade Center bombing, Yousef was convicted on all charges on February 12, 1997. The judge sentenced him to 240 years in prison, fined him $4.5 million, and imposed restrictions on his visitors. The severity of the sentence resulted in part from witness testimony that Yousef intended to blow up the World Trade Center to let Americans know that they were at war with Islam and to punish their government for its support of Israel. Yousef has been serving his sentence at the federal supermax prison in Florence, Colorado.

There has been considerable conjecture about Yousef's relationship with Osama bin Laden and Al Qaeda. Yousef undoubtedly had connections with Al Qaeda—he had stayed at Al Qaeda safe houses and received training at Al Qaeda camps. There is even evidence that he was personally acquainted with bin Laden. Despite these connections, Yousef seems to have been operating outside of Al Qaeda. Most of his operations lacked the sophistication associated with Al Qaeda, and his money problems would have been solved if he had had Al Qaeda funding. Yousef has never provided valuable information about anything but his own exploits, so it remains difficult to determine his relationship with other terrorists and terrorist groups. His close relationship with his uncle, Khalid Sheikh Mohammed—future architect of the September 11 operation—does indicate that

Yousef had a lasting impact among Islamist extremists.

Stephen E. Atkins

See also: Mohammed, Khalid Sheikh; World Trade Center Bombing (1993)

Suggested Reading

Bell, J. Bowyer. *Murders on the Nile: The World Trade Center and Global Terror.* San Francisco: Encounter Books, 2003.

Davis, Mike. *Buda's Wagon: A Brief History of the Car Bomb.* London: Verso, 2007.

Fouda, Yosri, and Nick Fielding. *Mastermind of Terror: The Truth behind the Most Devastating Terrorist Attack the World Has Ever Seen.* New York: Arcade, 2003.

McDermott, Terry. *Perfect Soldiers: The 9/11 Hijackers; Who They Were, Why They Did It.* New York: HarperCollins, 2005.

Miller, John, Michael Stone, and Chris Mitchell. *The Cell: Inside the 9/11 Plot and Why the FBI and CIA Failed to Stop It.* New York: Hyperion, 2002.

Reeve, Simon. *The New Jackals: Ramzi Yousef, Osama Bin Laden and the Future of Terrorism.* Boston: Northeastern University Press, 1999.

Z

Zawahiri, Ayman al- (1951–)

Ayman al-Zawahiri is the most important leader of Al Qaeda, in the aftermath of the death of Osama bin Laden in 2011. As the former leader of the Egyptian terrorism group Islamic Jihad, he has considerable influence over bin Laden. Al-Zawahiri merged his group into Al Qaeda in the late 1990s, making his contingent of Egyptians influential in the operations of Al Qaeda.

Al-Zawahiri came from a prominent Egyptian family of medical doctors and religious leaders. He was born on June 9, 1951, in al-Sharquiyyah, Egypt. Both sides of his family have roots going back to Saudi Arabia, and his mother's family claims descent from the Prophet Muhammed. His father was a professor at Cairo University's medical school. At an early age, al-Zawahiri joined the Muslim Brotherhood; his first arrest by the Egyptian police was at age 15 in 1966. After studying medicine at the University of Cairo, al-Zawahiri qualified as a physician in 1974, and then received a master's degree in surgical medicine in 1978.

Al-Zawahiri left medicine for political agitation against the Egyptian government of President Anwar Sadat. Inspiring his conversion to Islamic militancy were the writings of Sayyid Qutb, the ideological and spiritual leader of the Muslim Brotherhood. He was shocked by Qutb's execution in 1965 by the Nasser regime—enough so that he considered forming a clandestine Islamist group. While still in medical school, al-Zawahiri was instrumental in founding the terrorist group Islamic Jihad in 1973. This group's mission was to direct armed struggle against the Egyptian state. It did not take the Egyptian government long to ban activities of the Islamic Jihad.

In the aftermath of the 1981 assassination of President Anwar Sadat, Egyptian authorities arrested al-Zawahiri. He had learned of the plot against Sadat only a few hours before it went into operation and had advised against proceeding because the plot was premature and destined to fail. Al-Zawahiri has claimed that prison authorities treated him brutally. After a trial and acquittal for his role in the assassination plot against Sadat, al-Zawahiri served a three-year prison sentence for illegal possession of arms. His stay in prison only increased his militancy. It was in prison that al-Zawahiri and Sheikh Omar Abdel Rahman shared their views. Under torture al-Zawahiri assisted the police in capturing some of his associates in the Islamic Jihad.

After his release from prison, al-Zawahiri resumed his antigovernment activities. In 1984 he assumed the leadership of Islamic Jihad after its former head, Lieutenant Colonel Abbud al-Zumar, was arrested by the Egyptian police. Al-Zawahiri fled Egypt for Jeddah, Saudi Arabia, in 1985 in the middle of President Hosni Mubarak's purge of Egyptian dissidents. There he worked in a medical dispensary. It was in Jeddah in 1986 that al-Zawahiri first met Osama bin Laden. The ongoing war against the Soviets in Afghanistan attracted al-Zawahiri, and he decided to move to Pakistan.

Soon after arriving in Pakistan, al-Zawahiri started coordinating plans between his Islamic Jihad and the Afghan Arabs fighting against Soviet forces in Afghanistan. He served as the chief adviser to bin Laden in the creation of the Al Qaeda network in 1988. Al-Zawahiri also engaged in a campaign to undermine bin Laden's relationship with Abdullah Azzam. Azzam's assassination benefited al-Zawahiri, but there is no concrete evidence that he played any role in it. The Pakistani security service concluded that six associates of al-Zawahiri carried out the assassination.

For several years in the early 1990s al-Zawahiri played a dual role as a member of Al Qaeda and as a leader of the Islamic Jihad. Al-Zawahiri left Pakistan and moved to Sudan with bin Laden in 1992. His closeness to Egypt allowed him to plot against the Egyptian government of President Mubarak. Al-Zawahiri's goal from the beginning was to overthrow the Egyptian government and replace it with an Islamic state. As head of the Islamic Jihad, he planned the unsuccessful assassination attempt on Egyptian president Mubarak during his visit to Addis Ababa on June 25, 1995. This failure led to the Sudanese government expelling him and his followers from Sudan.

His activities for Al Qaeda kept him traveling around the world. Bin Laden sent al-Zawahiri to Somalia to aid the opposition to American intervention there. Then he was active in building support for the Bosnian Muslims in their separatist war against Yugoslavia. Next he coordinated aid for Albanian Muslims in the Kosovo War. Finally, al-Zawahiri received the assignment to set up terrorist operations in Europe and the United States. He visited the United States in 1996 to inspect sites for possible terrorist operations there. His conclusion was that major terrorist activities could be undertaken against American targets in the United States.

Al-Zawahiri returned to Afghanistan to join bin Laden. He decided to merge his Egyptian Islamic Jihad group into Al Qaeda in 1998 for a combination of political, financial, and operational reasons. In 1997 al-Zawahiri had been implicated in his group's participation in the terrorist massacre of 58 European tourists and 4 Egyptian security guards at Luxor, Egypt. This terrorist act was so brutal that it caused a backlash in both Egyptian public opinion and among the leadership of the Egyptian Islamic Jihad. It led to a schism within its leadership, with a significant number of the leaders concluding a ceasefire with the Egyptian government. Al-Zawahiri opposed the ceasefire with what he considered to be an apostate government. He led a much-weakened Egyptian Islamic Jihad into an alliance with Al Qaeda.

Al-Zawahiri's influence over bin Laden grew over the years. Bin Laden was neither as intellectual nor as militant as al-Zawahiri. Al-Zawahiri's views were expressed in the tract *Knights under the Prophet's Banner*. In this work al-Zawahiri justified the use of violence as the only way to match the brute military force of the West led by the United States. For this reason it is necessary to target American targets, the tract posits, and the most effective way to do this is by the use of human bombs. The proposed strategy is to inflict enough damage on the United States that its citizens will demand that their government change policies toward Israel and the Arab world. This treatise was written before the September 11 attacks, but such attacks were obviously in its author's mind.

In his position as number two in Al Qaeda, al-Zawahiri served as the chief adviser to bin Laden. Because of his more radical religious views, al-Zawahiri pushed bin Laden toward more radical positions.

Al-Zawahiri was aware of the September 11 plot from the beginning, but stayed in the background. The subsequent loss of Afghanistan as a staging area for Al Qaeda forced al-Zawahiri into hiding along with bin Laden. Al-Zawahiri and bin Laden kept in contact, but they stayed in separate areas to avoid the possibility of Al Qaeda's chief leaders being wiped out in a single attack by the Americans and their allies. On August 1, 2008, *CBS News* speculated that al-Zawahiri may have been seriously injured or even killed during a July 28 missile strike on a village in South Waziristan. This conjecture was based on an intercepted letter dated July 29 that urgently called for a doctor to treat al-Zawahiri. On August 2, however, senior Taliban commander Maulvi Omar dismissed the report as false.

It is assumed that al-Zawahiri became the leader of Al Qaeda following bin Laden's death during a firefight with U.S. special forces at a compound in Abbottabad, Pakistan, on May 1, 2011 (May 2 Pakistani local time). He has continued to release propaganda videos since that time, occasionally making references to current events to indicate that he is still alive. The U.S. State Department offers a reward of $25 million for information that leads to al-Zawahiri's capture.

Stephen E. Atkins

See also: Al Qaeda; Atta, Mohamed el-Amir Awad el-Sayed; Bin Laden, Osama; Mohammed, Khalid Sheikh

Suggested Reading

Atwan, Abdel Bari. *The Secret History of Al Qaeda.* Berkeley: University of California Press, 2006.

Bell, J. Bowyer. *Murders on the Nile: The World Trade Center and Global Terror.* San Francisco: Encounter books, 2003.

Kepel, Gilles. *The War for Muslim Minds: Islam and the West.* Cambridge, MA: Belknap, 2004.

Wright, Lawrence. *The Looming Tower: Al Qaeda and the Road to 9/11.* New York: Knopf, 2006.

Zubaydah, Abu (1971–)

When Abu Zubaydah was captured in March 2002, the U.S. government believed he was chief of operations for Al Qaeda and number three in its hierarchy. U.S. officials claimed that Zubaydah was in charge of Al Qaeda training camps that selected the personnel for the September 11, 2001, plot. However, in September 2009, the U.S. government reversed its position on Zubaydah, stating that it no longer believed he was a member of Al Qaeda or had anything to do with the September 11 terrorist attacks.

Zubaydah was born on March 12, 1971, in Saudi Arabia. He has reportedly engaged in extremist Islamist activities since his youth. His original name was Zayn al-Abidin Mohamed Husayn, but he adopted the name Zubaydah early in his career as a radical Islamist. Although born a Saudi, he grew up among the Palestinians in a refugee camp in the West Bank of Palestine. His first political association was with Hamas. Ayman Al-Zawahiri recruited him from Hamas to the Egyptian Islamic Jihad. When al-Zawahiri moved to Pakistan, Zubaydah went with him. As a teenager he fought with the Afghan Arabs in military operations against the Soviets. In one of these engagements in Afghanistan Zubaydah lost an eye.

The U.S. government initially reported that when Zubaydah became chief of operations, he played a role in all of Al Qaeda's military operations, including the selection of Mohamed Atta for an important future martyr mission while Atta was in training at Khaldan camp in 1998. U.S. officials asserted that Zubaydah was also active in planning the failed Millennium plots in Jordan and the United States and then became field commander for the attack on USS *Cole* on October 12, 2000. Khalid Sheikh Mohammed was the operational chief for the September 11 attacks, but the United States believed Zubaydah was a participant in the final draft of the plan, and was also active in post–September 11 plots. American authorities decided that Zubaydah was important enough to either capture or eliminate because of his alleged role in keeping all members' files, and in assigning individuals to specific tasks and operations.

A joint operation of Pakistani security, American Special Forces, and Federal Bureau of Investigation (FBI) Special Weapons and Tactics (SWAT) unit arrested Zubaydah in a suburb of Faisalabad, a town in western Pakistan, on March 28, 2002. From intercepted Al Qaeda communications, the National Security Agency (NSA) learned that Zubaydah might be at a two-story house owned by a leader of the Pakistani militant extremist group Laskar-e-Toiba. In the subsequent assault 35 Pakistanis and 27 Muslims from other countries were arrested. Among the captured was Zubaydah. He had been seriously wounded, with gunshots to the stomach, groin, and thigh. A medical unit determined that Zubaydah would survive, and he was taken into American custody.

Zubaydah has been held in American custody at various locations since his capture. The Americans decided to interrogate him as if they were in Saudi Arabia. Instead of being frightened, Zubaydah asked his phony "Saudi" interrogators to contact a senior member of the Saudi royal family—Prince Ahmed bin Salman bin Abdul-Aziz—who would save him from the Americans. This claim stunned the interrogators. They returned later to confront him for lying. Zubaydah instead gave more details about agreements among Al Qaeda, Pakistani, and Saudi high-level government leaders. He went so far as to indicate that certain Pakistani and Saudi leaders knew about September 11 before the attack occurred. According to him, these officials did not have the details and did not want them, but they knew the general outlines of the plot. After Zubaydah learned that the "Saudi" interrogators were really Americans, he tried to commit suicide. The attempt failed, and Zubaydah no longer volunteered information and denied what he had said earlier.

American investigators quizzed the Saudi government about Zubaydah's comments. Representatives of the Saudi government called his information false and malicious. In a series of strange coincidences three of the Saudis named by Zubaydah died in a series of incidents in the months after the inquiries—Prince Ahmed died of a heart attack at age 41; Prince Sultan bin Faisal bin Turki al-Said died in an automobile accident; and Prince Fahd bin Turki bin Saud al-Kabir died of thirst while traveling in the Saudi summer at age 25. The supposed Pakistani contact, Air Marshal Ali Mir, was killed in an airplane crash on February 20, 2003, with his wife and 15 senior officers.

Zubaydah remains in American custody, his eventual fate unknown. In September 2006 Zubaydah was transferred to the Guantánamo Bay Detention Camp. In 2006 Ron Suskind published the book *One Percent Doctrine,* which claimed that Zubaydah was not nearly as important in Al Qaeda as had been thought. Suskind claimed that Zubaydah was mentally ill and was only a minor figure in Al Qaeda. Suskind's assertions were countered by numerous others, including former Al Qaeda operatives.

Regardless of the controversy, Zubaydah appeared before a Combatant Status Review Tribunal in Guantánamo on March 27, 2007. There, he downplayed his role in Al Qaeda but still claimed some authority.

Zubaydah has also become part of another controversy because he was extensively tortured by Central Intelligence Agency (CIA) operatives. On May 30, 2005, a CIA memorandum stated that Zubaydah was subjected to waterboarding 83 times. A report concluded by the International Committee of the Red Cross in February 2007 and released to the public on April 7, 2009, found that Zubaydah had been subjected to 11 other forms of torture in addition to waterboarding. These included sleep deprivation, confinement in a small box, deprivation of food, and exposure to extreme cold. Videotapes showing the interrogation and torture of Zubaydah and another detainees were destroyed by the CIA in November 2005.

In September 2009, in a statement filed at Zubaydah's hearing for the reinstatement of habeas corpus protections, the U.S. government changed its position, claiming that it no longer believed Zubaydah was a member of Al Qaeda or had played any role in the African embassy bombings or the September 11 attacks. Despite this, Zubaydah remains in U.S. custody.

Stephen E. Atkins

See also: Al Qaeda; Zawahiri, Ayman al-

Suggested Reading

Corbin, Jane. *Al Qaeda: The Terror Network That Threatens the World.* New York: Thunder's Mouth, 2002.

Posner, Gerald. *Why America Slept: The Failure to Prevent 9/11.* New York: Ballantine, 2003.

Suskind, Ron. *One Percent Doctrine.* New York: Simon and Schuster, 2006.

Primary Documents

I. Osama bin Laden's Declaration of Jihad (August 23, 1996)

Introduction

Osama bin Laden had been disturbed by the Saudi government's granting of permission for American troops to be stationed on the holy soil of Saudi Arabia. He had gone to the Saudi government and volunteered his services, as well as those of Arabs who had fought in Afghanistan, to repulse Saddam Hussein's invasion of Kuwait. When the Saudis rejected his offer and invited American troops, bin Laden was infuriated. Bin Laden was a Wahhabi Sunni and believed that Christianity is a polytheistic religion because of the Christian belief in the Holy Trinity. He subscribed to a saying in the hadith (sayings of the Prophet Mohammad) that reads, "Expel the Polytheists from the Arabian peninsula." Bin Laden issued this judicial edict of jihad, or holy war, on August 23, 1996, with the assistance of the religious council of Al Qaeda. It was an open declaration of war against the United States for its presence in the Kingdom of Saudi Arabia. The declaration is a lengthy document, so only the most pertinent parts have been included here.

Primary Source

. . .

It is not concealed from you that the people of Islam had suffered from aggression, iniquity and injustice imposed on them by the Jewish-Christian alliance and their collaborators to the extent that the Muslims' blood became the cheapest and their wealth and assets looted by the hands of the enemies. Their blood was spilled in Palestine and Iraq. The horrifying pictures of the massacre of Qana, in Lebanon are still fresh in our memory. Massacres took place in Tajikistan, Burma, Kashmir, Assam, Philippine, Fattani, Ugadin, Somalia, Eritrea, Chechnya and in Bosnia-Herzegovina. Massacring Muslims that sent shivers in the body and shook the conscience. All of that happened and the world watched and heard, and not only did not respond to these atrocities, but also with a clear conspiracy between America and its allies prevented the weaklings from acquiring arms to defend themselves by using the United Nations as a cover. Muslims became aware that they were the main targets of the Jewish-Crusader alliance of aggression. The false propaganda regarding human rights have vanished under the tribulations and massacres that were committed against Muslims everywhere.

This last aggression was the worst catastrophe that was inflicted upon the Moslems since the death of the Prophet. That is, the occupation of the land of the two holiest sites, Islam's own grounds, the cradle of Islam, source of the Prophet's mission, site of the Ka'bah was launched by the Christian army of the Americans and their allies. There is no power and no strength save in God.

In light of these facts and the reality we live in, in light of this blessed and overwhelming awakening that swept the world, the Islamic world in particular, I meet with you today after a long absence imposed by the unjust Crusade under the leadership of America against the Islam scholars, fearing stirring up the Islamic Nation against its enemies as was guided by ancestoral scholars, like Ibn Tamimah and al-Iz Bin Abd-al-Salam, may Allah bless their souls. We do not justify anyone above God. They [alliance] murdered the Mujahid Sheikh/ Abdallah Azzam and arrested the Mujahid Sheikh/Ahmad Yasin. In the path of the prophet; praise and prayers be upon him, and Mujahid Sheikh/ Omar Abd-al-Rahman in America as well as many scholars, preachers and youth that were arrested in the land of the two Holiest sites upon the instructions of America. Most prominent were Sheikh/Salman al-Udah and Sheikh Safar al-Hawali. There is no power and no strength save by God. We were affected by some of that injustice by barring us from speaking with the Muslims, while being hunted in Pakistan, Sudan and Afghanistan; which caused our long absence. But by the grace of God there was a safe haven in Khurasan, under the protection of Hindukush Mountains. These mountains where the World's most powerful military and apostates were crushed, and where the legend of the great forces dissipated in front the cries of the Mujahideen.

God is Most Great. Today, from the same shelters in Afghanistan, we are working to lift off the injustice that was inflected upon the nation by the Jewish-Crusaders alliance, especially after their occupation of the Prophet's land, praise and peace be upon him, and their desecration of land of the two holiest sites. We ask Allah to grant us victory. He is the defender and the almighty.

Today we start talking, working and remembering to search for ways to reform whatever happened to the Islamic world in general, land of the two holiest sites in particular. We want to study all possible ways that can be established to restore the situation back to its origin and the rights to their owners, after what happened to the people from great misfortune and serious harm concerning their religion and worldly existence. People from all walks of life were stricken: civilians, military and security personnel, officials, merchants, young and old, school and university students, thousands of unemployed university graduates, who make up great number in society.

It also struck Industrial and agriculture groups, urbanites, nomads and desert inhabitants. Everyone is complaining about everything. The situation in the land of the two holy places became like a gigantic volcano ready to erupt, so it can annihilate the infidelity and corruption no matter where the source comes from. Riyadh and Khubar explosions were only a warning to this roaring flood, which was caused by suffering, bitter suppression, subjugation, excessive injustice, degrading oppression and poverty.

People are fully concerned about their every day livelihood, every one talks about the deterioration of the economy, inflation, high cost of living, ever-increasing debts, and prisons full of inmates. These employees are with limited income, talk about their debts of ten thousands and hundred thousands of Riyals. They complain that the value of the Riyal is greatly and continuously deteriorating against other major currencies. Even leading merchants and contractors talk about hundreds and thousands of million Riyals owed to them by the government. More than three hundred forty billions Riyals are owed by the government to the people, in addition to the daily-accumulated interest, let alone the foreign debt. People ask and wonder whether we are really the largest oil exporting country! They even feel and believe that this situation is punishment and curse put on them by Allah for their silence against the injustice, oppressive and illegitimate behavior and measures of the ruling regime. Most conspicuous is ignoring the divine Shari'ah law depriving people from their legitimate rights and allowing the Americans to occupy the land of the two holiest sites, and the unjust imprisonment of the devoted scholars and the successors of the prophet. Scholars, preachers, merchants, economists and dignitaries became aware of this great misfortune; every group did what they could and moved fast to correct the situation. All agreed that the country is heading toward a great catastrophe, the extent of which is not known except by Allah. One senior merchant said [the king is leading the country to a disaster]. There is no power and no strength save in God. Numerous princes share with the public their feelings, privately expressing their concerns and objecting to the corruption, repression and intimidation taking place in the country. Rivalry among the influential princes over personal interest and gains had destroyed the country. Through its course of actions, the regime has ripped apart its legitimacy the most important being:

1-Suspension of Islamic laws, and replacing it with statuary laws and embarking upon bloody confrontation with devoted scholars and righteous youths. We do not justify anyone above God.

2-Failure of the regime to protect the country, and allowing the enemy of Crusaders-American forces to occupy the land years present the main reason for our disaster in every aspect, especially economically. Because of the wasteful government spending, the imposed economic policies such as limiting the production of oil and controlling its selling price, and the high cost of arm deals, the people started wondering why does this regime exist?

Every group did its utmost to move swiftly to avert this deteriorating situation. They advised the government both privately and openly, in prose and in poetry, jointly and separately, they send letters and poems, reports after reports, reminders after reminders; they explored every way and enlist every influential person in their movement of reform and correction. They wrote with style of passion, diplomacy and wisdom asking for corrective measures and repentance from great wrong doings and corruption that had engulfed even the basic principles of the religion and the legitimate rights of the people. But unfortunately and to our deepest regret the regime refused to listen to the people accusing them of being ridiculous and silly. The matter got worse as previous wrong doings were followed by mischiefs of greater magnitudes. All of this took place in land of the two holiest sites!! Silence was no longer permissible nor connivance became unacceptable.

When the transgression reached this magnitude; and exceeded the limits of atrocity to contradict the solemn Islam, a group of scholars and preachers became fed up with the deafening sounds of deception and blinded their eyes from viewing bribery and blocked their noses from smelling corruption. Rejection vows were revived and demands for preventing the situation from deteriorating became loud. Dozens of educated dignitaries, merchants, and former officials joined in. They dispatched letters and memos to the king calling for reform. In 1411H, and during the Gulf war, a letter with over 400 signatures was sent to the king demanding reform, lifting oppression and the implementation of corrective measures. The king humiliated the people and ignored the letters. The bad situation of the country became even worse.

. . .

My Muslim brothers of the land of the two holiest sites: Does it make sense that our country is the largest buyer of arms from America and the area's biggest commercial partner of America, [who are occupying the land of the two holiest sites], and are assisting their Jewish brothers in occupying Palestine, and in evicting and killing the Muslims there, by providing them with financial aid, arms and men. To deny these occupiers from the enormous revenues of their trading with our country will help our Jihad war against them. It is an important moral expression to show our anger and hatred towards them. By doing that we would have contributed towards purging our sacred places from the Jews and Christians, and forcing them to leave our lands conquered and defeated, [Allah willing]. We expect the women in the land of the two holiest sites and other places to do their part by boycotting American goods.

. . .

Before I close, I have a very important message to the Muslim youths, men of the bright future of Muhammad's nation, [Allah's Blessings and Prayers be upon him]. My conversation with the youth is about their duty during this critical period of our nation's history; only the young [may Allah keep them] came forward to carry out their duty during this period. Some were hesitant to defend and protect Islam, and to save themselves and their wealth from the injustice, oppression, repression and terrorism that is carried out by the regime who used the media to mislead the people and conceal the truth. The youth [may Allah keep them] came to carry the banner of jihad high against the American-Jewish alliance that occupied the Islamic holy places,—some came out of fear from the tyranny of the regime, or stumbled as a result of greediness in an evanescent world. They proceeded to cast the legitimacy on this high treason and great misfortune of the occupation of the land of the two Holiest sites; there is no power and no strength save by God-. No wonder Muhammad's companions were all young, and these young people are the best successors for the best ancestors.

. . .

I tell the Islamic youth of the world who fought in Afghanistan, Bosnia-Herzegovina with their money, lives, tongues and pens that the battle has not yet ended. Remind them of the conversation between Gabriel and the prophet, after al-Ahzab campaign. (When the Messenger of Allah has left for Madinah, he put down his weapon, Gabriel then said: Did you put down the weapon? The angels have not put theirs down yet; get up with your people to Bani Quraythah, I will walk in front of you to shake down their stronghold, and spread fear in their hearts. These young people know, that he who is not killed for the cause of God will be considered as dead. The most honorable death is to die for the sake of God; like those four heroes who set off the explosives that killed the Americans in Riyadh. Those men disgraced the American occupiers by their courageous acts.

. . .

My Muslim Brothers of the world: Your brothers in land of the two holiest sites and Palestine are calling upon you for help and asking you to take part in fighting against the enemy, your enemy; the Israelis and Americans. They are asking you to do whatever you can within one's own means and ability, to expel the humiliate and defeat the enemy out of the sanctities of Islam. Almighty Allah said: {But if they seek your aid in religion, it is your duty to help them} [Al Anfal: 72]. You should know that your gathering and cooperation to liberate the sanctities of Islam is the right step to join forces under the banner of unity. We cannot but raise our hands in prayers, asking God to grant us wisdom and success in this matter.

. . .

Source: First published in *Al Quds Al Arabi*, a London-based newspaper, in August, 1996. Translation from the Harmony Program at the Combating Terrorism Center, West Point, Reference number AFGP-2002-003676. Online at https://ctc.usma.edu/harmony-program/declaration-of-jihad-against-the-americans-occupying-the-land-of-the-two-holiest-sites-original-language-2/

2. Declaration of the World Islamic Front (February 23, 1998)

Introduction

If the 1996 Declaration of Jihad was Osama bin Laden's personal declaration of war against the West and Israel, the Declaration of the World Islamic Front in 1998 was a group declaration of war by Al Qaeda and its supporters. Signatories of the declaration included bin Laden; Ayman al-Zawahiri, amir, or head, of the Egyptian

Islamic Jihad; Abu-Yasir Rifai Ahmad Taha, a leader of the Egyptian Islamic Group; Sheikh Mir Hamza, secretary of the Islamic Party of Religious Leaders in Pakistan; and Maulana Fazlur Rahman, a leader of the opposition in Pakistan's National Assembly. By having allies, bin Laden was able to answer criticism that he lacked the religious credentials to issue a judicial ruling, or fatwa. This document is an open declaration of hostilities by Al Qaeda and its allies that was to lead directly to the events of September 11, 2001.

Primary Source

Praise be to Allah, who revealed the Book, controls the clouds, defeats factionalism, and says in His Book: "But when the forbidden months are past, then fight and slay the pagans wherever ye find them, seize them, beleaguer them, and lie in wait for them in every stratagem (of war)"; and peace be upon our Prophet, Muhammad Bin-'Abdallah, who said: I have been sent with the sword between my hands to ensure that no one but Allah is worshipped, Allah who put my livelihood under the shadow of my spear and who inflicts humiliation and scorn on those who disobey my orders.

The Arabian Peninsula has never—since Allah made it flat, created its desert, and encircled it with seas—been stormed by any forces like the crusader armies spreading in it like locusts, eating its riches and wiping out its plantations. All this is happening at a time in which nations are attacking Muslims like people fighting over a plate of food. In the light of the grave situation and the lack of support, we and you are obliged to discuss current events, and we should all agree on how to settle the matter.

No one argues today about three facts that are known to everyone; we will list them, in order to remind everyone:

First, for over seven years the United States has been occupying the lands of Islam in the holiest of places, the Arabian Peninsula, plundering its riches, dictating to its rulers, humiliating its people, terrorizing its neighbors, and turning its bases in the Peninsula into a spearhead through which to fight the neighboring Muslim peoples.

If some people have in the past argued about the fact of the occupation, all the people of the Peninsula have now acknowledged it. The best proof of this is the Americans' continuing aggression against the Iraqi people using the Peninsula as a staging post, even though all its rulers are against their territories being used to that end, but they are helpless.

Second, despite the great devastation inflicted on the Iraqi people by the crusader-Zionist alliance, and despite the huge number of those killed, which has exceeded 1 million . . . despite all this, the Americans are once against trying to repeat the horrific massacres, as though they are not content with the protracted blockade imposed after the ferocious war or the fragmentation and devastation.

So here they come to annihilate what is left of this people and to humiliate their Muslim neighbors.

Third, if the Americans' aims behind these wars are religious and economic, the aim is also to serve the Jews' petty state and divert attention from its occupation of Jerusalem and murder of Muslims there. The best proof of this is their eagerness to destroy Iraq, the strongest neighboring Arab state, and their endeavor to fragment all the states of the region such as Iraq, Saudi Arabia, Egypt, and Sudan into paper statelets and through their disunion and weakness to guarantee Israel's survival and the continuation of the brutal crusade occupation of the Peninsula.

All these crimes and sins committed by the Americans are a clear declaration of war on Allah, his messenger, and Muslims. And ulema have throughout Islamic history unanimously agreed that the jihad is an individual duty if the enemy destroys the Muslim countries. This was revealed by Imam Bin-Qadamah in "Al-Mughni," Imam al-Kisa'i in "Al-Bada'i," al-Qurtubi in his interpretation, and the shaykh of al-Islam in his books, where he said: "As for the fighting to repulse [an enemy], it is aimed at defending sanctity and religion, and it is a duty as agreed [by the ulema]. Nothing is more sacred than belief except repulsing an enemy who is attacking religion and life."

On that basis, and in compliance with Allah's order, we issue the following fatwa to all Muslims:

The ruling to kill the Americans and their allies—civilians and military—is an individual duty for every Muslim who can do it in any country in which it is possible to do it, in order to liberate the al-Aqsa Mosque and the holy mosque [Mecca] from their grip, and in order for their armies to move out of all the lands of Islam, defeated and unable to threaten any Muslim. This is in accordance with the words of Almighty Allah, "and fight the pagans all together as they fight you all together," and "fight them until there is no more tumult or oppression, and there prevail justice and faith in Allah."

This is in addition to the words of Almighty Allah: "And why should ye not fight in the cause of Allah and of those who, being weak, are ill-treated (and oppressed)?—women and children, whose cry is: 'Our Lord, rescue us from this town, whose people are oppressors; and raise for us from thee one who will help!'"

We—with Allah's help—call on every Muslim who believes in Allah and wishes to be rewarded to comply with Allah's order to kill the Americans and plunder their money wherever and whenever they find it. We also call on Muslim ulema, leaders, youths, and soldiers to launch the raid on Satan's U.S. troops and the devil's supporters allying with them, and to displace those who are behind them so that they may learn a lesson.

Almighty Allah said: "O ye who believe, give your response to Allah and His Apostle, when He calleth you to that which will give you life. And know that Allah cometh between a man and his heart, and that it is He to whom ye shall all be gathered."

Almighty Allah also says: "O ye who believe, what is the matter with you, that when ye are asked to go forth in the cause of Allah, ye cling so heavily to the earth! Do ye prefer the life of this world to the hereafter? But little is the comfort of this life, as compared with the hereafter. Unless ye go forth, He will punish you with a grievous penalty, and put others in your place; but Him ye would not harm in the least. For Allah hath power over all things."

Almighty Allah also says: "So lose no heart, nor fall into despair. For ye must gain mastery if ye are true in faith."

Source: Federation of American Scientists. Available online at https://fas.org/irp/world/para/docs/980223-fatwa.htm

3. Al Qaeda's Instructions for Living in the Western World While on a Mission

Introduction

All Al Qaeda operatives received training on how to be inconspicuous while on a mission. Trainers identified the most intelligent trainees with the most potential to pass unnoticed in the Western world. Language expertise and personal appearance were of the utmost importance. To ensure that the training would last, a manual of behavior was prepared and given to those on operations in the Western world. This excerpt from a lengthy document gives insight into this training.

Primary Source
Member Safety

Defining Members' Safety:

This is a set of measures taken by members who perform undercover missions in order to prevent the enemies from getting to them.

It is necessary for any party that adopts Jihad work and has many members to subdivide its members into three groups, each of which has its own security measures. The three groups are: 1. The overt members; 2. The covert members; 3. The commander.

Measures that Should Be Taken by the Overt Member:

1. He should not be curious and inquisitive about matters that do not concern him.

2. He should not be chatty and talkative about everything he knows or hears.

3. He should not carry on him the names and addresses of those members he knows. If he has to, he should keep them safe.

4. During times of security concerns and arrest campaigns and especially if his appearance is Islamic, he should reduce his visits to the areas of trouble and remain at home instead.

5. When conversing on the telephone he should not talk about any information that might be of use to the enemy.

6. When sending letters, he should not mention any information that might be of use to the enemy. When receiving letters, he should burn them immediately after reading them and pour water on them to prevent the enemy from reading them. Further, he should destroy any traces of the fire so the enemy would not find out that something was burned.

Measures that Should Be Taken by the Undercover Member:
In addition to the above measures, the member should . . .

1. Not reveal his true name to the Organization's members who are working with him, nor to the [Islamic] Da'wa [Call].

2. Have a general appearance that does not indicate Islamic orientation [beard, toothpick, book, (long) shirt, small Koran].

3. Be careful not to mention the brothers' common expressions or show their behaviors (special praying appearance, "may Allah reward you," "peace be on you" while arriving and departing, etc.).

4. Avoid visiting famous Islamic places (mosques, libraries, Islamic fairs, etc.).

5. Carry falsified personal documents and know all the information they contain.

6. Have protection preceding his visit to any place while moving about (apartment, province, means of transportation, etc.).

7. Have complete and accurate knowledge of the security status related to those around him in his place of work and residence, so that no danger or harm would catch him unaware.

8. Maintain his family and neighborhood relationships and should not show any changes towards them so that they would not attempt to bring him back [from the Organization] for security reasons.

9. Not resort to utilizing letters and messengers except in an emergency.

10. Not speak loudly.

11. Not get involved in advocating good and denouncing evil in order not to attract attention to himself.

12. Break the daily routine, especially when performing an undercover mission. For example, changing the departure and return routes, arrival and departure times, and the store where he buys his goods.

13. Not causing any trouble in the neighborhood where he lives or at the place of work.

14. Converse on the telephone using special code so that he does not attract attention.

15. Not contacting the overt members except when necessary. Such contacts should be brief.

16. Not fall into the enemy's excitement trap either through praising or criticizing his Organization.

17. Performing the exercises to detect surveillance whenever a task is to be performed.

18. Not park in no-parking zones and not take photographs where it is forbidden.

19. Closing all that should be closed before departing the place, whether at home or his place of undercover work.

20. Not undergo a sudden change in his daily routine or any relationships that precede his Jihad involvement. For example, there should not be an obvious change in his habits of conversing, movement, presence, or disappearance. Likewise, he should not be hasty to sever his previous relationships.

21. Not meet in places where there are informers, such as coffee shops, and not live in areas close to the residences of important personalities, government establishments, and police stations.

22. Not write down on any media, specially [sic] on paper, that could show the

traces and words of the pen by rubbing the paper with lead powder.

Measures that Should Be Taken by the Commander:

The commander, whether in overt or covert work, has special importance for the following reasons.

The large amount of information that he possesses.

The difficulty of the command in replacing the commander.

Therefore, all previously mentioned security precautions regarding members should be heightened for the commander.

Important Note: Married brothers should observe the following:

Not talking with their wives about Jihad work.

The members with security risks should not travel with their wives. A wife with an Islamic appearance (veil) attracts attention.

Source: "UK/BM-40 Translation," U.S. Department of Justice, http://www.justice.gov/ag/manual part1_2.pdf, pp. 25–28.

4. Memorandum from Richard A. Clarke for Condoleezza Rice Informing Her about the Al Qaeda Network (January 25, 2001)

Introduction

On January 25, 2001, Richard A. Clarke, a holdover from the Bill Clinton administration and the head of counterterrorism efforts in that administration, sent a memorandum to Condoleezza Rice, then national security adviser to the George W. Bush administration, about Al Qaeda. This memo was Clarke's first effort to have the Bush administration take into account the danger emanating from Osama bin Laden and Al Qaeda.

Primary Source
Memorandum for Condoleezza Rice

FROM: Richard A. Clarke SUBJECT: Presidential Policy Initiative/Review—The Al-Qaida Network

Condi asked today that we propose major Presidential policy reviews or initiatives. We urgently need such a Principal level review on the al Qida network.

Just some Terrorist Group?

As we noted in our briefings for you, al Qida is not some narrow, little terrorist issue that needs to be included in broader regional policy. Rather, several of our regional policies need to address centrally the transnational challenge to the US and our interests posed by the al Qida network. By proceeding with separate policy reviews on Central Asia, the GCC, North Africa, etc. we would deal inadequately with the need for a comprehensive multi-regional policy on al Qida. Al Qida is the active, organized, major force that is using a distorted version of Islam as its vehicle to achieve two goals:

to drive the US out of the Muslim world, forcing the withdrawal of our military and economic presence in countries from Morocco to Indonesia;

to replace moderate, modern, Western regime in Muslim counties with theocracies modeled along the lines of the Taliban.

Al Qida affects centrally our policies on Pakistan, Afghanistan, Central Asia, North Africa and the GCC. Leaders in Jordan and Saudi Arabia see al Qida as a direct threat to them. The strength of the network of organizations limits the scope of support friendly Arab regimes can give to a range of US policies, including Iraq policy and the Peace Process. We would make a major error if we under-estimated the challenge al Qida poses, or over estimated the stability of the moderate, friendly regimes al Qida threatens.

Pending Time Sensitive Decisions

At the close of the Clinton Administration, two decisions about al Qaida were deferred to the Bush Administration.

First, should we provide the Afghan Northern Alliance enough assistance to maintain it as a viable opposition force to the Taliban/al Qida? If we do not, I believe that the Northern Alliance may be effectively taken out of action this Spring when fighting resumes after the winter thaw. The al Qida 55th Brigade, which has been a key fighting force for the Taliban, would then be freed to send its personnel elsewhere, where they would likely threaten US interests. For any assistance to get there in time to effect the Spring fighting, a decision is needed now.

Second, should we increase assistance to Uzbekistan to allow them to deal with the al Qida/IMU threat? [remainder of content of this section removed at the request of the CIA as operational detail]

Three other issues awaiting addressal now are:

First, what the new Administration says to the Taliban and Pakistan about the importance we attach to ending the al Qida sanctuary in Afghanistan. We are separately proposing early, strong messages to both.

Second, do we propose significant program growth in the FY02 budget for anti-al Qida operations by CIA and counter-terrorism training and assistance by State and CIA?

Third, when and how does the Administration choose to respond to the attack on the USS *Cole*? That decision is obviously complex. We can make some decisions, such as those above, now without yet coming to grips with the harder decision about the *Cole*. On the *Cole*, we should take advantage of the policy that we "will respond at a time, place, and manner of our own choosing/and not be forced into knee jerk responses."

Attached is the year-end 2000 strategy on al Qaida developed by the last Administration to give to you. Also attached is the 1998 strategy. Neither was a "covert action only" approach. Both incorporated diplomatic, economic, military, public diplomacy and intelligence tools. Using the 2000 paper as background, we could prepare a decision paper/guide for a PC review.

Threat Magnitude: Do the Principles agree that the al Qida network poses a first order threat to US interests in a number of regions, or is this analysis a "chicken little" over reaching and can we proceed without major new initiatives and by handling this issue in a more routine manner?

Strategy: If it is a first order issue, how should the existing strategy be modified or strengthened? Two elements of the existing strategy that have not been made to work effectively are a) going after al Qida's money and b) public information to counter al Qida propaganda.

FY02 Budget: Should we continue the funding increases into the FY02 for State and CIA programs designed to implement the al Qida strategy?

Immediate [blacked out] Decisions: Should we initiate [blacked out] funding to the Northern Alliance and to the Uzbek's?

Please let us know if you would like such a decision/discussion paper or any modifications to the background paper.

Concurrences by: Mary McCarthy, Dan Fried, Bruce Reidel, Don Camp

Source: National Security Archive. Available online at http://www.gwu.edu/~nsarchiv/NSAEBB /NSAEBB147/clarke%20memo.pdf.

5. Presidential Daily Briefing (August 6, 2001)

Introduction

Presidents receive daily briefings from various agencies. This particular President's Daily Brief (PDB) has become controversial because it included a warning from the Central Intelligence Agency (CIA) that Osama bin Laden wanted to strike at targets in the United States. A representative of the CIA presented the PDB to George W. Bush at Crawford, Texas, on August 6, 2001. This document was declassified and approved for release on April 10, 2004.

Primary Source

Bin Laden Determined to Strike in US

Clandestine, foreign government, and media reports indicate Bin Ladin since 1997 has wanted to conduct terrorist attacks in the US. Bin Ladin implied in US television interviews in 1997 and 1998 that his followers would follow the example of the World Trade Center bomber Ramzi Yousef and "bring the fighting to America."

After US missile strikes on his base in Afghanistan in 1998, Bin Ladin told followers he wanted to retaliate in Washington, according a [blacked out] service.

An Egyptian Islamic Jihad (EIJ) operative told an [blacked out] service at the same time that Bin Ladin was planning to exploit the operative's access to the US to mount a terrorist strike.

The millennium plotting in Canada in 1999 may have been part of Bin Ladin's first serious attempt to implement a terrorist strike in the US. Convicted plotter Ahmed Ressam has told the FBI that he conceived the idea to attack Los Angeles International Airport himself, but that Bin Ladin lieutenant Abu Zubaydah encouraged him and helped facilitate the operation. Ressam also said that in 1998 Abu Zubaydah was planning his own US attack.

Ressam says Bin Ladin was aware of the Los Angeles operation.

Although Bin Ladin has not succeeded, his attacks against the US Embassies in Kenya and Tanzania in 1998 demonstrate that he prepares operations years in advance and is not deterred by setbacks. Bin Ladin associates surveilled our Embassies in Nairobi and Dar es Salaam as early as 1993, and some members of the Nairobi cell planning the bombings were arrested and deported in 1997.

Al-Qaida members—including some who are US citizens—have resided in or traveled to the US for years, and the group apparently maintains a support structure that could aid attacks. Two al-Qaida members found guilty in the conspiracy to bomb our Embassies in East Africa were US citizens, and a senior EIJ member lived in California in the mid-1990s.

A clandestine source said in 1998 that a Bin Ladin cell in New York was recruiting Muslim-American youth for attacks.

We have not been able to corroborate some of the more sensational threat reporting, such as that from a (blacked out) service in 1998 saying that Bin Ladin wanted to hijack a US aircraft to gain the release of "Blind Shykh" 'Umar' Abdel-Rahman and other US-held extremists.

Nevertheless, FBI information since that time indicates patterns of suspicious activity in this country consistent with preparations for hijackings or other types of attacks, including recent surveillance of federal buildings in New York.

The FBI is conducting approximately 70 full field investigations throughout the US that it considers Bin Ladin-related. CIA and the FBI are investigating a call to our Embassy in the UAE in May saying that a group of Bin Ladin supporters was in the US planning attacks with explosives.

Source: "Bin Laden Determined to Strike in US." National Security Archive, https://nsarchive2.gwu .edu/NSAEBB/NSAEBB116/pdb8-6-2001.pdf

6. Mohamed Atta's Letter of Advice for Hijackers (September 2001)

Introduction

Mohamed Atta allegedly wrote a five-page document in Arabic to prepare the members of his Al Qaeda team for their mission on September 11, 2001. This letter was found in Atta's suitcase, which was left behind at Logan Airport with other papers because Atta was late in boarding American Airlines Flight 11. There is some question whether Atta wrote this document, but it is certainly written in language that he believed in. The document served as both a spiritual exhortation for the mission and a checklist for the teams.

Primary Source

The Last Night

1. Make an oath to die and renew your intentions. Shave excess hair from the body and wear cologne. Shower.

2. Make sure you know all aspects of the plan well, and expect the response, or a reaction from the enemy.

3. Read al-Tawba and Anfal [traditional war chapters from the Koran] and reflect on their meanings and remember all of the things that God has promised for the martyrs.

4. Remind your soul to listen and obey [all divine order] and remember that you will face decisive situations that might prevent you from 100 percent obedience, so tame your soul, purify it, convince it, make it understand and incite it. God said: "Obey God and his messenger, and do not fight amongst yourselves or else you will fail. And be patient, for God is with the patient."

5. Pray during the night and be persistent in asking God to give you victory, control and conquest, and that he may make your task easier and not expose us.

6. Remember God frequently, and the best way to do it is to read the Holy Koran, according to all scholars, as far as I know. It is enough for us that it [the Koran] are [*sic*] the words of the Creator of the Earth and the planets, the One that you will meet [on the Day of Judgment].

7. Purify your soul from all unclean things. Completely forget something called "this world" [or "this life"]. The time for play is over and the serious time is upon us. How much time have we wasted in our lives? Shouldn't we take advantage of these last hours to offer good deeds and obedience?

8. You should feel complete tranquility, because the time between you and your marriage [in heaven] is very short. Afterward begins the happy life, where God is satisfied with you, and eternal bliss "in the company of the prophets, the companions, the martyrs and the good people, who are all good company." Ask God for his mercy and be optimistic, because [the prophet], peace be upon him, used to prefer optimism in all his affairs.

9. Keep in mind that, if you fall into hardship, how will you act, and how will you remain steadfast and remember that you will return to God and remember that anything that happens to you could never be avoided, and what did not happen to you could never have happened to you. This test from Almighty God is to raise your level [a reference to the levels of heaven] and erase your sins. And be sure that it is a matter of moments, which will then pass, God willing, so blessed are those who win the great reward of God. Almighty God said: "Did you think you could go to heaven before God knows whom [*sic*] amongst you have fought for Him and are patient?"

10. Remember the words of Almighty God: "You were looking to the battle before you engaged in it, and now you see it with your own two eyes." Remember: "How many small groups beat big groups by the will of God." And his words: "If God gives you victory, no one can beat you. And if he betrays you, who can give you victory without Him? So the faithful put their trust in God."

11. Remind yourself of the supplications and of your brethren and ponder their meanings. [The morning and evening supplications, and the supplications of entering a town, and . . . the supplications said before meeting the enemy.]

12. Bless your body with some verses of the Koran [done by reading verses in one's hands and then rubbing the hands over whatever is to be blessed], the luggage, clothes, the knife, your personal effects, your ID, your passport, and all of your papers.

13. Check your weapons before you leave and long before you leave. (You must make your knife sharp and you must not discomfort your animal during the slaughter.)

14. Tighten your clothes [a reference to one making sure his clothes will cover his private parts at all times], since this is the way of the pious generations after the prophet. They would tighten their clothes before battle. Tighten your shoes. Also, do not seem confused or show signs well, wear socks so that your feet will be solidly in your shoes. All of these are worldly things [that humans can do to control their fate, although God decrees what will work and what will not] and the rest is left to God, the best One to depend on.

15. Pray the morning prayer in a group and ponder the great rewards of that prayer. Make supplications afterward, and do not leave your apartment unless you have performed ablution before leaving, because (The angels will ask for your forgiveness as long as you are in a state of ablution, and will pray for you). This saying of the prophet was mentioned by [Yaba ibn Shair] al-Nawawi in his book, *The Best of Supplications.* Read the words of God: "Did you think that We created you for no reason. . . ." from the al-Mu'minum chapter.

The Second Stage

When the taxi takes you to (M) [this initial could stand for *matar*, the Arabic term for "airport"] remember God constantly while in the car. (Remember the supplication for entering a car, for entering a town, the supplication of place and other supplications.) . . .

When you have reached (M) and have left the taxi, say a supplication of place ["O Lord, I ask you for the best of this place, and ask you to protect me from its evils"], and everywhere you go say that prayer and smile and be calm, for God is with the believers. And the angels protect you without you feeling anything. Say this supplication: "God is more dear than all of his creation." and Say: "O Lord, protect me from them as you wish." . . . [More supplications follow]:

They will come back [from battle] with God's blessings.

They were not harmed.

And God was satisfied with them.

[Many Koranic verses and statements of the Prophet follow.]

Fear is a great worship. The allies of God do not offer such worship except for the one God, who controls everything . . . with total certainty that God will weaken the schemes of the non-believers. God said: "God will weaken the schemes of the non-believers."

You must remember your brothers with all respect. No one should notice that you are making the supplication, "There is no God but God," because if you say it 1,000 times no one will be able to tell whether you are quiet or remember God. [More Koran verses]

Also, do not seem confused or show signs of nervous tension. Be happy, optimistic, calm because you are heading for a deed that God loves and will accept [as a good deed]. It will be the day, God willing, you spend with the women of paradise.

Smile in the face of hardship young man/ For you are heading toward eternal paradise.

You must remember to make supplications wherever you go, and anytime you do anything, and God is with his faithful servants, he will protect them and make their tasks easier, and give them success and control, and victory and everything. . . .

Third Stage—When You Ride the Plane

When you ride the (T) [probably for *tayyara*, the Arabic term for "airplane"], before your foot steps in it, and before you enter it, you make a prayer and supplications. Remember that this is a battle for the sake of God. As the prophet, peace upon him, said: An action for the sake of God is better than all of what is in this world, or as he said. When you step inside the (T), and sit in your seat begin with the known supplications that we have mentioned before. Be busy with the constant remembrance of God. God said: "Oh ye faithful, when you find the enemy be steadfast, and remember God constantly so that you may be successful." When the (T) moves, even slightly, toward (Q) [unknown reference], say the supplication of travel. Because you are traveling to Almighty God, so be attentive on this trip. . . .

And then it takes off. This is the moment that both groups come together. So remember God, as he said in his Book: "Oh Lord, pour your patience upon us and make our feet steadfast and give us victory over the infidels." And his works: "And the only thing they said Lord, forgive our sins and excesses and make our feet steadfast and give us victory over the infidels." And his prophet said: "O Lord, you have revealed the book, you move the clouds, you gave us victory over the enemy, conquer them and give us victory over them." Give us victory and make the ground shake under their feet. Pray for yourself and all of your brothers that they may be victorious and hit their targets and [unclear] and ask God to grant you martyrdom facing the enemy, not running away from it, and for him to grant you patience and the feeling that anything that happens to you is for him.

Then every one of you should prepare to carry out his role in a way that would satisfy God. You should clench your teeth, as the pious early generations did.

When the confrontation begins, strike like champions who do not want to go back to this world. Shout, "Allahu Akbar," because this strikes fear in the hearts of nonbelievers. God said: "Strike above the neck, and strike at all of their extremities."

Know that the gardens of paradise are waiting for you in all their beauty, and the women of paradise are waiting, calling out, "Come hither, friend of God." They have dressed in their most beautiful clothing.

If God decrees that any of you are to slaughter, you should dedicate the slaughter to your fathers . . . because you have obligations toward them. Do not disagree, and obey. If you slaughter, do not cause the discomfort of those you are killing, because this is one of the practices of the prophet, peace be upon him. On one condition: that you do not become distracted . . . and neglect what is greater, paying attention to the enemy. That would be reason, and would do more damage than good. If this happens, the deed at hand is more important than doing that, because the deed is an obligation, and [the other thing] is optional. And an obligation has priority over an option.

Do not seek revenge for yourself. Strike for God's sake. One time Ali bin Abi Talib [a companion and close relative of the Prophet Muhammad], may God bless him, fought with a nonbeliever. The nonbeliever spit on Ali, may God bless him. Ali . . . did not strike him. When the battle was over, the companions of the prophet asked him why he had not smitten the nonbeliever. He said, "After he spat at me, I was afraid that I would be striking at him in revenge for myself, so I lifted my sword." After he renewed his intentions, he went back and killed the man. This means that before you do anything, make sure that your soul is prepared to do everything for God only.

Then implement the way of the prophet in taking prisoners. Take prisoners and kill them. As Almighty God said, "No prophet should have prisoners until he has soaked the land with blood. You want the bounties of this world [in exchange for prisoners] and God wants the other world [for you], and God is all-powerful, all-wise."

If everything goes well, every one of you should pat the other on the shoulder in confidence. . . . Remind your brothers that this act is for Almighty God. Do not confuse your brothers or distract them. He should give them glad tidings and make them calm, and remind them [of God] and encourage them. How beautiful it is for one to read God's words, such as: "And those who prefer the afterlife over this world should fight for the sake of God." And his words: "Do not suppose that those who are killed for the sake of God are dead, they are alive. . . ." And others. Or they should sing songs to boost their morale, as the pious first generations did in the throes of battle, to bring calm, tranquility, and joy to the hearts of his brothers.

Do not forget to take a bounty, even if it is a glass of water to quench your thirst or that of your brothers, if possible. When the hour of reality approaches, the zero hour . . . wholeheartedly welcome death for the sake of God. Always be remembering God. Either end you life while praying, seconds before the target, or make your last words: "There is no God but God, Muhammad is his messenger."

Afterward, we will all meet in the highest heaven, God willing.

If you see the enemy as strong, remember the groups [that had formed a coalition to fight the Prophet Muhammad]. They were 10,000. Remember how God gave victory to his faithful servants. God said: "When the faithful saw the [size of the enemy army], they said, this is what God and the prophet promised, they said the truth. It only increased their faith."

And may the peace of God be upon the prophet.

Source: "Full Text of Notes Found after Hijackings." *New York Times*, September 29, 2001. Available online at https://www.nytimes.com/2001/09/29/us/a-nation-challenged-notes-found-after-the-hijackings.html

7. President George W. Bush's Address to the Nation (September 11, 2001)

Introduction

Americans were in a state of shock on September 11, 2001. The unthinkable had happened: a terrorist attack on the United States had killed thousands of Americans. President George W. Bush had been as startled as anybody else in the United States. In this speech, which he gave on the evening of September 11, 2001, he tried to reassure Americans that their government was going to help in the recovery and deal with the terrorists.

Primary Source

Today, our fellow citizens, our way of life, our very freedom came under attack in a series of deliberate and deadly terrorist acts. The victims were in airplanes or in their offices: secretaries, businessmen and -women, military and federal workers, moms and dads, friends and neighbors.

Thousands of lives were suddenly ended by evil, despicable acts of terror. The pictures of airplanes flying into buildings, fires burning, huge structures collapsing have filled us with disbelief, terrible sadness and a quiet, unyielding anger.

These acts of mass murder were intended to frighten our nation into chaos and retreat. But they have failed. Our country is strong. A great people has been moved to defend a great nation.

Terrorist attacks can shake the foundations of our biggest buildings, but they cannot touch the foundation of America. These acts shatter steel, but they cannot dent the steel of American resolve.

America was targeted for attack because we're the brightest beacon for freedom and opportunity in the world. And no one will keep that light from shining.

Today, our nation saw evil, the very worst of human nature, and we responded with the best of America, with the daring of our rescue workers, with the caring for strangers and neighbors who came to give blood and help in any way they could.

Immediately following the first attack, I implemented our government's emergency response plans. Our military is powerful, and it's prepared. Our emergency teams are working in New York City and Washington, DC, to help with local rescue efforts.

Our first priority is to get help to those who have been injured and to take every precaution to protect our citizens at home and around the world from further attacks.

The functions of our government continue without interruption. Federal agencies in Washington which had to be evacuated today are reopening for essential personnel tonight and will be open for business tomorrow.

Our financial institutions remain strong, and the American economy will be open for business as well.

The search is under way for those who are behind these evil acts. I've directed the full resources for our intelligence and law enforcement communities to find those responsible and bring them to justice. We will make no distinction between the terrorists who committed these acts and those who harbor them.

I appreciate so very much the members of Congress who have joined me in strongly condemning these attacks. And on behalf of the American people, I thank the many world leaders who have called to offer their condolences and assistance.

America and our friends and allies join with all those who want peace and security in the world, and we stand together to win the war against terrorism.

Tonight I ask for your prayers for all those who grieve, for the children whose worlds have been shattered, for all whose sense of safety and security has been threatened. And I pray they will be comforted by a power greater than any of us spoken through the ages in Psalm 23: "Even though I walk through the valley of the shadow of death, I fear no evil for you are with me."

This is a day when all Americans from every walk of life unite in our resolve for justice and peace. America has stood down enemies before, and we will do so this time.

None of us will ever forget this day, yet we go forward to defend freedom and all that is good and just in our world.

Thank you. Good night and God bless America.

Source: *Public Papers of the President of the United States. George W. Bush, 2001, Book 2.* Washington, DC: Government Printing Office, 2002, 1099–1100.

8. EPA's Press Release (September 13, 2001)

Introduction

One of the ongoing controversies stemming from September 11 has been the health problems experienced by workers who hunted for survivors, located bodies, and cleaned up the debris at the World Trade Center. There was a tremendous cloud of dust and debris in the air for weeks after the collapse of the Twin Towers and other buildings. One of the first actions of the U.S. government was to send Environmental Protection Agency (EPA) agents to test the air quality. In a series of press releases beginning on September 13, Christie Whitman, head of the EPA, reassured the rescue crews and the public that the level of air contaminants was low. This information was later questioned after a significant number of workers at the site began to have respiratory illnesses that led to long-term disabilities or death. The document presented here is the first of the EPA press releases, dated September 13.

Primary Source

EPA Initiates Emergency Response Activities, Reassures Public about Environment Hazards

U.S. Environmental Protection Agency Administrator Christie Whitman today announced that the EPA is taking steps to ensure the safety of rescue workers and the public at the World Trade Center and the Pentagon disaster sites, and to protect the environment. EPA is working with state, federal, and local agencies to monitor and respond to potential environmental hazards and minimize any environmental effects of the disasters and their aftermath.

At the request of the New York City Department of Health, EPA and the U.S. Department of Labor's Occupational Safety and Health Administration (OSHA) have been on the scene at the World Trade Center monitoring exposure to potentially contaminated dust and debris. Monitoring and sampling conducted on Tuesday and Wednesday have been very reassuring and potential exposure of rescue crews and the public to environmental contaminants [*sic*].

EPA's primary concern is to ensure that rescue workers and the public are not exposed to elevated levels of asbestos, acidic gases or other contaminants from the debris. Sampling of ambient air quality found either no asbestos or very low levels of asbestos. Sampling of bulk materials and dust found generally low levels of asbestos.

The levels of lead, asbestos and volatile organic compounds in air samples taken on Tuesday in Brooklyn downwind from the World Trade Center site, were not detectable or not of concern.

Additional sampling of both ambient air quality and dust particles was conducted Wednesday night in lower Manhattan and Brooklyn, and results were uniformly acceptable.

"EPA is greatly relieved to have learned that there appears to be no significant levels of asbestos dust in the air in New York City," said Administrator Whitman. "We are working closely with rescue crews to ensure that all appropriate precautions are taken. We will continue to monitor closely."

Public health concerns about asbestos contamination are primarily related to long-term exposure. Short-term, low-level exposure of the type that might have been produced by the collapse of the World Trade Center buildings is unlikely to cause significant health effects. EPA and OSHA will work closely with rescue and cleanup crews to minimize their potential exposure, but the general public should be very reassured by initial sampling.

EPA and OSHA will continue to monitor and sample for asbestos, and will work with the appropriate officials to ensure that rescue workers, cleanup crews and the general public are properly informed about appropriate steps that should be taken to ensure proper handling, transportation and disposal of potentially contaminated debris or materials.

EPA is taking steps to ensure that response units implement appropriate engineering controls to minimize environmental hazards, such as water sprays and rinsing to prevent or minimize potential exposure and limit releases of potential contaminants beyond the debris site.

EPA is also conducting downwind sampling for potential chemical and asbestos releases from the World Trade Center debris site. In addition, EPA has deployed federal On-Scene Coordinators to the Washington, DC. Emergency Operations Center, Fort Meade, and FEMA's alternative Regional Operations Center in Pennsylvania and has deployed an On-Scene Coordinator to the Virginia Emergency Operations Center.

Under its response authority, EPA will use all available resources and staff experts to facilitate a safe emergency response and cleanup.

EPA will work with other involved agencies as needed to:

- procure and distribute respiratory and eye protection equipment in cooperation with the Dept. of Health and Human Services;
- provide health and safety training upon request;
- design and implement a site monitoring plan;
- provide technical assistance for site control and decontamination; and
- provide some 3,000 asbestos respirators, 60 self-contained breathing apparatuses and 10,000 protective clothing suits to the two disaster sites.

New York Governor George E. Pataki has promised to provide emergency electric generators to New York City in efforts to restore lost power caused by Tuesday's tragedy, and EPA will work with State authorities to expedite any necessary permits for those generators.

OSHA is also working with Consolidated Edison regarding safety standards for employees who are digging trenches because of leaking gas lines underground. OSHA has advised Con Edison to provide its employees with appropriate respirators so they can proceed with emergency work, shutting off gas leaks in the city.

Source: "EPA Response to September 11," U.S. Environmental Protection Agency, https://archive .epa.gov/wtc/web/html/

9. Statements by FEMA on Its Response to September 11 before the U.S. Senate's Committee on Environment and Public Works (October 16, 2001)

Introduction

In 2001, the Federal Emergency Management Agency (FEMA) operated 28 teams from around the United States. It was FEMA's responsibility to react to the events of September 11, and following those events, FEMA mobilized 26 of those teams to travel to New York City and Washington, DC. Of these teams, 21 went to New York and 5 to Washington. Despite some deficiencies caused by the lack of equipment at times, these FEMA teams operated effectively under harsh conditions. These three statements, given on October 16, 2001, before the Senate's Committee on Environment and Public Works, show how FEMA performed and the difficulties that the teams had to deal with in a scene of destruction.

Primary Source
Statement of Joe M. Allbaugh, Director, Federal Emergency Management Agency

Actually, I'll be brief in my remarks because I know you have several questions. I'd just like to begin by telling that these folks sitting on the front row are the true heroes of everyday American life. They represent heroes, many men and women who put their lives on the line, whom we often take for granted, as Senator Voinovich said. They're always first in line for budget cuts and last in line for recognition. I think, as a result of September 11, that maybe these brave men and women will be due the admiration that they so richly deserve, putting their lives on the line every minute of every day all across this country.

Five weeks ago this morning, our world was transformed. At that time, President Bush told me to make sure that the Federal Government would provide whatever assistance was needed in New York, Pennsylvania and at the Pentagon. That mission is still a work in progress, but I can assure you and the American public that FEMA's response was swift and comprehensive and our commitment of continued support is unwavering.

Since September 11, I've spent many days at Ground Zero in New York City. I visited the site in Pennsylvania, was inside the Pentagon the Saturday after the event. Those places are where the true heroes are—those who were in their offices at work, grabbing a cup of coffee, on an airplane; and those who were first to respond to the tragic events—the firefighters, the police officers, the emergency medical technicians.

All are gone now, but I can assure you they're not forgotten. Our prayers are still with those folks and their families. Working hand-in-hand with Governor Pataki, Mayor Giuliani, Fire Commissioner Tommy Von Essen and Police Commissioner Bernard Kerik and many others, we've begun the painful process of recovery.

Beginning on September 11, FEMA deployed 26 of our 28 national urban search and rescue teams. Twenty-one went to New York, ultimately, the last one checking out of New York a week ago this last Sunday. Five went to northern Virginia at the Pentagon site. The New York City Office of Emergency Management's Task Force was among the first responders at the World Trade Center. Its leader, Chief Ray Downey, a person I was lucky to know, a great partner of FEMA, was on the scene. Tragically, he and his team never made it out.

I watched our rescue teams join New York City's finest and Virginia's finest, working shoulder to shoulder around the clock to find their brothers and sisters and fellow citizens. These sites are truly hallowed ground. Now our rescue teams have gone home and we are fully engaged in the recovery process. We have millions of tons of debris still to be moved out of New York City. It will take months. As of this morning, we've only moved out 300 million tons. It doesn't sound like very much compared to what we have to move.

Before and since the President signed the disaster declarations for Pennsylvania, for New Jersey, for Virginia and New York, FEMA activated the Federal response plan. To your point, Senator Voinovich, I think what we planned to do in this event worked just like it was supposed to, according to the Federal response plan.

We activated our emergency operations center here and in our 10 regions. We established disaster field offices in Virginia, New York and New Jersey and declared these disasters with public assistance at 100 percent for eligible cost. Our biggest concern currently is to make sure that the right assistance is getting to the right people. Many people need counseling; they will need counseling for a long time to come. Many qualify for individual assistance. I want to make sure that those people are helped.

In addition, we are there to help States and local governments with their public assistance needs, such as their public buildings, roads, streets, and emergency protective measures, making sure that these men and women are reimbursed for their time, material, their equipment in proper fashion.

In the past month, thousands of Federal employees have been working day and night at our disaster field offices at these three sites. Today we still have 1,300 employees deployed to New York City. Our job is not finished, but we will see it through to the end.

In the meantime, we're currently looking at all aspects of our disaster response in those three States to determine the lessons learned to be better prepared for the future. We're also working with President Bush and his Administration on any new legislative needs. As we continue to move forward with the recovery, I will let you know promptly if there is any new need for authorities.

Let me conclude on a personal note, if you don't mind. I attended about 10 days ago and spoke at the funeral of Captain Terry Haddon in New York City. Two weeks prior to that, on August 29, I had the fortune to sit down with his coworkers at Rescue One on 43rd Street in New York City to have a lunch with those individuals. Chief Ray Downey was there, with 13 or 14 of us around the table. We had a great time.

I try to stop in our country's firehouses every opportunity that I'm out on the road. It is amazing what I'm able to learn, what their needs are, what their wishes, wants, hopes. They are a true family in those fire-houses all across the country. In that short 1½–2 hours, I became, I thought, a small part of their family.

The night before Terry's funeral, I attended a wake in New York City, and his wife Beth, who subsequently found out that she was pregnant with their first child after September 11—Terry never knew—handed me a small card. On one side it was a short life history of Terry. On the back part of the card was the Fireman's Prayer. I'd like to close just with the last sentence of that prayer, because I think it says so much about men and women who wear the uniform of our country's military. It says so much about the firemen and firewomen and the police officers and the emergency responders and all those individuals who lost their lives on September 11.

It goes like this: "If, according to my fate, I am to lose my life, please bless with Your protecting hand my family, friends and wife." For Terry Haddon, Ray Downey, Joey Angelini, Dennis Mohica and thousands of other souls that were lost on that fateful day, I hope that those of us still living and thriving can help provide that protecting hand to all the families and loved ones.

Statement of Edward P. Plaugher, Chief, Arlington County, Virginia, Fire Department

Thank you very much. It is indeed a pleasure to be here this morning. It's also a great deal of pleasure and an honor to represent the men and women, not only of the Arlington County Fire Department, but also of the Nation. Hopefully my remarks will assist the cause of improving our capability to respond to any type of incident.

Again, I want to thank you [for] allowing me to be here today. I understand that you as a committee are deeply concerned, as are all of us, with the tragic events of September 11. These events have a profound impact on the men and women of my fire department and on the Nation's fire service as a whole.

I have prepared remarks which I hope will be entered into the record, and I'll just highlight a couple of the key points in order to be brief here this morning, to allow my colleagues ample time to testify.

It is an opportunity for me, however, to talk about the incident at the Pentagon. First of all, you need to know, I think, is that our response to the Pentagon began when one of our engine companies who was responding to another routine call noticed the plane and its route to the Pentagon and was actually a witness to the incident. Immediately, the northern Virginia automatic mutual aid program was activated. Units from Fort Myer, Alexandria, Fairfax County and the National Airport Fire Department responded from the initial alarm.

The second alarm units included units from the District of Columbia as well as from Montgomery County and Prince George's County, MD. These first responding fire units fought a fire that was triggered by 6,000 gallons of jet fuel in the world's largest office building.

The Federal Emergency Management Agency, in their response to the attack on the Pentagon and its aftermath, was superb. FEMA and their front line urban search and rescue teams, which were mobilized from Fairfax County, Virginia Beach, Montgomery County, MD; Memphis, TN, and then later on, we received assistance from New Mexico to provide relief for the exhausted rescue personnel.

I must tell you, Mr. Chairman and members of the committee, that the FEMA urban search and rescue teams made an outstanding contribution to our effort. These teams are comprised of dedicated professionals whose hard work and unyielding efforts should not be overlooked.

Two resources that were brought to bear to the incident scene by FEMA come to mind and stand out in my mind. First was the search dog capability. It's a unique and absolutely critical, necessary component of a structural collapse search that allows for swift and thorough search for victims that could not otherwise have been possible. Second, the urban search and rescue team brings in specially trained urban search and rescue structural engineers that allow us to then proceed into the building with safety being paramount to all the personnel on the scene.

However, there's a couple of areas that I think we can do to improve our business, and that is the business of response to our community, particularly in these types of incidents. That is what the director was just talking about, the ability to have a clear understanding of the local first responders, of what does the urban search and rescue team bring to an incident, and particularly the capability of this being taught at the National Fire Academy.

I also think that we need to have a clear understanding of the capability that is being developed for these urban search and rescue teams. In other words, what I mean is there needs to be a standardized list of equipment that is well understood and that we can count on when deployed. It also occurs to me that this complement of equipment and response capability should be developed with a panel of experts that seeks out local advice so that the folks of us who have been there will allow them to be able to adjust their response capability based upon our now new experiences.

We just heard again about the need for additional equipment. Most urban search and rescue teams—which in my earlier career in Fairfax County, I was fortunate enough to be one of the founding members of the team, and participated in its early structure—we realize that they are multiple deep in personnel, but not multiple deep in equipment. We think that now is the time that we could fix that.

We are, in fact, very lucky and very privileged in the Washington Metropolitan area to have two urban search and rescue teams in our midst, both Montgomery County, MD and Fairfax County, VA. This is a unique situation in our community.

However, one of the things that we also focused on, and we realized early on in this particular incident at the Pentagon, is that there was a need for some command overhead teams. These command overhead teams would be chief officers who would be experienced in dealing with these incidents and bring to bear that extra chief level officer capability. We think that maybe there's an opportunity for this to come out in the future.

The level of cooperation and mutual assistance between FEMA and the Arlington County Fire Department was excellent. There are many moving parts to an effective response to a terrorist incident. Each of us must have a good expectation of our own responsibilities of the different agencies.

In the final analysis, what transpired at the Pentagon, under the circumstances, was dealt with professionally and to the best of each of our abilities. We at the Arlington County Fire Department learned valuable lessons with regard to our own abilities and our limits. It is our hope that we can use those lessons to further a more effective preparedness approach.

I personally testified last spring before the House Transportation Committee on a piece of legislation designed to address this issue. A Senate companion bill, Senate bill 1453, the Preparedness Against Terrorism Act of 2001, was recently introduced by Senator Bob Smith and referred to this committee. This bill codifies the Office of National Preparedness at FEMA that President Bush created earlier this year. It creates a President's Council that will be charged with the development of a single national strategy on terrorism preparedness, that will include measurable preparedness goals.

We applaud President Bush's designation of Governor Tom Ridge of Pennsylvania as our new Homeland Security coordinator. However, it seems to us that Senate bill 1453 could and would bring focus and legal authority to this new effort. It is my understanding that the Bush Administration has significant input into this bill, and I urge you to make whatever modifications are necessary to address Governor Ridge's role and to act favorably on the bill in sending it to the full Senate for consideration as quickly as possible.

Statement of Jeffrey L. Metzinger, Fire Captain, Sacramento, Calif., Metropolitan Fire District; Member, Fema Urban Search and Rescue Team

Good morning Mr. Chairman and members of the committee. I'm Captain Jeff Metzinger. I'm with the Sacramento Metropolitan Fire District in northern California. I'm also a member of California's Urban Search and Rescue Team, California Task Force 7.

Like the others here, I am also honored and very humbled to be talking to you this morning, representing the thousands of firefighters across this country who put their lives on the line every day.

We were dispatched to the World Trade Center on the morning of September 11, as so many other teams were. I keep a journal with me wherever I go, and I brought it with me today and I'm going to read some excerpts for you. It's a habit I've had for a long time, and I think there's some value in there.

I'll start out on Wednesday, September 12.

We're finally leaving for New York City and everyone is anxious to get to work. As we approach the Hudson River from New Jersey, you can see a large column of smoke coming up from the site where the World Trade Center used to stand.

This is my first trip to New York City, and I feel sad about what I see. The traffic is incredible, even with a full police escort. The corners are filled with people, and we're just now a few blocks away from the large smoke column I had seen earlier. We arrive at the Javits Convention Center by 7 P.M. and set up our base of operations. There's other teams coming in as well, including teams from Los Angeles, Missouri, Indianapolis, Riverside, California, Pennsylvania, Massachusetts and Ohio.

Our 62 person team is divided into two teams, where we alternate 12-hour shifts, working 24 hours around the clock. It's assigned to the Blue team, working the night shift. The first night, on September 13, we loaded into the bus and headed into our sector to go to work. We met up with the Gray team and did a pass-on Street.

The scene was surreal. There were people everywhere. Smoke continued to drift from the massive piles of rubble. The expanse of the disaster is difficult to comprehend. Several searches were conducted by our search dogs in the vicinity of Tower Seven. The technical search cameras were also used, but we had no luck finding any victims.

The following night, our team was working again, looking for an assignment. The dogs alerted an area, but at a very dangerous location. It was too unstable to enter. That night there was thunder, lightning, wind and heavy rains pounding upon us. Frequently, debris—large pieces of metal were blowing off the roofs of adjacent buildings. Our task force leader determined it wasn't safe for us to go any farther, we didn't want to lose any further lives.

The next afternoon we had a briefing from our task force leader at our base and were told that President Bush would be visiting our facility that day. I was privileged to meet and shake hands with President Bush, with Senator Hillary Rodham Clinton, and the governor and the mayor were also present. It was quite an experience, and their visit was very much appreciated by all.

That night on the bus we were headed back to work, still hundreds of people lining the streets of New York City, cheering us as we go by. Traffic was so congested that we finally stopped the bus, got off and walked the last few blocks to the Church and Dey command post. Tonight our search team is finally getting to do some work, putting up a rope system to lower one of our members down into the debris crater near Church Street. The objective here is to place a cellular phone antenna down lower that might assist with victim locations.

The following night we were headed back to work and again people were lining the streets, cheering, waving flags, holding signs, lighting candles. It was a sight that warmed us even as we went in. This particular night, our search and rescue teams were assigned to search the buildings around the outer perimeter of the plaza area. There are several 30-plus story buildings around the World Trade Center plaza. We conducted searches from basement to roof, every door was opened, every space was checked. We climbed the stairwells, taking on one building at a time.

We didn't find any victims. Every floor of every building we searched was marked and completed. The assignment took a lot of toll on our legs that night.

On Sunday, during our briefing, we were told that three top New York fire chiefs were laid to rest that day. Firefighter Chaplain Ward Cockerton said a prayer for the victims and for the safety of the team members that are still working here.

Tonight we're going to work between buildings five and six, [possibly] going underground. We hear that there's up to six levels below the street grade. So we reported to the Church and Dey command post that night and I personally got assigned my first job as head rigger, which is my assignment with the team. Steve of Massachusetts Task Force One was there, and he and I worked with four New York City iron workers through the night, using a 90-10 crane, moving tons of debris all night long.

The following day we were back at work on the same crane, and a new group of iron workers. We made a connection with some guys by the name of Mike, Rich and Kevin. They're all great people. I found that the New York iron workers and construction workers are just incredibly great folks.

We cut and moved tons of steel again tonight. In the middle of the night I found a child's doll in the rubble, and I realized suddenly how much I missed my family. I heard our response team found a victim this morning, a police officer. Our hopes for a live rescue are starting to dim.

The next day we were back on the bus to the work site again. I'm already tired. We've averaged about 3 hours of sleep per night. Even when we get time to rest, you can't sleep.

Heading back to the crane, we worked all night again, moving steel, looking for bodies. I've noticed for several nights that there's very little debris that's recognizable. There's no desks, there's no chairs, carpet or sheet rock or anything else you'd associate with an office building, just the steel structure. There are still no victims in the area we're working in.

On September 18, we're back in the pile again, moving steel and searching for victims. Today the smell of death is more evident. I found a business card of a man with an office on the 83rd floor of one of the towers, and I wondered what his fate was at that moment. I said a prayer for him and hoped he is alive and well. I'm still not sure what his fate is.

Around midnight that night, the crane operation was halted while they were moving in a larger crane. When the crane shut down, I joined forces with some of the New York firefighters. Two of the battalion chiefs were out there with their sleeves rolled up, working right alongside of us. We were moving debris by hand, and that was a very solemn night. Went home tired that day.

The following day, Thursday, September 20, we started heading home, packing our equipment. It's been a long 10 days and everyone is exhausted. The team physician just diagnosed me with bronchitis. The dust we've been breathing all week finally caught up to us. Many others in the team had the same complaint of headache, sore throat, sinus congestion and sometimes fever. But most of all, everybody's troubled that we didn't find any victims.

Finally, on Friday, we land back in northern California, Travis Air Force Base, and we get a full police escort all the way back to Sacramento. Every freeway overpass for 40 miles was covered with fire engines,

police cars and citizens cheering us home. It was a warm reception.

We arrived in Sacramento to a similar greeting of family, friends, co-workers and media. I realized then for the people of Sacramento that we were their connection to this tragedy on the East Coast. It felt good to be home, but I felt like a part of me was still in New York. When I go to sleep, I still dream that I'm there. It doesn't leave us.

I just want to close and say that firefighters and law enforcement and EMS people are going to continue to be the first responders arriving at these incidents, and the toll is tremendous. The toll is tremendous on what I saw on the New York City firefighters, and for those of us who just came there and left, it took a toll as well, physically and mentally. We owe it to ourselves to be prepared for future incidents, to take care of our responders and make sure that we are afforded everything that we can possibly to do to be ready for the next one.

Source: U.S. Congress, Senate, Committee on Environment and Public Works, *FEMA's Response to the Sept. 11th Attacks* (Washington, DC: U.S. Government Printing Office, 2003), 7–12, 23–28.

10. USA PATRIOT Act (October 26, 200l)

Introduction

Less than seven weeks after the September 11 attacks, Congress voted on the Uniting and Strengthening America by Providing Appropriate Tools Required to Intercept and Obstruct Terrorism (USA PATRIOT) Act (PL 107-56), a major legislative package designed to enhance the ability of the United States to oppose terrorism at home and abroad. The lengthy act, drafted at great speed and in stressful circumstances, dramatically expanded the authority of the government to gather data through wiretaps, electronic surveillance, and other means, often covertly, on individuals and organizations suspected of being threats to the security of the United States. The act also imposed strict financial controls on the international movement of funds and tightened immigration controls. Although civil liberties organizations later successfully challenged in court various provisions of the act, in March 2006 Congress renewed and made permanent most of the USA PATRIOT Act's remaining surveillance provisions. As the initial impact of September 2001 receded, many Americans nonetheless feared that the legislation was too broad and imposed needless and undesirable restrictions on the civil liberties of both Americans and foreigners. A summary of the bill, written by the Congressional Research Service, is provided.

Primary Source

SUMMARY AS OF:

10/24/2001—Passed House without amendment.

Uniting and Strengthening America by Providing Appropriate Tools Required to Intercept and Obstruct Terrorism (USA PATRIOT ACT) Act of 2001—**Title I: Enhancing Domestic Security Against Terrorism**—Establishes in the Treasury the Counterterrorism Fund.

(Sec. 102) Expresses the sense of Congress that: (1) the civil rights and liberties of all Americans, including Arab Americans, must be protected, and that every effort must be taken to preserve their safety; (2) any acts of violence or discrimination against any Americans be condemned; and (3) the Nation is called upon to recognize the patriotism of fellow citizens from all ethnic, racial, and religious backgrounds.

(Sec. 103) Authorizes appropriations for the Federal Bureau of Investigation's (FBI) Technical Support Center.

(Sec. 104) Authorizes the Attorney General to request the Secretary of Defense to provide assistance in support of Department of Justice (DOJ) activities relating to the enforcement of Federal criminal code (code) provisions regarding the use of weapons of mass destruction during an emergency situation involving a weapon (currently, chemical weapon) of mass destruction.

(Sec. 105) Requires the Director of the U.S. Secret Service to take actions to develop a national network of electronic crime task forces throughout the United States to prevent, detect, and investigate various forms of electronic crimes, including potential terrorist attacks against critical infrastructure and financial payment systems.

(Sec. 106) Modifies provisions relating to presidential authority under the International Emergency Powers Act to: (1) authorize the President, when the United States is engaged in armed hostilities or has been attacked by a foreign country or foreign nationals, to confiscate any property subject to U.S. jurisdiction of a foreign person, organization, or country that he determines has planned, authorized, aided, or engaged in such hostilities or attacks (the rights to which shall vest in such agency or person as the President may designate); and (2) provide that, in any judicial review of a determination made under such provisions, if the determination was based on classified information such information may be submitted to the reviewing court ex parte and in camera.

Title II: Enhanced Surveillance Procedures—Amends the Federal criminal code to authorize the interception of wire, oral, and electronic communications for the production of evidence of: (1) specified chemical weapons or terrorism offenses; and (2) computer fraud and abuse.

(Sec. 203) Amends rule 6 of the Federal Rules of Criminal Procedure (FRCrP) to permit the sharing of grand jury information that involves foreign intelligence or counter-intelligence with Federal law enforcement, intelligence, protective, immigration, national defense, or national security officials (such officials), subject to specified requirements.

Authorizes an investigative or law enforcement officer, or an attorney for the Government, who, by authorized means, has obtained knowledge of the contents of any wire, oral, or electronic communication or evidence derived therefrom to disclose such contents to such officials to the extent that such contents include foreign intelligence or counterintelligence.

Directs the Attorney General to establish procedures for the disclosure of information (pursuant to the code and the FRCrP) that identifies a United States person, as defined in the Foreign Intelligence Surveillance Act of 1978 (FISA).

Authorizes the disclosure of foreign intelligence or counterintelligence obtained as part of a criminal investigation to such officials.

(Sec. 204) Clarifies that nothing in code provisions regarding pen registers shall be deemed to affect the acquisition by the Government of specified foreign intelligence information, and that procedures under FISA shall be the exclusive means by which electronic surveillance and the interception of domestic wire and oral (current law) and electronic communications may be conducted.

(Sec. 205) Authorizes the Director of the FBI to expedite the employment of personnel as translators to support counter-terrorism investigations and operations without regard to applicable Federal personnel requirements. Requires: (1) the Director to establish such security requirements as necessary for such personnel; and (2) the Attorney General to report to the House and Senate Judiciary Committees regarding translators.

(Sec. 206) Grants roving surveillance authority under FISA after requiring a court order approving an electronic surveillance to direct any person to furnish necessary information, facilities, or technical assistance in circumstances where the Court finds that the actions of the surveillance target may have the effect of thwarting the identification of a specified person.

(Sec. 207) Increases the duration of FISA surveillance permitted for non-U.S. persons who are agents of a foreign power.

(Sec. 208) Increases (from seven to 11) the number of district court judges designated to hear applications for and grant orders approving electronic surveillance. Requires that no fewer than three reside within 20 miles of the District of Columbia.

(Sec. 209) Permits the seizure of voice-mail messages under a warrant.

(Sec. 210) Expands the scope of subpoenas for records of electronic communications to include the length and types of service utilized, temporarily assigned network addresses, and the means and source of payment (including any credit card or bank account number).

(Sec. 211) Amends the Communications Act of 1934 to permit specified disclosures to Government entities, except for records revealing cable subscriber selection of video programming from a cable operator.

(Sec. 212) Permits electronic communication and remote computing service providers to make emergency disclosures to a governmental entity of customer electronic communications to protect life and limb.

(Sec. 213) Authorizes Federal district courts to allow a delay of required notices of the execution of a warrant if immediate notice may have an adverse result and under other specified circumstances.

(Sec. 214) Prohibits use of a pen register or trap and trace devices in any investigation to protect against international terrorism or clandestine intelligence activities that is conducted solely on the basis of activities protected by the first amendment to the U.S. Constitution.

(Sec. 215) Authorizes the Director of the FBI (or designee) to apply for a court order requiring production of certain business records for foreign intelligence and international terrorism investigations. Requires the Attorney General to report to the House and Senate Intelligence and Judiciary Committees semi-annually.

(Sec. 216) Amends the code to: (1) require a trap and trace device to restrict recoding or decoding so as not to include the contents of a wire or electronic communication; (2) apply a court order for a pen register or trap and trace devices to any person or entity providing wire or electronic communication service in the United States whose assistance may facilitate execution of the order; (3) require specified records kept on any pen register or trap and trace device on a packet-switched data network of a provider of electronic communication service to the public; and (4) allow a trap and trace device to identify the source (but not the contents) of a wire or electronic communication.

(Sec. 217) Makes it lawful to intercept the wire or electronic communication of a computer trespasser in certain circumstances.

(Sec. 218) Amends FISA to require an application for an electronic surveillance order or search warrant to certify that a significant purpose (currently, the sole or main purpose) of the surveillance is to obtain foreign intelligence information.

(Sec. 219) Amends rule 41 of the FRCrP to permit Federal magistrate judges in any district in which terrorism-related activities may have occurred to issue search warrants for searches within or outside the district.

(Sec. 220) Provides for nationwide service of search warrants for electronic evidence.

(Sec. 221) Amends the Trade Sanctions Reform and Export Enhancement Act of 2000 to extend trade sanctions to the territory of Afghanistan controlled by the Taliban.

(Sec. 222) Specifies that: (1) nothing in this Act shall impose any additional technical obligation or requirement on a provider of a wire or electronic communication service or other person to furnish facilities or technical assistance; and (2) a provider of such service, and a landlord, custodian, or other person who furnishes such facilities or technical assistance, shall be reasonably compensated for such reasonable expenditures incurred in providing such facilities or assistance.

(Sec. 223) Amends the Federal criminal code to provide for administrative discipline of Federal officers or employees who violate prohibitions against unauthorized disclosures of information gathered under this Act. Provides for civil actions against the United States for damages by any person aggrieved by such violations.

(Sec. 224) Terminates this title on December 31, 2005, except with respect to any particular foreign intelligence investigation beginning before that date, or any particular offense or potential offense that began or occurred before it.

(Sec. 225) Amends the Foreign Intelligence Surveillance Act of 1978 to prohibit a cause of action in any court against a provider of a wire or electronic communication service, landlord, custodian, or any other person that furnishes any information, facilities, or technical assistance in accordance with a court order or request for emergency assistance under such Act (for example, with respect to a wiretap).

Title III: International Money Laundering Abatement and Anti-Terrorist Financing Act of 2001—International Money Laundering Abatement and Financial Anti-Terrorism Act of 2001- Sunsets this Act after the first day of FY 2005 if Congress enacts a specified joint resolution to that effect.

Subtitle A: International Counter Money Laundering and Related Measures—Amends Federal law governing monetary transactions to prescribe procedural guidelines under which the Secretary of the Treasury (the Secretary) may require domestic financial institutions and agencies to take specified measures if the Secretary finds that reasonable grounds exist for concluding that jurisdictions, financial institutions, types of accounts, or transactions operating outside or within the United States, are of primary money laundering concern. Includes mandatory disclosure of specified information relating to certain correspondent accounts.

(Sec. 312) Mandates establishment of due diligence mechanisms to detect and report money laundering transactions through private banking accounts and correspondent accounts.

(Sec. 313) Prohibits U.S. correspondent accounts with foreign shell banks.

(Sec. 314) Instructs the Secretary to adopt regulations to encourage further cooperation among financial institutions, their regulatory authorities, and law enforcement authorities, with the specific purpose of encouraging regulatory authorities and law enforcement authorities to share with financial institutions information regarding individuals, entities, and organizations engaged in or reasonably suspected (based on credible evidence) of engaging in terrorist acts or money laundering activities. Authorizes such regulations to create procedures for cooperation and information sharing on matters specifically related to the finances of terrorist groups as well as their relationships with international narcotics traffickers.

Requires the Secretary to distribute annually to financial institutions a detailed analysis identifying patterns of suspicious activity and other investigative insights derived from suspicious activity reports and investigations by Federal, State, and local law enforcement agencies.

(Sec. 315) Amends Federal criminal law to include foreign corruption offenses as money laundering crimes.

(Sec. 316) Establishes the right of property owners to contest confiscation of property under law relating to confiscation of assets of suspected terrorists.

(Sec. 317) Establishes Federal jurisdiction over: (1) foreign money launderers (including their assets held in the United States); and (2) money that is laundered through a foreign bank.

(Sec. 319) Authorizes the forfeiture of money laundering funds from interbank accounts. Requires a covered financial institution, upon request of the appropriate Federal banking agency, to make available within 120 hours all pertinent information related to anti-money laundering compliance by the institution or its customer. Grants the Secretary summons and subpoena powers over foreign banks that maintain a correspondent bank in the United States. Requires a covered financial institution to terminate within ten business days any correspondent relationship with a foreign bank after receipt of written notice that the foreign bank has failed to comply with certain judicial proceedings. Sets forth civil penalties for failure to terminate such relationship.

(Sec. 321) Subjects to record and report requirements for monetary instrument transactions: (1) any credit union; and (2) any futures commission merchant, commodity trading advisor, and commodity pool operator registered, or required to register, under the Commodity Exchange Act.

(Sec. 323) Authorizes Federal application for restraining orders to preserve the availability of property subject to a foreign forfeiture or confiscation judgment.

(Sec. 325) Authorizes the Secretary to issue regulations to ensure that concentration accounts of financial institutions are not used to prevent association of the identity of an individual customer with the movement of funds of which the customer is the direct or beneficial owner.

(Sec. 326) Directs the Secretary to issue regulations prescribing minimum standards for financial institutions regarding customer identity in connection with the opening of accounts.

Requires the Secretary to report to Congress on: (1) the most timely and effective way to require foreign nationals to provide domestic financial institutions and agencies with appropriate and accurate information; (2) whether to require foreign nationals to obtain an identification number (similar to a Social Security or tax identification number) before opening an account with a domestic financial institution; and (3) a system for domestic financial institutions and agencies to review Government agency information to verify the identities of such foreign nationals.

(Sec. 327) Amends the Bank Holding Company Act of 1956 and the Federal Deposit Insurance Act to require consideration of the effectiveness of a company or companies in combating money laundering during reviews of proposed bank shares, acquisitions, or mergers.

(Sec. 328) Directs the Secretary take reasonable steps to encourage foreign governments to require the inclusion of the name of the originator in wire transfer instructions sent to the United States and other countries, with the information to remain with the transfer from its origination until the point of disbursement. Requires annual progress reports to specified congressional committees.

(Sec. 329) Prescribes criminal penalties for Federal officials or employees who seek or accept bribes in connection with administration of this title.

(Sec. 330) Urges U.S. negotiations for international cooperation in investigations of money laundering, financial crimes, and the finances of terrorist groups, including record sharing by foreign banks with U.S. law enforcement officials and domestic financial institution supervisors.

Subtitle B: Bank Secrecy Act Amendments and Related Improvements— Amends Federal law known as the Bank Secrecy Act to revise requirements for civil liability immunity for voluntary financial institution disclosure of suspicious activities. Authorizes the inclusion of suspicions of illegal activity in written employment references.

(Sec. 352) Authorizes the Secretary to exempt from minimum standards for anti-money laundering programs any financial institution not subject to certain regulations governing financial recordkeeping and reporting of currency and foreign transactions.

(Sec. 353) Establishes civil penalties for violations of geographic targeting orders and structuring transactions to evade certain recordkeeping requirements. Lengthens the effective period of geographic targeting orders from 60 to 180 days.

(Sec. 355) Amends the Federal Deposit Insurance Act to permit written employment references to contain suspicions of involvement in illegal activity.

(Sec. 356) Instructs the Secretary to: (1) promulgate regulations requiring registered securities brokers and dealers, futures commission merchants, commodity trading advisors, and commodity pool operators, to file reports of suspicious financial transactions; (2) report to Congress on the role of the Internal Revenue Service in the administration of the Bank Secrecy Act; and (3) share monetary instruments transactions records upon request of a U.S. intelligence agency for use in the conduct of intelligence or counterintelligence activities, including analysis, to protect against international terrorism.

(Sec. 358) Amends the Right to Financial Privacy Act to permit the transfer of financial records to other agencies or departments upon certification that the records are relevant to intelligence or counterintelligence activities related to international terrorism.

Amends the Fair Credit Reporting Act to require a consumer reporting agency to furnish all information in a consumer's file to a government agency upon certification that the records are relevant to intelligence or counterintelligence activities related to international terrorism.

(Sec. 359) Subjects to mandatory records and reports on monetary instruments transactions any licensed sender of money or any other person who engages as a business in the transmission of funds, including through an informal value transfer banking system or network (e.g., hawala) of people facilitating the transfer of money domestically or internationally outside of the conventional financial institutions system.

(Sec. 360) Authorizes the Secretary to instruct the United States Executive Director of each international financial institution to use his or her voice and vote to: (1) support the use of funds for a country (and its institutions) which contributes to U.S. efforts against international terrorism; and (2) require an auditing of disbursements to ensure that no funds are paid to persons who commit or support terrorism.

(Sec. 361) Makes the existing Financial Crimes Enforcement Network a bureau in the Department of the Treasury.

(Sec. 362) Directs the Secretary to establish a highly secure network in the Network that allows financial institutions to file certain reports and receive alerts and other information regarding suspicious activities warranting immediate and enhanced scrutiny.

(Sec. 363) Increases to $1 million the maximum civil penalties (currently $10,000) and criminal fines (currently $250,000) for money laundering. Sets a minimum civil penalty and criminal fine of double the amount of the illegal transaction.

(Sec. 364) Amends the Federal Reserve Act to provide for uniform protection authority for Federal Reserve facilities, including law enforcement officers authorized to carry firearms and make warrantless arrests.

(Sec. 365) Amends Federal law to require reports relating to coins and currency of more than $10,000 received in a nonfinancial trade or business.

(Sec. 366) Directs the Secretary to study and report to Congress on: (1) the possible expansion of the currency transaction reporting requirements exemption system;

and (2) methods for improving financial institution utilization of the system as a way of reducing the submission of currency transaction reports that have little or no value for law enforcement purposes.

Subtitle C: Currency Crimes— Establishes as a bulk cash smuggling felony the knowing concealment and attempted transport (or transfer) across U.S. borders of currency and monetary instruments in excess of $10,000, with intent to evade specified currency reporting requirements.

(Sec. 372) Changes from discretionary to mandatory a court's authority to order, as part of a criminal sentence, forfeiture of all property involved in certain currency reporting offenses. Leaves a court discretion to order civil forfeitures in money laundering cases.

(Sec. 373) Amends the Federal criminal code to revise the prohibition of unlicensed (currently, illegal) money transmitting businesses.

(Sec. 374) Increases the criminal penalties for counterfeiting domestic and foreign currency and obligations.

(Sec. 376) Amends the Federal criminal code to extend the prohibition against the laundering of money instruments to specified proceeds of terrorism.

(Sec. 377) Grants the United States extraterritorial jurisdiction where: (1) an offense committed outside the United States involves an access device issued, owned, managed, or controlled by a financial institution, account issuer, credit card system member, or other entity within U.S. jurisdiction; and (2) the person committing the offense transports, delivers, conveys, transfers to or through, or otherwise stores, secrets, or holds within U.S. jurisdiction any article used to assist in the commission of the offense or the proceeds of such offense or property derived from it.

Title IV: Protecting the Border—Subtitle A: Protecting the Northern Border— Authorizes the Attorney General to waive certain Immigration and Naturalization Service (INS) personnel caps with respect to ensuring security needs on the Northern border.

(Sec. 402) Authorizes appropriations to: (1) triple the number of Border Patrol, Customs Service, and INS personnel (and support facilities) at points of entry and along the Northern border; and (2) INS and Customs for related border monitoring technology and equipment.

(Sec. 403) Amends the Immigration and Nationality Act to require the Attorney General and the Federal Bureau of Investigation (FBI) to provide the Department of State and INS with access to specified criminal history extracts in order to determine whether or not a visa or admissions applicant has a criminal history. Directs the FBI to provide periodic extract updates. Provides for confidentiality.

Directs the Attorney General and the Secretary of State to develop a technology standard to identify visa and admissions applicants, which shall be the basis for an electronic system of law enforcement and intelligence sharing system available to consular, law enforcement, intelligence, and Federal border inspection personnel.

(Sec. 404) Amends the Department of Justice Appropriations Act, 2001 to eliminate certain INS overtime restrictions.

(Sec. 405) Directs the Attorney General to report on the feasibility of enhancing the Integrated Automated Fingerprint Identification System and other identification systems to better identify foreign individuals in connection with U.S. or foreign criminal investigations before issuance of a visa to, or permitting such person's entry or exit from, the United States. Authorizes appropriations.

Subtitle B: Enhanced Immigration Provisions—Amends the Immigration and Nationality Act to broaden the scope of aliens ineligible for admission or deportable due to terrorist activities to include an alien who: (1) is a representative of a political, social, or similar group whose political endorsement of terrorist acts undermines U.S. antiterrorist efforts; (2) has used a position of prominence to endorse terrorist activity, or to persuade others to support such activity in a way that undermines U.S. antiterrorist efforts (or the child or spouse of such an alien under specified circumstances); or (3) has been associated with a terrorist organization and intends to engage in threatening activities while in the United States.

(Sec. 411) Includes within the definition of "terrorist activity" the use of any weapon or dangerous device.

Redefines "engage in terrorist activity" to mean, in an individual capacity or as a member of an organization, to: (1) commit or to incite to commit, under circumstances indicating an intention to cause death or serious bodily injury, a terrorist activity; (2) prepare or plan a terrorist activity; (3) gather information on potential targets for terrorist activity; (4) solicit funds or other things of value for a terrorist activity or a terrorist organization (with an exception for lack of knowledge); (5) solicit any individual to engage in prohibited conduct or for terrorist organization membership (with an exception for lack of knowledge); or (6) commit an act that the actor knows, or reasonably should know, affords material support, including a safe house, transportation, communications, funds, transfer of funds or other material financial benefit, false documentation or identification, weapons (including chemical, biological, or radiological weapons), explosives, or training

for the commission of a terrorist activity; to any individual who the actor knows or reasonably should know has committed or plans to commit a terrorist activity; or to a terrorist organization (with an exception for lack of knowledge).

Defines "terrorist organization" as a group: (1) designated under the Immigration and Nationality Act or by the Secretary of State; or (2) a group of two or more individuals, whether related or not, which engages in terrorist-related activities.

Provides for the retroactive application of amendments under this Act. Stipulates that an alien shall not be considered inadmissible or deportable because of a relationship to an organization that was not designated as a terrorist organization prior to enactment of this Act. States that the amendments under this section shall apply to all aliens in exclusion or deportation proceedings on or after the date of enactment of this Act.

Directs the Secretary of State to notify specified congressional leaders seven days prior to designating an organization as a terrorist organization. Provides for organization redesignation or revocation.

(Sec. 412) Provides for mandatory detention until removal from the United States (regardless of any relief from removal) of an alien certified by the Attorney General as a suspected terrorist or threat to national security. Requires release of such alien after seven days if removal proceedings have not commenced, or the alien has not been charged with a criminal offense. Authorizes detention for additional periods of up to six months of an alien not likely to be deported in the reasonably foreseeable future only if release will threaten U.S. national security or the safety of the community or any person. Limits judicial review to habeas corpus proceedings in the

U.S. Supreme Court, the U.S. Court of Appeals for the District of Columbia, or any district court with jurisdiction to entertain a habeas corpus petition. Restricts to the U.S. Court of Appeals for the District of Columbia the right of appeal of any final order by a circuit or district judge.

(Sec. 413) Authorizes the Secretary of State, on a reciprocal basis, to share criminal- and terrorist-related visa lookout information with foreign governments.

(Sec. 414) Declares the sense of Congress that the Attorney General should: (1) fully implement the integrated entry and exit data system for airports, seaports, and land border ports of entry with all deliberate speed; and (2) begin immediately establishing the Integrated Entry and Exit Data System Task Force. Authorizes appropriations.

Requires the Attorney General and the Secretary of State, in developing the integrated entry and exit data system, to focus on the use of biometric technology and the development of tamper-resistant documents readable at ports of entry.

(Sec. 415) Amends the Immigration and Naturalization Service Data Management Improvement Act of 2000 to include the Office of Homeland Security in the Integrated Entry and Exit Data System Task Force.

(Sec. 416) Directs the Attorney General to implement fully and expand the foreign student monitoring program to include other approved educational institutions like air flight, language training, or vocational schools.

(Sec. 417) Requires audits and reports on implementation of the mandate for machine readable passports.

(Sec. 418) Directs the Secretary of State to: (1) review how consular officers issue visas to determine if consular shopping is a problem; and (2) if it is a problem, take steps to address it, and report on them to Congress.

Subtitle C: Preservation of Immigration Benefits for Victims of Terrorism— Authorizes the Attorney General to provide permanent resident status through the special immigrant program to an alien (and spouse, child, or grandparent under specified circumstances) who was the beneficiary of a petition filed on or before September 11, 2001, to grant the alien permanent residence as an employer-sponsored immigrant or of an application for labor certification if the petition or application was rendered null because of the disability of the beneficiary or loss of employment due to physical damage to, or destruction of, the business of the petitioner or applicant as a direct result of the terrorist attacks on September 11, 2001 (September attacks), or because of the death of the petitioner or applicant as a direct result of such attacks.

(Sec. 422) States that an alien who was legally in a nonimmigrant status and was disabled as a direct result of the September attacks may remain in the United States until his or her normal status termination date or September 11, 2002. Includes in such extension the spouse or child of such an alien or of an alien who was killed in such attacks. Authorizes employment during such period.

Extends specified immigration-related deadlines and other filing requirements for an alien (and spouse and child) who was directly prevented from meeting such requirements as a result of the September attacks respecting: (1) nonimmigrant status and status revision; (2) diversity immigrants; (3) immigrant visas; (4) parolees; and (5) voluntary departure.

(Sec. 423) Waives, under specified circumstances, the requirement that an alien spouse (and child) of a U.S. citizen must have been married for at least two years prior to such citizen's death in order to maintain immediate relative status if such citizen died as a direct result of the September attacks. Provides for: (1) continued family-sponsored immigrant eligibility for the spouse, child, or unmarried son or daughter of a permanent resident who died as a direct result of such attacks; and (2) continued eligibility for adjustment of status for the spouse and child of an employment-based immigrant who died similarly.

(Sec. 424) Amends the Immigration and Nationality Act to extend the visa categorization of "child" for aliens with petitions filed on or before September 11, 2001, for aliens whose 21st birthday is in September 2001 (90 days), or after September 2001 (45 days).

(Sec. 425) Authorizes the Attorney General to provide temporary administrative relief to an alien who, as of September 10, 2001, was lawfully in the United States and was the spouse, parent, or child of an individual who died or was disabled as a direct result of the September attacks.

(Sec. 426) Directs the Attorney General to establish evidentiary guidelines for death, disability, and loss of employment or destruction of business in connection with the provisions of this subtitle.

(Sec. 427) Prohibits benefits to terrorists or their family members.

Title V: Removing Obstacles to Investigating Terrorism—Authorizes the Attorney General to pay rewards from available funds pursuant to public advertisements for assistance to DOJ to combat terrorism and defend the Nation against terrorist acts, in accordance with procedures and regulations established or issued by the Attorney General, subject to specified conditions, including a prohibition against any such reward of $250,000 or more from being made or offered without the personal approval of either the Attorney General or the President.

(Sec. 502) Amends the State Department Basic Authorities Act of 1956 to modify the Department of State rewards program to authorize rewards for information leading to: (1) the dismantling of a terrorist organization in whole or significant part; and (2) the identification or location of an individual who holds a key leadership position in a terrorist organization. Raises the limit on rewards if the Secretary State determines that a larger sum is necessary to combat terrorism or defend the Nation against terrorist acts.

(Sec. 503) Amends the DNA Analysis Backlog Elimination Act of 2000 to qualify a Federal terrorism offense for collection of DNA for identification.

(Sec. 504) Amends FISA to authorize consultation among Federal law enforcement officers regarding information acquired from an electronic surveillance or physical search in terrorism and related investigations or protective measures.

(Sec. 505) Allows the FBI to request telephone toll and transactional records, financial records, and consumer reports in any investigation to protect against international terrorism or clandestine intelligence activities only if the investigation is not conducted solely on the basis of activities protected by the first amendment to the U.S. Constitution.

(Sec. 506) Revises U.S. Secret Service jurisdiction with respect to fraud and related activity in connection with computers. Grants the FBI primary authority to investigate specified fraud and computer related activity for cases involving espionage, foreign counter-intelligence, information protected against unauthorized disclosure for reasons of national defense or foreign relations, or restricted data, except for offenses affecting Secret Service duties.

(Sec. 507) Amends the General Education Provisions Act and the National Education Statistics Act of 1994 to provide for disclosure of educational records to the Attorney General in a terrorism investigation or prosecution.

Title VI: Providing for Victims of Terrorism, Public Safety Officers, and Their Families—Subtitle A: Aid to Families of Public Safety Officers—Provides for expedited payments for: (1) public safety officers involved in the prevention, investigation, rescue, or recovery efforts related to a terrorist attack; and (2) heroic public safety officers. Increases Public Safety Officers Benefit Program payments.

Subtitle B: Amendments to the Victims of Crime Act of 1984—Amends the Victims of Crime Act of 1984 to: (1) revise provisions regarding the allocation of funds for compensation and assistance, location of compensable crime, and the relationship of crime victim compensation to means-tested Federal benefit programs and to the September 11th victim compensation fund; and (2) establish an antiterrorism emergency reserve in the Victims of Crime Fund.

Title VII: Increased Information Sharing for Critical Infrastructure Protection—Amends the Omnibus Crime Control and Safe Streets Act of 1968 to extend Bureau of Justice Assistance regional information sharing system grants to systems that enhance the investigation and prosecution abilities of participating Federal, State, and local law enforcement agencies in addressing multi-jurisdictional terrorist conspiracies and activities. Authorizes appropriations.

Title VIII: Strengthening the Criminal Laws Against Terrorism—Amends the Federal criminal code to prohibit specific terrorist acts or otherwise destructive, disruptive, or violent acts against mass transportation vehicles, ferries, providers, employees, passengers, or operating systems.

(Sec. 802) Amends the Federal criminal code to: (1) revise the definition of "international terrorism" to include activities that appear to be intended to affect the conduct of government by mass destruction; and (2) define "domestic terrorism" as activities that occur primarily within U.S. jurisdiction, that involve criminal acts dangerous to human life, and that appear to be intended to intimidate or coerce a civilian population, to influence government policy by intimidation or coercion, or to affect government conduct by mass destruction, assassination, or kidnapping.

(Sec. 803) Prohibits harboring any person knowing or having reasonable grounds to believe that such person has committed or to be about to commit a terrorism offense.

(Sec. 804) Establishes Federal jurisdiction over crimes committed at U.S. facilities abroad.

(Sec. 805) Applies the prohibitions against providing material support for terrorism to offenses outside of the United States.

(Sec. 806) Subjects to civil forfeiture all assets, foreign or domestic, of terrorist organizations.

(Sec. 808) Expands: (1) the offenses over which the Attorney General shall have primary investigative jurisdiction under provisions governing acts of terrorism transcending national boundaries; and (2) the offenses included within the definition of the Federal crime of terrorism.

(Sec. 809) Provides that there shall be no statute of limitations for certain terrorism offenses if the commission of such an offense resulted in, or created a foreseeable risk of, death or serious bodily injury to another person.

(Sec. 810) Provides for alternative maximum penalties for specified terrorism crimes.

(Sec. 811) Makes: (1) the penalties for attempts and conspiracies the same as those for terrorism offenses; (2) the supervised release terms for offenses with terrorism predicates any term of years or life; and (3) specified terrorism crimes Racketeer Influenced and Corrupt Organizations statute predicates.

(Sec. 814) Revises prohibitions and penalties regarding fraud and related activity in connection with computers to include specified cyber-terrorism offenses.

(Sec. 816) Directs the Attorney General to establish regional computer forensic laboratories, and to support existing laboratories, to develop specified cyber-security capabilities.

(Sec. 817) Prescribes penalties for knowing possession in certain circumstances of biological agents, toxins, or delivery systems, especially by certain restricted persons.

Title IX: Improved Intelligence— Amends the National Security Act of 1947 to require the Director of Central Intelligence (DCI) to establish requirements and priorities for foreign intelligence collected under the Foreign Intelligence Surveillance Act of 1978 and to provide assistance to the Attorney General (AG) to ensure that information derived from electronic surveillance or physical searches is disseminated for efficient and effective foreign intelligence purposes. Requires the inclusion of international terrorist activities within the scope of foreign intelligence under such Act.

(Sec. 903) Expresses the sense of Congress that officers and employees of the intelligence community should establish and maintain intelligence relationships to acquire information on terrorists and terrorist organizations.

(Sec. 904) Authorizes deferral of the submission to Congress of certain reports on intelligence and intelligence-related matters until: (1) February 1, 2002; or (2) a date after February 1, 2002, if the official involved certifies that preparation and submission on February 1, 2002, will impede the work of officers or employees engaged in counterterrorism activities. Requires congressional notification of any such deferral.

(Sec. 905) Requires the AG or the head of any other Federal department or agency with law enforcement responsibilities to expeditiously disclose to the DCI any foreign intelligence acquired in the course of a criminal investigation.

(Sec. 906) Requires the AG, DCI, and Secretary of the Treasury to jointly report to Congress on the feasibility and desirability of reconfiguring the Foreign Asset Tracking Center and the Office of Foreign Assets Control to provide for the analysis and dissemination of foreign intelligence relating to the financial capabilities and resources of international terrorist organizations.

(Sec. 907) Requires the DCI to report to the appropriate congressional committees on the establishment and maintenance of the National Virtual Translation Center for timely and accurate translation of foreign intelligence for elements of the intelligence community.

(Sec. 908) Requires the AG to provide a program of training to Government officials regarding the identification and use of foreign intelligence.

Title X: Miscellaneous—Directs the Inspector General of the Department of Justice to designate one official to review allegations of abuse of civil rights, civil liberties, and racial and ethnic profiling by government employees and officials.

(Sec. 1002) Expresses the sense of Congress condemning acts of violence or discrimination against any American, including Sikh-Americans. Calls upon local and Federal law enforcement authorities to prosecute to the fullest extent of the law all those who commit crimes.

(Sec. 1004) Amends the Federal criminal code with respect to venue in money laundering cases to allow a prosecution for such an offense to be brought in: (1) any district in which the financial or monetary transaction is conducted; or (2) any district where a prosecution for the underlying specified unlawful activity could be brought, if the defendant participated in the transfer of the proceeds of the specified unlawful activity from that district to the district where the financial or monetary transaction is conducted.

States that: (1) a transfer of funds from one place to another, by wire or any other means, shall constitute a single, continuing transaction; and (2) any person who conducts any portion of the transaction may be charged in any district in which the transaction takes place.

Allows a prosecution for an attempt or conspiracy offense to be brought in the district where venue would lie for the completed offense, or in any other district where an act in furtherance of the attempt or conspiracy took place.

(Sec. 1005) First Responders Assistance Act—Directs the Attorney General to make grants to State and local governments to improve the ability of State and local law enforcement, fire department, and first responders to respond to and prevent acts of terrorism. Authorizes appropriations.

(Sec. 1006) Amends the Immigration and Nationality Act to make inadmissible into the United States any alien engaged in money laundering. Directs the Secretary of State to develop a money laundering watchlist which: (1) identifies individuals worldwide who are known or suspected of money laundering; and (2) is readily accessible to, and shall be checked by, a consular or other Federal official before the issuance of a visa or admission to the United States.

(Sec. 1007) Authorizes FY 2002 appropriations for regional antidrug training in Turkey by the Drug Enforcement Administration for police, as well as increased precursor chemical control efforts in South and Central Asia.

(Sec. 1008) Directs the Attorney General to conduct a feasibility study and report to Congress on the use of a biometric identifier scanning system with access to the FBI integrated automated fingerprint identification system at overseas consular posts and points of entry to the United States.

(Sec. 1009) Directs the FBI to study and report to Congress on the feasibility of providing to airlines access via computer to the names of passengers who are suspected of terrorist activity by Federal officials. Authorizes appropriations.

(Sec. 1010) Authorizes the use of Department of Defense funds to contract with local and State governments, during the period of Operation Enduring Freedom, for the performance of security functions at U.S. military installations.

(Sec. 1011) Crimes Against Charitable Americans Act of 2001—Amends the Telemarketing and Consumer Fraud and Abuse

Prevention Act to cover fraudulent charitable solicitations. Requires any person engaged in telemarketing for the solicitation of charitable contributions, donations, or gifts to disclose promptly and clearly the purpose of the telephone call.

(Sec. 1012) Amends the Federal transportation code to prohibit States from licensing any individual to operate a motor vehicle transporting hazardous material unless the Secretary of Transportation determines that such individual does not pose a security risk warranting denial of the license. Requires background checks of such license applicants by the Attorney General upon State request.

(Sec. 1013) Expresses the sense of the Senate on substantial new U.S. investment in bioterrorism preparedness and response.

(Sec. 1014) Directs the Office for State and Local Domestic Preparedness Support of the Office of Justice Programs to make grants to enhance State and local capability to prepare for and respond to terrorist acts. Authorizes appropriations for FY 2002 through 2007.

(Sec. 1015) Amends the Crime Identification Technology Act of 1998 to extend it through FY 2007 and provide for antiterrorism grants to States and localities. Authorizes appropriations.

(Sec. 1016) Critical Infrastructures Protection Act of 2001—Declares it is U.S. policy: (1) that any physical or virtual disruption of the operation of the critical infrastructures of the United States be rare, brief, geographically limited in effect, manageable, and minimally detrimental to the economy, human and government services, and U.S. national security; (2) that actions necessary to achieve this policy be carried out in a public-private partnership involving corporate and non-governmental organizations; and (3) to have in place a comprehensive and effective program to ensure the continuity of essential Federal Government functions under all circumstances.

Establishes the National Infrastructure Simulation and Analysis Center to serve as a source of national competence to address critical infrastructure protection and continuity through support for activities related to counterterrorism, threat assessment, and risk mitigation.

Defines critical infrastructure as systems and assets, whether physical or virtual, so vital to the United States that their incapacity or destruction would have a debilitating impact on security, national economic security, national public health or safety, or any combination of those matters.

Authorizes appropriations.

Source: USA PATRIOT Act of 2001, Public Law 107-56 (October 26, 2001). Summary at https://www.govtrack.us/congress/bills/107/hr3162/summary#libraryofcongress

---

II. Osama bin Laden's Letter to the American People (November 2002)

Introduction

In several public statements, including a "Letter to the American People," published in Arabic on the Internet in 2002 and later translated into English, Osama bin Laden enumerated what he viewed as American threats and enmity toward Islam. Bin Laden cited what he considered to be the immoral and irreligious character of American life, which was an affront to Muslim principles. Foremost among U.S. offenses, however, he placed American support for Israel, followed by its presence in the Persian Gulf, and American opposition to various Muslim governments and groups around the world. After the

September 11 attacks, U.S. president George H. W. Bush quickly declared that waging a global "War on Terror" wherever it raised its head was now by far the most significant U.S. foreign policy priority. The links bin Laden drew between his organization's attacks on American landmarks and other facilities and his adamant hostility to Israel, meant that the U.S. government and people were likely to view Palestinian and other terrorist operations against that country and its citizens and Israeli measures designed to repress them in the context of worldwide international efforts to combat the threat of armed Islamic militancy.

Primary Source

"Permission to fight (against disbelievers) is given to those (believers) who are fought against, because they have been wronged and surely, Allah is Able to give them (believers) victory" [Quran 22:39]

"Those who believe, fight in the Cause of Allah, and those who disbelieve, fight in the cause of Taghut (anything worshipped other than Allah e.g. Satan). So fight you against the friends of Satan; ever feeble is indeed the plot of Satan."[Quran 4:76]

Some American writers have published articles under the title 'On what basis are we fighting?' These articles have generated a number of responses, some of which adhered to the truth and were based on Islamic Law, and others which have not. Here we wanted to outline the truth—as an explanation and warning—hoping for Allah's reward, seeking success and support from Him.

While seeking Allah's help, we form our reply based on two questions directed at the Americans:

(Q1) Why are we fighting and opposing you?

Q2) What are we calling you to, and what do we want from you?

As for the first question: Why are we fighting and opposing you? The answer is very simple:

(1) Because you attacked us and continue to attack us.

a) You attacked us in Palestine:

(i) Palestine, which has sunk under military occupation for more than 80 years. The British handed over Palestine, with your help and your support, to the Jews, who have occupied it for more than 50 years; years overflowing with oppression, tyranny, crimes, killing, expulsion, destruction and devastation. The creation and continuation of Israel is one of the greatest crimes, and you are the leaders of its criminals. And of course there is no need to explain and prove the degree of American support for Israel. The creation of Israel is a crime which must be erased. Each and every person whose hands have become polluted in the contribution towards this crime must pay its price, and pay for it heavily.

(ii) It brings us both laughter and tears to see that you have not yet tired of repeating your fabricated lies that the Jews have a historical right to Palestine, as it was promised to them in the Torah. Anyone who disputes with them on this alleged fact is accused of anti-semitism. This is one of the most fallacious, widely-circulated fabrications in history. The people of Palestine are pure Arabs and original Semites. It is the Muslims who are the inheritors of Moses (peace be upon him) and the inheritors of the real Torah that has not been changed. Muslims believe in all of the Prophets, including Abraham, Moses, Jesus and Muhammad, peace and blessings of Allah be upon them all. If the followers of Moses have been promised a right to Palestine in the Torah, then the Muslims are the most worthy nation of this.

When the Muslims conquered Palestine and drove out the Romans, Palestine and Jerusalem returned to Islaam, the religion of all the Prophets peace be upon them. Therefore, the call to a historical right to Palestine cannot be raised against the Islamic Ummah that believes in all the Prophets of Allah (peace and blessings be upon them)—and we make no distinction between them.

(iii) The blood pouring out of Palestine must be equally revenged. You must know that the Palestinians do not cry alone; their women are not widowed alone; their sons are not orphaned alone.

(b) You attacked us in Somalia; you supported the Russian atrocities against us in Chechnya, the Indian oppression against us in Kashmir, and the Jewish aggression against us in Lebanon.

(c) Under your supervision, consent and orders, the governments of our countries which act as your agents, attack us on a daily basis;

(i) These governments prevent our people from establishing the Islamic Shariah, using violence and lies to do so.

(ii) These governments give us a taste of humiliation, and places us in a large prison of fear and subdual.

(iii) These governments steal our Ummah's wealth and sell them to you at a paltry price.

(iv) These governments have surrendered to the Jews, and handed them most of Palestine, acknowledging the existence of their state over the dismembered limbs of their own people.

(v) The removal of these governments is an obligation upon us, and a necessary step to free the Ummah, to make the Shariah the supreme law and to regain Palestine. And our fight against these governments is not separate from out fight against you.

(d) You steal our wealth and oil at paltry prices because of you international influence and military threats. This theft is indeed the biggest theft ever witnessed by mankind in the history of the world.

(e) Your forces occupy our countries; you spread your military bases throughout them; you corrupt our lands, and you besiege our sanctities, to protect the security of the Jews and to ensure the continuity of your pillage of our treasures.

(f) You have starved the Muslims of Iraq, where children die every day. It is a wonder that more than 1.5 million Iraqi children have died as a result of your sanctions, and you did not show concern. Yet when 3000 of your people died, the entire world rises and has not yet sat down.

(g) You have supported the Jews in their idea that Jerusalem is their eternal capital, and agreed to move your embassy there. With your help and under your protection, the Israelis are planning to destroy the Al-Aqsa mosque. Under the protection of your weapons, Sharon entered the Al-Aqsa mosque, to pollute it as a preparation to capture and destroy it.

(2) These tragedies and calamities are only a few examples of your oppression and aggression against us. It is commanded by our religion and intellect that the oppressed have a right to return the aggression. Do not await anything from us but Jihad, resistance and revenge. Is it in any way rational to expect that after America has attacked us for more than half a century, that we will then leave her to live in security and peace?!!

(3) You may then dispute that all the above does not justify aggression against civilians, for crimes they did not commit and offenses in which they did not partake:

(a) This argument contradicts your continuous repetition that America is the land of freedom, and its leaders in this world. Therefore, the American people are the ones who choose their government by way of their own free will; a choice which stems from their agreement to its policies. Thus the American people have chosen, consented to, and affirmed their support for the Israeli oppression of the Palestinians, the occupation and usurpation of their land, and its continuous killing, torture, punishment and expulsion of the Palestinians. The American people have the ability and choice to refuse the policies of their Government and even to change it if they want.

(b) The American people are the ones who pay the taxes which fund the planes that bomb us in Afghanistan, the tanks that strike and destroy our homes in Palestine, the armies which occupy our lands in the Arabian Gulf, and the fleets which ensure the blockade of Iraq. These tax dollars are given to Israel for it to continue to attack us and penetrate our lands. So the American people are the ones who fund the attacks against us, and they are the ones who oversee the expenditure of these monies in the way they wish, through their elected candidates.

(c) Also the American army is part of the American people. It is this very same people who are shamelessly helping the Jews fight against us.

(d) The American people are the ones who employ both their men and their women in the American Forces which attack us.

(e) This is why the American people cannot be not innocent of all the crimes committed by the Americans and Jews against us.

(f) Allah, the Almighty, legislated the permission and the option to take revenge. Thus, if we are attacked, then we have the right to attack back. Whoever has destroyed our villages and towns, then we have the right to destroy their villages and towns. Whoever has stolen our wealth, then we have the right to destroy their economy. And whoever has killed our civilians, then we have the right to kill theirs.

The American Government and press still refuses to answer the question:

Why did they attack us in New York and Washington?

If Sharon is a man of peace in the eyes of Bush, then we are also men of peace!!! America does not understand the language of manners and principles, so we are addressing it using the language it understands.

(Q2) As for the second question that we want to answer: What are we calling you to, and what do we want from you?

(1) The first thing that we are calling you to is Islam.

(a) The religion of the Unification of God; of freedom from associating partners with Him, and rejection of this; of complete love of Him, the Exalted; of complete submission to His Laws; and of the discarding of all the opinions, orders, theories and religions which contradict with the religion He sent down to His Prophet Muhammad (peace be upon him). Islam is the religion of all the prophets, and makes no distinction between them—peace be upon them all.

It is to this religion that we call you; the seal of all the previous religions. It is the religion of Unification of God, sincerity, the best of manners, righteousness, mercy, honour, purity, and piety. It is the religion of showing kindness to others, establishing justice between them, granting them their rights, and defending the oppressed and the persecuted. It is the religion of enjoining the good and forbidding the evil with the hand, tongue and heart. It is the religion of Jihad in the way of Allah so that Allah's Word and religion reign Supreme. And it is the religion of unity and agreement on the obedience to Allah, and total equality between all people, without regarding their colour, sex, or language.

(b) It is the religion whose book—the Quran—will remained preserved and unchanged, after the other Divine books and messages have been changed. The Quran is the miracle until the Day of Judgment. Allah has challenged anyone to bring a book like the Quran or even ten verses like it.

(2) The second thing we call you to, is to stop your oppression, lies, immorality and debauchery that has spread among you.

(a) We call you to be a people of manners, principles, honour, and purity; to reject the immoral acts of fornication, homosexuality, intoxicants, gambling's, and trading with interest.

We call you to all of this that you may be freed from that which you have become caught up in; that you may be freed from the deceptive lies that you are a great nation, that your leaders spread amongst you to conceal from you the despicable state to which you have reached.

(b) It is saddening to tell you that you are the worst civilization witnessed by the history of mankind:

(i) You are the nation who, rather than ruling by the Shariah of Allah in its Constitution and Laws, choose to invent your own laws as you will and desire. You separate religion from your policies, contradicting the pure nature which affirms Absolute Authority to the Lord and your Creator. You flee from the embarrassing question posed to you: How is it possible for Allah the Almighty to create His creation, grant them power over all the creatures and land, grant them all the amenities of life, and then deny them that which they are most in need of: knowledge of the laws which govern their lives?

(ii) You are the nation that permits Usury, which has been forbidden by all the religions. Yet you build your economy and investments on Usury. As a result of this, in all its different forms and guises, the Jews have taken control of your economy, through which they have then taken control of your media, and now control all aspects of your life making you their servants and achieving their aims at your expense; precisely what Benjamin Franklin warned you against.

(iii) You are a nation that permits the production, trading and usage of intoxicants. You also permit drugs, and only forbid the trade of them, even though your nation is the largest consumer of them.

(iv) You are a nation that permits acts of immorality, and you consider them to be pillars of personal freedom. You have continued to sink down this abyss from level to level until incest has spread amongst you, in the face of which neither your sense of honour nor your laws object.

Who can forget your President Clinton's immoral acts committed in the official Oval office? After that you did not even bring him to account, other than that he 'made a mistake,' after which everything passed with no punishment. Is there a worse kind of event for which your name will go down in history and remembered by nations?

(v) You are a nation that permits gambling in its all forms. The companies practice this as well, resulting in the investments becoming active and the criminals becoming rich.

(vi) You are a nation that exploits women like consumer products or advertising tools calling upon customers to purchase them. You use women to serve passengers, visitors, and strangers to increase your profit margins. You then rant that you support the liberation of women.

(vii) You are a nation that practices the trade of sex in all its forms, directly and indirectly. Giant corporations and establishments are established on this, under the name of art, entertainment, tourism and freedom, and other deceptive names you attribute to it.

(viii) And because of all this, you have been described in history as a nation that spreads diseases that were unknown to man in the past. Go ahead and boast to the nations of man, that you brought them AIDS as a Satanic American Invention.

(xi) You have destroyed nature with your industrial waste and gases more than any other nation in history. Despite this, you refuse to sign the Kyoto agreement so that you can secure the profit of your greedy companies and industries.

(x) Your law is the law of the rich and wealthy people, who hold sway in their political parties, and fund their election campaigns with their gifts. Behind them stand the Jews, who control your policies, media and economy.

(xi) That which you are singled out for in the history of mankind, is that you have used your force to destroy mankind more than any other nation in history; not to defend principles and values, but to hasten to secure your interests and profits. You who dropped a nuclear bomb on Japan, even though Japan was ready to negotiate an end to the war. How many acts of oppression, tyranny and injustice have you carried out, O callers to freedom?

(xii) Let us not forget one of your major characteristics: your duality in both manners and values; your hypocrisy in manners and principles. All manners, principles and values have two scales: one for you and one for the others.

(a) The freedom and democracy that you call to is for yourselves and for white race only; as for the rest of the world, you impose upon them your monstrous, destructive policies and Governments, which you call the 'American friends.' Yet you prevent them

from establishing democracies. When the Islamic party in Algeria wanted to practice democracy and they won the election, you unleashed your agents in the Algerian army onto them, and to attack them with tanks and guns, to imprison them and torture them—a new lesson from the 'American book of democracy'!!!

(b) Your policy on prohibiting and forcibly removing weapons of mass destruction to ensure world peace: it only applies to those countries which you do not permit to possess such weapons. As for the countries you consent to, such as Israel, then they are allowed to keep and use such weapons to defend their security. Anyone else who you suspect might be manufacturing or keeping these kinds of weapons, you call them criminals and you take military action against them.

(c) You are the last ones to respect the resolutions and policies of International Law, yet you claim to want to selectively punish anyone else who does the same. Israel has for more than 50 years been pushing UN resolutions and rules against the wall with the full support of America.

(d) As for the war criminals which you censure and form criminal courts for—you shamelessly ask that your own are granted immunity!! However, history will not forget the war crimes that you committed against the Muslims and the rest of the world; those you have killed in Japan, Afghanistan, Somalia, Lebanon and Iraq will remain a shame that you will never be able to escape. It will suffice to remind you of your latest war crimes in Afghanistan, in which densely populated innocent civilian villages were destroyed, bombs were dropped on mosques causing the roof of the mosque to come crashing down on the heads of the Muslims praying inside. You are the ones who broke the agreement with the Mujahideen when they left Qunduz, bombing them in Jangi fort, and killing more than 1,000 of your prisoners through suffocation and thirst. Allah alone knows how many people have died by torture at the hands of you and your agents. Your planes remain in the Afghan skies, looking for anyone remotely suspicious.

(e) You have claimed to be the vanguards of Human Rights, and your Ministry of Foreign affairs issues annual reports containing statistics of those countries that violate any Human Rights. However, all these things vanished when the Mujahideen hit you, and you then implemented the methods of the same documented governments that you used to curse. In America, you captured thousands the Muslims and Arabs, took them into custody with neither reason, court trial, nor even disclosing their names. You issued newer, harsher laws.

What happens in Guatanamo is a historical embarrassment to America and its values, and it screams into your faces—you hypocrites, "What is the value of your signature on any agreement or treaty?"

(3) What we call you to thirdly is to take an honest stance with yourselves—and I doubt you will do so—to discover that you are a nation without principles or manners, and that the values and principles to you are something which you merely demand from others, not that which you yourself must adhere to.

(4) We also advise you to stop supporting Israel, and to end your support of the Indians in Kashmir, the Russians against the Chechens and to also cease supporting the Manila Government against the Muslims in Southern Philippines.

(5) We also advise you to pack your luggage and get out of our lands. We desire for your goodness, guidance, and righteousness, so do not force us to send you back as cargo in coffins.

(6) Sixthly, we call upon you to end your support of the corrupt leaders in our countries. Do not interfere in our politics and method of education. Leave us alone, or else expect us in New York and Washington.

(7) We also call you to deal with us and interact with us on the basis of mutual interests and benefits, rather than the policies of sub dual, theft and occupation, and not to continue your policy of supporting the Jews because this will result in more disasters for you.

If you fail to respond to all these conditions, then prepare for fight with the Islamic Nation. The Nation of Monotheism, that puts complete trust on Allah and fears none other than Him. The Nation which is addressed by its Quran with the words: "Do you fear them? Allah has more right that you should fear Him if you are believers. Fight against them so that Allah will punish them by your hands and disgrace them and give you victory over them and heal the breasts of believing people. And remove the anger of their (believers') hearts. Allah accepts the repentance of whom He wills. Allah is All-Knowing, All-Wise." [Quran 9:13-1]

The Nation of honour and respect:

"But honour, power and glory belong to Allah, and to His Messenger (Muhammad-peace be upon him) and to the believers." [Quran 63:8]

"So do not become weak (against your enemy), nor be sad, and you will be superior (in victory) if you are indeed (true) believers" [Quran 3:139]

The Nation of Martyrdom; the Nation that desires death more than you desire life:

"Think not of those who are killed in the way of Allah as dead. Nay, they are alive with their Lord, and they are being provided for. They rejoice in what Allah has bestowed upon them from His bounty and rejoice for the sake of those who have not yet joined them, but are left behind (not yet martyred) that on them no fear shall come, nor shall they grieve. They rejoice in a grace and a bounty from Allah, and that Allah will not waste the reward of the believers." [Quran 3:169–171]

The Nation of victory and success that Allah has promised:

"It is He Who has sent His Messenger (Muhammad peace be upon him) with guidance and the religion of truth (Islam), to make it victorious over all other religions even though the Polytheists hate it." [Quran 61:9]

"Allah has decreed that 'Verily it is I and My Messengers who shall be victorious.' Verily Allah is All-Powerful, All-Mighty." [Quran 58:21]

The Islamic Nation that was able to dismiss and destroy the previous evil Empires like yourself; the Nation that rejects your attacks, wishes to remove your evils, and is prepared to fight you. You are well aware that the Islamic Nation, from the very core of its soul, despises your haughtiness and arrogance.

If the Americans refuse to listen to our advice and the goodness, guidance and righteousness that we call them to, then be aware that you will lose this Crusade Bush began, just like the other previous Crusades in which you were humiliated by the hands of the Mujahideen, fleeing to your home in great silence and disgrace. If the Americans do not respond, then their fate will be that of the Soviets who fled from Afghanistan to deal with their military defeat, political breakup, ideological downfall, and economic bankruptcy.

This is our message to the Americans, as an answer to theirs. Do they now know why we fight them and over which form of ignorance, by the permission of Allah, we shall be victorious?

Source: "Bin Laden's 'Letter to America,' Sunday, November 24, 2002." *Guardian Observer Worldview.* Extra. http://www.theguardian.com/world /2002/nov/24/theobserver

12. Testimony of Richard A. Clarke before the National Commission on Terrorist Attacks upon the United States (March 24, 2004)

Introduction

Richard A. Clarke was the leading counterterrorism expert for both the Bill Clinton and George W. Bush administrations. After he left office in 2003, Clarke became the leading critic of the Bush administration's handling of terrorism before September 11. Clarke is also famous for being the only U.S. government official who apologized to the families of the victims for the failures of government to prevent September 11. In his testimony before the National Commission on Terrorist Attacks upon the United States (better known as the 9/11 Commission), Clarke outlined the basics of the policies toward terrorism held by both the Clinton and Bush administrations. The following is an excerpt from that testimony.

Primary Source

I am appreciative of the opportunity the Commission is offering for me to provide my observations about what went wrong in the struggle against al Qida, both before and after 9-11. I want the families of the victims to know that we tried to stop those attacks, that some people tried very hard. I want them to know why we failed and what I think we need to do to insure that nothing like that ever happens again.

I have testified for twenty hours before the House-Senate Joint Inquiry Committee and before this Commission in closed hearings. Therefore, I will limit my prepared testimony to a chronological review of key facts and then provide some conclusions and summary observations, which may form the basis for further questions. My observations and answers to any questions are limited by my memory, because I do not have access to government files or classified information for purposes of preparing for this hearing.

I was assigned to the National Security Council staff in 1992 and had terrorism as part of my portfolio until late 2001. Terrorism became the predominant part of my duties during the mid-1990s and I was appointed National Coordinator for Counter-terrorism in 1998.

Terrorism without US Retaliation in the 1980s: In the 1980s, Hezbollah killed 278 United States Marines in Lebanon and twice destroyed the US embassy. They kidnapped and killed other Americans, including the CIA Station chief. There was no direct US military retaliation. In 1989, 259 people were killed on Pan Am 103. There was no direct US military retaliation. The George H. W. Bush administration did not have a formal counter-terrorism policy articulated in an NSC Presidential decision document.

Terrorism Early in the Clinton Administration: Within the first few weeks of the Clinton administration, there was terrorism in the US: the attack on the CIA gatehouse and the attack on the World Trade Center. CIA and FBI concluded at the time that there was no organization behind those attacks. Similarly, they did not report at the time that al Qida was involved in the planned attack on Americans in Yemen in 1992 or the Somali attacks on US and other peacekeepers in 1993. Indeed, CIA and FBI did not report the existence of an organization named al Qida until the mid-1990s, seven years after it was apparently created. Nonetheless, the 1993 attacks and then the terrorism in the Tokyo subway and the Oklahoma City bombing caused the Clinton Administration to increase its focus on terrorism and to expand funding for counter-terrorism programs.

As a result of intelligence and law enforcement operations, most of those involved in the World Trade Center attack of 1993, the planned attacks on the UN and New York tunnels, the CIA gatehouse shootings, the Oklahoma City bombing, and the attempted assassination of former President Bush were successfully apprehended.

The Clinton Administration responded to Iraqi terrorism against the US in 1993 with a military retaliation and against Iranian terrorism against the US in 1996 at Khobar Towers with a covert action. Both US responses were accompanied by warning that further anti-US terrorism would result in greater retaliation. Neither Iraq nor Iran engaged in anti-US terrorism subsequently. (Iraqis did, of course, later engage in anti-US terrorism in 2003–4.)

Identifying the al Qida Threat: The White House urged CIA in 1994 to place greater focus on what the Agency called "the terrorist financier, Usama bin Ladin." After the creation of a "virtual station" [Alec Station] to examine bin Ladin, CIA identified a multi-national network of cells and of affiliated terrorist organizations. That network was attempting to wage "jihad" in Bosnia and planned to have a significant role in a new Bosnian government. US and Allied actions halted the war in

Bosnia and caused most of the al Qida related jihadists to leave. The White House asked CIA and DOD to develop plans for operating against al Qida in Sudan, the country of its headquarters. Neither department was able successfully to develop a plan to do so. Immediately following Usama bin Ladin's move to Afghanistan, the White House requested that plans be developed to operate against al Qida there. CIA developed ties to a group which reported on al Qida activity, but which was unable to mount successful operations against al Qida in Afghanistan. CIA opposed using its own personnel to do so.

Sudan: While bin Ladin was in Sudan, he was hosted by its leader Hasan Turabi. Under Turabi, Sudan had become a safe haven for many terrorist groups, but bin Ladin had special status. He funded many development programs such as roads and dined often with Turabi and his family. Turabi and bin Ladin were ideological brethren. Following the assassination attempt on Egyptian President Mubarek, the US and Egypt successfully proposed UN sanctions on Sudan because of its support of terrorism. Because of the growing economic damage to Sudan due to its support of terrorism, bin Ladin offered to move to Afghanistan. Sudan at no time detained him, nor was there ever a credible offer by Sudan to arrest and render him. This is in contrast to Sudan's arrest of the terrorist known as Carlos the Jackal, who the Sudanese then handed over in chains to French authorities.

1998 Turning Point: In 1996, CIA had been directed to develop its capability to operate against al Qida in Afghanistan and elsewhere. CIA operations identified and disrupted al Qida cells in several countries. In 1997, a federal grand jury began reviewing evidence against al Qida and in 1998 indicted Usama bin Ladin. Several terrorists, including bin Ladin, issued a fatwa against the United States.

In August, al Qida attacked two US embassies in East Africa. Following the attacks, the United States responded militarily with cruise missile attacks on al Qida facilities.

President Clinton was widely criticized for doing so. A US Marine deployment combined with CIA activity, disrupted a third attack planned in Tirana, Albania.

President Clinton requested the Chairman of the Joint Chiefs to develop follow-on military strike plans, including the use of US Special Forces. The Chairman recommended against using US forces on the ground in Afghanistan, but placed submarines with cruise missile[s] off shore awaiting timely intelligence of the location of Usama bin Ladin.

The President also requested CIA to develop follow-on covert action plans. He authorized lethal activity in a series of directives which progressively expanded the authority of CIA to act against al Qida in Afghanistan.

Diplomatic activity also increased, including UN sanctions against the Taliban regime in Afghanistan and pressure on Pakistan to cooperate further in attempts to end the Taliban support for al Qida.

National Coordinator: In 1998, I was appointed by the President to a newly created position of National Coordinator for Security, Infrastructure Protection and Counter-terrorism. Although the Coordinator was appointed to the Cabinet level NSC Principals Committee, the position was limited at the request of the departments and agencies. The Coordinator had no budget, only a dozen staff, and no ability to direct actions by the departments or agencies. The President authorized ten security and counter-terrorism programs and assigned leadership on each program (e.g. Transportation Security) to an agency lead.

1999: The Clinton Administration continued to pursue intelligence, including covert action, military, law enforcement, and diplomatic activity to disrupt al Qida.

CIA was unable to develop timely intelligence to support the planned follow-on military strikes. On three occasions, CIA reported it knew where Usama bin Ladin was, but all three times the Director of Central Intelligence recommended against military action because of the poor quality of the intelligence. Eventually, the US submarines on station for the military operation returned to normal duties. CIA's assets in Afghanistan were unable to utilize the lethal covert action authorities and CIA recommended against placing its own personnel in Afghanistan to carry out the operations. Captures of al Qida personnel outside of Afghanistan continued.

In December 1999 intelligence and law enforcement information indicated that al Qida was planning attacks against the US. The President ordered the Principals Committee to meet regularly to prevent the attacks. That Cabinet level committee met throughout December 1999 to review intelligence and develop counter-measures. The planned al Qida attacks were averted.

Despite our inability to locate Usama bin Ladin in one place long enough to launch an attack, I urged that we engage in a bombing campaign of al Qida facilities in Afghanistan. That option was deferred by the Principals Committee.

Terrorists in the US: FBI had the responsibility for finding al Qida related activities or terrorists in the US. In the 1996–1999 timeframe, they regularly responded to me and to the National Security Advisor that there were no known al Qida operatives or activities in the US. On my trips to FBI offices, I found that al Qida was not a priority (except in the New York office). Following the Millennium Alert, FBI Executive Assistant Director Dale Watson attempted to have the field offices act more aggressively to find al Qida related activities. The Bureau was, however, less than proactive in identifying al Qida-related fund raising, recruitment, or other activities in the United States. Several programs to increase our ability to respond to terrorism in the US were initiated both in the FBI and in other departments, including programs to train and equip first responders.

2000: The President, displeased with the inability of CIA to eliminate the al Qida leadership, asked for additional options. The NSC staff proposed that the Predator, unmanned aerial vehicle, be used to find the leadership. CIA objected. The National Security Advisor, however, eventually obtained Agency agreement to fly the Predator on a "proof of concept" mission without any link to military or CIA forces standing by. CIA wanted to experiment with the concept before developing a command and control system that incorporated Predator information with attack capabilities. The flights ended when the high winds of winter precluded the operation of the aircraft. The experiment had proved successful in locating the al Qida leadership.

In October 2000, the USS *Cole* was attacked in Yemen. Following the attack, the Principals considered military retaliation. CIA and FBI were, however, unwilling to state that those who had conducted the attack were al Qida or related to the facilities and personnel in Afghanistan. The Principals directed that the Politico-Military Plan against al Qida be updated with additional options. Among those options were aiding Afghan factions to fight the Taliban and al

Qida and creating an armed version of the Predator unmanned aircraft to use against the al Qida leadership.

Military strike options, including cruise missiles, bombing, and use of US Special Forces were also included.

As the Clinton Administration came to an end, three attacks on the US had been definitively tied to al Qida (the World Trade Center 1993, the Embassies in 1998 and the *Cole* in 2000), in which a total of 35 Americans had been killed over eight years.

To counter al Qida's growing threat, a global effort had been initiated involving intelligence activities, covert action, diplomacy, law enforcement, financial action, and military capability. Nonetheless, the organization continued to enjoy a safe haven in Afghanistan.

2001: On January 24, 2001 I requested in writing an urgent meeting of the NSC Principals committee to address the al Qida threat. That meeting took place on September 4, 2001. It was preceded by a number of Deputies Committee meetings, beginning in April. Those meetings considered proposals to step up activity against al Qida, including military assistance to anti-Taliban Afghan factions.

In June and July, intelligence indicated an increased likelihood of a major al Qida attack against US targets, probably in Saudi Arabia or Israel. In response, the interagency Counter-terrorism Security Group agreed upon a series of steps including a series of warning notices that an attack could take place in the US. Notices were sent to federal agencies (Immigration, Customs, Coast Guard, FAA, FBI, DOD, and State), state and local police, airlines, and airports.

In retrospect, we know that there was information available to some in the FBI and CIA that al Qaeda operatives had entered the United States. That information

was not shared with the senior FBI counter-terrorism official (Dale Watson) or with me, despite the heightened state of concern in the Counter-terrorism Security Group.

Observations and Conclusions

Although there were people in the FBI, CIA, Defense Department, State Department, and White House who worked very hard to destroy al Qida before it did catastrophic damage to the US, there were many others who found the prospect of significant al Qida attacks remote. In both CIA and the military there was reluctance at senior career levels to fully utilize all of the capabilities available. There was risk aversion. FBI was, throughout much of this period, organized, staffed, and equipped in such a way that it was ineffective in dealing with the domestic terrorist threat from al Qida.

At the senior policy levels in the Clinton Administration, there was an acute understanding of the terrorist threat, particularly al Qida. That understanding resulted in a vigorous program to counter al Qida including lethal covert action, but it did not include a willingness to resume bombing of Afghanistan. Events in the Balkans, Iraq, the Peace Process, and domestic politics occurring at the same time as the anti-terrorism effort played a role.

The Bush Administration saw terrorism policy as important but not urgent, prior to 9-11. The difficulty in obtaining the first Cabinet level (Principals) policy meeting on terrorism and the limited Principals' involvement sent unfortunate signals to the bureaucracy about the Administration's attitude toward the al Qida threat.

The US response to al Qida following 9-11 has been partially effective. Unfortunately, the US did not act sufficiently quickly to insert US forces to capture or kill the al Qida leadership in Afghanistan. Nor did we employ sufficient US and Allied forces to stabilize that country. In the ensuing 30 months, al Qida has morphed into a decentralized network, with its national and regional affiliates operating effectively and independently. There have been more major al Qida related attacks globally in the 30 months since 9-11 than there were in the 30 months preceding it. Hostility toward the US in the Islamic world has increased since 9-11, largely as a result of the invasion and occupation of Iraq. Thus, new terrorist cells are likely being created, unknown to US intelligence.

To address the continuing threat from radical Islamic terrorism, the US and its allies must become increasingly focused and effective in countering the ideology that motivates that terrorism.

Source: "Testimony of Richard A. Clarke before the National Commission on Terrorist Attacks upon the United States, March 24, 2004," National Commission on Terrorist Attacks upon the United States, http://govinfo.library.unt.edu/911/hearings /hearing8/clarke_statement.pdf.

13. Executive Summary of the Final Report of the National Commission on Terrorist Attacks upon the United States (July 2004)

Introduction

In July 2004, the National Commission on Terrorist Attacks upon the United States (better known as the 9/11 Commission) released its final report, which was more than 560 pages in length. The report gave a detailed account of the events of September 11, and the previous growth during the 1990s of Al Qaeda and other Islamic extremist groups targeting the United States; identified weaknesses in U.S. security procedures, which if remedied might have prevented the attacks; stated that measures that the U.S. government had taken prior to September 2001 to address the dangers that Al Qaeda presented had been inadequate; highlighted failures to mobilize or pool intelligence resources; and warned that although the Al Qaeda headquarters in Afghanistan had been destroyed and many of the organization's top leaders had been killed, the United States was still not safe from terrorist threats.

Primary Source

We present the narrative of this report and the recommendations that flow from it to the President of the United States, the United States Congress, and the American people for their consideration. Ten Commissioners—five Republicans and five Democrats chosen by elected leaders from our nation's capital at a time of great partisan division—have come together to present this report without dissent.

We have come together with a unity of purpose because our nation demands it. September 11, 2001, was a day of unprecedented shock and suffering in the history of the United States. The nation was unprepared.

A Nation Transformed

At 8:46 on the morning of September 11, 2001, the United States became a nation transformed.

An airliner traveling at hundreds of miles per hour and carrying some 10,000 gallons of jet fuel plowed into the North Tower of the World Trade Center in Lower Manhattan. At 9:03, a second airliner hit the South Tower. Fire and smoke billowed upward. Steel, glass, ash, and bodies fell below. The Twin Towers, where up to 50,000 people worked each day, both collapsed less than 90 minutes later.

At 9:37 that same morning, a third airliner slammed into the western face of the Pentagon. At 10:03, a fourth airliner crashed in a field in southern Pennsylvania. It had been aimed at the United States Capitol or the White House, and was forced down by heroic passengers armed with the knowledge that America was under attack.

More than 2,600 people died at the World Trade Center; 125 died at the Pentagon; 256 died on the four planes. The death toll surpassed that at Pearl Harbor in December 1941.

This immeasurable pain was inflicted by 19 young Arabs acting at the behest of Islamist extremists headquartered in distant Afghanistan. Some had been in the United States for more than a year, mixing with the rest of the population. Though four had training as pilots, most were not well-educated. Most spoke English poorly, some hardly at all. In groups of four or five, carrying with them only small knives, box cutters, and cans of Mace or pepper spray, they had hijacked the four planes and turned them into deadly guided missiles.

Why did they do this? How was the attack planned and conceived? How did the U.S. government fail to anticipate and prevent it? What can we do in the future to prevent similar acts of terrorism?

A Shock, Not a Surprise

The 9/11 attacks were a shock, but they should not have come as a surprise. Islamist extremists had given plenty of warning that they meant to kill Americans indiscriminately and in large numbers. Although Usama Bin Ladin himself would not emerge as a signal threat until the late 1990s, the threat of Islamist terrorism grew over the decade.

In February 1993, a group led by Ramzi Yousef tried to bring down the World Trade Center with a truck bomb. They killed six and wounded a thousand. Plans by Omar Abdel Rahman and others to blow up the Holland and Lincoln tunnels and other New York City landmarks were frustrated when the plotters were arrested. In October 1993, Somali tribesmen shot down U.S. helicopters, killing 18 and wounding 73 in an incident that came to be known as "Black Hawk down." Years later it would be learned that those Somali tribesmen had received help from al Qaeda.

In early 1995, police in Manila uncovered a plot by Ramzi Yousef to blow up a dozen U.S. airliners while they were flying over the Pacific. In November 1995, a car bomb exploded outside the office of the U.S. program manager for the Saudi National Guard in Riyadh, killing five Americans and two others. In June 1996, a truck bomb demolished the Khobar Towers apartment complex in Dhahran, Saudi Arabia, killing 19 U.S. servicemen and wounding hundreds. The attack was carried out primarily by Saudi Hezbollah, an organization that had received help from the government of Iran.

Until 1997, the U.S. intelligence community viewed Bin Ladin as a financier of terrorism, not as a terrorist leader. In February 1998, Usama Bin Ladin and four others issued a self-styled fatwa, publicly declaring that it was God's decree that every Muslim should try his utmost to kill any American, military or civilian, anywhere in the world, because of American "occupation" of Islam's holy places and aggression against Muslims.

In August 1998, Bin Ladin's group, al Qaeda, carried out near-simultaneous truck bomb attacks on the U.S. embassies in Nairobi, Kenya, and Dar es Salaam, Tanzania.

The attacks killed 224 people, including 12 Americans, and wounded thousands more.

In December 1999, Jordanian police foiled a plot to bomb hotels and other sites frequented by American tourists, and a U.S. Customs agent arrested Ahmed Ressam at the U.S. Canadian border as he was smuggling in explosives intended for an attack on Los Angeles International Airport.

In October 2000, an al Qaeda team in Aden, Yemen, used a motorboat filled with explosives to blow a hole in the side of a destroyer, the USS *Cole,* almost sinking the vessel and killing 17 American sailors.

The 9/11 attacks on the World Trade Center and the Pentagon were far more elaborate, precise, and destructive than any of these earlier assaults. But by September 2001, the executive branch of the U.S. government, the Congress, the news media, and the American public had received clear warning that Islamist terrorists meant to kill Americans in high numbers.

Who Is the Enemy?

Who is this enemy that created an organization capable of inflicting such horrific damage on the United States? We now know that these attacks were carried out by various groups of Islamist extremists. The 9/11 attack was driven by Usama Bin Ladin.

In the 1980s, young Muslims from around the world went to Afghanistan to join as volunteers in a jihad (or holy struggle) against the Soviet Union. A wealthy Saudi, Usama Bin Ladin, was one of them. Following the defeat of the Soviets in the late 1980s, Bin Ladin and others formed al Qaeda to mobilize jihads elsewhere.

The history, culture, and body of beliefs from which Bin Ladin shapes and spreads his message are largely unknown to many Americans. Seizing on symbols of Islam's past greatness, he promises to restore pride to people who consider themselves the victims of successive foreign masters. He uses cultural and religious allusions to the holy Qur'an and some of its interpreters. He appeals to people disoriented by cyclonic change as they confront modernity and globalization. His rhetoric selectively draws from multiple sources—Islam, history, and the region's political and economic malaise.

Bin Ladin also stresses grievances against the United States widely shared in the Muslim world. He inveighed against the presence of U.S. troops in Saudi Arabia, which is the home of Islam's holiest sites, and against other U.S. policies in the Middle East.

Upon this political and ideological foundation, Bin Ladin built over the course of a decade a dynamic and lethal organization. He built an infrastructure and organization in Afghanistan that could attract, train, and use recruits against ever more ambitious targets. He rallied new zealots and new money with each demonstration of al Qaeda's capability. He had forged a close alliance with the Taliban, a regime providing sanctuary for al Qaeda.

By September 11, 2001, al Qaeda possessed

- leaders able to evaluate, approve, and supervise the planning and direction of a major operation;
- a personnel system that could recruit candidates, indoctrinate them, vet them, and give them the necessary training;
- communications sufficient to enable planning and direction of operatives and those who would be helping them;
- an intelligence effort to gather required information and form assessments of enemy strengths and weaknesses;

- the ability to move people great distances; and
- the ability to raise and move the money necessary to finance an attack.

1998 to September 11, 2001

The August 1998 bombings of U.S. embassies in Kenya and Tanzania established al Qaeda as a potent adversary of the United States.

After launching cruise missile strikes against al Qaeda targets in Afghanistan and Sudan in retaliation for the embassy bombings, the Clinton administration applied diplomatic pressure to try to persuade the Taliban regime in Afghanistan to expel Bin Ladin. The administration also devised covert operations to use CIA-paid foreign agents to capture or kill Bin Ladin and his chief lieutenants. These actions did not stop Bin Ladin or dislodge al Qaeda from its sanctuary.

By late 1998 or early 1999, Bin Ladin and his advisers had agreed on an idea brought to them by Khalid Sheikh Mohammed (KSM) called the "planes operation." It would eventually culminate in the 9/11 attacks. Bin Ladin and his chief of operations, Mohammed Atef, occupied undisputed leadership positions atop al Qaeda. Within al Qaeda, they relied heavily on the ideas and enterprise of strong-willed field commanders, such as KSM, to carry out worldwide terrorist operations.

KSM claims that his original plot was even grander than those carried out on 9/11—ten planes would attack targets on both the East and West coasts of the United States. This plan was modified by Bin Ladin, KSM said, owing to its scale and complexity. Bin Ladin provided KSM with four initial operatives for suicide plane attacks within the United States, and in the fall of 1999 training for the attacks began.

New recruits included four from a cell of expatriate Muslim extremists who had clustered together in Hamburg, Germany. One became the tactical commander of the operation in the United States: Mohamed Atta.

U.S. intelligence frequently picked up reports of attacks planned by al Qaeda. Working with foreign security services, the CIA broke up some al Qaeda cells. The core of Bin Ladin's organization nevertheless remained intact. In December 1999, news about the arrests of the terrorist cell in Jordan and the arrest of a terrorist at the U.S.-Canadian border became part of a "millennium alert." The government was galvanized, and the public was on alert for any possible attack.

In January 2000, the intense intelligence effort glimpsed and then lost sight of two operatives destined for the "planes operation." Spotted in Kuala Lumpur, the pair were lost passing through Bangkok. On January 15, 2000, they arrived in Los Angeles.

Because these two al Qaeda operatives had spent little time in the West and spoke little, if any, English, it is plausible that they or KSM would have tried to identify, in advance, a friendly contact in the United States. We explored suspicions about whether these two operatives had a support network of accomplices in the United States. The evidence is thin—simply not there for some cases, more worrisome in others.

We do know that soon after arriving in California, the two al Qaeda operatives sought out and found a group of ideologically like-minded Muslims with roots in Yemen and Saudi Arabia, individuals mainly associated with a young Yemeni and others who attended a mosque in San Diego. After a brief stay in Los Angeles about which we know little, the al Qaeda operatives lived openly in San Diego under their true names. They managed to avoid attracting much attention.

By the summer of 2000, three of the four Hamburg cell members had arrived on the East Coast of the United States and had begun pilot training. In early 2001, a fourth future hijacker pilot, Hani Hanjour, journeyed to Arizona with another operative, Nawaf al Hazmi, and conducted his refresher pilot training there. A number of al Qaeda operatives had spent time in Arizona during the 1980s and early 1990s.

During 2000, President Bill Clinton and his advisers renewed diplomatic efforts to get Bin Ladin expelled from Afghanistan. They also renewed secret efforts with some of the Taliban's opponents—the Northern Alliance—to get enough intelligence to attack Bin Ladin directly. Diplomatic efforts centered on the new military government in Pakistan, and they did not succeed. The efforts with the Northern Alliance revived an inconclusive and secret debate about whether the United States should take sides in Afghanistan's civil war and support the Taliban's enemies. The CIA also produced a plan to improve intelligence collection on al Qaeda, including the use of a small, unmanned airplane with a video camera, known as the Predator.

After the October 2000 attack on the USS *Cole,* evidence accumulated that it had been launched by al Qaeda operatives, but without confirmation that Bin Ladin had given the order. The Taliban had earlier been warned that it would be held responsible for another Bin Ladin attack on the United States. The CIA described its findings as a "preliminary judgment"; President Clinton and his chief advisers told us they were waiting for a conclusion before deciding whether to take military action. The

military alternatives remained unappealing to them.

The transition to the new Bush administration in late 2000 and early 2001 took place with the *Cole* issue still pending. President George W. Bush and his chief advisers accepted that al Qaeda was responsible for the attack on the Cole, but did not like the options available for a response.

Bin Ladin's inference may well have been that attacks, at least at the level of the *Cole,* were risk free.

The Bush administration began developing a new strategy with the stated goal of eliminating the al Qaeda threat within three to five years.

During the spring and summer of 2001, U.S. intelligence agencies received a stream of warnings that al Qaeda planned, as one report put it, "something very, very, very big." Director of Central Intelligence George Tenet told us, "The system was blinking red."

Although Bin Ladin was determined to strike in the United States, as President Clinton had been told and President Bush was reminded in a Presidential Daily Brief article briefed to him in August 2001, the specific threat information pointed overseas. Numerous precautions were taken overseas. Domestic agencies were not effectively mobilized. The threat did not receive national media attention comparable to the millennium alert.

While the United States continued disruption efforts around the world, its emerging strategy to eliminate the al Qaeda threat was to include an enlarged covert action program in Afghanistan, as well as diplomatic strategies for Afghanistan and Pakistan. The process culminated during the summer of 2001 in a draft presidential directive and arguments about the Predator aircraft, which was soon to be deployed with a missile of its own, so that it might be used to attempt to kill Bin Ladin or his chief lieutenants. At a September 4 meeting, President Bush's chief advisers approved the draft directive of the strategy and endorsed the concept of arming the Predator. This directive on the al Qaeda strategy was awaiting President Bush's signature on September 11, 2001.

Though the "planes operation" was progressing, the plotters had problems of their own in 2001. Several possible participants dropped out; others could not gain entry into the United States (including one denial at a port of entry and visa denials not related to terrorism). One of the eventual pilots may have considered abandoning the planes operation. Zacarias Moussaoui, who showed up at a flight training school in Minnesota, may have been a candidate to replace him.

Some of the vulnerabilities of the plotters become clear in retrospect. Moussaoui aroused suspicion for seeking fast-track training on how to pilot large jet airliners. He was arrested on August 16, 2001, for violations of immigration regulations. In late August, officials in the intelligence community realized that the terrorists spotted in Southeast Asia in January 2000 had arrived in the United States.

These cases did not prompt urgent action. No one working on these late leads in the summer of 2001 connected them to the high level of threat reporting. In the words of one official, no analytic work foresaw the lightning that could connect the thundercloud to the ground.

As final preparations were under way during the summer of 2001, dissent emerged among al Qaeda leaders in Afghanistan over whether to proceed. The Taliban's chief, Mullah Omar, opposed attacking the United States. Although facing opposition from many of his senior lieutenants, Bin Ladin effectively overruled their objections, and the attacks went forward.

September 11, 2001

The day began with the 19 hijackers getting through a security checkpoint system that they had evidently analyzed and knew how to defeat. Their success rate in penetrating the system was 19 for 19. They took over the four flights, taking advantage of air crews and cockpits that were not prepared for the contingency of a suicide hijacking.

On 9/11, the defense of U.S. air space depended on close interaction between two federal agencies: the Federal Aviation Administration (FAA) and North American Aerospace Defense Command (NORAD). Existing protocols on 9/11 were unsuited in every respect for an attack in which hijacked planes were used as weapons.

What ensued was a hurried attempt to improvise a defense by civilians who had never handled a hijacked aircraft that attempted to disappear, and by a military unprepared for the transformation of commercial aircraft into weapons of mass destruction.

A shootdown authorization was not communicated to the NORAD air defense sector until 28 minutes after United 93 had crashed in Pennsylvania. Planes were scrambled, but ineffectively, as they did not know where to go or what targets they were to intercept. And once the shootdown order was given, it was not communicated to the pilots. In short, while leaders in Washington believed that the fighters circling above them had been instructed to "take out" hostile aircraft, the only orders actually conveyed to the pilots were to "ID type and tail."

Like the national defense, the emergency response on 9/11 was necessarily improvised.

In New York City, the Fire Department of New York, the New York Police Department, the Port Authority of New York and New Jersey, the building employees, and the occupants of the buildings did their best to cope with the effects of almost unimaginable events unfolding furiously over 102 minutes. Casualties were nearly 100 percent at and above the impact zones and were very high among first responders who stayed in danger as they tried to save lives. Despite weaknesses in preparations for disaster, failure to achieve unified incident command, and inadequate communications among responding agencies, all but approximately one hundred of the thousands of civilians who worked below the impact zone escaped, often with help from the emergency responders.

At the Pentagon, while there were also problems of command and control, the emergency response was generally effective. The Incident Command System, a formalized management structure for emergency response in place in the National Capital Region, overcame the inherent complications of a response across local, state, and federal jurisdictions.

Operational Opportunities

We write with the benefit and handicap of hindsight. We are mindful of the danger of being unjust to men and women who made choices in conditions of uncertainty and in circumstances over which they often had little control.

Nonetheless, there were specific points of vulnerability in the plot and opportunities to disrupt it. Operational failures— opportunities that were not or could not be exploited by the organizations and systems of that time—included

- not watchlisting future hijackers Hazmi and Mihdhar, not trailing them after they traveled to Bangkok, and not informing the FBI about one future hijacker's U.S. visa or his companion's travel to the United States;
- not sharing information linking individuals in the *Cole* attack to Mihdhar;
- not taking adequate steps in time to find Mihdhar or Hazmi in the United States;
- not linking the arrest of Zacarias Moussaoui, described as interested in flight training for the purpose of using an airplane in a terrorist act, to the heightened indications of attack;
- not discovering false statements on visa applications;
- not recognizing passports manipulated in a fraudulent manner;
- not expanding no-fly lists to include names from terrorist watchlists;
- not searching airline passengers identified by the computer-based CAPPS screening system; and
- not hardening aircraft cockpit doors or taking other measures to prepare for the possibility of suicide hijackings.

General Findings

Since the plotters were flexible and resourceful, we cannot know whether any single step or series of steps would have defeated them. What we can say with confidence is that none of the measures adopted by the U.S. government from 1998 to 2001 disturbed or even delayed the progress of the al Qaeda plot. Across the government, there were failures of imagination, policy, capabilities, and management.

Imagination

The most important failure was one of imagination. We do not believe leaders understood the gravity of the threat. The terrorist danger from Bin Ladin and al

Qaeda was not a major topic for policy debate among the public, the media, or in the Congress. Indeed, it barely came up during the 2000 presidential campaign.

Al Qaeda's new brand of terrorism presented challenges to U.S. governmental institutions that they were not well-designed to meet. Though top officials all told us that they understood the danger, we believe there was uncertainty among them as to whether this was just a new and especially venomous version of the ordinary terrorist threat the United States had lived with for decades, or it was indeed radically new, posing a threat beyond any yet experienced.

As late as September 4, 2001, Richard Clarke, the White House staffer long responsible for counterterrorism policy coordination, asserted that the government had not yet made up its mind how to answer the question: "Is al Qida a big deal?"

A week later came the answer.

Policy

Terrorism was not the overriding national security concern for the U.S. government under either the Clinton or the pre-9/11 Bush administration.

The policy challenges were linked to this failure of imagination. Officials in both the Clinton and Bush administrations regarded a full U.S. invasion of Afghanistan as practically inconceivable before 9/11.

Capabilities

Before 9/11, the United States tried to solve the al Qaeda problem with the capabilities it had used in the last stages of the Cold War and its immediate aftermath. These capabilities were insufficient. Little was done to expand or reform them.

The CIA had minimal capacity to conduct paramilitary operations with its own personnel, and it did not seek a large-scale expansion of these capabilities before 9/11. The CIA also needed to improve its capability to collect intelligence from human agents.

At no point before 9/11 was the Department of Defense fully engaged in the mission of countering al Qaeda, even though this was perhaps the most dangerous foreign enemy threatening the United States.

America's homeland defenders faced outward. NORAD itself was barely able to retain any alert bases at all. Its planning scenarios occasionally considered the danger of hijacked aircraft being guided to American targets, but only aircraft that were coming from overseas.

The most serious weaknesses in agency capabilities were in the domestic arena. The FBI did not have the capability to link the collective knowledge of agents in the field to national priorities. Other domestic agencies deferred to the FBI.

FAA capabilities were weak. Any serious examination of the possibility of a suicide hijacking could have suggested changes to fix glaring vulnerabilities—expanding no-fly lists, searching passengers identified by the CAPPS screening system, deploying federal air marshals domestically, hardening cockpit doors, alerting air crews to a different kind of hijacking possibility than they had been trained to expect. Yet the FAA did not adjust either its own training or training with NORAD to take account of threats other than those experienced in the past.

Management

The missed opportunities to thwart the 9/11 plot were also symptoms of a broader inability to adapt the way government manages problems to the new challenges of the twenty-first century. Action officers should have been able to draw on all available knowledge about al Qaeda in the government. Management should have ensured that information was shared and duties were clearly assigned across agencies, and across the foreign-domestic divide.

There were also broader management issues with respect to how top leaders set priorities and allocated resources. For instance, on December 4, 1998, DCI Tenet issued a directive to several CIA officials and the DDCI for Community Management, stating: "We are at war. I want no resources or people spared in this effort, either inside CIA or the Community." The memorandum had little overall effect on mobilizing the CIA or the intelligence community. This episode indicates the limitations of the DCI's authority over the direction of the intelligence community, including agencies within the Department of Defense.

The U.S. government did not find a way of pooling intelligence and using it to guide the planning and assignment of responsibilities for joint operations involving entities as disparate as the CIA, the FBI, the State Department, the military, and the agencies involved in homeland security.

Specific Findings
Unsuccessful Diplomacy
Beginning in February 1997, and through September 11, 2001, the U.S. government tried to use diplomatic pressure to persuade the Taliban regime in Afghanistan to stop being a sanctuary for al Qaeda, and to expel Bin Ladin to a country where he could face justice. These efforts included warnings and sanctions, but they all failed.

The U.S. government also pressed two successive Pakistani governments to demand that the Taliban cease providing a sanctuary for Bin Ladin and his organization and, failing that, to cut off their support for the Taliban. Before 9/11, the United States could not find a mix of incentives and pressure that would persuade Pakistan to reconsider its fundamental relationship with the Taliban.

From 1999 through early 2001, the United States pressed the United Arab Emirates, one of the Taliban's only travel and financial outlets to the outside world, to break off ties and enforce sanctions, especially those related to air travel to Afghanistan. These efforts achieved little before 9/11.

Saudi Arabia has been a problematic ally in combating Islamic extremism. Before 9/11, the Saudi and U.S. governments did not fully share intelligence information or develop an adequate joint effort to track and disrupt the finances of the al Qaeda organization. On the other hand, government officials of Saudi Arabia at the highest levels worked closely with top U.S. officials in major initiatives to solve the Bin Ladin problem with diplomacy.

Lack of Military Options
In response to the request of policymakers, the military prepared an array of limited strike options for attacking Bin Ladin and his organization from May 1998 onward. When they briefed policymakers, the military presented both the pros and cons of those strike options and the associated risks. Policymakers expressed frustration with the range of options presented.

Following the August 20, 1998, missile strikes on al Qaeda targets in Afghanistan and Sudan, both senior military officials and policymakers placed great emphasis on actionable intelligence as the key factor in recommending or deciding to launch military action against Bin Ladin and his organization. They did not want to risk significant collateral damage, and they did not want to miss Bin Ladin and thus make the United States look weak while making Bin Ladin look strong. On three specific occasions in

1998–1999, intelligence was deemed credible enough to warrant planning for possible strikes to kill Bin Ladin. But in each case the strikes did not go forward, because senior policymakers did not regard the intelligence as sufficiently actionable to offset their assessment of the risks.

The Director of Central Intelligence, policymakers, and military officials expressed frustration with the lack of actionable intelligence. Some officials inside the Pentagon, including those in the special forces and the counterterrorism policy office, also expressed frustration with the lack of military action. The Bush administration began to develop new policies toward al Qaeda in 2001, but military plans did not change until after 9/11.

Problems within the Intelligence Community

The intelligence community struggled throughout the 1990s and up to 9/11 to collect intelligence on and analyze the phenomenon of transnational terrorism. The combination of an overwhelming number of priorities, flat budgets, an outmoded structure, and bureaucratic rivalries resulted in an insufficient response to this new challenge.

Many dedicated officers worked day and night for years to piece together the growing body of evidence on al Qaeda and to understand the threats. Yet, while there were many reports on Bin Laden and his growing al Qaeda organization, there was no comprehensive review of what the intelligence community knew and what it did not know, and what that meant. There was no National Intelligence Estimate on terrorism between 1995 and 9/11.

Before 9/11, no agency did more to attack al Qaeda than the CIA. But there were limits to what the CIA was able to achieve by disrupting terrorist activities abroad and by using proxies to try to capture Bin Ladin and his lieutenants in Afghanistan. CIA officers were aware of those limitations.

To put it simply, covert action was not a silver bullet. It was important to engage proxies in Afghanistan and to build various capabilities so that if an opportunity presented itself, the CIA could act on it. But for more than three years, through both the late Clinton and early Bush administrations, the CIA relied on proxy forces, and there was growing frustration within the CIA's Counterterrorist Center and in the National Security Council staff with the lack of results. The development of the Predator and the push to aid the Northern Alliance were products of this frustration.

Problems in the FBI

From the time of the first World Trade Center attack in 1993, FBI and Department of Justice leadership in Washington and New York became increasingly concerned about the terrorist threat from Islamist extremists to U.S. interests, both at home and abroad. Throughout the 1990s, the FBI's counterterrorism efforts against international terrorist organizations included both intelligence and criminal investigations. The FBI's approach to investigations was case-specific, decentralized, and geared toward prosecution. Significant FBI resources were devoted to after-the-fact investigations of major terrorist attacks, resulting in several prosecutions.

The FBI attempted several reform efforts aimed at strengthening its ability to prevent such attacks, but these reform efforts failed to implement organization-wide institutional change. On September 11, 2001, the FBI was limited in several areas critical to an effective preventive counterterrorism strategy. Those working counterterrorism matters did so despite limited intelligence collection and strategic analysis capabilities, a limited capacity to share information both internally and externally, insufficient training, perceived legal barriers to sharing information, and inadequate resources.

Permeable Borders and Immigration Controls

There were opportunities for intelligence and law enforcement to exploit Al Qaeda's travel vulnerabilities. Considered collectively, the 9/11 hijackers

- included known al Qaeda operatives who could have been watchlisted;
- presented passports manipulated in a fraudulent manner;
- presented passports with suspicious indicators of extremism;
- made detectable false statements on visa applications;
- made false statements to border officials to gain entry into the United States; and
- violated immigration laws while in the United States.

Neither the State Department's consular officers nor the Immigration and Naturalization Service's inspectors and agents were ever considered full partners in a national counterterrorism effort. Protecting borders was not a national security issue before 9/11.

Permeable Aviation Security

Hijackers studied publicly available materials on the aviation security system and used items that had less metal content than a handgun and were most likely permissible. Though two of the hijackers were on the U.S. TIPOFF terrorist watchlist, the FAA did not use TIPOFF data. The hijackers had to beat only one layer of security—the security checkpoint process. Even though several hijackers were selected for extra screening by the CAPPS system, this led only to greater scrutiny of their checked baggage. Once on board, the hijackers were faced with aircraft personnel who were trained to be nonconfrontational in the event of a hijacking.

Financing

The 9/11 attacks cost somewhere between $400,000 and $500,000 to execute. The operatives spent more than $270,000 in the United States. Additional expenses included travel to obtain passports and visas, travel to the United States, expenses incurred by the plot leader and facilitators outside the United States, and expenses incurred by the people selected to be hijackers who ultimately did not participate.

The conspiracy made extensive use of banks in the United States. The hijackers opened accounts in their own names, using passports and other identification documents. Their transactions were unremarkable and essentially invisible amid the billions of dollars flowing around the world every day.

To date, we have not been able to determine the origin of the money used for the 9/11 attacks. Al Qaeda had many sources of funding and a pre-9/11 annual budget estimated at $30 million. If a particular source of funds had dried up, al Qaeda could easily have found enough money elsewhere to fund the attack.

An Improvised Homeland Defense

The civilian and military defenders of the nation's airspace—FAA and NORAD— were unprepared for the attacks launched against them. Given that lack of preparedness, they attempted and failed to improvise an effective homeland defense against an unprecedented challenge.

The events of that morning do not reflect discredit on operational personnel. NORAD's Northeast Air Defense Sector personnel reached out for information and made the best judgments they could based on the information they received. Individual FAA controllers, facility managers, and command center managers were creative and agile in recommending a nationwide alert, ground-stopping local traffic, ordering all aircraft nationwide to land, and executing that unprecedented order flawlessly.

At more senior levels, communication was poor. Senior military and FAA leaders had no effective communication with each other. The chain of command did not function well. The President could not reach some senior officials. The Secretary of Defense did not enter the chain of command until the morning's key events were over. Air National Guard units with different rules of engagement were scrambled without the knowledge of the President, NORAD, or the National Military Command Center.

Emergency Response

The civilians, firefighters, police officers, emergency medical technicians, and emergency management professionals exhibited steady determination and resolve under horrifying, overwhelming conditions on 9/11. Their actions saved lives and inspired a nation.

Effective decisionmaking in New York was hampered by problems in command and control and in internal communications. Within the Fire Department of New York, this was true for several reasons: the magnitude of the incident was unforeseen; commanders had difficulty communicating with their units; more units were actually dispatched than were ordered by the chiefs; some units self-dispatched; and once units arrived at the World Trade Center, they were neither comprehensively accounted for nor coordinated. The Port Authority's response was hampered by the lack both of standard operating procedures and of radios capable of enabling multiple commands to respond to an incident in unified fashion. The New York Police Department, because of its history of mobilizing thousands of officers for major events requiring crowd control, had a technical radio capability and protocols more easily adapted to an incident of the magnitude of 9/11.

Congress

The Congress, like the executive branch, responded slowly to the rise of transnational terrorism as a threat to national security. The legislative branch adjusted little and did not restructure itself to address changing threats. Its attention to terrorism was episodic and splintered across several committees. The Congress gave little guidance to executive branch agencies on terrorism, did not reform them in any significant way to meet the threat, and did not systematically perform robust oversight to identify, address, and attempt to resolve the many problems in national security and domestic agencies that became apparent in the aftermath of 9/11.

So long as oversight is undermined by current congressional rules and resolutions, we believe the American people will not get the security they want and need. The United States needs a strong, stable, and capable congressional committee structure to give America's national intelligence agencies oversight, support, and leadership.

Are We Safer?

Since 9/11, the United States and its allies have killed or captured a majority of al Qaeda's leadership; toppled the Taliban, which gave al Qaeda sanctuary in Afghanistan; and severely damaged the organization. Yet terrorist attacks continue. Even as we have thwarted attacks, nearly everyone expects they will come. How can this be?

The problem is that al Qaeda represents an ideological movement, not a finite group of people. It initiates and inspires, even if it no longer directs. In this way it has transformed itself into a decentralized force. Bin Ladin may be limited in his ability to organize major attacks from his hideouts. Yet killing or capturing him, while extremely important, would not end terror. His message of inspiration to a new generation of terrorists would continue.

Because of offensive actions against al Qaeda since 9/11, and defensive actions to improve homeland security, we believe we are safer today. But we are not safe. We therefore make the following recommendations that we believe can make America safer and more secure.

Recommendations

Three years after 9/11, the national debate continues about how to protect our nation in this new era. We divide our recommendations into two basic parts: What to do, and how to do it.

What to Do? A Global Strategy

The enemy is not just "terrorism." It is the threat posed specifically by Islamist terrorism, by Bin Ladin and others who draw on a long tradition of extreme intolerance within a minority strain of Islam that does not distinguish politics from religion, and distorts both.

The enemy is not Islam, the great world faith, but a perversion of Islam. The enemy goes beyond al Qaeda to include the radical ideological movement, inspired in part by al Qaeda, that has spawned other terrorist groups and violence. Thus our strategy must match our means to two ends: dismantling the al Qaeda network and, in the long term, prevailing over the ideology that contributes to Islamist terrorism.

The first phase of our post-9/11 efforts rightly included military action to topple the Taliban and pursue al Qaeda. This work continues. But long-term success demands the use of all elements of national power: diplomacy, intelligence, covert action, law enforcement, economic policy, foreign aid, public diplomacy, and homeland defense. If we favor one tool while neglecting others, we leave ourselves vulnerable and weaken our national effort.

What should Americans expect from their government? The goal seems unlimited: Defeat terrorism anywhere in the world. But Americans have also been told to expect the worst: An attack is probably coming; it may be more devastating still.

Vague goals match an amorphous picture of the enemy. Al Qaeda and other groups are popularly described as being all over the world, adaptable, resilient, needing little higher-level organization, and capable of anything. It is an image of an omnipotent hydra of destruction. That image lowers expectations of government effectiveness.

It lowers them too far. Our report shows a determined and capable group of plotters. Yet the group was fragile and occasionally left vulnerable by the marginal, unstable people often attracted to such causes. The enemy made mistakes. The U.S. government was not able to capitalize on them.

No president can promise that a catastrophic attack like that of 9/11 will not happen again. But the American people are entitled to expect that officials will have realistic objectives, clear guidance, and effective organization. They are entitled to see standards for performance so they can judge, with the help of their elected representatives, whether the objectives are being met.

We propose a strategy with three dimensions: (1) attack terrorists and their organizations, (2) prevent the continued growth of Islamist terrorism, and (3) protect against and prepare for terrorist attacks.

Attack Terrorists and Their Organizations

- Root out sanctuaries. The U.S. government should identify and prioritize actual or potential terrorist sanctuaries and have realistic country or regional strategies for each, utilizing every element of national power and reaching out to countries that can help us.
- Strengthen long-term U.S. and international commitments to the future of Pakistan and Afghanistan.
- Confront problems with Saudi Arabia in the open and build a relationship beyond oil, a relationship that both sides can defend to their citizens and includes a shared commitment to reform.

Prevent the Continued Growth of Islamist Terrorism

In October 2003, Secretary of Defense Donald Rumsfeld asked if enough was being done "to fashion a broad integrated plan to stop the next generation of terrorists." As part of such a plan, the U.S. government should

- Define the message and stand as an example of moral leadership in the world. To Muslim parents, terrorists like Bin Ladin have nothing to offer their children but visions of violence and death. America and its friends have the advantage— our vision can offer a better future.
- Where Muslim governments, even those who are friends, do not offer opportunity, respect the rule of law, or tolerate differences, then the United States needs to stand for a better future.

- Communicate and defend American ideals in the Islamic world, through much stronger public diplomacy to reach more people, including students and leaders outside of government. Our efforts here should be as strong as they were in combating closed societies during the Cold War.
- Offer an agenda of opportunity that includes support for public education and economic openness.
- Develop a comprehensive coalition strategy against Islamist terrorism, using a flexible contact group of leading coalition governments and fashioning a common coalition approach on issues like the treatment of captured terrorists.
- Devote a maximum effort to the parallel task of countering the proliferation of weapons of mass destruction.
- Expect less from trying to dry up terrorist money and more from following the money for intelligence, as a tool to hunt terrorists, understand their networks, and disrupt their operations.

Protect against and Prepare for Terrorist Attacks

- Target terrorist travel, an intelligence and security strategy that the 9/11 story showed could be at least as powerful as the effort devoted to terrorist finance.
- Address problems of screening people with biometric identifiers across agencies and governments, including our border and transportation systems, by designing a comprehensive screening system that addresses common problems and sets common standards. As standards spread, this necessary and ambitious effort could dramatically strengthen the world's ability to intercept individuals who could pose catastrophic threats.

- Quickly complete a biometric entry-exit screening system, one that also speeds qualified travelers.
- Set standards for the issuance of birth certificates and sources of identification, such as driver's licenses.
- Develop strategies for neglected parts of our transportation security system. Since 9/11, about 90 percent of the nation's $5 billion annual investment in transportation security has gone to aviation, to fight the last war.
- In aviation, prevent arguments about a new computerized profiling system from delaying vital improvements in the "no-fly" and "automatic selectee" lists. Also, give priority to the improvement of checkpoint screening.
- Determine, with leadership from the President, guidelines for gathering and sharing information in the new security systems that are needed, guidelines that integrate safeguards for privacy and other essential liberties.
- Underscore that as government power necessarily expands in certain ways, the burden of retaining such powers remains on the executive to demonstrate the value of such powers and ensure adequate supervision of how they are used, including a new board to oversee the implementation of the guidelines needed for gathering and sharing information in these new security systems.
- Base federal funding for emergency preparedness solely on risks and vulnerabilities, putting New York City and Washington, DC, at the top of the current list. Such assistance should not remain a program for general revenue sharing or pork-barrel spending.
- Make homeland security funding contingent on the adoption of an incident command system to strengthen teamwork in a crisis, including a regional approach. Allocate more radio spectrum and improve connectivity for public safety communications, and encourage widespread adoption of newly developed standards for private-sector emergency preparedness—since the private sector controls 85 percent of the nation's critical infrastructure.

How to Do It? A Different Way of Organizing Government

The strategy we have recommended is elaborate, even as presented here very briefly. To implement it will require a government better organized than the one that exists today, with its national security institutions designed half a century ago to win the Cold War. Americans should not settle for incremental, ad hoc adjustments to a system created a generation ago for a world that no longer exists.

Our detailed recommendations are designed to fit together. Their purpose is clear: to build unity of effort across the U.S. government. As one official now serving on the front lines overseas put it to us: "One fight, one team."

We call for unity of effort in five areas, beginning with unity of effort on the challenge of counterterrorism itself:

- unifying strategic intelligence and operational planning against Islamist terrorists across the foreign-domestic divide with a National Counterterrorism Center;
- unifying the intelligence community with a new National Intelligence Director;
- unifying the many participants in the counterterrorism effort and their knowledge in a network-based information sharing system that transcends traditional governmental boundaries;
- unifying and strengthening congressional oversight to improve quality and accountability; and

- strengthening the FBI and homeland defenders.

Unity of Effort: A National Counterterrorism Center

The 9/11 story teaches the value of integrating strategic intelligence from all sources into joint operational planning—with both dimensions spanning the foreign-domestic divide.

- In some ways, since 9/11, joint work has gotten better. The effort of fighting terrorism has flooded over many of the usual agency boundaries because of its sheer quantity and energy. Attitudes have changed. But the problems of coordination have multiplied. The Defense Department alone has three unified commands (SOCOM, CENTCOM, and NORTHCOM) that deal with terrorism as one of their principal concerns.
- Much of the public commentary about the 9/11 attacks has focused on "lost opportunities." Though characterized as problems of "watchlisting," "information sharing," or "connecting the dots," each of these labels is too narrow. They describe the symptoms, not the disease.
- Breaking the older mold of organization stovepiped purely in executive agencies, we propose a National Counterterrorism Center (NCTC) that would borrow the joint, unified command concept adopted in the 1980s by the American military in a civilian agency, combining the joint intelligence function alongside the operations work.
- The NCTC would build on the existing Terrorist Threat Integration Center and would replace it and other terrorism "fusion centers" within the government. The NCTC would become the authoritative knowledge bank, bringing information to bear on common plans. It should task collection requirements both inside and outside the United States.

- The NCTC should perform joint operational planning, assigning lead responsibilities to existing agencies and letting them direct the actual execution of the plans.
- Placed in the Executive Office of the President, headed by a Senate-confirmed official (with rank equal to the deputy head of a cabinet department) who reports to the National Intelligence Director, the NCTC would track implementation of plans. It would be able to influence the leadership and the budgets of the counterterrorism operating arms of the CIA, the FBI, and the departments of Defense and Homeland Security.
- The NCTC should not be a policymaking body. Its operations and planning should follow the policy direction of the president and the National Security Council.

Unity of Effort: A National Intelligence Director

- Since long before 9/11—and continuing to this day—the intelligence community is not organized well for joint intelligence work. It does not employ common standards and practices in reporting intelligence or in training experts overseas and at home. The expensive national capabilities for collecting intelligence have divided management. The structures are too complex and too secret.
- The community's head—the Director of Central Intelligence—has at least three jobs: running the CIA, coordinating a 15-agency confederation, and being the intelligence analyst-in-chief to the president. No one person can do all these things.
- A new National Intelligence Director should be established with two main jobs: (1) to oversee national intelligence centers that combine experts from all the collection disciplines against common targets—like counterterrorism or nuclear

proliferation; and (2) to oversee the agencies that contribute to the national intelligence program, a task that includes setting common standards for personnel and information technology.

- The national intelligence centers would be the unified commands of the intelligence world—a long-overdue reform for intelligence comparable to the 1986 Goldwater-Nichols law that reformed the organization of national defense. The home services—such as the CIA, DIA, NSA, and FBI—would organize, train, and equip the best intelligence professionals in the world, and would handle the execution of intelligence operations in the field.

- This National Intelligence Director (NID) should be located in the Executive Office of the President and report directly to the president, yet be confirmed by the Senate. In addition to overseeing the National Counterterrorism Center described above (which will include both the national intelligence center for terrorism and the joint operations planning effort), the NID should have three deputies:
  - For foreign intelligence (a deputy who also would be the head of the CIA)
  - For defense intelligence (also the under secretary of defense for intelligence)
  - For homeland intelligence (also the executive assistant director for intelligence at the FBI or the under secretary of homeland security for information analysis and infrastructure protection)

- The NID should receive a public appropriation for national intelligence, should have authority to hire and fire his or her intelligence deputies, and should be able to set common personnel and information technology policies across the intelligence community.

- The CIA should concentrate on strengthening the collection capabilities of its clandestine service and the talents of its analysts, building pride in its core expertise.

- Secrecy stifles oversight, accountability, and information sharing. Unfortunately, all the current organizational incentives encourage overclassification. This balance should change; and as a start, open information should be provided about the overall size of agency intelligence budgets.

Unity of Effort: Sharing Information

The U.S. government has access to a vast amount of information. But it has a weak system for processing and using what it has. The system of "need to know" should be replaced by a system of "need to share."

- The President should lead a government-wide effort to bring the major national security institutions into the information revolution, turning a mainframe system into a decentralized network. The obstacles are not technological. Official after official has urged us to call attention to problems with the unglamorous "back office" side of government operations.

- But no agency can solve the problems on its own—to build the network requires an effort that transcends old divides, solving common legal and policy issues in ways that can help officials know what they can and cannot do. Again, in tackling information issues, America needs unity of effort.

Unity of Effort: Congress

Congress took too little action to adjust itself or to restructure the executive branch to address the emerging terrorist threat. Congressional oversight for intelligence—and counterterrorism—is dysfunctional. Both Congress and the executive [branch] need to do more to minimize national security risks during transitions between administrations.

- For intelligence oversight, we propose two options: either a joint committee on the old model of the Joint Committee on Atomic Energy or a single committee in each house combining authorizing and appropriating committees. Our central message is the same: the intelligence committees cannot carry out their oversight function unless they are made stronger, and thereby have both clear responsibility and accountability for that oversight.
- Congress should create a single, principal point of oversight and review for homeland security. There should be one permanent standing committee for homeland security in each chamber.
- We propose reforms to speed up the nomination, financial reporting, security clearance, and confirmation process for national security officials at the start of an administration, and suggest steps to make sure that incoming administrations have the information they need.

Unity of Effort: Organizing America's Defenses in the United States

We have considered several proposals relating to the future of the domestic intelligence and counterterrorism mission. Adding a new domestic intelligence agency will not solve America's problems in collecting and analyzing intelligence within the United States. We do not recommend creating one.

- We propose the establishment of a specialized and integrated national security workforce at the FBI, consisting of agents, analysts, linguists, and surveillance specialists who are recruited, trained, rewarded, and retained to ensure the development of an institutional culture imbued with a deep expertise in intelligence and national security.

At several points we asked: Who has the responsibility for defending us at home? Responsibility for America's national defense is shared by the Department of Defense, with its new Northern Command, and by the Department of Homeland Security. They must have a clear delineation of roles, missions, and authority.

- The Department of Defense and its oversight committees should regularly assess the adequacy of Northern Command's strategies and planning to defend against military threats to the homeland.
- The Department of Homeland Security and its oversight committees should regularly assess the types of threats the country faces, in order to determine the adequacy of the government's plans and the readiness of the government to respond to those threats.

* * *

We call on the American people to remember how we all felt on 9/11, to remember not only the unspeakable horror but how we came together as a nation—one nation. Unity of purpose and unity of effort are the way we will defeat this enemy and make America safer for our children and grandchildren.

We look forward to a national debate on the merits of what we have recommended, and we will participate vigorously in that debate.

Source: "The 9/11 Commission Report." National Commission on Terrorist Attacks upon the United States. Available online at https://www.9-11commission.gov/

14. Selected Excerpts from the Testimony of FBI Agent Harry Samit in the Zacarias Moussaoui Trial (March 9, 2006)

Federal Bureau of Investigation (FBI) agent Harry Samit was stationed at the FBI's

Minneapolis field office at the time that Zacarias Moussaoui was reported to be acting suspiciously. Samit also became suspicious; he suspected that Moussaoui was planning to use an aircraft for a terrorist act. This testimony reveals Samit's actions and the lack of response from FBI headquarters on obtaining a warrant to search Moussaoui's possessions. Samit tried for both a criminal warrant and a FISA warrant but was turned down for both. His testimony expresses his frustrations in dealing with his superiors in FBI headquarters. The questions in this testimony come from Mr. Novak, a federal prosecutor in the Moussaoui trial, and the answers come from Samit. The trial testimony of Mr. Samit took up 196 pages, so only about a third of his testimony is recorded here, but it covers most of the major points of his testimony. On May 3, 2006, Moussaoui was sentenced to life in prison without the possibility of parole.

Q. And could you tell the good folks on what—what kind of assignment do you have as a special agent with the FBI up there in Minneapolis?

A. I'm an investigator assigned to the Joint Terrorism Task Force.

Q. Tell the folks what the Joint Terrorism Task Force is.

A. The Joint Terrorism Task Force is an organization of law enforcement agents and officers who investigate international terrorism under the framework set up by the FBI. It's got personnel from a variety of different law enforcement agencies.

Q. Do you want to list some of the different agencies that work with you on that Joint Terrorism Task Force?

A. Immigration and Naturalization Service, United States Secret Service, local police officers, sheriff's deputies, a variety of different investigators.

Q. Beyond your assignment to the JTFF, can you tell us what else you do there as a special agent up there in Minnesota?

A. At the time in 1999, I was assigned as a pilot with the FBI as well.

Q. We're going to talk about your pilot training in a second, but your squad that you're assigned to is squad what?

A. Squad 5.

Q. And squad 5 up there includes the investigation of what types of crime?

A. In 2001, it included the investigation of international terrorism, domestic terrorism, and foreign counterintelligence.

Q. And would it be fair to say that since your inception into the FBI, your initial assignment up there in Minneapolis, you've basically been working full-time on terrorism investigations?

A. Yes, sir.

Q. Now, could you tell us, have you received any type of specialized training in the world of terrorism?

A. I have. During the FBI academy, the new agent training, there was a terrorism integrated case scenario which I participated in along with my class. I also attended a basic international terrorism in-service after graduating the FBI academy, and then later a double agent and recruitment in-service as well.

Q. Agent Samit, on August the 15th of 2001, were you assigned still as the special agent to the FBI in Minneapolis?

A. I was.

Q. And at that time did you have occasion to get assigned to the investigation of Zacarias Moussaoui?

A. I was.

Q. And at that time who was your supervisor?

A. I had an acting supervisor, Gregory Jones.

Q. And was there a fellow special agent by the name of Dave Rapp that also worked with you?

A. Yes, sir.

Q. Was he relatively new?

A. He was very new, yes, sir.

Q. Do you want to tell us how it is that you—how the investigation into Zacarias Moussaoui began?

A. Special Agent Rapp had complaint duty that day. It is a rotating shift. All the agents in the office have to answer phone calls from the public and other law enforcement agencies. Special Agent Rapp had occasion to take a call from Pan Am, and the person, the caller, Tim Nelson, provided some fairly significant information.

Q. What was the initial information that you-all received there from Pan Am?

A. That they had a student they were training at the flight academy on simulators for 747-400 series aircraft who was very unusual.

Q. Okay. Did they give you the student's name?

A. They did.

Q. And did they tell you why it is that the student was unusual?

A. Yes, sir. They said that he didn't have any ratings, any aviation ratings or licenses.

Q. What does that mean to you as a criminal investigator?

A. It means that for a person to want to do expensive aviation training, typically it is going to lead somewhere, to a job opportunity or to a job enhancement.

Q. And by not pursuing the ratings, that means they are just not doing it for the— benefit themselves financially; is that right?

A. Yes, sir.

Q. Not worth the investment, right?

A. Yes, sir.

Q. Did they tell you whether the student, Mr. Moussaoui, was employed by an airline?

A. They did. They said he was not. He had no affiliation with any airline.

Q. Was that unusual?

A. It was.

Q. Why was that unusual?

A. Because the typical student, as was explained to us, is an airline pilot or is seeking employment with an airline and is already qualified to do so.

Q. Why would that be unusual?

A. Because the airlines typically would pay for the student, or the student would be making an investment in their own training in order to become eligible to be hired by an airline.

Q. Okay. Did they tell you how much the training for Mr. Moussaoui cost?

A. The caller didn't know for sure, but said it was between 8- and 9,000 dollars.

Q. Okay, And what, if any, information did you get about the amount of hours or licensing that Mr. Moussaoui had?

A. It was low. It was less than 60 hours of flight time.

Q. All right. Did you receive information about what type of plane it was that Mr. Moussaoui was pursuing the training on?

A. Yes, sir.

Q. What type of plane was that?

A. 747-400 series airliner.

Q. All right. And could you tell us, are you familiar with the notion of a glass cockpit?

A. Yes, sir.

Q. Could you tell us what the glass cockpit means to you and the investigatory significance of that?

A. What it means to me as a pilot is the way the information is displayed to the pilot in the cockpit is different. Older airplanes, as compared to glass cockpit airplanes, have individual gauges that display the information, critical information that the pilot needs. When an airplane is said to have a glass cockpit, it relies on a much smaller number of multi-function displays, television screens in the cockpit.

Q. What, if any, impact did that have in terms of your thinking about whether criminality was afoot?

A. My initial thought was that it's a simpler interface for a relative novice, so that if someone had illegitimate purposes in mind for wanting to receive the flight training, that would be an ideal type of aircraft, because they wouldn't need as much training and experience if they were to try and fly it.

Q. And what if any impact would the glass cockpit have on the number of—if there was criminality afoot, the number of accomplices that would have to be involved?

A. The other issue would pertain to the number of crew members in the cockpit. Because the glass cockpit airplanes typically have increased automation, they need fewer people in the cockpit. And so in order to take over an airplane, it would be the difference between having to overwhelm one or two people as opposed to three or four.

Q. All right. Now, in addition to that information, did you ask for and receive any additional background information, identifiers or anything like that from the defendant?

A. We were able to get his name, his date of birth, and the fact that he was, said he lived in England and was from France, at least initially.

Q. Now, once you got that information, did you open up a case, an investigation?

A. We did.

Q. Could you explain to the ladies and gentlemen what kind of case that you opened up?

A. Within probably 30 minutes of receiving that telephone call we opened an intelligence investigation.

Q. Back in August of 2001, could you tell us what type of investigatory cases that you could open up?

A. During that time we had the intelligence investigation, which we did actually open on Mr. Moussaoui, and we also had a criminal investigation.

Q. All right. I want to ask you to explain the difference. Starting with the criminal, what is—criminal investigation, what was your goal back in 2001 if you were to open up just a standard criminal investigation?

A. Like any other type of crime that the FBI investigates, the goal of a criminal investigation pertaining to terrorism is to collect evidence of a crime relating to international terrorism.

Q. And would that—with a mind-set towards what?

A. Towards prosecution.

Q. All right. Now, contrast that with opening up an intelligence investigation, what's, what do you do there?

A. An intelligence investigation is designed to generate intelligence, intelligence whose goal would be to safeguard national security.

Q. And by safeguarding national security, what does that mean? What would you try to accomplish towards that goal?

A. We would attempt to use any information derived from a case, an intelligence investigation, to strengthen our ability to deal with threats to national security, whether it be espionage or terrorists, ways to implement countermeasures to deny them their objectives, without necessarily prosecuting anybody, but we would still take steps, countermeasures to prevent them from accomplishing their goals.

Q. Explain to us, if you are not going to arrest somebody, how is it that you could end up protecting national security during your investigation? What are the types of things you can do?

A. We can use that intelligence to deny personnel access to the United States, to certain classified information; we can use that intelligence to implement countermeasures, security countermeasures to make whole sectors safer. Any time information comes of a threat, or intelligence comes regarding a threat, the countermeasures which would counter that.

Q. Okay. Now, what if during the course of an investigation, an intelligence investigation, you decide that you have gathered enough information to charge somebody criminally? Are you allowed to do that?

A. Yes, sir. At the time we could, there was a mechanism by which a criminal investigation and prosecution could occur, but there were a number of steps that needed to be gone through before that could happen.

Q. Could you explain to us what those steps were?

A. There was a term called the wall. And the wall was supposed to be a barrier between intelligence and criminal investigations wherein information developed on the intelligence investigation could not be supplied at the wall to those working the criminal investigation.

Q. What was the purpose of the wall?

A. To prevent abuse, to prevent people in the FBI and law enforcement from utilizing information gathered under the auspices of national security to be used to prosecute someone, without safeguards and checks imposed on that.

Q. Now, we were talking about the wall there. Again, could you explain to us the amount of safeguards that you had to, or oversight that you had to go through, if you were working on the intelligence side versus the criminal side?

A. We could—the system was set up whereby there could be a group of, separate group of agents within the same office who were working criminal investigation against the same subject. It was important, especially for the people working the intelligence case against that person, to be very cognizant that they not share information that was derived directly. Instead what we were required to do during that time period was apply to our headquarters, who would then apply to the Department of Justice for authority to do that.

Q. Okay. And was there a particular unit within the Department of Justice that you needed approval from in order to switch the case from an intelligence to a criminal case?

A. Not to switch, not to switch the cases.

Q. Or share the information.

A. It was the Office of Intelligence Policy Review, OIPR.

Q. In a criminal case, who are the attorneys that you would normally deal with if you were to pursue a criminal investigation?

A. Assistant United States attorneys in the District of Minnesota.

Q. And if you opened an intelligence case, were you able to deal with the assistant United States attorneys that were located there in Minneapolis?

A. No, that would fall under the heading of our needing to go to the Office of Intelligence Policy Review first for authority.

Q. And they would have to approve that before you could share information with them; is that correct?

A. Yes, sir.

Q. Now, in addition to finding out that he was French, did Agent [John] Weess [special agent with the Immigration and Naturalization Service] determine, along with you, what Mr. Moussaoui's status was in terms of being an immigrant into the United States?

A. He did. He was able to determine very quickly that Mr. Moussaoui was out of status.

Q. Well, out of status means what?

A. Out of status means illegally in the United States.

Q. Can you tell us what it is that Mr. [Clancy] Prevost [Moussaoui ground school instructor] told you at that time?

A. Mr. Prevost was able to elaborate on his contact with Mr. Moussaoui, to describe his interest in aviation but his utter lack of experience and knowledge. He discussed the fact that they talked about Mr. Moussaoui was a resident of the U.K., originally from France. When we asked Mr. Prevost what sparked his suspicion that's when he related a story about Mr. Moussaoui's interest in the aircraft doors, the fact that he was surprised to learn that they couldn't be opened in flight, and then that led into the discussion about Mr. Moussaoui's religion.

Q. Okay, now, after you interviewed Mr. Prevost, could you tell us if you made any decision about how to proceed with your investigation?

A. We did. Special Agent Weess and I consulted and we decided that on the basis of the suspicious behavior discussed, provided to us by the school, that we were going to arrest Mr. Moussaoui.

Q. Okay. And why was that? You were going to arrest him for what?

A. We were going to arrest him on his visa waiver overstay.

Q. But were you focused upon that or were you focused on other concerns?

A. We were obviously focused on learning more about his plans. And we saw that as a way of preventing him from getting any simulator training, any meaningful aircraft training before we had the opportunity to talk to him and sort things out.

Q. Okay. Now, at the time that you arrested him, did you notice if Mr. Moussaoui had any other bags or any other items that were in the hotel room on the left side?

A. He did. The room was full of household goods, of clothing, of bags, backpacks, suitcases, and I noticed a considerable quantity of clothing and other materials like that on the left side of the room.

Q. Okay. And at that time did you search those items?

A. No, we did not.

Q. Okay. Why not?

A. We asked Mr. Moussaoui for permission to search. He became very upset at being informed he was being placed under arrest. He again noted to us that he had expensive flight training, urgent flight training he needed to attend. And I suggested to him that maybe there was a reply to that, that he had received—

Q. Reply to what?

A. To his request to adjust status.

Q. Okay.

A. That there might be other documents which would show that he was, in fact, in status.

Q. And what was his response to that?

A. His response was no, you may not search my things, you can't go through anything else. He was very insistent that we not do that.

Q. Why didn't you search them anyhow?

A. Because we're not allowed to do that under the law. Mr. Moussaoui was in custody. He had been patted down. He was, he was subsequently searched, his person was searched, but under the Fourth Amendment we're not allowed to search his room.

Q. All right. Now, could you tell us on August 17 of 2001, did you make some kind of notification to your headquarters?

A. We did.

Q. And could you tell us—first of all—would you explain to the ladies and gentlemen what ITOS is in the world of FBI?

A. ITOS stands for the International Terrorism Operations Section. It's a group of supervisors and analysts at headquarters . . . , who are assigned to oversee and support investigations in the field, like in Minneapolis.

Q. And within ITOS, are there various units dealing with particular groups of terrorists?

A. There are.

Q. Could you just summarize what some of the units are there that are within the ITOS division of the FBI?

A. Two important ones for this are the Usama Bin Laden Unit that deals with al Qaeda, or UBLU is the acronym, and the Radical Fundamentalist Unit, or RFU.

Q. And what do they deal with?

A. The Usama bin Laden Unit deals with al Qaeda. The Radical Fundamentalist Unit at the time dealt with Sunni extremists who are not al Qaeda, various other groups.

Q. And as a field agent out there, are you supposed to go to the, to the unit that deals with the particular terrorist that you're looking at?

A. Exactly.

Q. And—now, you believed that Mr. Moussaoui was a terrorist, and you've—you confronted him with, as you've testified; is that right?

A. Yes, sir.

Q. Did you know which terrorist organization he was a member of?

A. We did not.

Q. And so how did you know which unit to go to in the ITOS?

A. Well, we didn't originally, and the one that most logically fitted it was the Radical Fundamentalist Unit.

Q. And why is this that you went to the Radical Fundamentalist Unit?

A. We knew that Mr. Moussaoui was a Sunni Muslim, he was an extremist, and we believed he was involved in an ongoing plot. The Radical Fundamentalist Unit was the logical unit.

Q. Okay. And now could you tell us how is it that a field agent communicates with the headquarters? Do you just call them up on the telephone, or do you do something else.

A. Informal communications can be via telephone or e-mail, but in the FBI world, formalized communications were through a document that we call an electronic communication.

Q. Okay.

A. Or an EC is how we abbreviate it.

Q. This EC, did you send it then to the RFU unit?

A. Initially it was sent to the Iran unit and then routed to the RFU unit.

Q. Why did you go to the Iran unit then?

A. Because before speaking with Mr. Moussaoui, FBI database checks indicated that his name might be connected to Iran.

Q. Okay. And what happened when your EC got to Iran? Did you get kicked over to the RFU unit?

A. We did. By then there had been enough of a delay, the interviews had occurred, and we were well aware that it was not under the purview of the Iran unit but in fact the Radical Fundamentalist Unit.

Q. Where you should have been in the first place, all right. Now, could you tell us who was your contact in the RFU unit?

A. The supervisor who was assigned oversight and support responsibilities for Minneapolis was Supervisory Special Agent Mike Maltbie.

Q. Okay. And when you sent that electronic communication to Mr. Maltbie, what was it that your initial request was that you wanted to do?

A. My request to Mr. Maltbie was to apply to the Office of Intelligence Policy Review, to OIPR—

Q. That's in the Department of Justice. You talked about them before, right?

A. Yes, sir, that's correct.

Q. What did you want them—what did you want to occur?

A. I wanted them to grant permission to go to the United States Attorney's Office in the District of Minnesota so that we could pursue criminal charges.

Q. Are you trying to overcome the wall, so to speak?

A. Not overcome it. I'm trying to get permission to release selected information over it. The wall will still exist, and that will still be, certainly in August of 2001 will be a factor, but what I'm trying to do is pass information to criminal investigators so they can begin pursuing that type of investigation.

Q. Okay. And were you given permission to do that?

A. I was not.

Q. Okay. And why is it—were you told why it is you were not given permission?

A. I was told that, that our headquarters, FBI headquarters, Radical Fundamentalist Unit did not believe that sufficient evidence of a crime existed, and also there was a fear that if we were to try and go for a criminal case, to pursue a criminal search initially, and then we had to go back and use techniques under the intelligence world, that it might taint that.

Q. Could you tell us what the—would you describe for us what the process was then for you to go about procuring a FISA [Foreign Intelligence Surveillance Act] warrant back in August of 2001?

A. Once my investigation had convinced myself and supervisors, other agents working the case with me, that probable cause existed to believe that the subject of that warrant—of that search was acting as an agent of a foreign power, then I would prepare an electronic communication, an EC, and supporting documentation that would go to the Radical Fundamentalist Unit, or the FBI headquarters unit that was overseeing that investigation. They would, they would take that information, they would add whatever type—whatever information they could to amplify their request, and then they would take it to a headquarters unit, FBI headquarters unit called the National Security Law Unit, comprised of lawyers whose expertise is in the area of national security law. They would review it to ensure that probable cause did, in fact, exist to establish that that person was acting as an agent of a foreign power. When that was in agreement and the FBI agreed that the application had merit, it would then go to the Department of Justice, OIPR, Office of Intelligence Policy Review, where it would again be reviewed by attorneys, this time in the Department of Justice outside the FBI, and again, when all parties agreed that probable cause existed, it would go forward to the FISA court in the form of a declaration.

Q. Okay.

A. Which a judge would sign or not.

Q. Is the FISA court a local judge then in Minnesota, or is that somewhere else?

A. It's somewhere else.

Q. All right. And is it generally headquartered somewhere in the Washington area, with affiliates around the country?

A. Yes, sir.

Q. And, and even when the application goes to the FISA judge, the FISA judge still has the decision whether to approve it or disapprove it; is that right?

A. That's correct. There's many points along the way where it can be forwarded and not forwarded. The ultimate person who decides is a FISA court judge.

Q. After you were denied the authority to seek a criminal search warrant, did you take steps to try to get a FISA warrant?

A. Yes, sir.

Q. Could you explain what it is that—the steps that you took in order to do so?

A. We, we shifted—I personally shifted gears slightly, because now the nature of the information that I need is different. I no longer need to establish that, in fact, the person is engaged in an ongoing crime, but rather that they're doing any actions on behalf of a foreign power, that they are now acting as an agent of a foreign power, and so the focus changed slightly to that. The substance of the interviews was still useful to some extent and misleading to other extents, but the objective was the same, was the search of those belongings.

Q. Well, and specifically factually, are you trying to connect Mr. Moussaoui to a terrorist organization?

A. Yes, absolutely.

Q. Now, directing your attention to August 23, earlier on in your testimony, you had told us that you had made a request to your—to Jay Abbott, one of the French legats that the FBI has; is that correct?

A. Yes, sir, the assistant legal attaché in the Paris office.

Q. All right. And on August 23, did you get some information back from your French legat?

A. I did.

Q. All right. And did you get information from Mr. Abbott connecting Mr. Moussaoui to a dead Chechen fighter?

A. Yes, sir.

Q. Could you tell the folks what a Chechen fighter is?

A. Yes, sir. There was a conflict then going on in the former Soviet—the former Soviet, now Russian, region of Chechnya. They were seeking independence from the Russian Federation and, in fact, had seen an influx in the late '90s of foreign fighters from various Muslim countries. A number of these soldiers were trained in Afghanistan. They reported into Chechnya and began engaging the Russians in military combat.

Q. Well, let me ask you this: You had told us that al Qaeda was identified on a State Department list as a foreign terrorist organization. Were Chechen rebels identified as a foreign terrorist organization?

A. No, sir, they weren't.

Q. Now, on August 30, did you get additional information back through your French legat?

A. Yes, sir.

Q. And did you get specific information about Mr. Moussaoui's fundamentalism?

A. Yes.

Q. Could you describe what the extent of the information was about his religious views?

A. That he was extreme, that he was—had espoused violence, that he attempted to recruit and convert others to both the extreme view of Islam and to violence, and that he had followed closely the Wahhabi sect of Islam.

Q. And on August 19, did you send a request to the English government asking them to do investigation on your behalf?

A. To our legal attaché in London, yes, sir.

Q. Same type of thing you have in France, you've got one over there in England?

A. Correct.

Q. And what type of information was it that you were trying to gather in England?

A. The same type of information regarding associates, sources of funding. The one that was sent to London to our legal attaché carried particular weight and detail because those are the items not only that Mr. Moussaoui had disclosed to the associate, Ahmed Atif, but he had done so in such a way in the interview that made me believe that that was a person of significance.

Q. Now, on August 22, did you have—receive information from the Central Intelligence Agency?

A. I did.

Q. Well, what information did you get back from—summarizing what you got from the CIA at that time?

A. I received information from them that Mr. Moussaoui's dead associate was connected to the leader of the Chechen rebels by name, and that that—

Q. Who is the—what name did you receive of the leader of the Chechen rebels?

A. Ibn Khattab.

Q. Okay. Did you receive any other information about Ibn Khattab, the leader of the Chechen rebels?

A. From the Central Intelligence Agency I learned that Ibn Khattab and Usama Bin Laden had had a relationship based on their past history.

Q. Okay. Did you receive any information about Mr. Moussaoui being a member of al Qaeda?

A. No.

Q. Now, did you continue to try to accumulate the information that you had gotten through your French legat and from the Central Intelligence Agency in terms of pursuing your FISA warrant?

A. Yes. It was, it was the obsession of our squad, of the Joint Terrorism Task Force, was doing just that.

Q. When you say obsession, could you tell us what do you mean by that?

A. I mean that on the basis of the interviews that Special Agent Weess and myself had done on the 16th and the 17th, we were convinced that Mr. Moussaoui was involved in some type of plot, and so all of our energies were directed at accumulating whatever was required, evidence or intelligence, to get into his belongings and search them for information as to what was going to happen.

Q. Now, at some point, your request to get a FISA search warrant was denied by your headquarters; is that right?

A. Yes, sir.

Q. Okay. Do you know approximately when that was?

A. Approximately August 28.

Q. All right. At the time that your request for a search warrant was denied, could you explain to us what was the extent of the information that you had available that connected you to a terrorist organization?

A. Yes, sir.

Q. Or Mr. Moussaoui, I'm sorry.

A. Yes, sir. We had information from our legat in Paris that Mr. Moussaoui had recruited this fighter for the Chechens who had since been killed in Chechnya, that that fighter, in fact, was connected to Ibn Khattab, who was the leader of the Chechen fighters. The CIA was able to confirm that information and also to provide information that Ibn Khattab and Usama Bin Laden had a relationship.

Q. Let me ask you this: At any point, were you able to satisfy your headquarters' demands as to the proof as to what the foreign power was?

A. No.

Q. All right. Now, after your headquarters denied your efforts to try to get a FISA warrant, did you come up with a different plan in order to try to get a search into Mr. Moussaoui's bags, at least his bags that he had with him?

A. Yes, sir.

Q. And what was that plan?

A. Through consultation with our legal attaché's office in Paris, we learned that the French government had an interest in Mr. Moussaoui and, in fact, that they were willing to accept his being deported there with the provision of French law that his belongings could be searched upon his arrival.

Q. Now, you could lawfully deport him already based upon his overstay in the visa waiver program; is that right?

A. Yes, sir, that's correct.

Q. And through this series of days thereafter, did you set up plans in order to do so?

A. We did. We worked—that became the primary focus. We kept the other options, obviously mindful of the criminal and of the intelligence, the FISA option as well, but our primary focus then became the deportation of Mr. Moussaoui to France in order to allow his goods to be—his property to be—property to be searched.

Q. And when was that finally approved by all parties, that that was—that that could occur?

A. On the afternoon of September 10, 2001.

Q. And, and Mr. Moussaoui obviously as of September 11 had not been sent back to France; is that right?

A. That's correct.

Q. When was that to occur, do you know?

A. In the very near future. We had received authority to begin planning for that on the afternoon of September 10. Obviously, the time difference being what it was, the legal attaché's office in Paris was closed, so that next morning, we were going to set up the logistics, but it was going to be a matter of days.

Q. Now, in addition to taking those precautions, at any point did you ask your headquarters to notify the FAA about the threat that Mr. Moussaoui posed?

A. Yes, sir.

Q. And on August 31, did you send what is known as an LHM to Mr. Maltbie in the RFU unit?

A. I did.

Q. Do you want to tell the folks what an LHM is in the jargon of the FBI?

A. An LHM stands for letterhead memorandum, and a letterhead memorandum is a document authored by someone in the FBI that is intended to be released outside of the FBI, whether it's to another law enforcement agency in the United States, to another member of the intelligence community, or to a friendly foreign government.

Q. And why is that you wanted your headquarters to notify FAA about what was happening with Mr. Moussaoui?

A. Because of the, our investigative theory that he was involved in a plan to hijack a commercial airliner.

Q. And on September 5 of 2001, do you know if your headquarters did, in fact, make that notification?

A. They did. In fact, our headquarters issued a teletype, a message to a number of other government agencies, to include the FAA.

Q. Now, in addition to what you requested your headquarters to do, were you so concerned about the FAA being notified that you took steps on your own as a local guy on the ground out in Minnesota to make sure the FAA knew what was going on with Mr. Moussaoui?

A. Yes, sir, Special Agent Weess and myself on September 5 went to the FAA investigators in the Twin Cities, in Minneapolis–St. Paul, and provided them a personal briefing on the contents of the teletype, as well as case agent perspective on what we believed was actually going on.

Q. And as a result of those attacks [September 11], those crimes occurring, were you then authorized to go get a criminal search warrant?

A. Yes, sir.

Q. And did you go that very day, September 11, to the United States Attorney's Office in Minneapolis and procure a search warrant?

A. Within minutes of our being granted permission, I was on my way to the United States Attorney's Office at full speed, yes, sir.

Q. And did the U.S. Attorney's Office help you and your brother agents to get a search warrant then signed by a United States magistrate judge?

A. Yes, sir.

Q. Now, after you got a search warrant, now you had the legal ability to go in and search Mr. Moussaoui's items; is that right?

A. Yes, sir.

Q. And did you do so?

A. Yes, sir.

Q. Can you tell the folks what it is that you did finally with those bags that he had stored in INS for those three weeks?

A. Special Agent Weess went down to Immigration and was, was responding lights and sirens to bring those bags to the FBI office at full speed. The warrant was signed, and I had an FBI organization within our office call the evidence response team, agents who are specially trained in evidence recovery, standing by. When the goods arrived, when the personal property arrived and the warrant arrived, the evidence response team under my direction immediately began executing the search warrant.

Source: Testimony of FBI Agent Harry Samit in the Zacarias Moussaoui Trial (March 9, 2006): transcript pages 794–795, 802–818, 827–828, 845–846, and 922–952 (http://www.law.umkc.edu /faculty/projects/ftrials/moussaoui/zmsami/).

---

15. Confession of Khalid Sheikh Mohammed at the Combatant Status Review Tribunal at Guantánamo Bay Detention Camp (March 10, 2007)

Introduction

This testimony by Khalid Sheikh Mohammed at the Combatant Status Review Tribunal at Guantánamo Bay Detention Camp on March 10, 2007, answers many questions about the September 11, 2001, attacks. He takes complete responsibility for the planning and implementation of the attacks. In fact, Mohammed almost glorifies his role. He also takes responsibility for a number of other initiatives and operations of Al Qaeda, including some that never materialized. Mohammed considers his operations to be part of an ongoing war between the Muslim and Western worlds. Earlier in the proceedings, Mohammed complained about the use of torture on him. Mohammed and several other suspected 9/11 terrorists are at the center of an intense debate over whether they should be tried in military or civilian courts.

Primary Source

I hereby admit and affirm without duress to the following:

1. I swore Bay'aat (i.e., allegiance) to Sheikh Usama Bin Laden to conduct Jihad of self and money, and also Hijrah (i.e., expatriation to any location in the world where Jihad is required).
2. I was a member of the Al Qaida Council.
3. I was the Media Operations Director for Al-Sahab, or 'The Clouds,' under Dr. Ayman AL Zawahiri. Al-Sahab is the media outlet that provided Al-Qaida-sponsored information to Al Jazeera.
4. I was the Operational Director for Sheikh Usama Bin Laden for the organizing, planning, follow-up, and execution of the 9/11 Operation under the Military Commander, Sheikh Abu Hafs Al-Masri Subhi Abu Sittah.
5. I was the Military Operational Commander for all foreign operations around the world under the direction of Sheikh Usama Bin Laden and Dr. Ayman Al-Zawahiri.
6. I was directly in charge, after the death of Sheikh Abu Hafs Al-Masri Subhi Abu Sittah, of managing and following up on the Cell for the Production of Biological Weapons, such as anthrax and others, and following up on Dirty Bomb Operations on American soil.
7. I was Emir (i.e., commander) of Beit Al Shuhada (i.e., the Martyrs' House) in the state of Kandahar, Afghanistan, which housed the 9/11 hijackers. There I was responsible for their training and readiness for the execution of the 9/11 Operation. Also, I hereby admit and affirm without duress that I was a responsible participant, principal planner, trainer, financier (via the Military Council Treasury), executor, and/or a personal participant in the following;
   1. I was responsible for the 1993 World Trade Center Operation.
   2. I was responsible for the 9/11 Operation, from A to Z.
   3. I decapitated with my blessed right hand the head of the American Jew, Daniel Pearl, in the city of Karachi, Pakistan. For those who would like to confirm, there are pictures of me on the internet holding his head.
   4. I was responsible for the Shoe Bomber Operation to down two American airplanes.
   5. I was responsible for the Filka Island Operation in Kuwait that killed two American soldiers.
   6. I was responsible for the bombing of a nightclub in Bali, Indonesia, which was frequented by British and Australian nationals.
   7. I was responsible for planning, training, surveying, and financing the New (or Second) Wave attacks against the following skyscrapers after 9/11:
      1. Library Tower, California.
      2. Sears Tower, Chicago.
      3. Plaza Bank, Washington state.

   4. The Empire State Building, New York City.

8. I was responsible for planning, financing, & follow-up of Operations to destroy American military vessels and oil tankers in the Strait of Hormuz, the Strait of Gibraltar, and the Port of Singapore.

9. I was responsible for planning, training, surveying, and financing for the Operation to bomb and destroy the Panama Canal.

10. I was responsible for surveying and financing for the assassination of several former American Presidents, including President Carter.

11. I was responsible for surveying, planning, and financing for the bombing of suspension bridges in New York.

12. I was responsible for planning to destroy the Sears Tower by burning a few fuel or oil tanker trucks beneath it or around it.

13. I was responsible for planning, surveying, and financing for the operation to destroy Heathrow Airport, the Canary Wharf Building, and Big Ben on British soil.

14. I was responsible for planning, surveying, and financing for the destruction of many night clubs frequented by American and British citizens on Thailand soil.

15. I was responsible for surveying and financing for the destruction of the New York Stock Exchange and other financial targets after 9/11.

16. I was responsible for planning, financing, and surveying for the destruction of buildings in the Israeli city of Elat by using airplanes leaving from Saudi Arabia.

17. I was responsible for planning, surveying, and financing for the destruction of American embassies in Indonesia, Australia, and Japan.

18. I was responsible for surveying and financing for the destruction of the Israeli embassy in India, Azerbaijan, the Philippines, and Australia.

19. I was responsible for surveying and financing for the destruction of an Israeli EL AL Airlines flight on Thailand soil departing from Bangkok Airport.

20. I was responsible for sending several Mujahadeen into Israel to conduct surveillance to hit several strategic targets deep in Israel.

21. I was responsible for the bombing of the hotel in Mombasa that is frequented by Jewish travelers via EL AL airlines.

22. I was responsible for launching a Russian-made SA-7 surface-to-air missile on EL AL or other Jewish airliner departing from Mombasa.

23. I was responsible for planning and surveying to hit American targets in South Korea, such as American military bases and a few night clubs frequented by American soldiers.

24. I was responsible for financial, excuse me, I was responsible for providing financial support to hit American, Jewish, and British targets in Turkey.

25. I was responsible for surveillance needed to hit nuclear power plants that generate electricity in several U.S. states.

26. I was responsible for planning, surveying, and financing to hit NATO Headquarters in Europe.

27. I was responsible for the planning and surveying needed to execute

the Bojinka Operation, which was designed to down twelve American airplanes full of passengers. I personally monitored a round-trip, Manila-to-Seoul, Pan Am flight.

28. I was responsible for the assassination attempt against President Clinton during his visit to the Philippines in 1994 or 1995.
29. I shared responsibility for the assassination attempt against Pope John Paul the second while he was visiting the Philippines.
30. I was responsible for the training and financing for the assassination of Pakistan's President Musharaf.
31. I was responsible for the attempt to destroy an American oil company owned by the Jewish former Secretary of State, Henry Kissinger, on the Island of Sumatra, Indonesia.

Personal Representative: Sir, that concludes the written portion of the Detainee's final statement and as he has alluded to earlier he has some additional comments he would like to make.

President: Alright. Before you proceed, Khalid Sheikh Muhammad, the statement that was just read by the Personal Representative, were those your words?

Detainee: Yes. And I want to add some of this one just for some verification. It like some operations before I join al Qaida. Before I remember al Qaida which is related to Bojinka Operation I went to destination involve to us in 94, 95. Some Operations which means out of al Qaida. It's like beheading Daniel Pearl. It's not related to al Qaida. It was shared in Pakistani, other group, Mujahadeen. The story of Daniel Pearl, because he stated for the Pakistani group that he was working with the both. His mission was in Pakistan to track about Richard Reed trip to Israel. Richard Reed, do you have trip? You send it Israel to make set for targets in Israel. His mission in Pakistan from Israeli intelligence, Mosad, to make interview to ask about when he was there. Also, he mention to them he was both. He have relation with CIA people and were the Mosad. But he was not related to al Qaida at all or UBL. It is related to the Pakistan Mujahadeen group. Other operations mostly are some word I'm not accurate in saying. I'm responsible but if you read the heading history. The line there.

Personal Representative: Also hereby admit and affirm without duress that I was a responsible participant, principal planner, trainer, financier.

Detainee: For this is not necessary as I responsible, responsible. But with in these things responsible participant in finances.

In the name of God the most compassionate, the most merciful, and if any fail to retaliation by way of charity and. I apologize. I will start again. And if any fail to judge by the light of Allah has revealed, they are no better than wrong doers, unbelievers, and the unjust.

For this verse, I not take the oath. Take an oath is a part of your Tribunal and I'll not accept it. To be or accept the Tribunal as to be, I'll accept it. That I'm accepting American constitution, American law or whatever you are doing here. This is why religiously I cannot accept anything you do. Just to explain for this one, does not mean I'm not saying that I'm lying. When I not take oath does not mean I'm lying. You know very well peoples take oath and they will lie. You know the President he did this before he just makes his oath and he lied. So sometimes when I'm not making oath does not mean I'm lying.

Allah forbids you not with regards to those who fight you not for not for your faith nor drive you out of your homes from dealing kindly and justly with them. For Allah love those who are just. There is one more sentence. Allah only forbids you with regards to those who fight you for your faith and drive you out of your homes and support others in driving you out from turning to them for friendship and protection. It is as such to turn to them in these circumstances that do wrong.

So we are driving from whatever deed we do we ask about Koran or Hadith. We are not making up for us laws. When we need Fatwa from the religious we have to go back to see what they said scholar. To see what they said yes or not. Killing is prohibited in all what you call the people of the book, Jews, Judaism, Christianity, and Islam. You know the Ten Commandments very well. The Ten Commandments are shared between all of us. We all are serving one God. Then now kill you know it very well. But war language also we have language for the war. You have to kill. But you have to care if unintentionally or intentionally target if I have if I'm not at the Pentagon. I consider it is okay. If I target now when we target in USA we choose them military target, economical, and political. So, war central victims mostly means economical target. So if now American they know UBL. He is in this house they don't care about his kids and his. They will just bombard it. They will kill all of them and they did it. They kill wife of Dr. Ayman Zawahiri and his two daughters and his son in one bombardment. They receive a report that is his house be. He had not been there. They killed them. They arrested my kids intentionally. They are kids. They been arrested for four months they had been

abused. So, for me I have patience. I know I'm not talk about what's come to me. The American have human right. So, enemy combatant itself, it flexible word. So I think God knows that many who been arrested, they been unjustly arrested. Otherwise, military throughout history know very well. They don't war will never stop. War start from Adam when Cain he killed Abel until now. It's never gonna stop killing of people. This is the way of the language. American start the Revolutionary War then they starts the Mexican then Spanish War then World War One, World War Two. You read the history. You know never stopping war. This is life. But if who is enemy combatant and who is not? Finally, I finish statement. I'm asking you to be fair with other people.

Source: Department of Defense. Verbatim Transcript of Combatant Status Review Tribunal Hearing for ISN 10024. Available online at http://archive.defense.gov/news/transcript_ISN10024.pdf

16. President Barack Obama Announces the Death of Osama bin Laden (May 1, 2011)

Introduction

As a candidate, Barack Obama promised to focus added attention to capturing or killing bin Laden and, as president, instructed CIA chief Leon Panetta to recommit intelligence communities to those efforts. After months of running down intelligence leads, the White House had reason to believe that the United States had located bin Laden in Pakistan. Giving the order and monitoring the mission, Obama instructed U.S. forces to attack the compound where they believed bin Laden to be. On May 1, 2011, President Obama addressed the nation with the news of the killing of bin Laden.

Primary Source

THE PRESIDENT: Good evening. Tonight, I can report to the American people and to the world that the United States has conducted an operation that killed Osama bin Laden, the leader of al Qaeda, and a terrorist who's responsible for the murder of thousands of innocent men, women, and children.

It was nearly 10 years ago that a bright September day was darkened by the worst attack on the American people in our history. The images of 9/11 are seared into our national memory—hijacked planes cutting through a cloudless September sky; the Twin Towers collapsing to the ground; black smoke billowing up from the Pentagon; the wreckage of Flight 93 in Shanksville, Pennsylvania, where the actions of heroic citizens saved even more heartbreak and destruction.

And yet we know that the worst images are those that were unseen to the world. The empty seat at the dinner table. Children who were forced to grow up without their mother or their father. Parents who would never know the feeling of their child's embrace. Nearly 3,000 citizens taken from us, leaving a gaping hole in our hearts.

On September 11, 2001, in our time of grief, the American people came together. We offered our neighbors a hand, and we offered the wounded our blood. We reaffirmed our ties to each other, and our love of community and country. On that day, no matter where we came from, what God we prayed to, or what race or ethnicity we were, we were united as one American family.

We were also united in our resolve to protect our nation and to bring those who committed this vicious attack to justice. We quickly learned that the 9/11 attacks were carried out by al Qaeda—an organization headed by Osama bin Laden, which had openly declared war on the United States and was committed to killing innocents in our country and around the globe. And so we went to war against al Qaeda to protect our citizens, our friends, and our allies.

Over the last 10 years, thanks to the tireless and heroic work of our military and our counterterrorism professionals, we've made great strides in that effort. We've disrupted terrorist attacks and strengthened our homeland defense. In Afghanistan, we removed the Taliban government, which had given bin Laden and al Qaeda safe haven and support. And around the globe, we worked with our friends and allies to capture or kill scores of al Qaeda terrorists, including several who were a part of the 9/11 plot.

Yet Osama bin Laden avoided capture and escaped across the Afghan border into Pakistan. Meanwhile, al Qaeda continued to operate from along that border and operate through its affiliates across the world.

And so shortly after taking office, I directed Leon Panetta, the director of the CIA, to make the killing or capture of bin Laden the top priority of our war against al Qaeda, even as we continued our broader efforts to disrupt, dismantle, and defeat his network.

Then, last August, after years of painstaking work by our intelligence community, I was briefed on a possible lead to bin Laden. It was far from certain, and it took many months to run this thread to ground. I met repeatedly with my national security team as we developed more information about the possibility that we had located bin Laden hiding within a compound deep inside of Pakistan. And finally, last week, I determined that we had enough intelligence to take action, and authorized an operation to get Osama bin Laden and bring him to justice.

Today, at my direction, the United States launched a targeted operation against that compound in Abbottabad, Pakistan. A small team of Americans carried out the operation with extraordinary courage and capability. No Americans were harmed. They took care to avoid civilian casualties. After a firefight, they killed Osama bin Laden and took custody of his body.

For over two decades, bin Laden has been al Qaeda's leader and symbol, and has continued to plot attacks against our country and our friends and allies. The death of bin Laden marks the most significant achievement to date in our nation's effort to defeat al Qaeda.

Yet his death does not mark the end of our effort. There's no doubt that al Qaeda will continue to pursue attacks against us. We must—and we will—remain vigilant at home and abroad.

As we do, we must also reaffirm that the United States is not—and never will be—at war with Islam. I've made clear, just as President Bush did shortly after 9/11, that our war is not against Islam. Bin Laden was not a Muslim leader; he was a mass murderer of Muslims. Indeed, al Qaeda has slaughtered scores of Muslims in many countries, including our own. So his demise should be welcomed by all who believe in peace and human dignity.

Over the years, I've repeatedly made clear that we would take action within Pakistan if we knew where bin Laden was. That is what we've done. But it's important to note that our counterterrorism cooperation with Pakistan helped lead us to bin Laden and the compound where he was hiding. Indeed, bin Laden had declared war against Pakistan as well, and ordered attacks against the Pakistani people.

Tonight, I called President Zardari, and my team has also spoken with their Pakistani counterparts. They agree that this is a good and historic day for both of our nations. And going forward, it is essential that Pakistan continue to join us in the fight against al Qaeda and its affiliates.

The American people did not choose this fight. It came to our shores, and started with the senseless slaughter of our citizens. After nearly 10 years of service, struggle, and sacrifice, we know well the costs of war. These efforts weigh on me every time I, as Commander-in-Chief, have to sign a letter to a family that has lost a loved one, or look into the eyes of a service member who's been gravely wounded.

So Americans understand the costs of war. Yet as a country, we will never tolerate our security being threatened, nor stand idly by when our people have been killed. We will be relentless in defense of our citizens and our friends and allies. We will be true to the values that make us who we are. And on nights like this one, we can say to those families who have lost loved ones to al Qaeda's terror: Justice has been done.

Tonight, we give thanks to the countless intelligence and counterterrorism professionals who've worked tirelessly to achieve this outcome. The American people do not see their work, nor know their names. But tonight, they feel the satisfaction of their work and the result of their pursuit of justice.

We give thanks for the men who carried out this operation, for they exemplify the professionalism, patriotism, and unparalleled courage of those who serve our country. And they are part of a generation that has borne the heaviest share of the burden since that September day.

Finally, let me say to the families who lost loved ones on 9/11 that we have never forgotten your loss, nor wavered in our commitment to see that we do whatever it takes to prevent another attack on our shores.

And tonight, let us think back to the sense of unity that prevailed on 9/11. I know that it has, at times, frayed. Yet today's achievement is a testament to the greatness of our country and the determination of the American people.

The cause of securing our country is not complete. But tonight, we are once again reminded that America can do whatever we set our mind to. That is the story of our history, whether it's the pursuit of prosperity for our people, or the struggle for equality for all our citizens; our commitment to stand up for our values abroad, and our sacrifices to make the world a safer place.

Let us remember that we can do these things not just because of wealth or power, but because of who we are: one nation, under God, indivisible, with liberty and justice for all.

Thank you. May God bless you. And may God bless the United States of America.

Source: Obama, Barack. Remarks on the Death of Al Qaida Terrorist Organization Leader Usama bin Laden. May 1, 2011. *Public Papers of the Presidents of the United States: Barack Obama (2011, Book 1)*. Washington, DC: Government Printing Office, 480–482.

17. Commemorating the 10th Anniversary of 9/11 (September 11, 2011)

Introduction

In the ten years following the attacks of 9/11, the United States was moving on. A war had been fought, and the leader of the enemy vanquished. A new president was in office, and a new building was underway at the World Trade Center. In these remarks made at a concert commemorating the anniversary, President Barack Obama addressed how far the country had come.

Primary Source

The Bible tells us, "Weeping may endure for a night, but joy cometh in the morning."

Ten years ago, America confronted one of our darkest nights. Mighty towers crumbled. Black smoke billowed up from the Pentagon. Airplane wreckage smoldered on a Pennsylvania field. Friends and neighbors, sisters and brothers, mothers and fathers, sons and daughters, they were taken from us with a heartbreaking swiftness and cruelty. And on September 12, 2001, we awoke to a world in which evil was closer at hand and uncertainty clouded our future.

In the decade since, much has changed for Americans. We've known war and recession, passionate debates and political divides. We can never get back the lives that were lost on that day or the Americans who made the ultimate sacrifice in the wars that followed.

And yet today it is worth remembering what has not changed. Our character as a nation has not changed. Our faith in God and in each other, that has not changed. Our belief in America, born of a timeless ideal that men and women should govern themselves, that all people are created equal and deserve the same freedom to determine their own destiny, that belief, through tests and trials, has only been strengthened.

These past 10 years have shown that America does not give in to fear. The rescue workers who rushed to the scene, the firefighters who charged up the stairs, the passengers who stormed the cockpit, these patriots defined the very nature of courage. Over the years, we've also seen a more quiet form of heroism: in the ladder company that lost so many men and still suits up and saves lives every day, the businesses that have been rebuilt from nothing, the burn victim who has bounced back, the families who press on.

Last spring, I received a letter from a woman named Suzanne Swaine. She had lost her husband and brother in the Twin Towers and said that she had been robbed of "so many would-be proud moments where a father watches their child graduate, or tend a goal in a lacrosse game, or succeed academically." But her daughters are in college, the other doing well in high school. "It has been 10 years of raising these girls on my own," Suzanne wrote. "I could not be prouder of their strength and resilience." That spirit typifies our American family. And the hopeful future for those girls is the ultimate rebuke to the hateful killers who took the life of their father.

These past 10 years have shown America's resolve to defend its citizens and our way of life. Diplomats serve in far-off posts, and intelligence professionals work tirelessly without recognition. Two million Americans have gone to war since 9/11. They've demonstrated that those who do us harm cannot hide from the reach of justice anywhere in the world. America has been defended not by conscripts, but by citizens who choose to serve: young people who signed up straight out of high school, guardsmen and reservists, workers and businesspeople, immigrants and fourth-generation soldiers. They are men and women who left behind lives of comfort for two, three, four, five tours of duty. Too many will never come home; those that do carry dark memories from distant places and the legacy of fallen friends.

The sacrifices of these men and women and of our military families reminds us that the wages of war are great, that while service to our Nation is full of glory, war itself is never glorious. Our troops have been to lands unknown to many Americans a decade ago, to Kandahar and Kabul, to Mosul and Basra. But our strength is not measured in our ability to stay in these places, it comes from our commitment to leave those lands to free people and sovereign states and our desire to move from a decade of war to a future of peace.

These 10 years have shown that we hold fast to our freedoms. Yes, we're more vigilant against those who threaten us, and there are inconveniences that come with our common defense. Debates about war and peace, about security and civil liberties, have often been fierce these last 10 years. But it is precisely the rigor of these debates, and our ability to resolve them in a way that honors our values and our democracy, that is the measure of our strength. Meanwhile, our open markets still provide innovators the chance to create and succeed, our citizens are still free to speak their minds, and our souls are enriched in churches and temples, our synagogues and our mosques.

These past 10 years underscores the bonds between all Americans. We have not succumbed to suspicion, nor have we succumbed to mistrust. After 9/11, to his great credit, President Bush made clear what we reaffirm today: The United States will never wage war against Islam or any other religion. Immigrants come here from all parts of the globe. And in the biggest cities and the smallest towns, in schools and workplaces, you still see people of every conceivable race and religion and ethnicity, all of them pledging allegiance to the flag, all of them reaching for the same American Dream. *E pluribus unum*—out of many, we are one.

These past 10 years tell a story of our resilience. The Pentagon is repaired and filled with patriots working in common purpose. Shanksville is the scene of friendships forged between residents of that town and families who lost loved ones there. New York–New York remains the most vibrant of capitals of arts and industry and fashion and commerce. Where the World Trade Center once stood, the sun glistens off a new tower that reaches towards the sky.

Our people still work in skyscrapers. Our stadiums are still filled with fans, and our parks full of children playing ball. Our airports hum with travel, and our buses and subways take millions where they need to go. And families sit down to Sunday dinner, and students prepare for school. This land pulses with the optimism of those who set out for distant shores and the courage of those who died for human freedom.

Decades from now, Americans will visit the memorials to those who were lost on 9/11. They'll run their fingers over the places where the names of those we loved are carved into marble and stone, and they may wonder at the lives that they led. And standing before the white headstones in Arlington and in peaceful cemeteries and small-town squares in every corner of the country, they will pay respects to those lost in Iraq and Afghanistan. They'll see the names of the fallen on bridges and statues, at gardens and schools.

And they will know that nothing can break the will of a truly United States of America. They will remember that we've overcome slavery and civil war, we've overcome breadlines and fascism and recession and riots and communism and, yes, terrorism. They will be reminded that we are not perfect, but our democracy is durable, and that democracy—reflecting, as it does, the imperfections of man—also give us the opportunity to perfect our Union. That is what we honor on days of national commemoration, those aspects of the American

experience that are enduring and the determination to move forward as one people.

More than monuments, that will be the legacy of 9/11: a legacy of firefighters who walked into fire and soldiers who signed up to serve; of workers who raised new towers and citizens who faced down their private fears; most of all, of children who realized the dreams of their parents. It will be said that we kept the faith, that we took a painful blow and we emerged stronger than before.

"Weeping may endure for a night, but joy cometh in the morning." With a just God as our guide, let us honor those who have been lost, let us rededicate ourselves to the ideals that define our Nation, and let us look to the future with hearts full of hope.

May God bless the memory of those we lost, and may God bless the United States of America.

Source: *Public Papers of the President of the United States. Barack Obama (2011, Book 2).* Washington, DC: Government Printing Office, 1049–1051.

18. Testimony of Jon Stewart on Health Care for First Responders (June 11, 2019)

Introduction

Eighteen years after the events of 9/11, those who had been first on the scene were continuing to suffer the effects of toxic exposure. With cases of cancer and respiratory diseases on the rise, Congress was due to reauthorize the James Zadroga 9/11 Health and Compensation Act of 2010. However, funding the act became a political battlefield, with some balking at the idea of a permanent compensation fund.

Comedian (and lifelong New Yorker) Jon Stewart had been an advocate for those first responders since the early days after 9/11.

In June 2019, he was invited to testify in Congress, and he brought several of the first responders with him. However, the committee's seats were nearly empty; few had shown up.

In this emotional speech, Stewart lashed out at Congress's disrespect, and begged them to pass the bill. His testimony was widely aired, and the bill passed the next day, extending funding to 2090.

Primary Source

Chairman Nadler, Ranking Member Collins and Members of the Committee, thank you for letting me join these 9/11 responders and survivors, these heroes, today on this panel.

And thank you for this hearing today on the September 11th Victim Compensation Fund and the legislation Never Forget the Heroes: Permanent Authorization of the September 11th Victim Compensation Fund—that would fully fund the program and extend its authorization.

You have just heard in agonizing detail why you need to act on this legislation.

Many talk about 9/11 and how the country responded to it, but frankly the response on the impact of the toxins at Ground Zero, as these men and women have outlined, has not been as good as it should have been—to say the least.

First, the issues these heroes face is squarely the fault of terrorists. But in the rush to get Wall Street open again and move people back in, mistakes were made.

People—local residents, students and commuters into the area (as well as responders)— were told that the air was safe. But it was not. Children were brought back to school next to a toxic pit—and then it was denied—for years—that there was a health problem. Those who responded and worked in the pit—and had the most exposure—were of course the first to feel the effects. But soon residents became ill, too—with persistent coughs or rare cancers.

So, for many years since 9/11, these responders and residents had to walk the halls of Congress, looking to see if "Remember 9/11" is more than a cheap twitter slogan senators and representatives use to nod in the direction of empathy without having to do anything.

They had to work to get Congress to provide health care for these injuries from toxins; they had to work to get compensation for the injuries so that their families would not suffer.

First responders, firefighters, police, construction workers, Red Cross volunteers, transit workers, FBI agents and schoolteachers have had to go door to door down your gold- and marble-lined hallways, because 17 years after the attacks on 9/11, they and their families are still dealing with the impact of the toxins at Ground Zero.

They are in every state and 433 out of 435 Congressional Districts.

The fact that they have had continue to do this is beyond my comprehension. But I have to say that my impression of Washington might be changing.

Some things are getting done. Just a few weeks ago I said that the Trump Justice Department was doing a good job running the program, I would never have thought that I would say it, but I did because it is true.

The fact that this hearing is happening in this committee today is heartening. I understand there has been some recent unpleasantness.

This legislation has over 300 bipartisan sponsors. 300 members of the House agreeing to take action is pretty good.

I want to thank Ranking Member Collins for his support today; he and Mr. Nadler have set an example that the parties can come together. All of the support gives me some hope.

There seems to be a general understanding and agreement that compensating the 9/11 heroes through this bill needs to happen. I thank all of you—Republicans and Democrats—for that.

These people can't wait—the cuts to them or their survivors are happening now. I know that this is going to cost a lot, but you need [to] figure out how to pay for it. It is not their job to tell you how to pay for it—they did their job.

I ask you to move this bill and get it to the floor. Two weeks ago, I was at Ground Zero for the dedication of the National September 11th Memorial, for the dedication of a new memorial glade, with ragged stone monoliths that honor those who have become ill and those that have died from 9/11 related illnesses.

The space will never bring closure to those who have lost so much and continue to suffer so deeply, but it recognizes the great courage and strength they gave so willingly and the price they continue to pay.

But they need this bill. Please help them.

Source: Testimony of Jon Stewart. House Judiciary Committee Hearing. The Need to Reauthorize the September 11th Victim Compensation Fund. June 11, 2019. Available online at https://docs.house.gov/meetings/JU/JU10/20190611/109609/HHRG-116-JU10-Wstate-StewartJ-20190611.pdf

Chronology

October 25, 1978
President Jimmy Carter signs the Foreign Intelligence Surveillance Act, which allows investigations of foreign persons who are engaged in espionage or international terrorism.

December 26, 1979
Soviet forces invade Afghanistan, beginning the Soviet-Afghan War.

August 11, 1988
Osama bin Laden and Sheikh Abdullah Azzam start the Al Qaeda organization in Afghanistan.

November 24, 1988
An unknown group assassinates Islamist leader Sheikh Abdullah Azzam in Peshawar, Pakistan, with a car bomb, leaving Osama bin Laden in control of Al Qaeda.

February 15, 1989
Soviet forces withdraw from Afghanistan.

November 5, 1990
El Sayyid Nosair assassinates Rabbi Meir Kahane in New York City.

July 24, 1992
Mohamed Atta arrives in Germany to begin graduate work.

September 1, 1992
Ramzi Ahmed Yousef arrives in the United States at the request of Sheikh Abdel Rahman.

February 26, 1993
The bombing of the World Trade Center in New York City by an Islamist terrorist team led by Ramzi Ahmed Yousef kills 6 and wounds 1,042.

March 4, 1993
The Federal Bureau of Investigation (FBI) discovers the VIN number of the Ryder van used in the World Trade Center bombing, leading to the arrest of some of those involved.

March 4, 1994
Three of the World Trade Center bombers are convicted.

April 9, 1994
The Saudi government revokes Osama bin Laden's Saudi citizenship.

December 11, 1994
Ramzi Ahmed Yousef plants a bomb on Philippine Air Lines Flight 434 that kills a Japanese engineer.

January 6, 1995
Ramzi Ahmed Yousef accidentally causes a fire in a Manila apartment that exposes his plot to assassinate the pope.

January 20, 1995
Abdul Hakim Murad confesses to a plot to fly a small plane into Central Intelligence Agency (CIA) headquarters in Langley, Virginia.

February 7, 1995
Pakistani authorities arrest Ramzi Ahmed Yousef, the head of the 1993 World Trade Center bombing, in Islamabad, Pakistan.

September 22, 1995
Ramzi Bin al-Shibh arrives in Germany.

January 17, 1996
Sheikh Abdel Rahman receives a life sentence for his role in planning the bombing of New York City landmarks.

April 3, 1996
Zaid Jarrah arrives in Germany to continue his education.

April 28, 1996
Marwan al-Shehhi arrives in Germany with a military scholarship to further his studies.

May 18, 1996
Sudan expels Osama bin Laden, who leaves for Afghanistan.

June 25, 1996
Al Qaeda operatives explode a truck bomb at the al-Khobar in Dhahran, Saudi Arabia, killing 19 Americans and wounding hundreds of others.

July 17, 1996
An explosion downs TWA Flight 800 near Long Island, New York.

August 23, 1996
Osama bin Laden issues his Declaration of Jihad against the Americans Occupying the Land of the Two Holiest Sites world.

May 26, 1997
The Saudi government is the first to recognize the Taliban government in Afghanistan.

January 8, 1998
Ramzi Ahmed Yousef receives a sentence of 240 years for his role in the World Trade Center bombing in 1993.

February 23, 1998
The World Islamic Front issues its Declaration of War against Jews and Crusaders, written by Osama bin Laden and others.

August 7, 1998
Bombing of U.S. embassies in Nairobi, Kenya, and Dar es Salaam, Tanzania, by Al Qaeda operatives.

August 20, 1998
U.S. Tomahawk cruise missiles strike Al Qaeda base camps in Afghanistan and Sudan.

October 8, 1998
The Federal Aviation Administration (FAA) warns U.S. airports and airlines of Al Qaeda's threat to U.S. civil aviation.

November 1, 1998
Mohamed Atta, Said Bahaji, and Ramzi Bin al-Shibh move into 54 Marienstrasse in the Harburg area of Hamburg, beginning the Hamburg Cell.

December 1, 1998
U.S. intelligence makes the assessment that Osama bin Laden has been planning attacks inside the United States.

June 7, 1999
The FBI puts Osama bin Laden on its 10 Most Wanted list.

October 1999
Creation of the special intelligence unit Able Danger.

2000
Pentagon lawyers block Able Danger reporting to FBI three times during the year.

January–February 2000
Special intelligence unit Able Danger identifies Mohamed Atta and three associates as possible Al Qaeda agents.

January 5–8, 2000
Al Qaeda holds a summit conference in Kuala Lumpur, Malaysia, where plans for September 11 are discussed.

January 15, 2000
The logistical team of Khalid al-Mihdhar and Nawaf al-Hamzi arrives in Los Angeles to prepare for the September 11 operation.

June 3, 2000
Mohamed Atta arrives in the United States at Newark International Airport from Prague, Czech Republic.

July 2000
Mohamed Atta and Marwan al-Shehhi begin flying lessons at Huffman Aviation in Venice, Florida.

July–August 2000
Defense Intelligence Agency (DIA) employees destroy evidence gathered by Able Danger.

August 12, 2000
Italian intelligence wiretaps an Al Qaeda terrorist cell in Milan, Italy, whose members talk about a massive strike involving aircraft.

October 12, 2000
Al Qaeda operatives place a bomb next to the American destroyer USS *Cole*, killing 17 sailors and injuring 39 others.

October 24–26, 2000
An emergency drill is held at the Pentagon on the possibility of a hijacked airliner crash into the building.

December 20, 2000
Richard Clarke proposes a plan to attack Al Qaeda, but it is postponed and later rejected by the new George W. Bush administration.

December 21, 2000
Mohamed Atta and Marwan al-Shehhi receive their pilot's licenses.

December 26, 2000
Mohamed Atta and Marwan al-Shehhi abandon a rented plane on the taxiway of Miami Airport after the plane's engine fails during takeoff.

January 2001
Lieutenant Colonel Anthony Shaffer, a member of Able Danger, briefs General Hugh Shelton on the group's findings.

January 4, 2001
Mohamed Atta travels to Spain.

January 10, 2001
Mohamed Atta returns to the United States.

February 23, 2001
Zacarias Moussaoui arrives in the United States.

March 7, 2001
Government leaders discuss a plan to fight Al Qaeda, but there is no urgency to proceed.

Spring 2001
The Able Danger program is terminated.

April 1, 2001
Oklahoma police give a speeding ticket to Nawaf al-Hazmi.

April 16, 2001
Mohamed Atta receives a traffic ticket for driving without a license.

April 18, 2001
The FAA warns airlines about possible Middle Eastern hijackers.

April 18, 2001
Marwan al-Shehhi flies to Amsterdam.

April 30, 2001
Deputy Defense Secretary Paul Wolfowitz downplays the importance of Osama bin Laden at a meeting on terrorism.

May 10, 2001
Attorney General John Ashcroft omits counterterrorism from a list of goals of the Justice Department.

May 15, 2001
The CIA refuses to share information with the FBI about the Al Qaeda meeting in Malaysia in January 2000.

June 10, 2001
The CIA notifies all its station chiefs of a possible Al Qaeda suicide attack on U.S. targets over the next few days.

June 11, 2001
A CIA analyst and FBI agents have a shouting match over sharing terrorists' identification information.

June 20, 2001
FBI agent Robert Wright sends a memo that charges the FBI of not trying to catch known terrorists living in the United States.

June 21, 2001
Osama bin Laden tells a Muslim journalist that an attack on the United States is imminent.

June 28, 2001
CIA director George Tenet issues a warning of imminent Al Qaeda attack.

July 2, 2001
The FBI warns of possible Al Qaeda attacks abroad but also possibly in the United States.

July 5, 2001
Richard Clarke briefs senior security officials on the Al Qaeda threat at the White House and tells them Al Qaeda is planning a major attack.

July 8–19, 2001
Mohamed Atta, Ramzi Bin al-Shibh, and Marwan al-Shehhi travel to Spain to finalize attack plans.

July 10, 2001
FBI agent Ken Williams sends a memo about the large number of Middle Eastern men taking flight training lessons in Arizona.

July 10, 2001
CIA director George Tenet briefs Condoleezza Rice and warns of the possibility of an Al Qaeda attack in the United States.

July 17, 2001
Mohamed Atta and Marwan al-Shehhi meet with Al Qaeda leaders in Taragona, Spain, to make final plans for the September 11 attacks.

July 18, 2001
Both the FBI and FAA issue warnings about possible terrorist activity.

August 6, 2001
President Bush receives a briefing entitled "Bin Laden Determined to Strike in U.S." at his Crawford, Texas, ranch.

August 15, 2001
FBI agents in Minneapolis request a FISA search warrant for Zacarias Moussaoui.

August 16, 2001
Arrest of Zacarias Moussaoui by Harry Samit in Minneapolis for visa violation.

August 19, 2001
The FBI's top Al Qaeda expert, John O'Neill, resigns from the FBI under pressure.

August 20, 2001
Harry Samit sends a memo to FBI headquarters in Washington, DC, citing Zacarias Moussaoui as a terrorist threat for an aircraft hijacking.

August 23, 2001
The FBI adds two of the September 11 conspirators, Nawaf al-Hazmi and Khalid al-Mihdhar, to the Terrorist Watch List.

August 23, 2001
Israel's Mossad gives the CIA a list of terrorists living in the United States, on which are named four 9/11 hijackers.

August 23, 2001
John O'Neill begins work as head of World Trade Center security.

August 24, 2001
Khalid al-Mihdhar buys his 9/11 ticket.

August 25, 2001
Nawaf al-Hazmi buys his 9/11 ticket.

August 28, 2001
The FBI's New York office requests to open a criminal investigation of Khalid al-Mihdhar, but FBI headquarters turns down the request.

August 28, 2001
Mohamed Atta buys his 9/11 ticket.

August 29, 2001
Khalid Sheikh Mohammed gives the go-ahead for the September 11 attacks in a call from Afghanistan.

August 29, 2001
Mohamed Atta tells Ramzi Bin al-Shibh the date of the attack in code.

September 4, 2001
Cabinet-level advisers approve of Richard Clarke's plan, proposed eight months earlier, to attack Al Qaeda.

September 9, 2001
Maryland police give Ziad Jarrah a ticket for speeding.

September 10, 2001

Attorney General John Ashcroft turns down an increase of $58 million for the FBI's counterterrorism budget.

September 10, 2001

At a dinner John O'Neill warns that there is a distinct probability of an Al Qaeda attack on New York City in the near future.

September 10, 2001

Mohamed Atta and Abdulaziz al-Omari check in at a motel in Portland, Maine.

September 11, 2001

Assault on World Trade Center and the Pentagon.

12:45 a.m. Willie Brown, the mayor of San Francisco, receives a call from security at San Francisco International Airport warning him about air travel on September 11.

6:45 a.m. Two workers at the instant messaging company Odigo, an Israeli-owned company housed in the World Trade Center, receive messages warning of a possible attack on the World Trade Center.

6:50 a.m. Mohamed Atta and Abdulaziz al-Omari's flight from Portland, Maine, arrives at Boston Logan International Airport.

7:45 a.m. Mohamed Atta and Abdulaziz al-Omari board American Airlines Flight 11.

7:59 a.m. American Airlines Flight 11 leaves Boston Logan Airport, headed for Los Angeles.

8:13:31 a.m. Last routine radio communication from American Airlines Flight 11; the aircraft begins climbing to 35,000 feet.

8:14 a.m. United Airlines Flight 175 leaves Boston Logan Airport, headed for Los Angeles, after a 16-minute delay.

8:17 a.m. Daniel Lewin, former member of the Israel Defense Forces' counterterrorist unit Sayeret Matkal, is killed.

8:20 a.m. American Airlines Flight 77 leaves Washington, DC, headed for Los Angeles.

8:21 a.m. The transponder in American Airlines Flight 11 stops transmitting identification.

8:21 a.m. Flight attendant Betty Ong, on American Airlines Flight 11, notifies American Airlines of the hijacking.

8:25 a.m. The Boston air traffic control center becomes aware of the hijacking of American Airlines Flight 11 and notifies several air traffic control centers that a hijacking is in progress.

8:26 a.m. American Airlines Flight 11 makes a 100-degree turn to the south, toward New York City.

8:37:08 a.m. Boston flight control asks the pilots of United Airlines Flight 175 whether they can see American Airlines Flight 11, and they answer to the affirmative.

8:38 a.m. The Boston air traffic control center notifies North American Aerospace Defense Command (NORAD) of the hijacking of American Airlines Flight 11.

8:40 a.m. The FAA notifies NORAD of the American Airlines Flight 11 hijacking.

8:42 a.m. Last radio communication from United Airlines Flight 175 with New York air traffic control; afterward, the transponder is inactive.

8:43 a.m. The FAA notifies NORAD of the United Airlines Flight 175 hijacking.

8:43 a.m. United Airlines Flight 93 takes off from Newark International Airport, headed for San Francisco after a 41-minute delay.

8:46 a.m. NORAD scrambles Otis fighter jets in search of American Airlines Flight 11.

8:46 a.m. The transponder signal from United Airlines Flight 175 stops transmitting.

8:46:40 a.m. American Airline Flight 11 crashes into the North Tower of the World Trade Center in New York City.

8:47 a.m. NORAD learns about American Airlines Flight 11 striking the World Trade Center.

8:49 a.m. United Airlines Flight 175 deviates from its assigned flight path.

8:50 a.m. A female flight attendant from United Airlines Flight 175 reports to a San Francisco mechanic that the flight had been hijacked.

8:50:51 a.m. Last radio communication from American Airlines Flight 77.

8:52 a.m. A flight attendant on United Airlines Flight 175 notifies United Airlines of hijacking.

8:53 a.m. Otis fighter jets become airborne.

8:54 a.m. American Airlines Flight 77 makes an unauthorized turn south.

8:55 a.m. Barbara Olson, a passenger on American Airlines Flight 77, notifies her husband, Solicitor General Theodore Olson, at the Justice Department that her aircraft has been hijacked.

8:56 a.m. The transponder on American Airlines Flight 77 stops sending signals.

8:56 a.m. American Airlines Flight 77 begins making a 180-degree turn over southern Ohio and heads back to the Washington, DC, area.

8:57 a.m. The FAA formally informs the military about the crash of American Airlines Flight 11 into the World Trade Center.

9:00 a.m. The FAA starts contacting all airliners to warn them of the hijackings.

9:01 a.m. An aide informs President Bush of the crash of American Airlines Flight 11 into the World Trade Center at Emma E. Booker Elementary School in Sarasota, Florida.

9:02:54 a.m. United Airlines Flight 175 crashes into the South Tower of the World Trade Center in New York City.

9:03 a.m. Boston air traffic control center halts traffic from its airports to all New York area airspace.

9:05 a.m. American Airlines becomes aware that American Airlines Flight 77 has been hijacked.

9:05 a.m. An aide informs President Bush about the second plane hitting the World Trade Center, and he understands that the United States is under attack.

9:06 a.m. The FAA formally informs the military that United Airlines Flight 175 has been hijacked.

9:08 a.m. The FAA orders all aircraft to leave New York airspace and orders all New York–bound aircraft nationwide to stay on the ground.

9:11 a.m. Two F-15 Eagles from Otis Air National Guard Base arrive over New York City airspace.

9:15 a.m. The New York air traffic control center advises NORAD that United Airlines Flight 175 has also crashed into the World Trade Center.

9:16 a.m. American Airlines becomes aware that American Airlines Flight 11 has crashed into the World Trade Center.

9:17 a.m. The FAA shuts down all New York City area airports.

9:20 a.m. United Airlines headquarters becomes aware that United Airlines Flight 175 has crashed into the World Trade Center.

9:21 a.m. The Port Authority of New York and New Jersey orders all bridges and tunnels in the New York area closed.

9:24 a.m. The FAA informs NORAD that American Airlines Flight 77 has been hijacked.

9:24 a.m. NORAD scrambles Langley fighter jets to search for American Airlines Flight 77.

9:24 a.m. United Airlines Flight 93 receives a warning from United Airlines about possible cockpit intrusion by terrorists.

9:25 a.m. Herndon Command Center orders the nationwide grounding of all commercial and civilian aircraft.

9:26 a.m. Barbara Olson calls her husband again to give him details about the hijacking.

9:27 a.m. Last routine radio communication from United Airlines Flight 93.

9:28 a.m. Likely takeover of United Airlines Flight 93 by terrorists.

9:29 a.m. Jeremy Glick, a passenger on United Airlines Flight 93, calls his wife, who informs him about the attacks in New York City.

9:30 a.m. President Bush states in an informal address at the elementary school in Sarasota, Florida, that the country has suffered an apparent terrorist attack.

9:30 a.m. F-16 Fighting Falcons take off from Langley Air Force Base and head toward New York City until redirected to Washington, DC.

9:32 a.m. Dulles Tower observes the approach of a fast-moving aircraft on radar.

9:32 a.m. Secret Service agents take Vice President Dick Cheney to the underground bunker in the White House basement.

9:34 a.m. The FAA advises NORAD that American Airlines Flight 77's whereabouts are unknown.

9:34 a.m. Herndon Command Center advises FAA headquarters that United Airlines Flight 93 has been hijacked.

9:35 a.m. United Airlines Flight 93 begins making a 135-degree turn near Cleveland, Ohio, and heads for the Washington, DC, area.

9:36 a.m. A flight attendant on United Airlines Flight 93 notifies United Airlines of hijacking.

9:36 a.m. Ronald Reagan Washington National Airport asks a military C130 aircraft that has just departed Andrews Air Force Base to locate American Airlines Flight 77, and it answers that a 767 was moving low and very fast.

9:37:46 a.m. American Airlines Flight 77 crashes into the Pentagon.

9:40 a.m. Transportation Secretary Norman Y. Mineta orders the FAA to ground all 4,546 airplanes in the air at the time.

9:41 a.m. The transponder on United Airlines Flight 93 stops functioning.

9:42 a.m. Mark Bingham, a passenger on United Airlines Flight 93, calls his mother and reports the hijacking.

9:45 a.m. The White House evacuates all personnel.

9:45 a.m. President Bush leaves the elementary school in Sarasota to board Air Force One.

9:45 a.m. Todd Beamer, a passenger on United Flight 93, tells a Verizon supervisor that the passengers have voted to storm the hijackers.

9:47 a.m. Military commanders worldwide are ordered to raise their threat alert status to the highest level to defend the United States.

9:49 a.m. The F-16s arrive over the Washington, DC, area.

9:57 a.m. The passenger revolt begins on United Airlines Flight 93.

9:57 a.m. President Bush departs from Florida.

9:58 a.m. After receiving authorization from President Bush, Vice President Cheney gives instructions to engage United Airlines Flight 93 as it approaches the Washington, DC, area.

10:03:11 a.m. United Airlines Flight 93 crashes in a field in Shanksville, Pennsylvania.

10:05 a.m. The South Tower of the World Trade Center collapses.

10:07 a.m. The Cleveland air traffic control center advises NORAD of the United Airlines Flight 93 hijacking.

10:10 a.m. A portion of the Pentagon collapses.

10:15 a.m. United Airlines headquarters becomes aware that Flight 93 has crashed in Pennsylvania.

10:15 a.m. The Washington air traffic control center advises Northeast Air Defense Sector (NEADS) that Flight 93 has crashed in Pennsylvania.

10:24 a.m. The FAA orders that all inbound transatlantic aircraft flying into the United States be diverted to Canada.

10:28:31 a.m. The North Tower of the World Trade Center collapses.

10:30 a.m. American Airlines headquarters confirms American Airlines Flight 77 has crashed into the Pentagon.

10:31 a.m. Presidential authorization to shoot down hijacked aircraft reaches NORAD.

10:32 a.m. Vice President Cheney tells President Bush that a threat against Air Force One has been received.

10:50 a.m. Five stories of the Pentagon collapse due to the blast and fire.

11:02 a.m. New York City mayor Rudolph Giuliani asks New Yorkers to stay home and orders an evacuation of the area south of Canal Street.

11:40 a.m. Air Force One lands at Barksdale Air Force Base in Louisiana.

12:04 p.m. Los Angeles International Airport is evacuated and shut down.

12:15 p.m. San Francisco International Airport is evacuated and shut down.

1:04 p.m. President Bush, speaking from Barksdale Air Force Base in Louisiana, announces that all appropriate security measures are being taken and all U.S. military has been put on high alert worldwide.

1:48 p.m. President Bush flies to Offutt Air Force Base in Nebraska.

2:00 p.m. Senior FBI sources tell CNN that they are assuming that the aircraft hijackings are part of a terrorist attack.

4:10 p.m. Reports surface that Building Seven of the World Trade Center complex is on fire.

4:30 p.m. President Bush leaves Offutt Air Force Base to return to Washington, DC.

5:20:33 p.m. The 47-story Building Seven of the World Trade Center collapses.

6:00 p.m. Northern Alliance launches a bombing campaign against the Taliban in Kabul, Afghanistan.

6:54 p.m. President Bush arrives at the White House in Washington, DC.

8:30 p.m. President Bush addresses the nation about the events of the day.

September 18, 2001

The first of several anthrax-infected letters is sent through the U.S. mail. In all, 5 individuals will die and 17 more will become infected. Public fears that these attacks are being perpetrated by Al Qaeda prove groundless, however.

September 20, 2001

President Bush issues his "Justice Will Be Done" speech before a joint session of Congress.

September 22, 2001

The Air Transportation Safety and System Stabilization Act is signed into law. The act creates the September 11th Victim Compensation Fund, which will eventually award some $7 billion to survivors and family members of victims of the 9/11 attacks in exchange for agreeing not to file lawsuits against the airline companies involved.

October 7, 2001

U.S. and British forces begin airstrikes against Taliban targets in Afghanistan after repeated refusals by Taliban officials to relinquish Osama bin Laden to the United States.

October 2001–February 2002

Khalid Sheikh Mohammed plans a series of airline hijackings similar to those of 9/11 that will target West Coast buildings such as the Library Tower in Los Angeles; his plan fails after one recruit is arrested and others drop out.

October 21, 2001

Osama bin Laden gives his justification for the 9/11 attacks in an interview with an al-Jazeera journalist.

October 24, 2001

The House of Representatives passes the USA PATRIOT Act.

October 25, 2001

The Senate passes the USA PATRIOT Act.

October 26, 2001

President Bush signs the USA PATRIOT Act.

November 19, 2001

The Aviation and Transportation Security Act is signed into law. The act creates the Transportation Security Administration (TSA), which will be responsible for ensuring security in all modes of transportation, particularly air travel.

December 22, 2001

Richard Reid, who later claims to be a follower of Osama bin Laden, is arrested after attempting to blow up American Airlines Flight 63 with a shoe bomb that fails to detonate.

December 26, 2001

Osama bin Laden issues a statement of homage to the 19 martyrs of September 11.

July 2002

The Lower Manhattan Development Corporation (LMDC) is formed and tasked with overseeing reconstruction efforts at Ground Zero and surrounding areas of New York City.

October 12, 2002

Suicide bombers kill more than 200 people, including 7 Americans, at two discotheques and outside the U.S. consulate in Bali. Osama bin Laden claims that the attacks were committed in retaliation for the United States' and Australia's involvement in the War on Terror.

November 2002

The Homeland Security Act, which creates the Department of Homeland Security and grants it sweeping powers, is signed into law.

November 2002

Osama bin Laden issues his "Letter to the American People."

November 15, 2002

The National Commission on Terrorist Attacks upon the United States (the 9/11 Commission) is chartered over the objection of President Bush.

December 12, 2002

The *Washington Post* runs a front-page article by Barton Gellman titled "US Suspects Al-Qaeda Got Nerve Agent from Iraqis" that, although unfounded, helps reinforce the commonly held misconception among Americans that Iraqi president Saddam Hussein is closely tied to Al Qaeda and the 9/11 attacks.

December 20, 2002

Final Report of the Senate Select Committee on Intelligence and the House of

Representatives Permanent Select Committee on Intelligence Joint Inquiry into the Terrorist Attacks of September 11 is issued.

March 20, 2003
U.S.-led invasion of Iraq begins.

March 31–April 2003
First public hearings by the 9/11 Commission.

May 1, 2003
President Bush declares that major combat operations in Iraq are at an end. U.S. and increasingly smaller numbers of allied troops have, however, remained in the country, combating a growing Iraqi insurgency and attempting to establish lasting stability.

March 11, 2004
Four trains in Madrid, Spain, are bombed, killing more than 190 people. Although not specifically ordered by Al Qaeda's leadership, the attacks appear to be inspired by the terrorist organization.

June 2004
The September 11th Victim Compensation Fund closes, after providing more than $7 billion in compensation to victims or families of victims. (It would be reopened with the passage of the Zadroga Act in 2011.)

June 26–28, 2004
Opening weekend of filmmaker Michael Moore's controversial documentary *Fahrenheit 9/11*, which is highly critical of the Bush administration. The film pulls in more than $20 million in these three days, instantly becoming the highest-grossing documentary.

July 22, 2004
Final report of the 9/11 Commission is issued.

December 2004
The September 11th Fund, created by the New York Community Trust and the United Way of New York City shortly after 9/11, distributes the last of its 559 grants. The grants, totaling $528 million, provided monetary assistance, counseling, and other services to survivors and family members of victims of the 9/11 attacks.

June 2005
Representative Curt Weldon (R-Penn.) gives a floor speech about Able Danger.

July 7, 2005
Four Al Qaeda–affiliated suicide bombers attack three subway trains and one double-decker bus in London, killing more than 50 people.

August 12, 2005
The 9/11 Commission issues a statement dismissing the Able Danger information as not "historically significant."

August 17, 2005
Lieutenant Colonel Anthony Shaffer, a member of Able Danger, issues a public statement about the identification of Mohamed Atta and others as Al Qaeda agents by Able Danger as early as 2000.

September 21, 2005
The Senate Judiciary Committee holds a hearing on Able Danger, but the Defense Department prohibits Able Danger officers from participating in the hearings.

January 5, 2006
James Zadroga, a New York City police officer who helped in rescue and recovery operations at Ground Zero after the September 11 attacks, dies of respiratory

illness. He is the first police officer whose death is attributed to breathing harmful toxins and debris in the days and weeks following 9/11.

March 2006
Construction starts on the National September 11 Memorial & Museum, which will be located at Ground Zero and may cost upwards of $1 billion.

March 9, 2006
President Bush reauthorizes the USA PATRIOT Act.

April 27, 2006
Construction begins on the Freedom Tower, the largest building in the planned reconstruction of the World Trade Center. When finished, the tower will exceed 1,700 feet, making it the largest building in the Western Hemisphere.

May 3, 2006
Zacarias Moussaoui is sentenced to life in prison without the possibility of parole for conspiring to commit acts of terrorism in conjunction with the September 11 attacks.

March 2007
At a Combatant Status Review Tribunal Hearing at Guantánamo Bay Detention Camp, Khalid Sheikh Mohammed confesses to masterminding the September 11 attacks, the 2002 Bali bombings, and a number of other terrorist actions.

September 11, 2008
The Pentagon Memorial opens.

February 4, 2009
Representative Carolyn Maloney introduces H.R. 847, also known as the James Zadroga Health and Compensation Act, in Congress.

If passed, the bill would provide $7.4 billion in medical care to first responders, cleanup workers, and New York City residents exposed to toxins caused by the destruction of the World Trade Center.

March 30, 2009
The Port Authority of New York and New Jersey announces that the Freedom Tower will be renamed One World Trade Center.

May 1, 2010
Pakistani-born Faisal Shahzad plants a car bomb at Times Square in New York City, but the bomb is detected and defused before it can be detonated. Government officials suggest that Shahzad was acting in conjunction with a terrorist organization closely allied with Al Qaeda.

May 2010
Plans to build a Muslim community center, dubbed the "Ground Zero Mosque," several blocks from the World Trade Center sparks nationwide controversy.

June 10, 2010
A lawsuit brought against the New York City by rescue and recovery workers is settled for $712 million.

September 23, 2010
Iranian president Mahmoud Ahmadinejad delivers a speech before the United Nations (UN) General Assembly in which he claims that while most American politicians advance the idea that September 11 was carried out by Al Qaeda, most Americans believe that the terrorist attacks were in fact orchestrated by the U.S. government for economic and political gain. Ahmadinejad's comments trigger a mass walkout at the UN, and political leaders around the world criticize his speech.

January 2, 2011
The James Zadroga 9/11 Health and Compensation Act becomes law.

May 2, 2011 (Pakistan time)
Osama bin Laden is killed by U.S. Navy Seals in Abbottabad, Pakistan.

September 10, 2011
The Flight 93 National Memorial opens.

September 11, 2011
The 10th anniversary of the 9/11 attacks is recognized across the country.

May 15, 2014
The 9/11 Memorial Museum opens.

November 3, 2014
One World Trade Center opens to tenants. It is the tallest building in New York City, the tallest office building in the world, and the sixth tallest skyscraper in the world.

December 18, 2015
The James Zadroga 9/11 Health and Compensation Reauthorization Act is reauthorized, extending medical benefits until 2090.

July 15, 2016
U.S. government declassifies a previously redacted portion of the 9/11 Commission report (called "the 28 pages") which covered and discussed financial and logistical support provided to the hijackers by the Kingdom of Saudi Arabia (KSA). The KSA and elements of the U.S. intelligence community had long fought against declassification.

July 29, 2019
The September 11th Victim Compensation Fund (Zadroga Act) is permanently authorized and funded.

August 30, 2019
A military judge sets the date for the trial of Khalid Sheikh Mohammed to January 11, 2021.

March 15, 2020
The USA PATRIOT Act expires, after several reauthorizations.

Annotated Bibliography

The controversy surrounding the events of September 11, 2001, rivals that of Pearl Harbor and the John F. Kennedy assassination as a source of conflicting views. Besides the usual partisan infighting between the adherents of the Clinton presidency and those of the George W. Bush administration, there is a growing industry of authors eager to cast doubt on the official version. They examine each incident and come up with a conspiracy theory to explain any discrepancies. Some of the most extreme authors have charged that the Bush administration orchestrated 9/11 to erode constitutional liberties. The reader of this encyclopedia needs to approach each book on 9/11 listed in this bibliography with an understanding of the author's concentration and/or bias. Most of the works here are authoritative and objective, but several are efforts to cast doubts on the facts of the September 11 attacks. Consequently, each book listed has an annotation to help the reader understand the background and point of view of the author. It is estimated that there are around 3,000 books that deal with one aspect or another of September 11. This bibliography is selective, as it cannot accommodate all of them.

Ahmed, Nafeez Mosaddeq. *The War on Freedom: How and Why America Was Attacked September 11, 2001* (Joshua Tree, CA: Tree of Life Publications, 2002).

Nafeez M. Ahmed, a British political scientist and executive director of the Institute for Policy Research and Development in Brighton, England, advances the theory that the U.S. government instigates terrorism as a pretext to justify an aggressive foreign policy. He claims that the Bush administration allowed September 11 to happen so that the American government would have an excuse to invade Afghanistan. The author poses some tantalizing conjectures, but his treatment lacks objectivity.

Atwan, Abdel Bari. *The Secret History of Al Qaeda* (Berkeley, CA: University of California Press, 2006). The author is a Palestinian journalist and the editor-in-chief of the influential *Al-Quds al-Arabi* publication. He has lived in London for over thirty years. He suggests that Al Qaeda is becoming bigger and stronger because of current American foreign policy. There is considerable material in this book that contributes to the understanding of the strategy and tactics of both Osama bin Laden and Al Qaeda.

Ausmus, David W. *In the Midst of Chaos: My 30 Days at Ground Zero* (Victoria, Canada: Trafford, 2004). The author is a construction safety official who was working at Oak Ridge, Tennessee, when word came that he was needed at the World Trade Center site. He recorded his impression of the site and related safety issues. Although Ausmus spent only thirty days at the World Trade Center site, he was able to record the horrors of the debris pile and the hazards of those working in that environment.

Aust, Stefan, et al. *Inside 9/11: What Really Happened* (New York: St. Martin's Press, 2001). Nineteen reporters, writers, and editors of the German magazine *Der Spiegel* combined their talents to write a narrative of the events leading to September 11 and the events of the day. Emphasis of the authors is on the human interest aspects of 9/11. This book is an excellent introduction to the state of knowledge in the months following September 11.

Barbash, Tom. *On Top of the World: The Remarkable Story of Howard Lutnick, Cantor Fitzgerald and the Twin Towers Attack* (London: Headline, 2003). The author, a former newspaper reporter, recounts the story of the brokerage firm Cantor Fitzgerald and its loss of 658 employees on September 11. This company is a huge international brokerage firm that handled most of the bond activity for the New York Stock Exchange. This book tells of its resurrection as a company and its efforts to compensate the families of employees lost on September 11.

Barrett, Jon. *Mark Bingham: Hero of Flight 93* (Los Angeles, CA: Advocate Books, 2002). This laudatory biography explains the complex personality of Mark Bingham, a passenger on United Airlines Flight 93. His participation in the attempt to overthrow the flight's hijackers placed him on a hero's pedestal.

Barrett, Wayne, and Adam Fifield. *Rudy! An Investigative Biography of Rudolph Giuliani* (New York: Basic Books, 2000). Wayne Barrett, senior editor at the *Village Voice,* has written a critical biography of Rudolph "Rudy" Giuliani. Although the biography ends before September 11, it gives a critical analysis of his lengthy career as mayor of New York City. This book provides background on one of the leading figures in New York City during and after September 11.

Beamer, Lisa, and Ken Abraham. *Let's Roll! Ordinary People, Extraordinary Courage* (Wheaton, IL: Tyndale Publishing, 2002).

The author is the widow of Todd Beamer, one of the heroes of United Airlines Flight 93. She explains the background of Todd Beamer and why he was one of the leaders of the attempt to regain control of the cockpit on September 11, 2001. She subscribes to the theory that it was his religious faith and his desire to return to his family that motivated Todd Beamer to do what he did.

Bell, J. Bowyer. *Murders on the Nile: The World Trade Center and Global Terror* (San Francisco: Encounters Books, 2003). J. Bowyer Bell, an adjunct professor at the School of International and Public Affairs at Columbia University and a member of the Council on Foreign Relations, has used his lifetime of research on terrorism to examine the origins of Jihadi terrorism that led to September 11. It is his thesis that the origin of Jihadi terrorism was in Egypt, and the expansion to the rest of the Middle East has been led by Egyptians such as Sayyid Qutb, Sheikh Omar Abdel Rahman, and Ayman al-Zawahiri. This book is a good introductory source on the personalities and events surrounding the September 11 attacks.

Benjamin, Daniel, and Steven Simon. *The Age of Sacred Terror* (New York: Random House, 2004). Two former Clinton administration officials in Richard Clarke's National Security Council's Directorate of Transnational Threats have written this book on the terrorist threat to the United States before September 11. As key members of Clarke's staff they participated in most of the decisions regarding counterterrorist operations. This book is a good source for actions taken by the Clinton administration.

Bergen, Peter L. *The Osama bin Laden I Know: An Oral History of Al Qaeda's Leader* (New York: Free Press, 2006). The author is CNN's terrorism analyst and an adjunct professor at the School of Advanced International Studies at Johns Hopkins University. He has used his extensive contacts in the Middle East to produce an oral history of the career of Osama bin Laden. Bergen interviewed bin Laden once, but the strength of the book is the interviews with the associates of bin Laden. This book is a gold mine of information about bin Laden and how he is viewed by Muslims both inside and outside of Al Qaeda.

Bernstein, Richard. *Out of the Blue: The Story of September 11, 2001: From Jihad to Ground Zero* (New York: Times Books, 2002). The author, a journalist with the *New York Times*, has, with the help of the staff of the *Times*, produced this history of the conspirators of September 11 and the impact of the attack on the lives of Americans. He followed the lives of heroes, victims, and terrorists in considerable detail. This survey is strong on human interest stories that give perspective to the tragedy of September 11.

Bin Laden, Osama. *Messages to the World: The Statements of Osama bin Laden* (London: Verso, 2005). An American professor at Duke University, Bruce Lawrence, and a British specialist on Arab affairs and language, James Howarth, united to compile a book on the messages, writings, and interviews of Osama bin Laden, the head of Al Qaeda. In this work all of bin Laden's principal messages appear, including the famous August 23, 1996, *Declaration of Jihad* and the equally famous February 23, 1998, *The World Islam Front*. This book is an indispensable tool for the understanding of Osama bin Laden and his worldview.

Breitweiser, Kristen. *Wake-Up Call: The Political Education of a 9/11 Widow* (New York: Warner Books, 2006). Kristen Breitweiser lost her husband on September 11, 2001, in the North Tower of the World Trade Center. She allied with three other New Jersey widows to form the Jersey Girls, whose mission was to find out what happened on September 11 and hold people accountable. To do this Breitweiser and her allies joined the Family Steering Committee to help form and guide the 9/11 Commission.

Bull, Chris, and Sam Erman (eds.). *At Ground Zero: 25 Stories from Young Reporters Who Were There* (New York: Thunder's Mouth Press, 2002). The editors have compiled the stories from reporters and photographers who were active at the World Trade Center complex on September 11, 2001, and afterward. Most of the accounts came from young news professionals fresh to the field of journalism and concern how they coped with the disaster. Each of them attests to the fact that they experienced a range of emotions from anger and excitement to terror and depression covering September 11 and the victims' families.

Burgat, François. *Islamism in the Shadow of al-Qaeda*, Tr. Patrick Hutchinson (Austin: University of Texas Press, 2008). The author teaches political science at the Institute for Research on the Arab and Muslim World and is a renowned authority on Islamic movements. Bringing his expertise to the current situation with Al Qaeda, Burgat concludes that most of the political and media rhetoric in the West has only created a breeding ground for terrorism, having led to a lack of comprehension of the violence that divides the Middle East, and has only strengthened Al Qaeda's cause. Burgat's new roadmap for stability and historical perspective, however, makes this book a valuable resource for anyone trying to understand the post-9/11 world.

Burnett, Deena, and Anthony Giombetti. *Fighting Back: Living Life beyond Ourselves* (Altamonte Springs, FL: Advantage Books, 2006). The widow of Tom Burnett, a passenger on United Airlines Flight 93 on September 11, 2001, recounts her life with her husband and the events of September 11. He was one of those who fought for control of the cockpit on that fateful day. She recounts her cell phone conversations with her husband until the moment when he participated with the other passengers to regain control of the airliner.

Butler, Gregory A. *Lost Towers: Inside the World Trade Center Cleanup* (New York:

iUniverse, 2006). Gregory Butler is a carpenter in New York City, and in this book he has compiled his impressions about the cleanup at Ground Zero. His tidbits of information give a somewhat different perspective on the cleanup. Butler's insights on work at Ground Zero make this book a valuable resource on the aftermath of September 11.

Calhoun, Craig, Paul Price, and Ashley Timmer (eds.). *Understanding September 11* (New York: New Press, 2002). Three editors with support from the Social Science Research Council, New York, have united a host of experts on terrorism and international security to produce a book that attempts to understand why September 11 happened. The authors of the articles tackle such topics as Islamic radicalism, globalism, and terrorism as part of their analysis. This book's value is in the quality of the contributions by experts in the field.

Caran, Peter. *The 1993 World Trade Center Bombing: Foresight and Warning* (London: Janus Publishing, 2001). Peter Caran had been a detective and antiterrorist officer with the Port Authority of New York and New Jersey at the World Trade Center complex until 1998. Caran was one of the investigators at the 1993 World Trade Center bombing, and he was critical of the lack of security that allowed terrorists to plant a bomb at the World Trade Center complex so easily. It was his thesis before September 11, 2001, that the terrorists had bungled the first bombing, and they were going to come back for another try.

Chermak, Steven, Frankie Y. Bailey, and Michelle Brown. *Media Representations of 9/11* (Santa Barbara: Praeger, 2003). The images of the events of 9/11, while disturbing and surreal, provide an important vehicle for interdisciplinary dialogue within media studies, showing us how horrific national disasters are depicted in various media. Each contributor to this volume discusses how the media transformed the 9/11 crisis into an ideological tour de force, examining why certain readings of these events were preferred, and discussing the significance of those preferred meanings.

Chomsky, Noam. *9-11* (New York: Seven Stories Press, 2001). In a series of questions and answers, the noted critic of the U.S. government and its policies Noam Chomsky gives his views on the events surrounding the September 11 attacks. He believes the U.S. government view on Al Qaeda's responsibility for the attacks is correct, but in his eyes the attacks are also a product of American support for repressive Middle Eastern regimes, which has allowed Al Qaeda to constitute a danger to the United States. This book shows his fear that the Bush administration would take advantage of the desire for revenge to worsen the situation in the Middle East by invading Iraq.

Clarke, Richard A. *Against All Enemies: Inside America's War on Terror* (New York: Free Press, 2004). The author was the counterterrorism expert in both the Clinton and Bush administrations before and after September 11, and in this post he could evaluate each administration's efforts against Osama bin Laden and Al Qaeda. Although a lifetime Republican, Clarke is more critical of the Bush administration's counterterrorism actions than those of the Clinton administration. He also maintains that the Iraq War has emboldened terrorists because most of the leadership of Al Qaeda and the Taliban remain at large to exploit the chaos of war.

Clinton, Bill. *My Life* (New York: Vintage Books, 2005). President Bill Clinton (1993–2001) presents in this memoir his version of the events in his life and his presidency. He chronicles his efforts to fight terrorism before September 11, including his clashes with a Republican Congress and his rocky relationship with the FBI.

Cole, David, and James X. Dempsey. *Terrorism and the Constitution: Sacrificing Civil Liberties in the Name of National Security*

(New York: New Press, 2002). David Cole, a professor of law at Georgetown University, and James X. Dempsey, deputy director at the Center for Democracy and Technology, have collaborated on a book that shows how the war on terrorism threatens civil liberties. They are critical of how the FBI has acted in the past and present in dealing with those suspected of terrorism. Their thesis is that even after September 11 curtailing civil liberties does not enhance security.

Coll, Steve. *Ghost Wars: The Secret History of the CIA, Afghanistan, and Bin Laden, from the Soviet Invasion to September 10, 2001* (New York: Penguin Books, 2004). The author won the 2005 Pulitzer Prize for this balanced treatment of the history of the CIA's war against Osama bin Laden and Al Qaeda. He starts his story with the 1979 Soviet invasion of Afghanistan and ends with the assassination of Ahmed Shah Massoud on September 10, 2001. This book is the best source available for understanding the complexities of dealing with terrorism in the modern world.

Congressional Research Service. FBI Intelligence Reform since September 11, 2001: Issues and Options for Congress (Washington, DC: The Library of Congress, 2004). This report, prepared for Congress by the Federal Bureau of Investigation (FBI) after the 9/11 Commission found the FBI negligent in not preventing the terrorist attacks of 9/11, offers suggested changes within the FBI's intelligence capabilities subject to approval by Congress. Repeatedly discussed are issues such as whether or not the intelligence reforms, already underway, are enough to correct the problems, and whether Director Robert Mueller is qualified to oversee an intelligence overhaul.

Corbin, Jane. *Al-Qaeda: The Terror Network That Threatens the World* (New York: Thunder's Mouth Press, 2002). Jane Corbin, a senior reporter for the BBC's (British Broadcasting Corporation) current affairs program Panorama, traveled around the Middle East interviewing former associates of Osama bin Laden and other Al Qaeda operatives in an attempt to understand how Al Qaeda operates. Besides these interviews, she depended heavily on the testimony of former Al Qaeda member Jamal al-Fadl. This book gives an excellent background treatment of Al Qaeda's role in the September 11 attacks.

Danieli, Yael, and Robert L. Dingman (eds.). *On the Ground after September 11: Mental Health Responses and Practical Knowledge Gained* (New York: Haworth Maltreatment and Trauma Press, 2005). The editors, one a clinical psychologist and the other a retired professor of counseling at Marshall University, have compiled a book that contains the experiences of medical and health professionals who worked at the various sites of the September 11 attacks. These responses show the intensity of feeling and the stress felt even from health professionals. This book fills a necessary void in understanding the psychological impact of September 11.

Davis, Mike. *Buda's Wagon: A Brief History of the Car Bomb* (London: Verso, 2007). Mike Davis, a freelance writer of numerous nonfiction titles, turns his attention to the use of car bombings as a terrorist weapon. He begins with the bombing by an Italian anarchist in 1920 and continues to the use of car bombs in Iraq. His treatment of Ramzi Yousef's truck bomb at the World Trade Center Complex in 1993, and Al Qaeda's 1998 African Embassy bombings, makes this book a valuable resource on how Al Qaeda conducted operations before September 11, 2001.

DiMarco, Damon. *Tower Stories: An Oral History of 9/11*, 2nd ed. (Solano Beach, CA: Santa Monica Press, 2007). Damon DiMarco has put together an impressive collection of firsthand accounts of what happened during the 9/11 attacks. Weeks after the World Trade Center attacks DiMarco wandered New York collecting stories from New Yorkers who had witnessed the events. The themes of heroism and the rigors of loss permeate the accounts and offer an excellent oral history of the event.

Defede, Jim. *The Day the World Came to Town: 9/11 in Gander, Newfoundland* (New York: HarperCollins, 2011). The story of a tiny community's week-long hospitality to thousands of passengers on 38 jets that were re-routed to Canada when U.S. airspace was closed.

Drumheller, Tyler, and Elaine Monaghan. *On the Brink: An Insider's Account of How the White House Compromised American Intelligence* (New York: Carroll and Graf, 2006). Tyler Drumheller was a senior CIA operations officer for more than twenty-five years before retiring in 2005. He uses this book to defend the CIA's intelligence-gathering efforts and criticize how the intelligence information was misused by the Bush administration. Although much of the material in the book covers the post–September 11 era, there are valuable insights into intelligence-gathering problems in the CIA that led up to the September 11 attacks.

Dudziak, Mary L. (ed.). *September 11 in History: A Watershed Moment* (Durham, NC: Duke University Press, 2003). The editor has recruited a group of cross-disciplinary scholars to examine the question of whether the September 11, 2001, attacks have changed American politics and society as a seminal event in history. They question this assumption in various ways, and they conclude that there is more continuity than change.

This book is a good counterweight against much current political opinion about September 11.

Dunbar, David, and Brad Reagan. *Debunking 9/11 Myths: Why Conspiracy Theories Can't Stand Up to the Facts* (New York: Hearst Books, 2006). The investigative staff of the magazine *Popular Mechanics*, under the two editors, tackle the myths coming out of the 9/11 conspiracy movement. They consulted more than 300 experts in aviation and scientific fields before publishing this book. This book is the best source available to counter some of the wild theories coming out of the conspiracy theorists.

Dwyer, Jim, and Kevin Flynn. *102 Minutes: The Untold Story of the Fight to Survive inside the Twin Towers* (New York: Times Books, 2005). Jim Dwyer and Kevin Flynn are both reporters for the *New York Times*, and they spent four years researching the story of what happened between the time the first commercial aircraft hit the North Tower of the World Trade Center and the collapse of the twin towers. They give a personalized picture of the dilemmas facing the 14,000 or so workers faced with the chaos of an unfolding disaster. This book also discusses New York City's institutions and their handling of the emergency.

Emerson, Steven. *American Jihad: The Terrorists Living among Us* (New York: Free Press, 2002). The author is an investigative journalist and executive director of the Investigative Project, which specializes in the study of Islamic militants. In this book Emerson traces the control of the mosques in the United States by partisans of militant Islamist groups—Abu Sayyaf, Algerian Armed Islamic Group, Hamas, Hezbollah, Islamic Jihad, and Al Qaeda. He warns that these terrorists living in the United States constitute a constant danger because they consider the United States to be the enemy, and September 11, 2001, is an example of what they want to do.

Ensalaco, Mark. *Middle Eastern Terrorism: From Black September to September 11* (Philadelphia: University of Pennsylvania Press, 2007). Mark Ensalaco, Raymond A. Roesch Chair in the Social Sciences at the University of Dayton, in this well-researched book seeks to trace Middle Eastern terrorism from its origins to the September 11, 2001, attacks. Focusing on when and why terrorists began attacking Americans and American interests, and how terrorist attacks changed from spectacle to atrocity, this book is an excellent source for any reader trying to understand the origins and the rise of terrorism in the Middle East.

Farren, Mick. *CIA: Secrets of "The Company"* (New York: Barnes and Noble, 2004). This book is an expose of the history of the Central Intelligence Agency (CIA). It has a chapter on how the CIA was hampered in the 1990s by poor leadership, low morale, and the departure of key personnel with experience in intelligence. It is critical of intelligence chiefs in the organization who, it asserts, did not properly heed early warnings about Al Qaeda and terrorist threats.

Fink, Mitchell, and Louis Mathias. *Never Forget: An Oral History of September 11, 2001* (New York: ReganBooks, 2002). A husband and wife team from New York City conducted a series of nearly eighty interviews of survivors of the events of September 11. These interviews began just days after September 11, and each story gives a different personal perspective of what happened on that day. This book gives a view of September 11 that most books only attempt to do.

Finn, Jonathan. *Capturing the Criminal Image: From Mug Shot to Surveillance Society* (Minneapolis: University of Minnesota Press, 2009). This book offers a history of photography as it pertains to law enforcement and criminality. By tracing its use in identifying criminals from its inception in the 19th century, it serves as a foreground to the newer technologies of fingerprinting, DNA analysis, and surveillance systems, and how they are used by law enforcement today in complementing photography in criminal identification. By bringing together work from multiple fields into one study, Finn details the problems of interpreting identification data according to highly mutable and sometimes dubious conceptions of criminality. While not dealing directly with 9/11, the study ties in closely with airport security, profiling, and a surveillance society.

Forst, Brian. *Terrorism, Crime, and Public Policy* (Cambridge: Cambridge University Press, 2008). In this book, Brian Forst brings his extensive background of law, social research, and policing to the subject of terrorism. By giving a broad but comprehensive overview, he also draws the distinction between terrorism and other forms of crime, while taking a multidisciplinary approach to public policy methodologies for how to combat it. This book would be a valuable resource both for someone experienced in the field and for a newcomer.

Fouda, Yosri, and Nick Fielding. *Masterminds of Terror: The Truth behind the Most Devastating Terrorist Attack the World Has Ever Seen* (New York: Arcade Publishing, 2003). Yosri Fouda, a journalist with the Arab television service al-Jazeera, and Nick Fielding, a journalist with the British newspaper *The Sunday Times*, combined to write a book on the operational heads of the September 11 attacks in the United States: Khalid Sheikh Mohammed and Ramzi Bin al-Shibh. In a series of interviews in Pakistan in 2002, Mohammed and Bin al-Shibh confessed to their role as planners of the attacks. This is an important book because of Fouda's interviews with Mohammed and Bin al-Shibh.

Freeh, Louis J., and Howard Means. *My FBI: Bringing Down the Mafia, Investigating Bill Clinton, and Fighting the War on Terror* (New York: St. Martin's Press, 2005). Louis Freeh, the head of the FBI during the Clinton administration and the early Bush administration, gives his interpretation of the events during his tour of duty. He recounts his successes and offers his own explanation for the failures of the FBI before September 11. His blaming of Congress for the FBI's outdated computer system is only one of the symptoms of the FBI's malaise in the years before September 11.

Gerges, Fawaz A. *The Far Enemy: Why Jihad Went Global* (Cambridge, UK: Cambridge University Press, 2005). Fawaz Gerges, a professor of international affairs and Middle Eastern studies at Sarah Lawrence College, uses his contacts among followers of jihad to explain why Al Qaeda declared war on the West. It is his thesis that there are two competing jihadist schools: those that want to overthrow Arab regimes and those that want to expand the war against the West. In this excellent and informative book, the author concludes that Al Qaeda's attack on September 11 was not universally approved of by the jihadists who want to overthrow Arab regimes and are fearful of a war with the United States.

Gertz, Bill. *Breakdown: The Failure of American Intelligence to Defeat Global Terror*, rev. ed. (New York: Plume Book, 2003). The author is the defense and national security reporter for the *Washington Times*. In this book Gertz uses his inside connections in the American intelligence community to back his thesis that American security was compromised by failures of the American bureaucracies and by political blunders. He traces what he perceives to be past failures and argues that unless significant reforms take place, another September 11–type of terrorist event will take place.

Gohari, M. J. *The Taliban: Ascent to Power* (Oxford: Oxford University Press, 1999). M. J. Gohari teaches Islam and Middle Eastern cultures at Oxford University. In this book, Gohari traces the ascendancy to power of the Taliban in Afghanistan. Particularly important is his treatment of Osama bin Laden's relationship with the Taliban, and the negotiations between the United States and the Taliban over bin Laden before September 11.

Goldberg, Alfred, et al. *Pentagon 9/11* (Washington, DC: Historical Office, Office of the Secretary of Defense, 2007). This book is the official U.S. government version of what happened in the attack on the Pentagon on September 11, 2001. A team of historians interviewed 1,300 survivors and had access to government sources to write the definitive account on what happened on that day.

Graff, Garrett M. *The Only Plane in the Sky: An Oral History of 9/11* (New York: Simon and Shuster, 2019). Garrett Graff is a journalist and the book reads like a riveting magazine article, with a dramatic tick-tock of the events of 9/11. The title refers to the sight from space available to the only American not on planet earth on 9/11. A few hours after the attacks, Frank Culbertson saw only a single plane crossing the country: Air Force One returning to Washington.

Graham, Bob. *Intelligence Matters: The CIA, the FBI, Saudi Arabia, and the Failure of America's War on Terror* (New York: Random House, 2004). Former Senator Robert Graham (D–Fla.) was the chair of the Senate's Committee on Intelligence, and he was instrumental in the setting up of the Senate-House Joint Inquiry on Intelligence that studied American intelligence failures leading up to September 11. It remains his thesis that systemic failure in the U.S. government contributed to the intelligence failures. He also criticizes the Bush administration for trying to evade responsibility for September 11 and for taking the United States into the Iraq War before wiping out Al Qaeda.

Griffin, David Ray. *The 9/11 Commission Report: Omissions and Distortions* (Northampton, MA: Olive Branch Press, 2005). Dr. Griffin, a retired and respected postmodernist theology professor, has gathered a number of so-called experts to challenge the official treatment of the events surrounding September 11. It is their contention that the U.S. government, rather than hijackers, planned and implemented the attacks on September 11. This book, much as other works by conspiracy theorists, is of limited value except to study the thought processes of conspiracy advocates.

Gunaratna, Rohan. *Inside Al Qaeda: Global Network of Terror* (New York: Columbia

University Press, 2002). Rohan Gunaratna, a terrorist scholar who has contacts with both the United Nations and several scholarly institutions, spent five years in the field researching the Al Qaeda organization from its beginnings in 1989 to September 11, 2001. This book covers information from Al Qaeda's financial infrastructure to how it trains its soldiers and operatives. Although the research in this book predates September 11, it is an indispensable source in understanding how Al Qaeda operated in the decade before September 11.

Habeck, Mary. *Knowing the Enemy: Jihadist Ideology and the War on Terror* (New Haven, CT: Yale University Press, 2006). Mary Habeck, a professor at the School of Advanced International Studies at Johns Hopkins University, gives an analysis of the jihadist political thought that led to the September 11 attacks. The jihadists around Al Qaeda and other Islamist groups are the extremist wing of the Islamist movement, but they constitute a danger to the West. She maintains that it is necessary to understand jihadist ideology to be able to fight it.

Hagen, Susan, and Mary Carouba. *Women at Ground Zero: Stories of Courage and Compassion* (New York: Alpha Books, 2002). The authors, who have backgrounds in professional writing and investigative social work, rushed to New York to interview women who had worked at Ground Zero in the aftermath of the September 11 attacks. They interviewed thirty women from different organizations. At the end of the book, the authors pay tribute to the three women who lost their lives on September 11 while performing their duties: Captain Kathy Mazza, Yamel Merino, and Moira Smith.

Halberstam, David. *Firehouse* (New York: Hyperion, 2002). David Halberstam, a Pulitzer Prize–winning journalist-author, wrote this study of the firefighters of Fire House 40/35 in mid-Manhattan. This Fire House became famous for the loss of twelve out of thirteen of its firefighters sent to the World Trade Center on September 11, and a serious injury to the thirteenth. This book is full of human interest, and how the loss of these men affected their families and others.

Hayes, Stephen F. *The Connection: How al Qaeda's Collaboration with Saddam Hussein Has Endangered America* (New York: HarperCollins, 2004). Stephen Hayes, a staff writer for the *Weekly Standard* and a frequent commentator on CNN, Fox News, and The McLaughlin Group, has compiled information to support his argument that Saddam Hussein and Al Qaeda collaborated to attack American interests. He asserts that the Saddam Hussein regime had no role in the September 11, 2001, attacks in the United States, but that there had been contact between the Hussein regime and Al Qaeda over training and others issues.

Henshall, Ian, and Rowland Morgan. *9/11 Revealed: Challenging the Facts behind the War on Terror* (London: Robinson, 2005). Two British journalists question both the official version of the September 11, 2001, attacks, and the report from the 9/11 Commission. They believe that certain facts do not make sense, and they wonder why no one has been held accountable for misjudgments. This book does not fall into the realm of the 9/11 conspiracy movement, but it gives considerable ammunition to the conspiracy theorists for often unsupported theories and theses.

Hersh, Seymour M. *Chain of Command: The Road from 9/11 to Abu Ghraib* (New York: HarperCollins, 2004). Seymour M. Hersh is a Pulitzer Prize–winning author for *The New Yorker*, and this book is his treatment of the decision-making processes in the Bush administration. In his eyes the Bush administration has been so blinded by neoconservative ideology that it has made a series of blunders. Hersh argues that it took political momentum from the September 11 attacks to pursue policies that have made the United States more vulnerable to terrorism, rather than less.

Holloway, David. *Cultures of the War on Terror: Empire, Ideology, and the Remaking of 9/11* (Montreal, Quebec, Canada: McGill-Queen's University Press, 2008). David Holloway, senior lecturer in American Studies at the University of Derby, has written an interdisciplinary study of the period between the September 11, 2001, terrorist attacks and the 2006 midterm elections. In it he discusses how representations of 9/11 and the War on Terror have been treated in politics and the media, and how these representations have been used to prompt international crises and legitimize or stifle the broader meanings of 9/11 and the War on Terror.

Jacquard, Roland. *In the Name of Osama bin Laden: Global Terrorism and the Bin Laden Brotherhood* (Durham, NC: Duke University Press, 2002). In a book that has been updated since it made its appearance the week before September 11, Roland Jacquard, terrorist expert and president of the Paris-based International Observatory on Terrorism, gives an assessment of Osama bin Laden and Al Qaeda. He presents evidence that bin Laden has been interested in acquiring biological, chemical, and nuclear weapons, making him and his organization an ongoing danger to the Western world. Jacquard has collected forty key documents, including a British intelligence report on extremist base camps in Afghanistan in 2000.

Jefferson, Lisa, and Felicia Middlebrooks. *Called: "Hello, My Name Is Mrs. Jefferson. I Understand Your Plane Is Being Hijacked?"—9:45 AM, Flight 93. September 11, 2001* (Chicago: Northfield Publishing, 2006). Lisa Jefferson was the Verizon Airfone supervisor whom Todd Beamer talked to during the last twenty minutes of his life on September 11, 2001. It gave Beamer an opportunity to tell authorities what was going on during the hijacking but also to pass on his love for his family. The author also spends a considerable amount of the book explaining what an impact this conversation had on her life and religious beliefs.

Joint Inquiry into Intelligence Community Activities before and after the Terrorist Attacks of September 11, 2001. *Hearings before the Select Committee on Intelligence U.S. Senate and the Permanent Select Committee on Intelligence House of Representatives*, 2 volumes (Washington, DC: U.S. Government Printing Office, 2004). The reports of the Joint Inquiry into Intelligence Community Activities before and after the Terrorist Attacks of September 11, 2001, provide the best source for understanding the actions and, in some cases, perceived failure of American intelligence agencies before September 11. These reports and the testimony of leaders of the intelligence community show that the most serious deficiency was the failure of the various intelligence agencies to communicate with each other.

Kashurba, Glenn J. *Quiet Courage: The Definitive Account of Flight 93 and Its Aftermath* (Somerset, PA: SAJ Publishing, 2006). The author is a Board Certified Child and Adolescent Psychiatrist who wrote this book to bring closure to the families of the victims of the hijacking of United Airlines Flight 93 on September 11, 2001. He counseled and interviewed the families of the victims and the inhabitants of Somerset County, where the plane crashed. His goal is to establish an accurate picture of the events of that day and to build a lasting memorial to those who lost their lives on that fateful day.

Kean, Thomas H., Lee H. Hamilton, and Benjamin Rhodes. *Without Precedent: The Inside Story of the 9/11 Commission* (New York: Knopf, 2006). The co-chairs of the 9/11 Commission, Thomas Kean and Lee Hamilton, recount their trials and tribulations during the start, middle, and end of the life of the 9/11 Commission. From the beginning of the 9/11 Commission, they believed that the Commission had been set up to fail. Kean and Hamilton refused to allow the 9/11 Commission to fail, but it was a long, hard struggle that is told in this book.

Keegan, William Jr., and Bart Davis. *Closure: The Untold Story of the Ground Zero Recovery Mission* (New York: Touchstone Books, 2006). William Keegan is a lieutenant in the Port Authority police department, and he served as the night swing supervisor at Ground Zero for nine months. He recounts in depth the search and recovery efforts at the World Trade Center site during those months. His treatment is balanced, but he does display some resentment over how the Port Authority police were ignored in the early days of the cleanup.

Kepel, Gilles. *The War for Muslim Minds: Islam and the West* (Cambridge, MA: Belknap Press, 2004). Gilles Kepel, professor at the Institute for Political Studies in Paris and an eminent scholar on Middle East politics, gives his assessment of the motivation of the planners of September 11. In his eyes they considered it the initial blow in an ongoing battle, leading ultimately to the West's submission to Islam. Kepel is one of the leading authorities in the West on Islamist studies, and his work is an indispensable source for understanding the jihadist Muslim mind.

Kessler, Ronald. *The CIA at War: Inside the Secret Campaign against Terror* (New York: St. Martin's Griffin, 2003). The author, a former *Washington Post* and *Wall Street Journal* investigative reporter now affiliated with the *New York Times*, has compiled a book that is a defense of the Central Intelligence Agency (CIA) in its war against terrorism. He is critical of the Clinton administration for its inaction against Osama bin Laden and Al Qaeda but has nothing but praise for the actions of the Bush administration in its attempts to combat terrorism. The author also expresses criticism of the FBI.

Kushner Harvey, and Bart Davis. *Holy War on the Home Front: The Secret Islamic Terror Network in the United States* (New York: Sentinel, 2004). Harvey Kushner, an academic and chairman of a university department of criminal justice, uses his expertise as a scholar of terrorism to survey secret Islamic terrorist activities in the United States. Little of the material in this book refers directly to the conspiracy of September 11, but it does show the motivations of those who consider martyrdom missions. This book has value in that it traces many of the organizations in the United States that sponsor terrorist activities.

Lance, Peter. *1000 Years for Revenge: International Terrorism and the FBI—the Untold Story* (New York: ReganBooks, 2003). Peter Lance is an award-winning investigative reporter who has intertwined the careers of FBI agent Nancy Floyd, New York City Fire Department fire marshal Ronnie Bucca, and the terrorist Ramzi Yousef to tell the story of the events leading up to September 11, 2001. The author presents Floyd's and Bucca's attempts to warn authorities about the dangers of terrorism. This book is well researched and is well worth reading for anyone interested in the history of September 11.

Langewiesche, William. *American Ground: Unbuilding the World Trade Center* (New York: North Point Press, 2002). William Langewiesche, a writer for the *Atlantic Monthly* and author of several nonfiction books, has written a detailed story of his six months covering the cleanup of the World Trade Center site. An accurate and objective treatment, his account of all of the ups and downs of the cleanup nonetheless caused some controversy among those involved.

Lansford, Tom. *9/11 and the Wars in Afghanistan and Iraq: A Chronology and Reference Guide* (Santa Barbara: ABC-CLIO, 2011). Through narrative chapters, a chronology of events, biographical sketches of principal players, and annotated primary documents, Lansford documents the domestic impact of the terrorist attacks that stunned the world as well as the subsequent "War on Terror" and the invasions and occupations of Afghanistan and Iraq. This book addresses the rise of global terrorism and the concurrent histories of Afghanistan, Iraq, and the broader Middle East, as well as the interaction of the United States with the region.

Ledeen, Michael A. *The War against the Terror Masters: Why It Happened, Where We Are Now, How We'll Win* (New York: Truman Talley Books, 2002). The author is a member of the American Enterprise Institute, a conservative think tank. He has written his version of why something like September 11 happened. In his treatment, the Clinton administration was at fault for the events of September 11.

Lioy, Paul J. *Dust: The Inside Story of Its Role in the September 11th Aftermath* (Lanham, MD: Rowman & Littlefield Publishers, 2010). Paul Lioy, director of the Exposure Science Division at the Environmental & Occupational Health Sciences Institute at Rutgers University, gives this detailed analysis of the World Trade Center dust exposure to rescue workers and people in the surrounding areas. Having been one of the first environmental health scientists on the scene, he was able to see firsthand the successes and failures of the response teams in assessing and responding to the situation, and gives in-depth preparedness suggestions for future environmental disasters.

Longman, Jere. *Among the Heroes: United Flight 93 and the Passengers and Crew Who Fought Back* (New York: HarperCollins, 2002). The author is a journalist at the *New York Times* who conducted hundreds of interviews in an attempt to re-create the events on United Airlines Flight 93 on September 11, 2001. His thesis is that the reaction of the passengers was a heroic act that saved lives in the long run. The strength of the book is that it covers the human side of the story.

Markham, Ian, and Ibrahim M. Abu-Rabi (eds.). *11 September: Religious Perspectives on the Causes and Consequences* (Oxford: One World, 2002). Religious leaders attempt in this book to bring together the moral and religious aspects of September 11. This book of readings by religious scholars gives insight into the moral dimension of September 11 but offers no conclusions regarding the events of the day. This book is for those looking at how the events of September 11 fit into a moral and religious context.

Marrs, Jim. *The Terror Conspiracy: Deception, 9/11, and the Loss of Liberty* (New York: Disinformation, 2006). Jim Marrs, a former investigative journalist and now a freelance writer, is a veteran conspiracy theorist going back to the John F. Kennedy assassination conspiracy. Much as in his other books, Marrs believes that there was a U.S. government conspiracy leading to September 11. This book has marginal value except as an example of how conspiracy advocates look for any discrepancies to prove their points.

McCole, John. *The Second Tower's Down* (London: Robson Books, 2002). John McCole, a lieutenant in the Fire Department of New York, recounts his experience at the World Trade Center complex beginning on September 11 and for the six months afterward. He tells of the emotional toll on the firefighters with the loss of 343 of their colleagues. This book is another of the personal accounts of the aftermath of September 11 that should be read to understand the impact of September 11.

McDermott, Terry. *Perfect Soldiers: The 9/11 Hijackers: Who They Were, Why They Did It* (New York: Harper, 2005). Terry McDermott, a journalist for the *Los Angeles Times*, has compiled extensive information about the conspirators of the September 11, 2001, attacks. He conducted interviews in twenty countries in the course of writing this book. This book is the best source available on the backgrounds of the Al Qaeda conspirators leading up to September 11.

Miller, John, Michael Stone, and Chris Mitchell. *The Cell: Inside the 9/11 Plot, and Why the FBI and CIA Failed to Stop It* (New York: Hyperion, 2002). Three veteran journalists produced this book as an explanation for the failure of the American intelligence community to stop the 9/11 plot. Their explanation is that it was a combination of risk-averse bosses and a bureaucratic structure that prevented information from being shared and coordinated. They cover the 9/11 plot from its conception to its execution.

Mohamedou, Mohammad-Mahmoud Ould. *Understanding Al Qaeda: The Transformation of War* (London: Pluto Press, 2007). Mohammad-Mahmoud Ould Mohamedou, the associate director of the Program on Humanitarian Policy and Conflict Research at Harvard University, traces the development of Al Qaeda from its beginnings. It is his contention that from the beginning the leaders of Al Qaeda have had a plan to challenge the West but that the West has been slow to understand. The attacks on September 11, 2001, were only one stage of this plan to confront the West.

Moussaoui, Abd Samad, and Florence Bouquillat. *Zacarias, My Brother: The Making of a Terrorist* (New York: Seven Stories Press, 2003). The author is the brother of the Al Qaeda operative Zacarias Moussaoui, and in this book he traces the change of a French-born Moroccan secularist into an Islamist extremist. Abd Samad Moussaoui is a moderate Muslim, and he has difficulty in understanding how his younger brother could make this transition into an extremist, but he tries. This book is an excellent source for understanding why young Muslims are attracted to extremist causes.

Murawiec, Laurent. *The Mind of Jihad* (New York: Cambridge University Press, 2008). In this new look at militant jihad, Laurent Murawiec acknowledges that although the ideology of militant jihad is essentially Islamic, it shares a number of similarities with historical Western antecedents. Bringing together history, anthropology, and theology, Murawiec ties the current movements to medieval millenarians and apocalyptics who, as now in the Middle East, were experiencing intense social dislocation. In addition he traces the political constructs used by militant jihadists to the Russian Bolsheviks. While controversial, the book offers a repudiation of the War on Terror as a failure to capture the essence of terror as a continuation of politics.

Murphy, Dean E. *September 11: An Oral History* (New York: Doubleday, 2002). Dean Murphy has compiled a lengthy list of oral histories from the survivors of September 11. These oral histories help give context to the events of that day. This book is an invaluable source to understand how some survived while others did not, and the serendipity of survival.

Murphy, Tom. *Reclaiming the Sky: 9/11 and the Untold Story of the Men and Women Who Kept America Flying* (New York: AMACOM, 2007). The author, an aviation trainer for the Port Authority of New York and New Jersey's aviation division, recounts the impact on aviation caused by the September 11 attacks. He describes what happened at the airports and on the airliners that day, and how members of the aviation industry responded to the tragedy. This book provides a valuable insight into how the aviation industry dealt with the aftermath of September 11.

Naftali, Timothy. *Blind Spot: The Secret History of American Counterterrorism* (New York: Basic Books, 2005). The author, a professor at the University of Virginia's Miller Center of Public Affairs and a contractor for the 9/11 Commission, has written a survey of American counterterrorism efforts since 1945. He traces his assertion that American counterterrorism policy has lurched from one crisis to another as American presidents have failed to recognize the dangers of terrorism. This book is a strong source for the study of American counterterrorism.

Office of Inspector General. *EPA's Response to the World Trade Center Collapse: Challenges, Successes, and Areas for Improvement: Evaluation Report* (Washington, DC: Government Printing Office, 2003). A team from the Office of Inspector General investigated the successes and failures of the Environmental Protection Agency (EPA) during its supervision of the cleanup of the World Trade Center complex site and the Pentagon. This team concluded that the press statements issued by the EPA to reassure the cleanup crew and the public were misleading because at the time the air-monitoring data were lacking for several pollutants of concern, especially for particulate matter and polychlorinated biphenyls (PCBs). This report is also critical of the influence of the White House Council on Environmental Quality on statements issued by the EPA.

Peek, Lori. *Behind the Backlash: Muslim Americans after 9/11* (Philadelphia: Temple University Press, 2010). Lori Peek, assistant professor of Sociology and co-director of the Center for Disaster and Risk Analysis at Colorado State University, has written a book that seeks to explain why blame and scapegoating occur after a catastrophe. In it 140 ordinary Muslim Americans describe their experiences both before and after the September 11, 2001, terrorist attacks, detailing discrimination, harassment, and exclusion.

Picciotto, Richard. *Last Man Down: A Firefighter's Story of Survival and Escape from the World Trade Center* (New York: Berkley Books, 2002). The author was a Battalion Commander of FDNY 11 in New York City on September 11, 2001. Responding to the aircraft crash into the North Tower of the World Trade Center, he was busy leading the evacuation when the tower began to show signs that it was about to come down. His miraculous escape allowed the death toll for the New York Fire Department to stay at 343.

Posner, Gerald. *Why America Slept: The Failure to Prevent 9/11* (New York: Ballantine Books, 2003). Gerald Posner, a former Wall Street lawyer who is now a freelance journalist, gives his assessment why American agencies and government failed to prevent the September 11 attacks. He is critical of all the agencies, and in particular the Clinton administration, but is kinder to the Bush administration. This book presents the material in a rapid-fire fashion, and some of its instant assessments have been overtaken by further research.

Powers, Richard Gid. *Broken: The Troubled Past and Uncertain Future of the FBI* (New York: Free Press, 2004). Richard Gid Powers, a professor of history at CUNY Graduate Center and the College of Staten Island, and an acknowledged expert on the FBI, writes a history of the FBI from its beginnings until September 11, 2001. He posits the question of whether the FBI can handle the intelligence burden of combating terrorism when its entire culture has been reactive to solving crimes rather than proactive in preventing them. The section on the FBI during the Freeh administration is particularly valuable.

Quay, Sarah, and Amy Damico. *September 11 in Popular Culture: A Guide* (Santa Barbara: Greenwood, 2010). This book offers an exploration of the comprehensive impact of the events of September 11, 2001, on every aspect of American culture and society.

Randal, Jonathan. *Osama: The Making of a Terrorist* (New York: Knopf, 2004). The author, a former correspondent for the *Washington Post*, used his extensive contacts in the Middle East to write this biography/analysis of Osama bin Laden. Bin Laden has been able to build a legend in the Muslim world mostly because of the ineptness of the Americans. He concludes that even the capture or death of bin Laden will not end terrorism from Al Qaeda or similar organizations.

Redfield, Marc. *The Rhetoric of Terror: Reflections on 9/11 and the War on Terror* (New York: Fordham University Press,

2009). Marc Redfield is a professor of English and dean of Arts and Humanities at Claremont Graduate University. In this book he focuses on not just the literal damage of 9/11 but also on the symbolic, or virtual, damage. He proposes that the phrase itself, "9/11," points to the cultural wound that the event describes, which makes it at the same time real and ephemeral. In addition he argues that the "War on Terror" makes the two terms seem tautological, and the War on Terror becomes crazed and somewhat fictional, though damaging, war.

Reuters. *After September 11: New York and the World* (New York: Prentice Hall, 2003). Reuters, the international wire service, commissioned members of its staff to produce this combination of text and photography. It chronicles the weeks and months of the recovery in New York City through commentary and photos. Although this work adds little to the information surrounding September 11, it does add visual evidence to show the recovery following September 11.

Ridgeway, James. *The 5 Unanswered Questions about 9/11: What the 9/11 Commission Report Failed to Tell Us* (New York: Seven Stories Press, 2005). James Ridgeway, Washington correspondent for the *Village Voice* and a prolific writer in newspapers, magazines, and books, posed five key questions that he believes were not covered adequately by the 9/11 Commission. These questions are fundamental to answering the ultimate question of accountability for failure to uncover and stop the September 11 plot.

Risen, James. *State of War: The Secret History of the CIA and the Bush Administration* (New York: Free Press, 2006). James Risen, a journalist specializing in national security for the *New York Times*, has investigated the relationship between the Bush administration and the CIA. He argues that the Bush administration pressured the CIA to comply with the administration's agenda. A valuable feature of the book is its discussion of the activities of the National Security Administration (NSA).

Robinson, Adam. *Bin Laden: Behind the Mask of the Terrorist* (New York: Arcade Publishing, 2001). This biography of Osama bin Laden appeared shortly after September 11, 2001, but the author, a veteran Middle East journalist, had been working on this book for over a year at that time. Because he had already concluded that bin Laden was an imminent danger to the United States, the events of September 11 did not surprise him. This book is an important look at bin Laden and his ambitions, but the author is sometimes a little sloppy with his facts.

Rubin, Barry, and Judith Colp Rubin (eds.). *Anti-American Terrorism and the Middle East: A Documentary Reader* (New York: Oxford University Press, 2002). Barry Rubin, the director of the Global Research in International Affairs Center and editor of *Middle East Review of International Affairs*, and Judith Colp Rubin, a journalist specializing in the Middle East, compiled a documentary reader that covers the variety of anti-American opinion in the Middle East. The editors filled this book with primary documents, many of which were hard to find, that scholars studying Middle East studies will find useful. Several of these are part of the September 11 story, and they need to be read for understanding September 11.

Ruthven, Malise. *A Fury for God: The Islamist Attack on America* (London: Granta Books, 2002). The author, a PhD from Cambridge University with extensive teaching and writing experience on Islamic subjects, has written this book to explain the motivation in the Islamic world for September 11. He believes that the lack of democracy in the Middle East has made the United States a convenient target for Islamist militants as they are unable to overturn the regimes of their own countries. This book is a balanced assessment from a scholar with expertise on Muslim culture and society.

Saar, Erik, and Viveca Novak. *Inside the Wire: A Military Intelligence Soldier's Eyewitness Account of Life at Guantánamo* (New York: Penguin Press, 2005). Erik Saar, an enlisted linguist specialist in the U.S. Army, tells about his stay at the Guantánamo Bay Detention Camp as an Arab linguist dealing with detainees there. He documents tensions between the Military Police and the linguists, and he discusses what he perceived as problems in the handling of detainees.

Sageman, Marc. *Understanding Terror Networks* (Philadelphia: University of Pennsylvania Press, 2004). The author, a former Foreign Service officer and forensic psychiatrist, traces the terrorist network of Al Qaeda and how it operated in carrying out the September 11 attacks. He concludes that the Hamburg Cell was part of a cluster of four terrorist cells—Central Staff Cluster Cell (Osama bin Laden and Al Qaeda central command), Core Arab Cluster Cell (Hamburg Cell and other Arab groups), Southeastern Asian Cluster Cell (Jemaah Islamiyya in Indonesia), and the Maghreb Arab Cluster Cell (North African groups). This book is an invaluable study in the type of terrorist networking that produced September 11.

Salter, Mark B., ed. *Politics at the Airport* (Minneapolis: University of Minnesota Press, 2008). In this book Mark Salter brings together academics from such diverse fields as political science and urban planning to examine the modern airport, particularly after the September 11, 2001, terrorist attacks. In analyzing how airports have become increasingly securitized, the essays focus on specific practices and technologies that serve to socially sort the safe from the potentially dangerous travelers. At the heart of the evaluation is establishing the airport as critical to the study of politics and global life.

Scheuer, Michael. *Imperial Hubris: Why the West Is Losing the War on Terror* (Washington, DC: Brassey's, 2004). Michael Scheuer continued his assessment of the American War on Terror in this book written after he left the CIA. His thesis is that the U.S. government needs to change its foreign policy to undercut the appeal that Osama bin Laden and Al Qaeda have in the Muslim world. Unless it does so, there is the possibility that the United States will lose its war on terrorism.

Scheuer, Michael. *Through Our Enemies' Eyes: Osama Bin Laden, Radical Islam, and the Future of America* (Washington, DC: Brassey's, 2002). The author was the former head of the CIA's Alec Station, a unit charged with capturing or assassinating Osama bin Laden. In this CIA-vetted book Scheuer tries to inform the American public how bin Laden and the leaders of Al Qaeda view the United States and the West. This book became so controversial that the CIA revamped its policy on CIA officials writing books.

Sharma, Arvind. *The World's Religions after September 11*, 4 vols. (Westport, CT: Praeger, 2008). This four-volume, comprehensive set explores the positive and negative possibilities of the religious dimension of life, particularly after the shift the concept of religion took after the 9/11 terrorist attacks. Following those attacks the book posits that the very word "religion" became inextricably linked with aggression and terror, and even evil, and that it has come into question whether the world's religions can coexist, as the future of religion has come to be seen as uncertain, or at least suspect. This set addresses religion's intersection with all aspects of the rest of human life, and is an excellent resource for anyone interested in examining religio-political relationships.

Simpson, David. *9/11: The Culture of Commemoration* (Chicago: University of Chicago Press, 2006). David Simpson, a professor of English at the University of California–Davis, examines the way America commemorated the dead on and after September 11, 2001. He puts the process of commemorating the dead into a historical context of how the dead have been handled in previous wars and catastrophes. His thesis is that the 9/11 commemorations have been overtaken by ideas of revenge.

Smith, Ennis. *Report from Ground Zero: The Story of the Rescue Efforts at the World Trade Center* (New York: Viking, 2002). Dennis Smith, a former firefighter and founder of *Firehouse Magazine*, gives his insight on what the New York Fire Department's (NYFD) firefighters went through on September 11. As an eighteen-year veteran of the NYFD, he had access to information that the firefighters were reluctant to share with outsiders. This book gives a good picture of the firefighters on September 11 and later, and it is recommended reading.

Spencer, Lynn. *Touching History: The Untold Story of the Drama That Unfolded in the Skies over America on 9/11* (New York: Simon & Schuster, 2008). A commercial pilot and flight instructor herself, Lynn Spencer weaves together a painstakingly detailed narrative of what developed in the air traffic controllers' stations as they realized that a coordinated terrorist attack was taking place. Taking the reader into the lives of air traffic controllers, airline pilots, fighter pilots, and military battle cabs, Spencer distills three years of interviews into one account in order to recreate what happened in a largely undocumented facet of the 9/11 attacks.

Springer, Paul J. *9/11 and the War on Terror: A Documentary and Reference Guide* (Santa Barbara: Greenwood, 2016). This book showcases key primary documents that follow the trajectory of events of the 9/11 attacks and the subsequent War on Terror. Each primary source is prefaced by an introduction and followed by an analysis written by a scholar specializing in the field. The accompanying analyses enable readers to better gauge the role of diplomacy, military strategy, national security concerns, and ideological propaganda in the Global War on Terror.

Stewart, James B. *Heart of a Soldier: A Story of Love, Heroism, and September 11th* (New York: Simon & Schuster, 2002). The author, a Pulitzer Prize–winning journalist, has written a biography of Rick Rescorla from his birth in Hayle, Cornwall, England, to his death on September 11, 2001, in the World Trade Center complex. Rescorla was a heavily decorated Vietnam veteran of the 2nd Battalion, 7th Cavalry, but he was also a writer and security specialist with a law degree. He died heroically, evacuating people from the South Tower, and his body was never found.

Stout, Glenn, Charles Vitchers, and Robert Gray. *Nine Months at Ground Zero: The Story of the Brotherhood of Workers Who Took on a Job Like No Other* (New York: Scribner, 2006). A journalist and two construction workers compiled this book from their experiences working at Ground Zero of the World Trade Center. In the months that Vitchers and Gray worked there, they developed a close working relationship with the New York City Fire Department. At the end they considered the nine months spent at Ground Zero working seven twelve-hour days per week "the most precious and most painful time of their lives."

Sulmasy, Glenn. *The National Security Court System: A Natural Evolution of Justice in an Age of Terror* (New York: Oxford University Press, August 2009). Glenn Sulmasy is an expert in national security law and a professor of law and judge advocate for the U.S. Coast Guard. After giving a history of America's military court system, Sulmasy offers a third option that would combine civilian and military courts in a post-Guantánamo world in order to try terror suspects. This book provides an excellent, well-documented solution in a cogent, non-partisan way.

Suskind, Ron. *The One Percent Doctrine: Deep Inside America's Pursuit of Its*

Enemies since 9/11 (New York: Simon and Schuster, 2007). Ron Suskind is a former Pulitzer Prize–winning journalist who uses his contacts in the Washington, DC, area to write about the war between the U.S. government and the terrorists in the aftermath of 9/11. The title of the book comes from Vice President Dick Cheney's remark that, if there is a 1 percent chance of a threat to the security of the United States, then it is necessary to take action against that threat.

Sweet, Christopher (ed.). *Above Hallowed Ground: A Photographic Record of September 11, 2001* (New York: Viking Studio, 2002). The photographers of the New York City Police Department took photos of the World Trade Center complex from minutes after the first aircraft hit the North Tower until the last steel beam was removed in May 2002. These never-before-published photos give a sense of reality about what happened on September 11 and its aftermath. It is a tribute to the loss of twenty-three members of the New York City Police Department and to all the others who died that day.

Sylvester, Judith, and Suzanne Huffman. *Women Journalists at Ground Zero: Covering Crisis* (Lanham, MD: Rowman and Littlefield, 2002). Two journalism professors, Sylvester at Louisiana State University and Huffman at Texas Christian University, were intrigued at how many women journalists risked their lives over the September 11, 2001, story. They decided to interview twenty-four women journalists ranging from TV reporters to newspaper journalists. These journalists recorded their horror at the loss of life and the devastation, but they believed that they were just doing their jobs.

Tenet, George, and Bill Harlow. *At the Center of the Storm: My Years at the CIA* (New York: HarperCollins, 2007). George Tenet, the head of the CIA for most of the Clinton and Bush administrations, uses this book to counter what he considers misrepresentations of how the CIA operated during his years in command. Although Tenet admits mistakes on the part of the CIA and himself, he maintains that the CIA has been used as a scapegoat by the Bush administration. Though there has been debate over some of the details, this is a must-read for anybody interested in how the CIA operated and its limitations in the period before September 11.

Thomas, R. Andrew. *Aviation Insecurity: The New Challenges of Air Travel* (Amherst, NY: Prometheus Books, 2003). Thomas, a global business expert and an aviation security analyst, uses his expertise on aviation matters to expose the inadequacies of commercial airline security. It is his thesis that the FAA's weaknesses in regulating security compliance by the commercial airline industry contributed to what happened on September 11. This book is an invaluable resource on security issues before and after September 11.

Thompson, Paul. *The Terror Timeline: Chronicle of the Road to 9/11—and America's Response* (New York: ReganBooks, 2004). Paul Thompson, a political activist and the founder of the Center for Cooperative Research, has combed newspapers and reports on events before and after September 11. His analysis of more than five thousand articles and reports points out the contradictions in the media. This book is also the most detailed chronology of the events surrounding September 11, and it is marred only by the author's acceptance of sometimes dubious sources.

Trento, Susan B., and Joseph J. Trento. *Unsafe at Any Altitude: Failed Terrorism Investigations, Scapegoating 9/11, and the Shocking Truth about Aviation Security Today* (Hanover, NH: Steerforth Press, 2006). This husband and wife team with experience in investigative journalism has produced a book on commercial airline security before and after September 11. The authors assert that the airline industry and other lobbyists worked against improved airline security before September 11, and that private security companies have since been used as scapegoats.

Von Essen, Thomas, with Matt Murray. *Strong of Heart: Life and Death in the Fire Department of New York* (New York: ReganBooks, 2002). Thomas Von Essen was the Commissioner of the Fire Department of New York (FDNY) on September 11. As a former firefighter and firefighter union official, he traces the events of September 11 and how the loss of 343 firefighters impacted the FDNY. Von Essen's viewpoint and his close association with Mayor Giuliani make this book a valuable source.

Weiss, Murray. *The Man Who Warned America: The Life and Death of John O'Neill, the FBI's Embattled Counterterror Warrior* (New York: ReganBooks, 2003). The author traces the colorful career of FBI counterterrorism expert John O'Neill through its ups and downs. Weiss traces O'Neill's clashes with the upper levels of the FBI hierarchy and his position as head of security at the World Trade Center complex.

Woodward, Bob. *Bush at War* (New York: Simon and Schuster, 2002). Bob Woodward has been a longtime investigative journalist for the *Washington Post* and the author of many books on American politics. In this book he examines the reaction to September 11 by President George W. Bush and the Bush administration. It covers the period from September 11 through the overthrow of the Taliban to the eve of the invasion of Iraq.

Wright, Lawrence. *The Looming Tower: Al-Qaeda and the Road to 9/11* (New York: Knopf, 2006). The author is a freelance journalist with extensive contacts in the Middle East that he used to write this book, which traces the origins of the September 11 conspiracy. The strength of the book is the numerous interviews of people close to the leaders of Al Qaeda. This book is an excellent treatment of Al Qaeda's role in the conspiracy, and it won the 2007 Pulitzer Prize for General Nonfiction.

Zuckoff, Michael. *Fall and Rise: The Story of 9/11* (New York: Harper, 2019). Classic minute-by-minute account—from multiple perspectives—of the terrible day's events.

About the Editor and Contributors

Editor

Stephen E. Atkins served as head of collection development at Texas A&M Libraries in College Station, Texas, for 15 years. In addition to *The 9/11 Encyclopedia*, his published works include Greenwood's *Encyclopedia of Modern American Extremists and Extremist Groups* and *Historical Encyclopedia of Atomic Energy*, which received a *Booklist* Editors' Choice Award in 2000. Additional published works include *Writing the War: My Ten Months in the Jungles, Streets, and Paddies of South Vietnam, 1968*.

Contributors

Elliot P. Chodoff is a military and political analyst at the University of Haifa, currently as a doctoral candidate writing a dissertation on international relations. He also serves as a Population Officer for the IDF Northern Command and a lecturer for Hamartzim Educational Services. Chodoff has provided contributions to *The Encyclopedia of Middle East Wars: The United States in the Persian Gulf, Afghanistan, and Iraq Conflicts* (ABC-CLIO, 2010), regularly freelances for popular publications on issues of national security and foreign policy, and is the editor and founder of the e-journal *MidEast: On Target*. He received his MA in sociology at the University of Chicago and his BA in sociology at the University of New York at Stony Brook.

Lawrence Davidson is Professor Emeritus at West Chester University, West Chester, Pennsylvania.

Paul W. Doerr is Professor and Department Head of the Department of History and Classics at Acadia University, Nova Scotia, where he teaches courses in British and European history. He was previously a lecturer at McMaster University. Doerr received his PhD from the University of Waterloo in British foreign policy. He is the author of *British Foreign Policy, 1919–1939* (1998) as well as "Munich Sixty Years Later" in *Chronicle Herald*.

Andrea Harrington is Associate Professor at the Air Command and Staff College, Air University, Montgomery, Alabama.

Arne Kislenko is associate professor of history at Ryerson University and adjunct professor in the International Relations Program at Munk School for International Studies at the University of Toronto. Dr. Kislenko earned his PhD at the University of Toronto. His courses focus on 19th- and 20th-century diplomatic history, national security, and U.S. foreign policy. Along with Margaret MacMillan, Kislenko is the coauthor of *Culture and Customs of*

Laos (Greenwood, 2009), *Culture and Customs of Thailand* (Greenwood, 2004), and has contributed to *Global Perspectives on the United States: Issues and Ideas Shaping International Relations* (2008).

Tom Lansford is a professor of political science at the University of Southern Mississippi. From 2009 to 2014 he served as the academic dean of the University of Southern Mississippi, Gulf Coast. His areas of expertise include homeland security, international relations and security, U.S. foreign and security policy, and U.S. government and politics. Dr. Lansford is a member of the governing board of the National Social Science Association and an associate editor for the journal *White House Studies*. He has published articles in such journals as *Defense Analysis*, *The Journal of Conflict Studies*, *European Security*, *International Studies*, *Security Dialogue*, and *Strategic Studies*. Dr. Lansford is the author, coauthor, editor, or coeditor of 31 books and the author of more than 100 essays, book chapters, and reviews. His books include *9/11 and the Wars in Afghanistan and Iraq: A Chronology and Reference Guide* (ABC-CLIO, 2011), *A Bitter Harvest: U.S. Foreign Policy and Afghanistan* (2003), and the edited work, the *Political Handbook of the World* (2015).

Keith A. Leitich is a part-time instructor in the Business and Social Science Department at Pierce College, Puyallup.

Jerry D. Morelock, Colonel, U.S. Army, retired, PhD, is the managing editor and senior historian for *Armchair General* magazine, an acclaimed military history publication. Morelock is a decorated combat veteran of Vietnam who spent 36 years in uniform. His military assignments included service in Germany, Korea, Russia, China,

Republic of Georgia, Estonia, Romania, and Ukraine. His final active duty tour was as the head of the History Department at the U.S. Army Command and General Staff College (CGSC). He earned a Masters Degree from Purdue University, a Master of Military Art and Science Degree from CGSC, and a PhD in history from the University of Kansas. From 2000 to 2004 he was the Executive Director of the Winston Churchill Memorial & Library at Westminster College in Fulton, Missouri, and remains a member of Westminster's adjunct faculty teaching history and political science.

Gregory W. Morgan is a PhD candidate at University of Southern Mississippi. He is also the proofreader for a website, chinika.com. He is interested in European history, specifically British imperialism into the Middle East.

Bradley F. Podliska is Assistant Professor of Military and Security Studies at the Air Command and Staff College at Maxwell Air Force Base in Montgomery, Alabama.

Frank Shanty, PhD, is the director of research and a co-founder of the Cobra Institute in Maryland. He is a counterterrorism expert and author of *The Nexus: International Terrorism and Drug Trafficking from Afghanistan* (ABC-CLIO, 2011) and editor of the *Encyclopedia of World Terrorism* (2004), and *Organized Crime: From Trafficking to Terrorism* (ABC-CLIO, 2007).

Spencer C. Tucker graduated from the Virginia Military Institute and was a Fulbright scholar in France. Dr. Tucker was a U.S. army captain and intelligence analyst in the Pentagon during the Vietnam War, then taught for 30 years at Texas Christian University before returning to his alma mater for 6 years as the holder of the John

Biggs Chair of Military History. He retired from teaching in 2003. He is now Senior Fellow of Military History at ABC-CLIO. Dr. Tucker has written or edited more than 50 books, including ABC-CLIO's award-winning *The Encyclopedia of the Cold War* and *The Encyclopedia of the Arab-Israeli Conflict* as well as the comprehensive *A Global Chronology of Conflict*.

Jeremy S. Weber is Colonel, U.S. Air Force, Air Force JAG Corps, at Maxwell Air Force Base in Montgomery, Alabama.

Index

Page numbers with bold indicate main entries in the encyclopedia.